# Science Fiction

# Science Fiction

## Toward a World Literature

George Slusser

Edited by Gary Westfahl
Foreword by N. Katherine Hayles
Afterword by Gregory Benford

LEXINGTON BOOKS
*Lanham • Boulder • New York • London*

Published by Lexington Books
An imprint of The Rowman & Littlefield Publishing Group, Inc.
4501 Forbes Boulevard, Suite 200, Lanham, Maryland 20706
www.rowman.com

86-90 Paul Street, London EC2A 4NE

British Library Cataloguing in Publication Information Available

**Library of Congress Cataloging-in-Publication Data**

Names: Slusser, George Edgar, author. | Westfahl, Gary, editor.
Title: Science fiction : toward a world literature / George Slusser ; edited by Gary
    Westfahl ; foreword by N. Katherine Hayles ; afterword by Gregory Benford.
Description: Lanham : Lexington Books, [2022] | Includes bibliographical references
    and index.
Identifiers: LCCN 2021044028 (print) | LCCN 2021044029 (ebook) | ISBN
    9781666905359 (cloth) | ISBN 9781666905366 (ebook)
Subjects: LCSH: Science fiction—History and criticism. | LCGFT: Literary criticism.
Classification: LCC PN3433.5 .S55 2021 (print) | LCC PN3433.5 (ebook) | DDC
    809.3/8762—dc23/eng/20211027
LC record available at https://lccn.loc.gov/2021044028
LC ebook record available at https://lccn.loc.gov/2021044029

# Contents

*Contents*

# Foreword

## *A Novel Method for Constructing Science Fiction's Origins*

### N. Katherine Hayles

In this enormously ambitious posthumous volume, George Slusser conceives of science fiction in its grandest terms: as a *world* literature. With erudite discussion of French, German, British, and Russian science fiction, Slusser interrogates its origins with a powerful methodology. To see its advantages, we can compare his method with more conventional attempts. All too often, these begin with a contemporary sense of science fiction as a well-established genre, identify its characteristics, and then retrospectively seek to find the same characteristics in earlier texts. The problems with these typical approaches are multiple. By working backward, they import into the search assumptions that emerged at a later time, giving the erroneous impression that the trajectory from past to present was, if not exactly deterministic, at least smoothly coherent and predictable. Slusser, by contrast, looks not for a set of genre characteristics but rather starts from a far more interesting question: what ideational and conceptual formations made it possible to think the genre of science fiction? As he puts it, what are the "ideas and processes" that made science fiction a thinkable thought?

His inquiry turns on the evolving meanings of the two key terms "science" and "fiction." For "science," one of the necessary ingredients was a belief that rational inquiry could, through verifiable experiments, discover truths about the world. Tracing how this was possible requires deep dives into historical ideas about the relation of mind to body and both to the material conditions of the physical universe. For "fiction," a key idea was the thought that storytelling itself is an experimental practice. Citing Zola in particular, Slusser shows how the scope of fiction was enlarged so that it is not merely about science's "impact" but rather a parallel investigation into the conditions of human existence.

With historical contexts this broad, it should be no surprise that Slusser's account includes discussions of an enormous variety of texts not usually associated with the historical development of science fiction. In his introduction, Gary Westfahl suggests that the initial readers' reports on the manuscript regarded this as a flaw and requested extensive revisions, which Slusser was undertaking by writing new chapters when he died. Wisely, Westfahl questions this judgment and briefly suggests that Slusser's initial idea was superior to the more conventional approach that the readers evidently preferred. I agree wholeheartedly with this assessment, and I very much appreciate that Westfahl took as his primary text Slusser's original version, working in portions from the revised manuscript when possible. One of the primary virtues of this book, in my view, is its refusal to remain in the conceptual ghetto to which the origin stories of science fiction are normally confined and to break out into the open air of larger intellectual and philosophical discussions.

That said, the encyclopedic scope of the work makes its omissions the more telling. With a few notable exceptions, almost all the writers discussed here are male. Largely absent are early feminist writers such as Margaret Cavendish, Elizabeth Burgoyne Corbett, and Frances Harper; even later well-known writers such as Octavia Butler and Margaret Atwood are not mentioned, much less discussed at length. One of the exceptions is Ursula K. Le Guin, acknowledged both for her Earthsea fantasy series and later novels such as *The Dispossessed* (1974), but here discussed thematically rather than in terms of her accomplishments in introducing some of the "soft" sciences, such as anthropology, into the science fiction tradition.

Also largely absent are discussions of how the entire notion of "science" have been deconstructed and reconstructed within the social studies of science by writers such as Bruno Latour, Steve Shapin and Simon Schaffer, John Law, Andy Pickering, Steve Woolgar, and others. Other than acknowledging that the vaulted "scientific method" has now been recognized as a plurality of methods and *sciences,* the book lacks a deep discussion of how the presumed distinction between scientific "fact" and literary "fiction" has been reconfigured in the contemporary era. Similarly, one looks in vain for any mention of the Anthropocene and its implications for the humanistic values often on display in science fiction texts. In particular, science fiction's ability to use the viewpoints of aliens to critique the limits of human perceptions, here represented perhaps most astutely in Slusser's discussion of Ted Chiang's novella "The Story of Your Life" (1999), could easily have been extended to the implications of anthropogenic climate change, so this must also be counted as a missed opportunity.

These caveats notwithstanding, the book remains a remarkable achievement in envisioning science fiction as a world literature, with all that implies.

Slusser's work as co-founder establishing the remarkable Eaton Collection at the University of California at Riverside is a similar endeavor, in the sense that it provides the archives that enable the serious study of science fiction's world evolution and development. Moreover, without the dedicated work of Gary Westfahl in undertaking the final revision and publication of the manuscript, this book would never have seen the light of day. The book itself is inspiring in its ambition, scope, and achievement; the circumstances of its publication add an implicit story of friendship and dedication that is also inspiring in a quieter and more modest way. Both enrich the science fiction community, and for both we are grateful.

# Notes on the Text

Gary Westfahl

After retiring as a professor of comparative literature at the University of California, Riverside, George Slusser set out, among other projects, to write a definitive account of the history and development of science fiction as he viewed it, integrating previous published analyses with new material. He completed a manuscript and submitted it to the University of Illinois Press. Although the peer reviewer reports cannot be located, they were evidently supportive but nonetheless requested extensive revision; one of their concerns, I am told, was that Slusser's book was devoting too much attention to authors and texts that were not really part of the genre of science fiction.

Slusser decided to postpone revising the manuscript in order to focus on another task, researching and writing his author study *Gregory Benford*, published in 2014 as part of Illinois's Modern Masters of Science Fiction series. By the time he returned to work on this manuscript, however, the health problems that would ultimately take his life were already taking their toll. He did manage, in evident haste, to create some new chapters, largely copied from old essays, and combine them with previous chapters to provisionally produce a second version of the book, but he never had the opportunity to thoroughly rework this variegated material in a manner that would make the entire revised text presentable as a unified argument.

To provide a suitable manuscript for publication, from the materials given to me by his widow Danièle Slusser (who published as Danièle Chatelain), I have employed the first version as its basis while integrating some of the contents of the second version by means of some minimal connective language. I have also imposed consistent formatting conventions, added documentation where needed, edited some passages to slightly reduce their length, and corrected minor errors. Otherwise, however, everything here represents what Slusser originally wrote. I should note that, in the two versions of the manuscript, Slusser included discussions of other topics relevant to the devel-opment of science fiction, including the quest for immortality and the roles played by food and music in science fiction; however, to produce a volume of publishable length, I was obliged to omit these materials, though his thoughts on these subjects and others are available in his numerous other publications. For those with a further interest in his work, I include in this volume a list of his books and summary of his other accomplishments, and a complete bibliography of his works will be available at the Lexington Books website.

I should finally comment on the primary objection of the peer reviewers, which I regard as misguided. In the twentieth century, when works were first labeled and published as science fiction, it became reasonable to posit that science fiction writers, before beginning their careers, had focused their at-tention primarily, or exclusively, on reading science fiction, and that those earlier texts constituted the major influence on their own writings. Prior to the twentieth century, however, such a reading regimen was simply not possible, since there was no ready way for readers to identify certain texts as science fiction in the modern sense; instead, one must assume that the individuals we now regard as science fiction writers read, and were affected by, a broad range of authors and texts. Yet the implicit logic of most histories of science fiction, discussing earlier works in chronological order, is that each writer was principally responding to the preceding texts designated after the fact as science fiction, which was almost certainly not the case. By reminding us that earlier writers were surely familiar with the key ideas of many other authors like Descartes, Pascal, Constant, and DeQuincey, and by explaining works of science fiction within this larger context, Slusser's work, I think, provides a valuable corrective and supplement to other histories of science fiction; and his is an argument that, at least, merits a wide audience.

# Introduction

## *Science Fiction:*
## *Toward a World Literature*

This study will examine the origins and fortunes of science fiction. These are dynamically interrelated questions, for we cannot understand what science fiction is today until we determine where it came from and speculate on where it is going. In terms of origins, as will be discussed, science fiction is an eminently international literature. In turn, the literary and cultural dynamics that gave rise to science fiction reveal that it is well on its way to becoming what Goethe, at the beginning of the nineteenth century, called a "world literature." For it is a form of fiction shaped in an ongoing transformational dialectic between various national cultures and literatures, and an international set of themes, methods, and what we might call world systems. The shared element is science in its modern sense.

Science fiction has had a local habitation since 1926, when editor Hugo Gernsback provided readers of his new magazine *Amazing Stories* with a name and definition for the fiction they were reading, and "scientifiction" was his first choice. But what is named is clearly no airy nothing. Something was already there, recognizable if not totally definable. At the end of the nineteenth century, Wells called his fiction "scientific romance," while his Belgian counterpart J.-H. Rosny aîné described his as "le merveilleux scientifique." Rosny's mentor Edmond de Goncourt, seeking a name for Rosny's speculative fictions, called them "fantastic-scientifico-phono-littéraire," foreseeing the generic jungle we witness today in the vast body of works that are called science fiction, but assimilate long strings of hyphenated opposites, such as fantasy *and* science fiction. Science fiction remains notoriously undefined, if not undefinable. Damon Knight offers tautology: science fiction "means what we point to when we say it."[1] Most other definitions remain descriptive, such as Robert A. Heinlein's "realistic speculation about possible future events, based solidly on adequate knowledge of the real world, past and present, and on a thorough understanding of the nature and significance of the scientific method."[2]

What is needed, however, to explore the origins of science fiction, is a dynamic definition allowing us to locate and define the process whereby fiction became *science* fiction. Science is notably present in all early attempts to name the form—Wells, Rosny, Goncourt's comments on Poe's "scientific" fiction—as well as national designations—the Russian *nauchnaya fantastika*. An adequate definition therefore will enable us to measure when and how science enters the picture in terms of themes, world views, and ultimately forms of conventional narrative. Isaac Asimov's definition seems to fit this bill: "Science fiction is that branch of literature which is concerned with the impact of scientific advance upon human beings."[3] This definition calls for historical locations. Where and when is science first seen as *advancing* knowledge, becoming an open-ended process of experimentation? In the Western world, this occurs in the seventeenth century, the same century when the word "fiction" takes its modern meaning of prose narrative. This "fiction" derives from conventional forms of story that, in Asimov's sense, deal with "human beings." Different "world systems" contribute to the history of story. But before this scientific "revolution," these systems—mythic, Christian, national epic, dynastic—offer cosmologies that are closed and bounded. They involve love affairs or personal ambitions in conflict with sets of fixed boundaries or rules.

Yet in Asimov's definition, scientific and technological advancement, in the modern sense, does not simply impact systems; it impacts *human beings*. In conventional stories, humans represent a dynamic element. So, it seems that, in combining science and fiction, Asimov proposes a creative encounter between two dynamics, one (in Heinlein's words) the method of science, the other the vital forces of human biology and mental activity, now liberated in the sense that they are asked to deal, in fictional situations, with *new* ways of seeing the world and new relationships between mind and nature. What is called for, essentially, is a fiction that is *experimental*—encounters between what are now variable elements, in which science tests fiction, and fiction science.

But this process of science impacting fiction does not occur, across the span of modern scientific culture in the Western world, in a single place or at a single time. Just as modern science is seen to operate by "paradigm shifts," so it appears that the history of the origins and genesis of science fiction has its own shifts—moments when ideas or world views, born of new scientific inquiry, become so prevalent that they challenge reigning national or cultural models of fiction and generate the kind of fictional experiment that will ultimately become science fiction. Modern physicist-writer Robert

L. Forward, from his position in the history of science fiction, had a radical view of this, claiming not only that "science writes the fiction" but also seeing the process of writing a science fiction novel as one of simply writing a scientific paper—when all the physical details are worked out, the novel is written.[4] But between total absence of science and Forward's view, there are many national and cultural variations on this dialectic between the modalities of conventional fiction and those of advancing scientific visions.

The first paradigm shift we identify occurs in France, with Descartes's science-driven reordering of the Christian system, creating a set of coordinates whereby the unaided rational mind relates, via the physical body, with an "extended" physical world both alien and accessible through quantitative analysis. The impact of this system, in both fiction and science, is immediate and continues to this day. The most powerful contemporary reaction is perhaps that of Pascal, whose ensuing formulation of a science-driven "human condition" had a powerful and enduring impact on French thought and fiction.

In rival England, it seems that the point of impact occurs much later. Bacon, Descartes's counterpart, also urges modern mankind to abandon authority for unaided, rational examination of physical nature. He remains however skeptical as to the ability of human reason to (in Descartes's terms) "master" nature. Perhaps because no new active sense of a human condition issues from Bacon's *Novum Organum* (1620), English fiction continues to evolve within conventional parameters, on a parallel track with scientific discovery. Milton in the seventeenth century explains the ways of God to man; Pope in the eighteenth century declares that the proper study of Mankind is Man. In terms of fiction, religion appears to morph into the moral secularism that regulates society in fiction from Fielding down through the nineteenth century. With few exceptions (Sterne), the English novel remains impermeable to science. In the wake of Samuel Johnson, works dealing with science were relegated to "low" genres such as the Gothic. It is not until the end of the nineteenth century that, with evolutionary theory, science effects the violent cultural schism we see in Matthew Arnold's "Literature and Science" (1882). In light of this paradigm shift, one can argue that Wells's *The Time Machine* (1895) is the seminal work of English science fiction. The evolutionary paradigm shift seems catastrophic, whereas in France the rationalist paradigm continues, subtly, to open the door to fictional experiments that, throughout the nineteenth century, assimilate new and changing world models proposed by the advancement of science.

The study identifies other paradigm shifts which represent key moments in the assimilation of scientific method and ideas, across a broad spectrum of national cultures. There is Kant's "Copernican Revolution," which attempts to reconcile the all-but-irreconcilable currents of Continental rationalism, British empiricism, and experimental science, leading to fictional experiments such as E. T. A. Hoffmann's "Der Sandmann" (1816). But if this shift leads nowhere in nineteenth-century German fiction, the paradigm shift that occurs with Emerson in the United States—which synthesizes international scientific activities in areas such as thermodynamics (occurring in German universities under the direction of figures like Helmholz) with Eastern and Indian cosmologies—has vast consequences for the development of science fiction. Emerson's self-reliant monad displaces the static Cartesian center, dynamizing the self as expansive entity capable of generating its own circumference, so form becomes a product of power. Literary experiments of this period—from writers like Hawthorne and Twain—led directly to Heinlein and the central current of American science fiction.

Historians of science fiction tend to focus on "seminal" works, generally limited to those of nineteenth-century England. The classic example is Brian W. Aldiss and David Wingrove's *Trillion Year Spree* (1986) which (despite its title) locates origin in a single literary tradition and work: the nineteenth-century British Gothic and Mary Shelley's *Frankenstein; or, The Modern Prometheus* (1818). Later histories of science fiction display more sophisticated methods—Roger Luckhurst's excellent *Science Fiction* (2005)—and in one case a broader national-historical and cultural vision—Adam Roberts's *The History of Science Fiction* (2006). As he advances through the seventeenth and eighteenth centuries, Roberts deals with French works. He also, in the encyclopedic manner of Pierre Versins, seeks to trace the "roots" of science fiction back to ancient Greece and India. Yet most of his examples are British. Even so, one interesting aspect of his history is an origin-based definition of science fiction treading much the same ground as my first paradigm shift: "SF is the genre that mediates between the discoveries of 'science' (or 'fact') and magic (or subsequently, imagination, 'fiction'), and it comes into being at precisely the historical moment when competing cosmic discourses were in the process of separating themselves into rationalist-Protestant and ritual-magic Catholic religious idioms."[5] Again, if on a larger scale, we have a "precise" seminal moment.

My approach is comparative. It seeks a field of fictional works rather than a single point of origin. Nor are my paradigm shifts precise defining moments so much as enablers. They create patterns of reception for scientific ideas or "competing cosmic discourses" within given national cultures and literatures. They are preconditions for a science fiction, and within their contexts generate many potentially significant works, examples of fiction's capacity to absorb and dialogue with the impact of science and technology. Both Luckhurst and Roberts examine the material and social causes that led to the creation of science fiction; I begin with ideas and processes, which are powerful shaping factors as well. Alfred North Whitehead sees all modern science issuing from what he calls the "Cartesian apparatus." The ideas and "apparatuses" of Pascal, Locke, Hume, Kant, and Emerson are important elements in both the development of modern science and the scientific "world view." The "big ideas" of modern science—evolution, relativity, quantum theory—that have radically changed the way we see our position in the extended world are simply more recent examples of earlier shifts that invite fiction to change the parameters of its own human-oriented story.

Roberts speaks of a science fiction *genre* in relation to its seventeenth-century origins. It is a long way however from science fiction's origins to the moment when all its generic markers are recognizably in place. This study attempts to trace the journey, on a comparative scale, through a series of fictional works rarely if ever before associated with science fiction. In these by-ways, at a deep level of literary transformation, we witness the development of the elements necessary for a science fiction: a character, a setting, a modus operandi or method for expanding closed systems of thought, a reading code that defines it as a specific genre, and finally a masterplot that allows it to investigate mankind's place in the material universe.

Chapter 1 begins with the seventeenth and eighteenth centuries, which witness interconnections between France and England in terms of scientific ideas and fictional models. By the nineteenth century, however, with its rapid expansion of science and technology, all our paradigm shifts are, in varying degrees, operational and interactive. Chapter 2 explores how concepts of space, which would become key elements in science fiction, began developing during the same period later emerged interestingly in French graphic novels. Chapter 3 charts the expansion, from the European nineteenth century to modern French and American science fiction, of the idea of scientific liberty, from specific national contexts to future possibilities. It compares *Frankenstein* with Balzac's little known *Le Centenaire* (1822) to plot the emergence of a common protagonist and theme—the fictional scientist and the genre's claim to "future liberty," to wield new technologies and generate new "creations" that impact the course of future societies and worlds. Following national paradigms, it traces very different developments of this figure and theme in France, England, and the United States. Chapter 4 discovers the functional nexus between mind, mechanical vehicle, and accelerated motion in DeQuincey's "The English Mail-Coach" (1849), a work written fifty years before *The Time Machine*. Here vehicular technology literally forces the "poetic" mind out of its fantasy refuge to engage the forces of mechanical transformation, hurtling down the ringing grooves of change. DeQuincey fictionalizes scientific mankind's future collision with material limits. In doing so, he presents what will become perhaps the central *theme* of science fiction—the reprieve: the dispensation that allows science fiction protagonists to continue pushing the "envelope" of human limits. To explore the synchronicity of development of science fiction models, comparison is made with a contemporary work, Mark Twain's *Adventures of Huckleberry Finn* (1884), and Heinlein's fiction.

Chapter 5 focuses on a specific generic crossroads that forms at the end of the nineteenth century around scientific theories of disease transmission, the theme of invisibility, and fears of alien "invasion." It examines the expectations and protocols that allow readers, in diverse works such as Guy de Maupassant's "Le Horla" (1887), Stoker's *Dracula* (1897), and Wells's *The Invisible Man* (1897), to either place them in established genres such as Gothic horror or the *fantastique*, or recharacterize them as works of science fiction. The determining element in this decision seems what I call the material imperative—the necessity on readers' part to take external events, however unlikely or absurd-seeming in terms of conventional modes of thought, as things *literally physically* present. Just as accelerated motion in DeQuincey forced mind out of its fantasy circle, here the science fiction genre seems born as mind is obliged to abandon metaphor and adopt science's experimental method to engage and understand its material environment.

Across the nineteenth century, in works from different cultures, a science-fictional *gestalt* seems to take shape. We have a new character—the scientist; new themes—scientific liberty and the reprieve; and a clear generic marker. What is now needed, for an international science fiction to develop in the twentieth century, is a masterplot that can be shared by all the national paradigms. For this to function as masterplot, it must probe the limits, of not simply human activity through science and technology, but human physical and mental *capacity*. Can mankind, by means of science, ever know more that our physical brains allow us to know? Can we advance beyond our physical limits as established by evolution to achieve a transhuman or "posthuman" condition? Chapter 6 takes J. D. Bernal's *The World, the Flesh, and the Devil* (1929) as a convenient "roadmap" that allows us to see how the Cartesian paradigm, evolutionary theory, and Western mankind's Judeo-Christian legacy all contribute to define the aspirations and limitations to scientific humanity's pursuit of the transhuman promise. Central to all major Western science fictions of the twentieth century—British, American, French, and Russian—is the quest to extend our environment, bodies, and mental capacity to "enhance" and hopefully transcend our human condition. The process that begins with Descartes's unaided reason seems to end with Bernal's "dimorphic split."

Bernal's "devil"—the human mind fatally divided between what we are and what we might become, between conservation and transformation, stasis and advancement—appears to mark the end point of science's, and science fiction's, adventure. As fiction pursuing the open-ended process of the scientific method, science fiction seems to meet a final barrier—that of the myth of science itself, science as hubris, as defiance of God's plan or nature's order. Finally, chapter 7 argues that Emerson's American paradigm, because of its ability to challenge—if not overcome—such material, cultural, and mythic limits, generates the Golden Age model that dominates science fiction in the twentieth century. At this point we see clearly how the fortunes of national science fictions depend on their origins. For example, the rationalist paradigm gives mind a privileged position in relation to external nature. Assailed by materialist science, mind remains not only unmovable, but in French science fiction, takes refuge in mind worlds that offer alternate fields of action. In British science fiction, the pessimism of evolution yields to a retreat to a social space, much as in conventional English novels. It is the distance between Wells's *The Time Machine* and *Star Begotten* (1937). In the case of both France and England, science fiction (if for different cultural reasons) tends to adhere to a fictional mainstream, tacking away from rich currents of pulp adventure. In the United States however (whose national novel is in essence a "boys' book"), the dime novel and popular fiction carry American romanticism and Emerson's paradigm into the twentieth century, where they claim the status of a separate form of literature in opposition to the academic mainstream. Emerson's dynamic, as product of new scientific vistas of his time and place, energizes the Cartesian mind, making it an active rather than rational force in the universe. Further, it makes the Western individual potential master of Eastern cosmic energy. I seek to show that, not only did it generate a science fiction—American and beyond—whose basic principle is that humans have no limits, and that ceaseless exploration and discovery are the destiny of the self-reliant individual, but that this dynamic may have contributed to the expanding circumference of science fiction to visual and "mediatized" forms easily accessible to world audiences. At the same time, in an age of increasingly ahuman models of physical order, Emerson's "representative men" play a role in allowing conventional fiction to narrate otherwise unnarratable "quantum worlds."

The study concludes with reflections on science fiction in the twenty-first century, and the difference between "global" and world science fiction. Goethe argued at the beginning of the nineteenth century that national literatures—each defending its language and cultural patterns it incarnates—tend to closure, to define themselves by excluding other literary traditions. An internationalist at the beginning of the scientific nineteenth century, he proposed an "anmarschierende Weltliteratur" [an advancing and/or approaching world literature] to be the dynamic open-ended product of an "erweiteres Vaterland" [extended fatherland] of what very well could be science itself. Goethe's idea of world literature as the ongoing dialectic between localizing and globalizing tendencies not only describes the international origins of science fiction but gives us a sense of how it might develop in the twenty-first century. In terms of scientific impact, the same creative matrix exists today as existed at the formation of national identities in Europe. In the case of science fiction, however, the encounter of global and national tendencies now plays out in terms of cultural *and* language resistance.

## NOTES

1. Damon Knight, *In Search of Wonder: Essays on Modern Science Fiction*, Revised and Enlarged (Chicago: Advent: Publishers, 1967), 1.

2. Robert A. Heinlein, "Science Fiction: Its Nature, Faults and Virtues," *The Science Fiction Novel: Imagination and Social Criticism*, edited by Basil Davenport (Chicago: Advent: Publishers, 1959), 22.

3. Isaac Asimov, "Social Science Fiction," *Modern Science Fiction: Its Meaning and Its Future*, edited by Reginald Bretnor (New York: Coward-McCann, 1953), 158.

4. See Robert L. Forward, "When Science Writes the Fiction," *Hard Science Fiction*, edited by George Slusser and Eric S. Rabkin (Carbondale: Southern Illinois University Press, 1986), 1–7.

5. Adam Roberts, *The History of Science Fiction* (London: Palgrave Macmillan, 2006), 28.

# Chapter One

# The Paradigms of Science Fiction

Attempts to locate a time and place of origin for science fiction have generally been too imprecise, or too precise—because critics seem to be looking for different things. When Pierre Versins calls science fiction a "literature of rational conjecture," he is describing a mode or method of dealing with physical nature. Yet in his first example of science fiction, *The Epic of Gilgamesh* (c. 2100 BCE) one has difficulty finding either reason or conjecture. Gilgamesh loses the possibility of eternal life, not by a *defaut de méthode*, but because he cannot stay awake long enough. His are physical, not cognitive limits. Critics at the other end of the spectrum do not look for a mode of apprehension, but a literary form. Thus can Brian W. Aldiss and many others locate the origin of science fiction at a specific time and a specific literary form: Mary Shelley's *Frankenstein; or, The Modern Prometheus* (1818), and the English Gothic.

A more precise way of proceeding, perhaps, is to seek to define the historical and cultural conditions that allow something called "science-fiction" to exist. Critics today have a clear idea of what "science" means. But when and where did that meaning become current? Some critics insist on the hyphen that connects the words "science" and "fiction" (as in John W. Campbell, Jr.'s *Astounding Science-Fiction*). Does this imply that the two elements thus joined were, at the origin, somehow incompatible? But what occurred, and when, to make them compatible? The modern sense of "science" came with the Scientific Revolution in seventeenth-century Europe. The word "fiction" acquired its present meaning in that century as well. But what was the nature of story and narrative before the advent of "fiction"? And, as narrative became "fiction," what changes in story, characterization, and "world view" might have resulted from this encounter with science? I pose these basic questions hypothetically, as starting points. Insofar as the term "science fiction" is a twentieth-century coinage, nothing in these preceding centuries can be easily labeled or pointed to. The coming-together of science and fiction occurred within pre-existing forms, at different moments of convergence, across the literary landscape of Western Europe, often in works that have never been considered "ancestors" of science fiction. This study seeks to identify, and examine, these points of convergence.

Thomas S. Kuhn, in *The Structure of Scientific Revolutions* (1962), saw the advancement of science not as a straight-line process, but one that moves through revolutionary moments he calls "paradigm shifts." Importantly, he saw these shifts as cultural moments, driven by both scientific discovery and social factors. It becomes a matter of choosing a model on the basis of its future possibilities. The shift is not just a matter of overthrowing old systems but is also a way to streamline the procedures and methods that allow science and culture alike to advance. The seventeenth-century Scientific Revolution was his model, and here, it seems, the possibility of a science-fiction begins. The term "paradigm" is helpful in studying the origins and development of science fiction, for it points not just at the scientific "apparatus"—the Copernican system, Descartes's quantitative geometry, tools like the calculus—but to the concurrence of social and national factors that not only favored adoption of the new paradigm but brought it, particularly in France, to interact with the world of fiction.

## PARADIGM FOUND

The Scientific Revolution that began in the sixteenth century and extended into the eighteenth century with Newton and the Enlightenment was an international phenomenon. The shape that science took in France, however, is the product of precise, perhaps unique, cultural factors. A strong current of rationalism informed medieval scholasticism in France, as observed in the Renaissance figure Rabelais. If on one hand he celebrates the linguistic and creative freedom of the Classical revival, on the other he subjects his unruly Gargantua to a regimen where he is taught that the trained and balanced mind, not authority, governs individual destiny. This awareness and exercise of the individual "moi" leads Montaigne to discover the relative nature of things. As opposed to Rabelais's anti-clericalism, Montaigne's sense of the centrality of the rational self—the "que sais-je?"—develops almost organically. It leads, in the early seventeenth century, to Corneille's radical transformation of the Renaissance theater in *Le Cid* (1636), where a woman wields reason against all elements of the monarchical stage—king, royalty, honor, love—

and essentially holds them at bay—as she proceeds to act on no authority but that of individual reason. Corneille's play was performed the same year that Descartes published his *Discours de la méthode*. Descartes's treatise, fully informed by the new sciences of his time, radically realigned the relation of mind to the natural world, and ultimately, the mind's own body. This was a quiet revolution but had massive consequences for the Christian world view. For by means of his "method," through exercise of reason, Montaigne's "je" can literally create itself. Once this occurs, this rational self is given the task, now unaided by any power except its own "right reason," of mastering the material world, and finally its own bodily passions. Descartes's method represents a science-driven paradigm shift for not only philosophy, but fiction as well.

It is in Descartes's France that our two terms—science and fiction—take on their modern meanings. The OED dates the first usage of the word "science" in the sense we understand today in France to 1725. Bacon still spoke of "natural philosophy" and used terms such as "new *organon*." Descartes himself rarely used the new word "science," but when he did, along with the word "method," it was in the modern sense of experimental science, to describe the tools by which he proposed to examine nature and relocate humanity in relation to that natural world. Descartes did not use the world "fiction." But in his *Les passions de l'âme* (1649), he spoke of "faiseurs de romans," referring to the form of prose narrative that, within this same century, becomes synonymous with the "roman" or novel.

"Fiction" as we understand it today is also a modern coinage. The word derives from the Latin "fictus," past participle of "fingere"—to form, invent, shape in the mind. *The American Heritage Dictionary of the English Language* (Fourth Edition, 2000) states that "Our first instance of 'fiction,' recorded in a work composed around 1412, was used in the sense of 'invention of the mind, that which was imaginatively invented.' It is not a far step from this meaning to the sense 'imaginative literature,' first recorded in 1599." When Littré's *Dictionnaire de la langue française* (1863–1876) defines "fiction" as the "invention de choses fictives," it refers specifically to "romans" in the modern sense of "novels." His citation of the earliest known use of the term in this sense is from Bossuet's *Oraison funèbre d'Henriette de France* (1669). It is not clear here whether the author is referring to something untrue, or the narrative form that conveys such untruths. The latter sense however seems the right one: "Elle y perdait [dans la lecture de l'histoire] insensiblement le goût des romans et de leurs fades héros; et soigneuse de se former sur le vrai, elle méprisait ces froides et dangereuses *fictions*." [Through the reading of history, she gradually, imperceptibly, lost all interest in novels and their insipid heroes; desirous to educate her mind by adhering to that which

was true, she came to despise these cold and dangerous *fictions*.] The historical terrain is prepared (even if the terms that will define it are not yet completely in place), in seventeenth-century France, for an encounter of between
"science" and "fiction" in their modern senses.

The term Scientific Revolution designates the historical moment when
observation and experimental examination of the physical world replace
authority, dogma, closure. We must find a modern definition of science
fiction that defines the form in terms of such a paradigm shift. The terms
in Asimov's definition, already cited, merits analysis in the context of the
Scientific Revolution in general, and the Cartesian response in particular. In
considering the origins of what Asimov calls a "branch of literature," his term
"impact" demands we fix a locus: When, in the history of Western culture,
might the word *impact* mean something in the sense of an interactive relation between science and fiction? Descartes not only sets new parameters to
mankind's interaction with external nature, but elaborates, in *Les passions
de l'âme*, a material model whereby mind can explore, and seek to master,
its body as seat of potentially destructive emotions. These "passions" are the
traditional stuff of literature—epics, tragedies, and their seventeenth-century
counterpart, fiction. Descartes's treatise offers a visible vector by which the
new world view of science might "impact" the world of fiction. The new
story of material science actively challenges the old story of authority. A
shift in human thought occurs that, in its impact on moral or religious world
views, proves potentially capable of *rewriting* the fundamental structure of
imaginative narratives about human relations.

The second important term in Asimov's definition is scientific *advance.*
The science that emerges from Galileo's cry "but it moves," from Descartes's
call for ideas that are not "true" in the old doctrinal sense, but simply "clear
and distinct," proposes a dynamic and open-ended process of experiment
and discovery that "advances" knowledge because the relationship between
mankind and physical nature, through successive hypotheses, is seen as ever-
changing, advancing in what will become the Enlightenment sense of this
word. This new vision of the relation between mind and world proves capable
of radically changing the way human stories are conceived and told. A new
model for structuring fictional stories is possible. Where and when was this
model first embraced?

The corollary question is: what sort of fiction might this model produce?
The conventional story of the hero's journey, trials, and homecoming, outlined in Vladimir Propp's *The Morphology of the Folktale* (1928), governs
the broad structure of fiction from Homer's *Odyssey* (c. eighth century BCE)
to Dante's *Divine Comedy* (1320).[1] Ironically, in this latter work, the actions
of Ulysses reveal conventional narrative on the verge of the scientific revo-

lution. Ulysses sails beyond the known world, thinks and acts "outside the box." For Dante to place him in the overall structure of his *Comedy*, he must sentence him for crimes other than scientific experimentation. Only in the seventeenth century does experimental science's radical new way of conceiving mankind's place in that world begin to generate new ways of telling the human story. We remember Robert L. Forward's statement: "I just write a scientific paper about some strange place—and by the time I have the science correct—the science has written the fiction."[2] This idea of writing a scientific paper about "some strange place" has uncanny resonance for the seventeenth century, for the emerging science of this century creates just such a "strange" new place—the uncharted realm of *res extensa*. Once Descartes gets "the science correct" and the world around us becomes a place of extended *things,* it becomes necessary to rewrite the way humans relate to the new sense of physical reality. Such a rewrite, on the level of narrative form, brings about corresponding transformations. What these are, and where they first occur, is our concern here.

The elements of the Cartesian "revolution" are well known. Instead of the authority of the Church—which still dictated, in the seventeenth century, the way humans conceived their relation to nature and God—Descartes proposed a *tabula rasa*, a method of thought whereby each and every person capable (as he put it) of *bon sens* could locate (and therefore define) his or her place in a material universe now seen as *res extensa*—comprised of things exterior to, and of another order than, the rational mind. The language necessary "pour acquérir la bonne science" would be one of simple, clear, mathematical precision.[3] The means of achieving this, available to all can think clearly and distinctly—in other words, "de ne recevoir aucune chose pour vrai que je ne connusse évidemment être telle" [to never accept anything as being true except for that which I completely know as being such]—is Descartes's "méthode" of systematic doubt. (*Discours de la méthode* 137)[4] The endpoint of this process—after we doubt away all dubious attachment to old ideas and systems of thought, even all bodily connections to the physical world—is the famous *cogito ergo sum*: "Je connus de là que j'étais une substance dont toute l'essence ou la nature n'est que de penser." [From this I concluded that I was a substance of which the entire being or nature is to think.] (*Discours* 148)

Descartes generates not only a mind-matter duality, but a complicated, paradoxical relationship between mind and body. Consistent with his duality, the latter is said to be a material "machine," separate from mind, part of *res extensa*: "En sorte que ce moi, c'est-à-dire l'âme, par laquelle je suis ce que je suis, est entièrement distincte du corps." [Such that this "me," that is, the soul by which I am what I am, is entirely distinct from the body.] (*Discours* 148) But as his analysis of this "machine" proceeds, Descartes comes to see that his rational soul is materially connected to it. What results is a new *dramatic* situation that was not present under Christian doctrine. There the body was simply the temporary abode of the soul, which leaves the body at death, bound for heaven or hell. But if Descartes still asserts mind to be of a different order, scientific fact leads him to see that the mind can only *extend* itself by means of bodily functions, which constitute its necessary interface with greater *res extensa.* Descartes is obliged to admit that the act of "penser" includes not only "douter," "vouloir," and "imaginer," but "sentir." The body, although material in substance, is somehow permeable to secondary aspects of pure thought.

Descartes devotes his entire *Les passions de l'âme* to the problem of how unextended mind can interact with the "mechanisms" of the physical body. The interface, he asserts, takes place by means of the sole singularity in the body, the so-called "pineal gland": the "petite glande qui est le principal siège de l'âme" of Art. 34 of *Les passions de l'âme,* or the "glande H" that figures in numerous drawings of the human brain in his *Traité de l'homme.* (*Passions* 711)[5] It is never clear how this gland, a material object, can act as point of passage between two qualitatively different entities. Given the attention Descartes pays to the means whereby the rational mind controls the mechanical functions of the body and passions, he clearly felt, as a matter of practical reason [*bon sens*], a fundamental need to define what today would be called an existential connection between them. For in the end, Descartes concedes that mind must die with the body. Descartes's last work, his *Les passions de l'âme,* is in fact a compendium of situations in which mind is called upon to master the bodily "passions" that threaten to overwhelm it. Once removed from its Christian and moral context, and radically *re-located* by the Cartesian duality as a purely physical struggle between a "higher" rational will and a physical process whereby external forces "stimulate" the nerves and humors of the material body, the Cartesian system offers a new paradigm to the "makers" of novels, whose key subject is traditionally the human passions.

At this point, the central element becomes Descartes's idea of the self-constructed rational mind, realized by means of a process of disconnecting itself from all external constraints, including morality and (openly stated in the eighteenth century) God itself. Descartes gives this rational self all the authority of the new sciences, making it *the* unique human quality in a world of material things. Recast in this Cartesian matrix, the experience of fiction, which previously involved action on a human stage conceived in religious or moral terms, is radically refocused along the lines of this coordinate system of mind, body, and *res extensa*—a refocusing full of potential fictional drama. For if Descartes gives human reason great powers, by the same token, in designating the theater of mankind's actions a place of extended *things,* he alienates mankind from its environment, opening the door to Pascal's terror of infinite spaces, whereby mankind's central position in the scheme of things is threatened. In terms of fiction, what is immediately significant is this redefined relation between mind and body. This new sense of body becomes the conduit whereby science can begin to write the fiction.

It is probable, given evidence in the text, that Descartes's final treatise was a shaping force for Mme de Lafayette's *La Princesse de Clèves* (1678), generally hailed as the "first French novel." Descartes set forth a coordinate system, whereby x is horizontal movement or location in *res extensa*, y is vertical resistance of mind, and z (the body) is the meeting point of x and y. Too much reason brings to a standstill one's normal relations with society or nature and stymies the course of passions like love. If we turn the proposition around, excess of passion bends the vector of mind from vertical to horizontal, letting body be swept away in *res extensa.* The first scenario is that of *Le Cid.* The second is that of Jean Racine's *Phèdre* (1677), where the heroine literally "loses her mind" to fatal passion. *La Princesse de Clèves* strikes a dynamic balance between these coordinates. Madame de Clèves, threatened by potentially devastating passion for the Duc de Nemours, is able to conquer her passions through reason and retreats to a convent. She does so not in the name of religion, moral values, or even social rank and order, but for the purely selfish reason of self-mastery, of finding "repos"—a physical solution to a problem now cast in purely material terms. In the passage from Bossuet, we saw that triumph of the rational mind has become, by the second half of the seventeenth century, the prescription for good fiction. The unfortunate Henriette is seen as one who, despising the "dangerous fictions" of popular novels of the time full of intrigue and amorous adventure, instead *formed her mind* in terms of the "vrai," truth achieved in Cartesian terms by mastery of self.

But it would be simplistic to see the "impact" of the Cartesian system as simply rewriting the fiction here. In terms of story, de Lafayette's work taps into a vogue of "historical" narratives which, in the France of Louis XIV, seek to establish lineage and legitimacy, adapting epic figures to "real" historical events. At the core of her story are not only human passions, but the question of human time. The idea of the *cogito* evolves very differently in a descriptive work of analytical science than the story situation of a novel. Descartes offers an anatomy of the different bodily passions that effect the operation of his "rational soul." At several places in his description, we seem on the verge of materialist determinism, as these passions appear to overwhelm the actions of the "higher" rational mind. In the end, however, Descartes simply follows the logic of his deductive argument and declares the mastery of body by the rational mind. Time is not an element in Descartes's analytical method. But in novels we are in worlds of human time, bodily time, where a passion mastered today can return with destructive force tomorrow. The Princesse de Clèves struggles to control her "fatal" passion and ultimately can renounce her love for Nemours. To do so, however, she isolates herself in a convent, with daily fears that, were she to see him again, his physical presence would shatter her self-control. As she lives this struggle day by day, it takes a physical toll on her body. This novel, in fact, seems to have been written to *test* the Cartesian *cogito* in a fictional matrix that takes on—perhaps itself inspired by the experimental sciences—an experimental function of its own.

No one would call Mme de Lafayette's novel science fiction as we understand it today. Yet in the novel's relationship to the science of the time, as mediated by Descartes, it fits Asimov's definition. Moreover, if this is (as most critics say) the first French novel, then the novel in France evolves from a thought experiment. Only in 1880 did Émile Zola, in his *Le roman expérimental*, identified clearly the form of fiction French writers had been practicing since *La Princesse de Clèves*. Zola openly called upon novelists to vie with scientists in the sense that each novel is itself a form of experimentation. Zola's "theme" however remains that of the majority of previous French fiction writers—testing the pretensions and limits of the rational mind in its attempts to master an external world increasingly seen as governed by the iron laws of matter. Perhaps one reason French science fiction, as it seeks to define itself after World War II, resembles its "mainstream" counterpart, to the point of "not being seen" by French critics, is that it remains fixated on the same Cartesian duality of mind and matter it shares with French fiction in general. As evidence for scientific materialism becomes overwhelming, the rational self is increasingly seen as powerless, its actions irrelevant. Yet its presence is constantly maintained, often as the sole remaining refuge of the *cogito* that continues to define humanity in a world of repressive materiality.

This Cartesian paradigm shift locates a point of origin for a "science-fiction" that is some 200 years before the time and place conventional wisdom generally fixes the point of departure: nineteenth-century England and *Frankenstein*. As stated, Adam Roberts argues that the origins of science fiction lie in the intellectual struggle between Catholicism and Protestantism in seventeenth-century Europe. To test this idea, one need not go as far as England. For in France, the rudiments of such a struggle are discernable in Blaise Pascal's thought-experiments. Pascal reacted violently to the Cartesian system but did not reject the mind-matter duality. Instead, he *experimented* with it. To simplify things, we can see his angle of vision as "Protestant" in contrast to Descartes's residual Catholicism. Ultimately, however, Pascal's response to Descartes, in his fragmentary *Pensées* (1670), is a *fictional* response, in that it offers a series of mini-narratives that confront the scientific concepts of rational mind and *res extensa* with a human story, one again borrowed from Montaigne—the story of the "human condition." Usually, passages like the "thinking reed" are considered metaphors, or parables. But in essence they stand for nothing other than themselves. They are compressed versions of the story of the human condition in a new age of material science. They are best seen, given their elaboration by hosts of later writers, as mini-narratives, embryonic examples of something that again can be called a "science-fiction."[6]

In this sense, Pascal follows Descartes, who also produced mini-scenarios which form a crucial part of the deep narrative of both French culture and French fiction. If less incisively than Pascal, Descartes presents his scientific vision of mankind's epistemological adventure in proto-fictional situations. These again are more than mere exempla. He launches his discussion of the famous "method" with the fictional story of his night in the "stove," an event with a precise date and location. The most striking passages in his scientific writings are scenarios with real narrative potential. For example, in his *Méditations touchant la première philosophie . . .* (1642), Descartes reframes the old tempter story as he recounts how the process of doubt leads the rational mind to understand that its own acts of "right reason," not God's truth, provide the sole fixed point in a world of shifting appearances: "Je supposerai donc qu'il y a, non point un vrai Dieu, qui est la souveraine source de vérité, mais un certain mauvais génie, non moins rusé et trompeur que puissant, qui a employé toute son industrie à me tromper." [I will posit therefore that there is no true God, who is the sovereign source of truth, but rather a certain evil genius, no less cunning and deceitful than he is powerful, who has used all of his activity in order to deceive me.] (273) The workings of mind are fictionalized as radical physical *actions* that not only remove "toutes les choses extérieures que nous voyons" [all exterior things that we see] but those very body parts that physically attach mind to this world of deception: "Je me considérerai moi-même comme n'ayant point de mains, point d'yeux, point de chair, point de sang." [I will consider myself as not having any hands at all, no eyes, no flesh, no blood.] (272) The struggle with the "mauvais génie" is a physical one, the removal of his physical parts a means of literally denying this being ways of "getting a handle" on him. The scientist abandons his role as descriptor to become a *narrator* with a story to tell, of how his own "obstinate attachment" to the reality of mind gives him the means of tricking the master of illusion in turn: "Et si par ce moyen [doubt] il n'est pas en mon pouvoir de parvenir à la connaissance d'aucune vérité, à tout le moins il est en ma puissance de suspendre mon jugement." [And if by means of such doubt, it is not in my power to arrive at the knowledge of any truth whatsoever, it is nonetheless in my power to suspend my judgment.] (272) In the world of this "evil genius," our ability *not* to judge ultimately leads to apprehension of the sole remaining fixed point, the thinking mind. Here and only here positive judgment can occur: "Il suffit de bien juger pour bien faire." [It is sufficient to judge well in order to do good.] The story of the *cogito* has a happy end.

An interesting sidelight is the way Descartes's scenario has traveled across centuries and oceans to be given a new story treatment, this time in a work of twentieth-century science fiction—Ray Bradbury's "No Particular Night or Morning" (1951). The same systematic doubting away of one's entire physical being now takes place in a materialist world with no possibility of a metaphorical escape hatch. Bradbury's protagonist Hathaway is a failed Cartesian in the world of Bishop Berkeley, looking for a Cartesian absolute—"mental evidence"—to anchor his existence in the flux of phenomena: "I want evidence that you can carry in your mind and always smell and touch and feel. But there's no way to do that."[7] He comes to accept that, because nothing exists but percepts in the present, the void of space is his ideal habitat, a place where there is no particular night or morning. Bradbury's science fiction story goes one step beyond Descartes, giving Cartesian doubt the power to *physically* to remove all the limbs, legs and arms, that attach it to its material locus. In fact, Bradbury's story arguably makes fully literal a narrative of the body that begins with Descartes. The latter's method is not a logical maneuver so much as an experiment to determine what can and cannot be "detached" from one's essential self: "et je trouve ici que la pensée est un attribut qui m'appartient; elle seule ne peut être détachée de moi." [and I find here that thought is an attribute that belongs to me; it alone cannot be detached from my being.] (277) Descartes discovers that, though thought alone defines the rational soul, it nevertheless *exists* in the world of extension and duration, the world of the body: "*Je suis, j'existe*: cela est certain; mais combien de temps? A savoir, autant de temps que je pense." [*I am, I exist:* that is certain; but for how long? As long as I am thinking.] (277) When Descartes, in his later *Les passions de l'âme*, addresses the relations between mind and material body, he is forced to admit that mind cannot survive the death of body.

Descartes held to his mind-matter duality all his life. Yet increasingly, his scientific investigations brought him to realize that, if the "soul" as seat of reason is to challenge *res extensa,* it must first achieve *absolute* mastery over the passions, the imponderables of the body: "Qu'il n'y a point d'âme si faible qu'elle ne puisse, étant bien conduite, acquérir un pouvoir absolu sur ses passions." [And that there is absolutely no soul that is not capable, provided it is *well directed*, of establishing absolute control over its passions.] To *tell* the process of how mind controls the passions, Descartes invents another fiction—that of the "fontenier"—the master of the waterworks in the royal gardens. Again, what seems simply a metaphor holds the germ of a story. As entities, the master of the waters and the rational mind are not simply comparative terms. We are told they *function* in like manner. Given the state of description in seventeenth-century physiology, it is not far-fetched to present the flow of fluids and humors in the body as a waterworks: "Et enfin quand l'âme raisonnable sera en cette machine, elle y aura son siège principal dans le cerveau, et sera là comme le fontenier, qui doit être dans les regards où se vont rendre tous les tuyaux de ces machines, quand il veut exciter, ou empêcher, ou changer en quelque façon leurs mouvements." [And finally when the rational soul will be in that machine (the body), its principal seat will be in the brain, and it will act there like the master of waters, who must know precisely where all the pipes of his machines go.] (*Traité de l'Homme* 815) Science yields to story here; the "fontenier" is an exploratory fiction designed to reach out to the bodily unknown. Again, later science fiction writers will retell this same story, now in a completely literal manner. Works like Asimov's *Fantastic Voyage* (1966) or Norman Spinrad's "Carcinoma Angels" (1967) literally inject material "fonteniers," miniaturized masters of the water, into the waterworks of a human body to explore, and physically master, the flow of molecules and chemicals through its arteries and organs.

One can argue that the paradigm shift initiated by the Cartesian system has continued right down to modern times to shape French culture and fiction. The key element is the insistence on the rational soul as anchor of the mind-matter duality in the face of overwhelming scientific evidence that no such "Cartesian ghost" exists. The Cartesian pendulum has swung back and forth between extremes. Descartes's mechanist fictions lead to La Mettrie's *L'homme machine* (1748) and the Great Machine of the eighteenth-century materialists. At the other extreme is Laplace's "demon," a super Cartesian intellect so vast that it can process all the data in the universe at a given instant, from the infinitely great to the tiniest atom. The history of French science is one of oscillation between the positivist and classifying sciences, characterized by Cuvier, and the experimental science of figures like Lavoisier, Sadi Carnot, Claude Bernard, and Louis Pasteur. Reading the small print in the work of the latter, we still find hints of the Cartesian ghost, the sense that the rational soul, in the face of evidence to the contrary, still assures our human role in the scheme of things. The final assault, now on the Cartesian mind per se, comes in neuroscience. Jean-Pierre Changeux, in *L'homme neuronal* (1983), says this about the problem: "Les possibilités combinatoires liées au nombre et à la diversité des connexions du cerveau de l'homme paraissent effectivement suffisantes pour rendre compte des capacités humaines. Le clivage entre activités mentales et neuronales ne se justifie pas. Désormais, à quoi bon parler d'Esprit." [The possible combinations linked to the number and diversity of human cerebral connections appear to be sufficient to account for the capacity of human reason. The distinction between neuronal and "mental" activities is no longer tenable. Why do we need to speak of "rational mind" anymore?][8] Yet at the end of Changeux's study, we see this neuronal brain, apparently dissatisfied with the limits matter has placed on "mind," transcending itself in an "apocalypse neuronal."

French science fiction itself operates at the extreme ends of Descartes's mind-matter coordinate system. As with the "apocalypse neuronal," at the point where matter seems to obliterate mind, a "reversal" occurs, the landscape is turned inside out, and mind encompasses matter. French science fiction produces stories that literally transpose the extended world inside the confines of the brain, creating a mental landscape where activities can again be regulated by the mind. Mind becomes the space of alternate worlds and temporal manipulations, models of a rational order it substitutes for an increasingly uncontrollable world of irrational phenomena. These mind-worlds are the terrain of both the "nouveau roman" and French science fiction. They are found in science fiction works like Philippe Curval's *Cette chère humanité* (1976), where the entire Common Market reduces itself to a mind space no larger than the protagonist's bathroom. We have numerous titles like that of Francis Berthelot's *La Ville au fond de l'oeil* (1986). It is not a question here of perceiving the external world, but of transposing it literally into the space of the eye, the window into the Cartesian soul.

To gauge the depth of dialogue, post-Descartes, in France, one need only turn to his contemporary Pascal, who sums up his relation to Descartes in the following phrase: "Descartes, inutile, incertain." Descartes's metaphysical concept of the rational mind can be said to be "uncertain," therefore "useless" in the material world because mind, in Descartes, has no physical location. To call it *res cogitans* is contradictory, for how can it be a "thing" if it has no existence in extended space? In *Pensées,* Pascal conducts what could be called a science-fictional experiment before its time: he re-attaches this Cartesian *cogito* to its physical body to measure that body, as finite entity, against the vertiginous scale of the material universe. Pascal "extrapolates" from Galileo's heavens and Cyrano's plurality of worlds the infinite vastness of the cosmos; from Leeuwenhoek's microscope, he extrapolates the realm of the infinitely small. Through this maneuver, the "mystical" authority of the rational soul is abolished. In this new context of *total* human insignificance, Pascal re-narrates the mind-matter question.

Descartes's text is useless because, like "scripture," it is static. Pascal animates and transforms it with some striking fictions. To present Descartes's abstract system, he animates its positions in a sort of back-and-forth dialogue: "Descartes. Il faut dire en gros: Cela se fait par figure et mouvement. Car cela est vrai, mais de dire quelles et composer la machine, cela est ridicule. . . . Et quand cela serait vrai, nous n'estimons pas que toute la philosophie vaille une heure de peine." [Descartes. In general (his ideas) reduce to this: everything is a product of geometry and movement. There is truth in this, but to say what those truths are and to build the machine on this basis, that is ridiculous. And even if what he says were true, we esteem that all of philosophy is not worth even an hour of effort.][9] This "heure de peine" echoes Pascal's famous statement that human beings cannot stay an hour in a room alone. Here he trumps Descartes's story of the "stove" with a mini-narrative of his own. Pascal's comments on *divertissement* address the same problem Descartes discusses in his *Les passions de l'âme*: "Je voudrais donc porter l'homme . . . a être prêt et dégagé des passions . . . sachant combien sa connaissance s'est obscurcie par les passions." [I would like therefore to bring mankind to the point where (it is) ready and disengaged from its passions . . . knowing just how much its ability to know is obscured by the passions.] (119) Pascal however turns this situation against Descartes, as if in a duel of contending story scenarios. For by dramatically presenting human beings as "embarqués," body and soul in the material course of things, Pascal narrates rather than demonstrates that the *cogito* is itself a "fiction," as is the claim that mind can be separated from body. In Pascal's text, we witness a dialogue going on between science and fiction. As rational scientist, Pascal knows that we are nothing in relation to the "all" of the physical universe. But as creator of fictions, Pascal seeks scenarios whereby mankind, also by "figure et mouvement," hopes to compensate for the physical "disproportion" between itself and the material infinities. In the scientist's version of the story, reason will never master the new infinite universe. In the fictional version, however, this same reason is bid to search for means, through grammatical and mathematical "feintes," of creating some form of parity with the physical universe.

Where Descartes is seen as merely *describing* mankind's place in the universe, Pascal invents a *fiction* he calls the "human condition"—a dynamic construct, where mankind exists in a state of endless contradiction. Pascal's formulations, like Descartes's mind-matter duality, are extremes, but they are not so much mutually exclusive as mutually "repelling" entities. Pascal calls these extremes "contrairiétés." As such they are endless oscillations, not between ideas or categories, but between contrary conditions of human *existence*: "grandeur de l'homme," and "misère de l'homme." In itself, our physical condition is totally, hopelessly miserable. Pascal recounts this as a mini-narrative: "Notre âme est jetée dans le corps où elle trouve nombre, temps, dimensions, elle raisonne là-dessus et appelle cela nature . . . et ne peut croire autre chose." [Our soul is thrown into a body where it finds number, time, dimensions, it reasons thereupon, and calls this nature . . . and cannot believe anything else.] (418) In this condition, our imaginations remain powerless to grasp even the slimmest fraction of material truth: "Mais si notre vue s'arrête là que l'imagination passe outre, elle se lassera plutôt de concevoir que la nature de fournir. Tout le monde n'est qu'un trait imperceptible dans l'ample sein de la nature. Nulle idée n'en approche, nous avons beau enfler nos conceptions au-delà des espaces imaginables, nous n'enfantons que des atomes au prix de la réalité des choses." [But if our power of sight stops there where imagination moves beyond, this latter will sooner become more tired of conceiving than nature of furnishing data. Every person is nothing more than an imperceptible mark on the ample busom of nature. No idea can even come close to grasping what nature is, in vain do we expand our ideas beyond what is spatially imaginable, we come up with nothing but atoms in relation to what the reality of things might be.] (199)

What then is mankind's "grandeur"? Pascal's "feinte" here is not to follow Descartes as he describes mind gradually becoming mired in its passions, but to have mind simply reject these as insignificant. Pascal recognizes the role of the passions and their ability to expel us physically from the Cartesian room of mind. But he dismisses them (and with them Descartes's entire treatise) with a bluntly material action: "Nous sommes pleins de choses qui nous jettent au-dehors." [We are full of things that cast us outside ourselves.] (143) Descartes describes this "pleins de choses" in great detail. Pascal instead creates a mathematical comparison of dramatic proportions, where the problem of the passions becomes a matter of *scale*, in this case the relation of finite to infinite quantities. Given this, reason cannot, in purely physical terms, "master" *res extensa,* either in the large or small world. Pascal at this point no longer thinks as a physical scientist but as a mathematician. Negating the mind-body problem, he posits the human condition (mind *and* body) as a question of mathematical proportionality (or disproportionality), where both physical extremes recede infinitely as we move toward them: "Mais comme c'est nous qui surpassons les petites choses nous croyons plus capables de les posséder, et cependant il ne faut pas moins de capacité pour aller jusqu'au néant que jusqu'au tout. Il la faut infinie pour l'un et l'autre . . ." [But insofar as it is us who surpass in size the little things, we believe ourselves more capable of possessing them, and yet just as much capacity is needed to go to the zero point as to the totality of things. For the one or the other, that capacity has to be infinite . . .] (199)

Extrapolating his human condition from mathematical formulas rather than scientific description, Pascal sketches the scenario for a stunningly dramatic narrative. In the story he constructs, Pascal restates the *cogito* as a situation whereby the mind reasons itself into absolute isolation: "Enfin les choses extremes sont pour nous comme si elles n'étaient point et nous ne sommes point à leur égard; elles nous échappent ou nous à elles." [Finally things at their extremities are for us as if they did not exist at all, and in turn we are nothing at all in relation to them. They escape us as we do them.] (199) In

Pascal's scenario, the ultimate act of reason is to realize that reason is infinitely powerless: "La dernière démarche de la raison est de reconnaître qu'il y a une infinité de choses qui la surpassent." [The final action of reason is to recognize that there are an infinite number of things that surpass it.] (188)

If the "stove" is at the center of Descartes's narrative, Pascal's center is the prison cell. But this cell, in his dramatic game of proportion, becomes our entire universe, just as that universe becomes a small speck in an infinity of receding universes: "ce petit cachot où il [l'homme] se trouve logé, j'entends l'univers." [this small prison cell where mankind finds itself living, I mean the universe.] (199) If for Descartes in his stove, the process of reason was a liberating act, for Pascal, reason leads mankind to understand the absolute nature of its imprisonment in extended space. Pascal now speaks openly in fictional terms, and the fiction is one of absolute hopelessness: "Le dernier acte est sanglant quelque belle que soit la comédie en tout le reste. On jette enfin de la terre sur la tête et en voilà pour jamais." [The final act is always bloody no matter how beautiful the comedy has been in all the rest. In the end, they throw dirt on the head, and everything is over forever.] (165)

This is the condition of "man without God," and the condition of Descartes's man. But unlike the God of Catholicism, with its levels of intercession, this Jansenist God is absent—*deus absconditus*—His designs and grace inscrutable to human reason. These are totally different levels of reality, as are the faculties that, respectively, can access them: "le coeur a ses raisons, que la raison ne connaît point." The negative "point" marks absolute separation. We notice however that the same word—"reason," or rather "reasons," a sort of indeterminate human middle between extremes—crosses the absolute boundary between head and heart. If the cold equations of Pascal's mathematical science imprison us, that same science appears to offer us a way out of the material prison, this time by means of a *feinte* whereby logic tricks itself.

Pascal, a writer admired for his *literary* qualities, has absorbed the impact of Descartes's scientific vision, and, in the manner of the thought experiment, reshaped it in the matrix of his fiction of the *condition humaine.* And indeed thought—the "reason" that he diminishes on one hand—becomes the means whereby he hopes to reinstate the role of the Cartesian mind in the human equation. This he accomplishes by restating, at a different level of apprehension, Descartes's two levels of reality—mind and matter. Pascal's famous *contrariétés*—his process of "renversement continuel du pour au contre" [a continual reversal of terms, from for to against, against to for] (93)—is itself a method, but one that Pascal proceeds to fictionalize, as the climax of his story of the human condition, at which time humanity simultaneously understands the misery of its grandeur and grandeur of its misery. Pascal's French prose is written, at one and the same time, with the precision of a mathematical formula and slipperiness of the *double entendre.* This is something difficult to render in translation. Take the following "first person narrative": "S'il se vante, je l'abaisse. S'il s'abaisse, je le vante. Et je le contredit toujours. Jusqu'à ce qu'il comprenne/Qu'il est un monstre incomprehensible." [If he praises himself, I bring him down. If he lowers himself, I praise him. And I contradict him always. Until he finally comprehends/That he is an incomprehensible monster.] (130) The "I" speaking in this passage must be (this side of God) Pascal himself. Animated by this "narrator," what begins as a mathematical statement—a proportional equation—turns into the description of a *someone* subjecting a human object (a "him") to a series of contrary actions designed to make the human object know its place in the physical world. But as human logic displaces that of pure number, a turn occurs on the word "comprendre." It has two meanings: first, to contain physically; second, to understand by act of mind. But here, in this play of words, if we are "contained" by the physical world, we can because of this "comprehend" our condition; we know ourselves in this play of contraries, but only as an "incomprehensible" monster. This is verbal sleight of hand, mind using mind to extricate itself from the inextricable.

We now come to Pascal's most famous fiction, that of the "roseau pensant." [thinking reed] Here again the word "comprendre" provides the bridge between mind and matter. But the play is more complex yet. The sign of absolute negation "ne . . . point" indicates *total* separation between human concepts like "dignity" and a totally *unhuman* world of *res extensa.* But there is another "point" in the equation, this time not a negative pronoun, but a noun, "a point." The point can be a mathematical entity or can indicate a physical location, the place where the human mind stakes out an (infinitesimally small) foothold in the absolute void that literally "engulfs" it: "Ce n'est point par l'espace que je dois chercher ma dignité, mais c'est du règlement de ma pensée. . . . Par l'espace l'univers me comprend et m'engloutit comme un point: par la pensée je la comprends." [It is not at all in terms of space that I must seek my dignity, but it is by putting my reason in order. In terms of space, the universe encompasses and swallows me up like a point; (on the other hand) it is through reason that I understand the universe.] (113) As climax to this evolving story of mankind's condition, the "thinking reed" exists at the crossroads between metaphor and narrative as defined by Gerald Prince, where "in a narrative sequence the last situation or event constitutes a *partial* repetition of the first" (52): "L'homme est un roseau, le plus faible de la nature, mais c'est un roseau *pensant.*" Both man and reed are the weakest things in the world, but once we add "thinking" to the equation, there is movement forward, a potential story in Prince's sense. The extreme logic of our *mathematical* condition (man = reed) gives way to the tentative condition of "thinking" reed. We may be the *weakest* thing in nature, but because we think and nature does not, we may claim a *comparative* advantage: man is *"encore plus noble* que ce que le tue, parce qu'il sait qu'il meurt . . . l'univers n'en sait rien." [mankind is still more noble than that which kills it, because it knows it dies . . . the universe knows nothing of this] If reason traps itself in its equations, reason also learns to *use* that same reason to circumvent these equations. For now, the weakest thing, because it possesses reason, is somehow, magically, more than the sum of the universe's parts. By such gambits, Pascal brings the Cartesian mind back into nature's absolute equations.

Two things in the Descartes-Pascal dialectic are crucial to the creation of a science fiction. One is the mind-matter duality which, in writings like *Les passions de l'âme*, becomes a mind-body *problem,* the physical location where advancing world views born of science will "impact" the religious, moral, and ultimately "humanist" narrative of Western culture. The other is the problem created by Descartes's adherence, despite scientific evidence to the contrary, to the idea of the "otherness" of human reason. This adherence generates, in the complex reaction of scientist-writer Pascal, what is possibly the first example of a science-fictional mode of *thinking,* in Western or in any literature. What does it mean to *think* in a science fiction manner? It means to take a new, science-driven vision of the world, which like Descartes's paradigm opens up previous closed systems, and extrapolate from it *further* human situations and conditions of existence. It is with Pascal that fiction—the human story—begins to respond and adapt to scientific advancement. Pascal's mini-narratives—as the first genuine works of science fiction—have proven so cogent (and in a sense so "modern") that they are still being rewritten today, bringing a terrifying, yet somehow comforting adaptation of the scientific vision of things to numerous fiction writers. For instance, Pascal's "thinking reed," his dramatization of the human condition as humans chained in a dark cave awaiting death by fire, or his terrifying portrayal of the silence of space ("le silence éternel de ces espaces infinis m'effraie") have provided the scientific "kernel" for numerous fictions, from André Malraux's *Le condition humaine* (1933) to science fiction works from J.-H. Rosny aîné's *Les navigateurs de l'infini* (1925) to Jean-Pierre Andrevon's "Comme une étoile solitaire et fugitive" (1981), and Gregory Benford's "Exposures" (1981) and "Mozart on Morphine" (1989). Benford sees Pascal's two infinities not just as a theme or plot, but at the center of science's and science fiction's "sense of wonder." In his essay, "Pascal's Terror," Benford extols that form of science fiction "that does not subvert the infinite": "Perhaps humanity equally cannot stand emptiness, the flip side of infinity. For Pascal feared the meaninglessness of it, the absence of any hint that human effort had pith and substance. Nearly all science fiction attempts to answer this supreme agoraphobia by populating the yawning abyss."[10]

## PARADIGM LOST:
## E. T. A. HOFFMANN'S "COPERNICAN REVOLUTION"

German culture and science made an amazing leap into prominence in the last decades of the eighteenth and early decades of the nineteenth century—telescoping a "classical" and "romantic" period into a few short years. Germany found itself in the position of mediator between two dominant cultures—France and England—and, in the areas of science and philosophy of science, at the crossroads between three distinct and contradictory currents. Two are clearly defined: Cartesian rationalism on one hand, with its adherence to *a priori* ideas, and the powerful assault on rationalist systems from Newtonian science. Newton's mechanical model derives knowledge from sense experience, proceeding by inductive, not deductive, reasoning to general "laws" whereby natural phenomena are explained in terms of cause and effect. A rationalist *a priori* such as Descartes's *cogito* cannot be given a causal explanation (one sees this in *Les passions de l'âme*, whereas material evidence mounts to the contrary, he resorts to simply reaffirming the existence of the rational soul). Science seems to invalidate metaphysics. In response, we have Kant's question: can metaphysical speculation lead to knowledge at all?

The third current, that of Berkeley, Hume, and empirical skepticism, can be seen as a counterattack on Newtonian science. For Hume, we know only our percepts; we perceive things in sequence, thus can assume, at best, that they exist in the physical world in chronological succession. But we cannot prove that causality exists. Rather, within our minds, we organize our impressions according to mental categories such as constancy and coherence. These are categories we bring to nature; from them we cannot prove that such a thing as causality exists in the external world. Berkeley carried this even farther with his famous statement: *esse est percipi*, to be is to be perceived. The only world we know is the one we perceive; if we turn our backs, will that world still exist? Skepticism, for Hume, doubts away not only causality but the existence of a "self," and with it the substance said to subtend the existence of self and world alike. He therefore challenges both the inductive method of science and the existence of *a priori* entities like the Cartesian self. Limited to the world of percepts, we can never know that such a thing as the rational soul exists. Any idea of a "self" is a construct after the fact, a mental fantasy. The skeptic's refusal of both scientific method and rationalism leads to a second of Kant's questions: Can reason know anything apart from the experience of direct perception?

Empiricism, then, threatens the basis of both physics and metaphysics. Neither *res cogitans* nor *res extensa* offer fixed points in the flux of percepts, because we can never know the *Ding an sich*. We have here a potential paradigm shift where both science and philosophy must engage a totally different sense of mankind's relation to the universe. The science that derives from this shift will wait until the twentieth century to be formulated—in probability and quantum theory, or Goedel's theorem, which states that no system, rational or physical, is ever closed. Hume's theory of perception leads away from both rationalist systems of organization and the laws of Newtonian physics, looking forward to modern physics, where perception becomes a means of participating in the creation of an event, where we cannot observe a phenomenon without changing it, and changing our perception of self in turn.

The implications of Hume's theory of perception leads to an impasse that plays itself out in thought experiments like the Einstein-Podolsky-Rosen paradox. It challenges the idea of "locality," the principle that what happens in one location does not depend on variables subject to control by an experimenter in a distant and separated location. Einstein-Podolsky-Rosen seems to reveal an unexplained interconnectedness between particles in two different localities, as if the particle in area A were instantaneously to *know* the spin direction of the particle in area B. The barrier that sustains both locality and the discrete nature of percepts in Hume's theory—the speed of light—appears to fail. There appears here an order that links localized phenomena but transcends concepts such as causality—a "superluminary" connection between things that lies beyond both quantum probability and (on the macroscopic level of Hume's percepts) the complex structures of chaos theory. Einstein did not hesitate to call this connection "telepathic," throwing the idea of an order beyond locality into the realm of the paranormal.

This takes us back to two late-eighteenth-century reactions to Hume's theory. One is Kant's famous "Copernican revolution," where in concepts such as the "synthetic *a priori*," he seeks to negotiate what seems an insurmountable divide between physics and metaphysics, between locality and "transcendental" order. The other is E. T. A. Hoffmann's strikingly original fictional response to this dilemma, his story "Der Sandmann" (1816). Kant took up the challenge of Hume's skeptical empiricism as a problem of "critical" philosophy but came down on the side of science. His fundamental question— what can reason know apart from experience?—revisits the Cartesian *cogito* from a non-metaphysical point of view. For though he admits that knowledge begins with experience, he goes on to argue that knowledge is not entirely *from* or *of* experience. An example is causality. No one has experienced every possible instance of causal connection. Yet from what experience we have, we posit a law of causality. This, to Kant, is not a statement of an absolute but rather a "judgment," what science today calls a hypothesis. Kant's term for ideas like causality is "synthetic a priori." Here, if the process of statement is initiated in the realm of percept and experience (the predicate is not contained in the subject), it moves as far as it can in the *noumenal* realm of the idea. The outer limit however remains the *Ding an sich,* the thing in itself, which exists outside perception and thus remains unknowable. Kant's sense of how the mind functions—as faculty of judgment where perceptions pass through fixed structures that require choice (for example "quantity" where we must choose in terms of more or less, or "modality" where we must decide whether a given phenomenon is possible or impossible)—appears to mediate between the rationalists and science. But does it really address Hume, who sees mind as conforming to objects of perception, isolated in an internal "theater" where imagination roams infinite realms, yet remains bound in its own space? Descartes's stove has become Hamlet's nutshell.

Kant claims to bring about a "Copernican Revolution" but leaves unanswered two extreme positions. One is perceptual isolation, itself a radical form of "locality." The other is the thing-in-itself, guarantor of an order beyond knowing, in modern terms an "implicate" order that lies beyond judgmental barriers such as the speed of light. Kant's offers the philosopher's response to the implications of Hume's skepticism for science. But is there a fictional response as well? The giant of German classicism and romanticism, Goethe, was throughout his long life fascinated with scientific activity in Europe. His *Farbenlehre* [*The Theory of Colors*] (1810) challenged Newton's optics. But there is little evidence of any deep structural impact of science or scientific method on his fiction. His novel *Die Wahlverwandtschaften* [*Elective Affinities*] (1809), though its title refers to a chemical theory of mutual attraction of the time, does little more than use chemistry as a metaphor for human relationships. The novel explores a running parallel between material science and emotional life. But problems arise when critics attempt to see human actions in the novel as being determined in the same way chemical reactions would be. Science simply overlays the fiction here; in no way does it (as with the novels that issue from Cartesian France) cause a radical transformation of the themes and structures of narrative.

There is however one literary event in early nineteenth-century Germany which, all by itself, comes close to affecting a paradigm shift in the relation of fiction to science. This is Hoffmann's "Der Sandmann." Hoffmann's fiction existed on the margins of what had rapidly become a literary canon in Germany (Goethe found its style grating to the ear). Originally a musician and music critic, Hoffmann segued into prose fiction as creator of such forms as the "musikalische Erzählung" [literally "the musical narrative"], "Nachtstucke" [night pieces], and most famously the "Fantastiestücke in Callots Manier" [literally "fantasy pieces in the manner of (Jacques) Callot], where later generations saw him as inventor of the *fantastique,* more a fictional mode than fixed genre. Working outside the mainstream of what would become the bourgeois "realist" novel, Hoffmann's "minor" and invented forms appear more open to new ideas, many of which reflected scientific discoveries of the time, notably the association of paranormal phenomena with the emerging fluid sciences. England too had a brief moment when minor forms seemed freer to respond to radical shifts in ideas about the human mind and nature. An example is Laurence Sterne's *A Sentimental Journey through France and Italy* (1768), which put to the fictional test ideas of Locke and Hume concerning perception and reason. Sterne demonstrates, in what claims to be a simple travelogue, the power of unexpected sensations to shatter what we believe to be our rational control of self. We turn a corner and see a moving scene, we smell a strong odor, we swoon or burst into tears, and all sense of purpose and order collapses. The mind is seen here to conform to, to be shaped by, objects of perception. Sterne's fictional treatment of these ideas, here and (on a vast scale) in *The Life and Opinions of Tristram Shandy, Gentleman* (1759–1769), influenced the vogue of "sentimental" novels in Germany, under the conceptual banner of *Empfindsamkeit*.[11] But a vogue is not a paradigm shift, something capable of transforming the deep structures of fictional experience. This transformation is left to Hoffmann.

"Der Sandmann" adopts the minor genre of the "literary fairy tale" or *Kunstmärchen*. Yet, in this inconspicuous setting, Hoffmann takes up the central problem generated by science in his time, Hume's theory of perception and Kant's response. Kant and Hoffmann shared a cultural climate and city—Königsberg—where young Hoffmann may have seen Kant on his famous walks to the university. In any event, where Kant's Copernican revolution consisted of the "synthetic a priori," a sophisticated logical maneuver, Hoffmann's revolution occurs at the level of narrative structure. "Der Sandmann" asks readers to consider whether one can tell a coherent story of a life in a world where there is neither causality (the logic of actions and events) nor the unified sense of self that comprises a fictional character. Hoffmann's story rejects not only the assumptions but the physical premises of the idea of *Bildung* that dominated classical German culture at the time. Instead, its concern is the disintegration of the subject and subsequent collapse of narrative in a world governed (as in Hume) by the material activity of perception alone. We have a protagonist whose sole horizon is the percept, whose limits deny him all possibility of "synthesizing" the world he lives in, unable to make Kantian judgments concerning what seems an ever-shifting sense of reality.

Hoffmann's story begins with a set of letters written between the various characters: Nathanael, his fiancée Clara, and his confidant Lothar. Clara writes to Nathanael; he never writes directly to her but describes her, as in a vacuum, in varying perspectives in the theater of his imagination. Neither Nathanael nor Clara (note the Latinate "C"), as they present themselves in

letters, display any consistency of personality, but seem governed by immediate perceptual moments. As they do so, they contradict the cultural roles
placed on them by their names. Clara should display bourgeois "reason" and
measure, yet her responses are often, and unpredictably, irrational. With the
Hebrew name Nathanael, readers expect to find the Romantic *Schwärmer*,
the opposite of Clara's "classical" restraint. Yet his responses can be as
coldly logical as they are otherwise effusive and inconsistent. Characters are
presented in a precise cultural setting, but none of the expected categories
of that culture seem to stick. Readers have nothing to rely on but their own
perceptions of the moment.

Hoffmann's narrator does not appear until the middle of the story. Here,
suddenly, the narrator claims to take control and *begin* the story. But the narrative is already half over and seemed up to now to be moving forward as an
epistolary fiction. The narrator weighs possibilities: should I begin with "once
upon a time" or "in the town of . . . at such and such a date" or *in medias res*?
He rapidly realizes, however, as he attempts to define his characters, that he
too is trapped in a perceptual play of mirrors. Attempting to describe Clara,
he compares her eyes to a lake in a Ruysdael painting. This lake however is
only another mirror, reflecting a cloudless sky that itself reflects backs the
trees and flowers of the landscape. Human forms are absent from this endless
play of mirrors. He asks his "readers" for "opinions" about Clara's eyes, but
these, as reported, all contradict each other. In the end, Clara remains indescribable to her supposed creator, a *Ding as sich.* All the while, the narrative
itself continues, as a sequence of perceived instants. These, like the isolated
letters of the opening pages, are all "bundles of different perceptions" that
unfold in sequential manner but otherwise have no apparent order, through
neither external causality nor a coherent "self" that claims to order them.

Hoffmann's story turns around two series of scientific experiments. Readers expect, as in a conventional narrative, that these experiments will lead
somewhere, to some meaningful discovery in terms of a self and its relation
to the natural world. But not only do they mirror each other, but they do so
in a glass that remains hopelessly clouded. As with the names Nathanael and
Clara, the names of the scientists seem to promise opposing cultures—Germany and Italy. As such they promise to mark distinct stages in Nathanael's
*Bildung*, his development from superstitious child to responsible adult. Coppelius seems a figure out of an *Ammenmärchen*, here the old nurse's tale of
the sinister Sandman who steals eyes by casting sand in them. Spalanzani
on the other hand is a university professor who makes automata (there was
a real Lazzaro Spallanzani [1729–1799], a biologist who studied *in vitro*
fertilization in animals). The link between these two experimenters (and their
"worlds") however is a lens grinder named Giuseppe Coppola, whose name

and actions provide a strange mirror in which each of the above presents a blurred identity. Such mirrorings reflect the narrator's warning to those who seek to know "reality" through the dark medium of perception: "Vielleicht wirst du, O mein leser! dann glauben, dass nichts wunderlicher und toller sei, als das wirkliche Leben und dass dieser Dichter doch nur, wie in eines matt geschliffnen Spiegels dunklem Widerschein, auffassen könne." [Perhaps, my dear reader, you will then believe that there is nothing more wonderful and crazy than real life itself, and which your author need only capture, as in the dark reflection of a dully polished mirror.][12]

In the first experiment, Nathanael as child spies on his father and the sinister Coppelius as they perform an alchemical procedure aimed at creating, in a fiery crucible, a living being out of inert matter.[13] Nathanael learns, as he overhears the two, that his own eyes are to be used to provide the spark of life for this creation, eyes that first must be torn from his head. Coppelius discovers Nathanael, and in a scene that could either be a dream or (given Coppelius's seemingly real powers) a waking experience, sand is hurled in his eyes, they pop out, and go into the sockets of the android, who comes alive. In the second experiment, Professor Spalanzani, creates another automaton, but this time the optician Coppola supplies its eyes.[14] Nathanael is once again involved in giving "life" by means of his eyes, but in this case the "eyes" are the optical glasses that Coppola strews, like sand, on Nathanael's table. Nathanael chooses one at random. Looking through it out the window, he spies the automaton Olimpia, whom he perceives in the glass as a beautiful woman. In Coppelius's first experiment, Nathanael sees the loss of his eyes as the loss of his self. But the narrator as well, we remember, loses himself in Clara's eyes, that become blank—"matt geschliffen"—like the mutually reflecting lake and sky in the Ruysdael painting. And so, with Coppola, Nathanael at random picks up one of the lens grinder's "sköne Oke" [corrupt German "beautiful eyes"]. Staring into it, he not only perceives an alternate "reality," but now must inhabit it, because his own eye, through this dark glass, has given life to this automaton. The "life" in question however is nothing more than a *perceived* life. The eyeglass offers Nathanael a "world" of percepts, but none of these touch any bedrock of material reality.

Readers at this point find themselves in a perceptual, and in Kantian terms, judgmental maze. In terms of the conventional (i.e., causal) logic of narrative, Coppelius and Coppola have no connection except the sound of their names. "Sand" and "eye" have nothing in common except the fairy tale. In a fictional world where narrator and characters alike appear to wander in a perceptual maze, unable to fix either their beings or their world, the burden is placed on readers. The only decision one can make is whether each perceptual situation is unique, a fragment in a dark glass in which no human being can assemble a *gestalt* offering the possibility of a purposeful, self-directed life, or whether, behind this dark mirror, there exists some higher, non-human order—a "fatality" that runs through this otherwise meaningless concatenation of similar names and scenarios. Is it fated that Nathanael turn in perceptual circles until, in his fatal leap from the tower, he encounters physical death—the "thing in itself" that extinguishes all percepts?

Kant offers two possible ways of going beyond the mirrors of perception. One is to posit the existence of the *Ding an Sich,* the unknowable thing that Nathanael encounters as cold, hard pavement. The other is to invoke what Kant calls "the transcendental unity of apperception"—the point where we must accept the *idea* of a unified self as the necessary condition that guarantees the further necessity of accepting an external reality obeying the laws of causality. This is the late-eighteenth-century equivalent of Heinlein's Waldo deciding to "set the pace," collapse the wave in favor of order. Hoffmann's narrator, in telling his story, cannot assert the idea of a unified self needed to guarantee the coherence of its narrative. At one point, however, the story describes an act of perception that seemingly offers the possibility of breaking this solipsistic perceptual loop. Just as Nathanael will later look into Coppola's eyeglass, the narrator describes looking into the "glass" of Clara's eyes: "Kônnen wir den das Mädchen anschauen, ohne das uns aus ihrem Blick wunderbare, himmlische Gesänge und Klänge entgegenstrahlen, die in unser inneres dringen, das da alles wach und rege wird?" [Can we then look at this girl, without wonderful heavenly songs and harmonies streaming out at us from her eyes, which penetrate our innermost being, so that everything within becomes awake and vital?] The description is all about eyes and perception. Yet the narrator admits here that he/she is nothing more than an opaque surface, incapable of rendering back this "heavenly" music triggered by the act of gazing into Clara's eyes. Moreover, when the narrator attempts to return this heavenly song as verbal image to its "sender," Clara's face responds with mocking blankness: "und das lesen wir denn auch deutlich in dem um Claras Lippen schewebenden feinen Lächeln, wenn wir uns unterfangen, ihr etwas vorzuquinkelieren, das so tun will als sei es Gesang, unerachtet nur einzelne Töne verworren durcheinander springen." [and this we read clearly in the sly smile that hovers around Clara's lips, as we undertake to stammer something back that seeks to act as though it were song, even though what springs from our lips is only a series of confused scattered sounds] Clara's eyes send forth heavenly music, but narrator (and reader) as dark mirrors cannot reflect it. Floundering in this chaotic existence, they expend and disperse what they believed to be their inner "selves" in cacophony. This chaos is mirrored as her eyes and face, responding to this confusion, become blank in turn. Yet in her "sly" smile, perceptual mankind perceives something that mocks its attempts to escape from its perceptual isolation. Descartes has his *malin genie*. Hoffmann's fiction has its "Teufel," its devil, whose role is to confront fallen mankind with its mirror condition, to reveal its disconnection from any sense of a higher order or understanding of the natural world.

But if Hoffmann's mankind here is "fallen," it is a condition far grimmer than Pascal's. Reason can no longer claim parity with the material order of things, because reason remains trapped in its "apperceptions." Instead, any possible order here belongs to the realm of Kant's *Ding an sich*, an order forever beyond our cognitive reach. What is more, there are no synthetic a prioris in Hoffmann's world. If the *Ding an sich* is the "heavenly" music we occasionally hear, we can neither sing it nor render it in words or percepts. Hoffmann embeds this separation in the "music" of his prose. We have the self-cancelling extremes of Romantic "Schwärerei" ("wunderbare, himmlische Gesänge") and grating dissonance (Goethe objected mightily to words like "vorzuquinkelieren"), contrasts which do little more than provide more mirrors to our helpless condition. As the narrator gazes into Clara's eyes, he/she discovers that the higher order here has no "face." This enigma corresponds neither to human logic nor (to use Kant's word) to human imperatives. It regulates our world, we do not regulate it.

Throughout the narrative, a web of interconnecting elements takes shape independently of the actions and desires of the characters. These are words, sounds, and linguistic structures that recur in apparently meaningless order. We find them in the rhyming doublings of words—"Gesänge und Klänge," "Nebler und Schwebler." They occur in the absurd metonymy of "eyes" and "sand," a connection born of an old wives' tale which later proves to be a grim physical reality. If on the level of story, a pattern of mirroring relations seems to build between eye and socket, on the level of language this neat opposition is confounded. Coppola appears to be the Italian equivalent for the German Coppelius, thus his mirror double, apparently offering a neat way for the mind to organize this situation. Yet there is a further, non-rational connection between these names. For at the root of both is the Italian word "coppo," "eye socket." The socket and the maker of eyes, absurdly, become one and the same. When Nathanael stares at Clara through Coppola's glass, he sees a "wooden doll"; when he looks at the automaton Olimpia, he sees a beautiful living woman. The reader believes it can explain this as an insane reversal of the facts. But what facts are there to reverse here? The name "Olimpia," with its odd spelling, appears to have as its root "limpia," whose Spanish twin is "Clara," spelled here with a "c" rather than the German "k."[15] Opposites turn out to be twins; doubles turn out to be singularities; human categories of organization fail. In conventional fiction we have to choose, to "legislate," between fatality or free will as the order that governs the actions of human

characters. We cannot do so here, for all we have is seemingly random connections, embedded in the phonetics and grammar of language itself, a system
that mutates independently of all willed human control.

Freud later sought in his essay "The Uncanny" [Über das Unheimliche]
(1919) to restore human order to this story by seeing it as an Oedipal drama.
Psychoanalysis is timid science however compared to what Hoffmann's
story suggests, as he transposes Kant's problematic into fictional structures
that point toward paradigm shifts in modern science that in his time were
centuries away. Sitting on a historical cusp, Hoffmann reorients the synthetic
*a priori* toward what has become a divide in modern science. Hoffmann's
narrative on one hand seems to vector Hume's skeptical empiricism toward a
modern relativistic vision where we deal with "localities," strings of discrete
percepts in spacetime, where events "have no meaning in the universe at large
unless they are tied to a specific frame of reference."[16] Taking the idea of discrete localities farther, we see Hoffmann presenting something like a world
of quanta, a world in which there are not only no fixed things but in fact no
things at all, only measurements of things now said to exist only in reference
to the locality where they are perceived in the "now." On the other hand, in
the chains of associations that tie together this world of disjointed percepts,
Hoffmann hints at hyperstructures, looking forward to a world view such as
that of Bell's Theorem. This theorem, in challenging the principle of local
causes, denies both relativity and the conventional and consensual bedrock on
which our sense of the macroscopic world, the one in which we live and act,
rests. Scientists see here experimental evidence for the possibility of superlu-
minal communication of information, "a new notion of unbroken wholeness
which denies the classical idea of analyzability of the world into separately
and independently existent parts."[17]

Hoffmann's story is a prime example of fiction responding to new and
complex scientific and philosophical models and pushing beyond them, in the
sense that the implications of Hoffmann's fictional structures seem far in advance of the formulated theories that might someday explain them. At a time
when the spacetime world of narrative fiction was conventionally Newtonian,
"Der Sandmann" tests the possibility of using narrative devices proper to one
paradigm to tell a story in a world where that paradigm has radically shifted.
But where the Cartesian paradigm seemed eminently suited to narrative in its
time and culture, Hoffmann's masterpiece had no following in the nineteenth
century, and certainly not in Germany. In the nineteenth century, and first half
of the twentieth century, the novel of bourgeois "realism" reigned in German-
speaking countries. In such novels, there was no place for science, except
as topic of discussion. There is, for example, a world of difference between
Hoffmann's attempt to integrate new, science-driven ideas into the *structures*

of his narrative, and the long disquisitions on scientific theory in a work like Thoman Mann's *Der Zauberberg* (*The Magic Mountain*) (1924). Science here plays a figurative or allegorical role, as indicator of the *Zeitgeist*, but in no way impacts the way characters might interact with a radically changed world around them. Hoffmann's early work of science fiction asks its reader: Can we, given what science reveals about the changing nature of the physical world, still tell meaningful stories? By asking such a question, Hoffmann marginalizes his work in a time and place not ready to ask such questions.

Hoffmann's paradigm however is not so much lost as delayed. As discussed later, East German science fiction, in its post-war isolation, turned to Hoffmann and his "fantastic" science for inspiration. On the other hand, the paranormal sciences, a muted presence in the Golden Age, return to later Anglophone science fiction as writers become increasingly aware of the limitations of conventional narrative, not only in the wake of Clarke's "sufficiently advanced" sciences that seem like magic, but of scientific world views, such as quantum theory, that seem to leave little or no room for human participation. Science fiction rediscovers the barrier of the *Ding an sich* almost two centuries after Hoffmann.

One of the first science fiction works to carry on Hoffmann's dialectic between mental percepts and an implicate order of things is Brian W. Aldiss's British "new wave" novel *An Age* (U.S. *Cryptozoic!*) (1967). Protagonist Edward Bush is a "mind-travelling" artist. Mind travelers' bodies lie in suspended animation in their present, while their minds pass as insubstantial ghosts through distant eras of time. Their travel is directed by the Institute, a scientific body suspected to be in the hands of an increasingly totalitarian regime using the "minders" for covert purposes, notably to break through "the prohibitions of the human mind" itself.[18] These "prohibitions" remind one of the barrier of Hume's mind theater. Mind travelers are described as being explorers within themselves. A "biosphere" unto themselves, they are "analogue[s] of the world." Entire oceans "wash in the arteries of man." (35) In their voyage to the "Amniote Egg" (146), time is seen as measured, as with Augustine, solely in the mind: "In te, anima meus, tempora metior." Clock time, the discrete units that mark the irreversible arrow of time, is declared to have no physical reality outside that mind: "I do not measure the things themselves whose passage produced the impress; it is the impress that I measure when I measure time." (154) Professor Silverstone—imagining infinite space (as Hume put it) bounded in his mind—carries this theory of internalized spacetime to insane extremes. In his vision, once the measuring "overmind" collapses, the "undermind" becomes totally free to reverse the course of physical time, so that now "acorns from giant trees grow": "Human life bursts in upon the world in countless ways! . . . Before road accidents, you will see ambulances rush backwards, with broken limbs that are strewn over the road to join themselves into a living being . . ." (166) With Silverstone's death in the cryptozoic, we are said to "attend the birth of a great man." (171)

Yet there are signs that the world of Bush's bodily present, each time he returns from a mind jaunt, is changing in linear fashion, and for the worse. Commodities are scarcer, police control tighter. Bush leaves behind Dr. Franklin in charge of the Institute; he returns to find a certain Frankland in charge, and a stricter regime in place. After the epiphanic "death" of Silverstone in the cryptozoic, Bush's father, seeking news of his son, finds the same Frankland now supervisor of something called the Advanced Mental Disturbances Institution, where Bush is interned. Once the mind world and physical world are seen as hopelessly severed from one another, the state can use this separation as pretext for interning its opponents—people like Bush—in mental institutions. Even so, beyond state manipulation, readers begin to perceive, in a world that seems a schizoid version of the mind-matter duality, another form of order operating—as with Hoffmann on a level of non-human associations—that links these two realms, breaching a schism that appears absolute on the human level. Once again, this order emerges as a seemingly random play of sound shifts and alliterative associations. Franklin becomes Frank*land*; the good Howes becomes Howells the evil temporal agent. The title of the book is "An Age"; Bush's lady companion is named Ann. In fact, the workings of the action, both in and out of mind travel, is tied together by a series of "an" word sounds which, if not quite random, form a pattern that escapes easy decryption. This is the "cryptozoic" of the novel's U.S. title. The widow friend of Bush Sr. is Mrs Annivale. The Amniote Egg is the place of rendezvous in the Jurassic. Augustine's word for "mind," "soul," is *anima.* Frankland, describing Bush's "illness" to his father, speaks of him as anosmic, "meaning without the sense of smell—the olfactory centers of the brain are the most ancient ones." (184) Frankland attempts to put these elements into analytic order: "He experiences his anima—his *anima,* or female actuating spirit, not to be confused with anomia or anosmia—as he detached from himself, as a separate entity." (188) He goes on: "The mind plays strange tricks with names. And, of course, there are strange coincidences to be accounted for. Ann, Annivale, anomia. . . . Do you know what an amnion is?" (189) Hoffmann's chain of "coincidences" marks the intrusion of a sinister fatality into the compartmented lives of his characters. But in Aldiss's novel, this subliminal patterning seems to offer hope instead. For in the final scene Ann is seen waiting outside the hospital, possibly to free Bush. In this novel the chains of words and sounds appear linked, if in some inscrutable way, to a lost human sense of the order of things.

Let us turn to a more recent science fiction novel, Greg Egan's *Permutation City* (1996). Here the problems raised by Hume's theory of perception have mutated into the realm of computer simulations and mathematical theories of the Ultimate Ensemble. Coppola's welter of glasses, thrown on the table before Nathanael, is now a dizzying array of auto-generated "worlds," where perception of reality has *become* reality. Egan's is a near-future world where the mirror existence of Hoffmann's characters is now a function of electronic cloning, where (wealthy) humans avoid death by making computerized simulations at the synaptic level—mind entities—that can be "run" in "VRs" (virtual realities), simulated environments that are increasingly simplified due to the cost of "running" them. These VRs are either computed at speeds slower than human biotime. Or, in a same computing space, details are simply, in the manner of Berkeley, rubbed out when not perceived, when we turn our backs on them. VRs are inhabited by Copies, digital renderings of human brains, "scanned" into these virtual worlds as an advanced form of cryonics. Scientists in Egan's future are experimenting with "Autoverses," self-sustaining, self-consistent "automata," computerized systems capable of sustaining not just virtual realities, but entire worlds in evolution, with their own chemistry and physical and biological laws.

This is a scientific elaboration of Aldiss's Augustinian mind world. But again, there is, in this maze of simulations, a physical world from which these self-contained perceptual constructs are increasingly disjuncted. Physical pressures are felt. For example, it takes increasing computer space-time to construct VRs that can only strive to become like the complex environments we experience in "real" life. These VRs consume increasing quantities of energy, whose sources are dwindling in Egan's post-climate-change world. Computing units are traded on the stock market; the "copies" that inhabit these worlds, if their worlds are complex, need foundations to insure monetary support for their sustainability. And just as these assets are subject to financial crises, so "copies," with these crises, find their worlds increasingly diminished, sterile like Homer's land of shades, and eventually elect to terminate themselves. The story involves two protagonists—the entrepreneur-con man-visionary Durham and bioengineer Maria—whose projects become intertwined. Durham's is to realize a supercomputer automaton world he calls Permutation City, generated from a "Garden of Eden configuration," thus given a computational starting point that is *ex nihilo* in relation to other simulations. But if his dream is to emulate God the creator, he finds himself simply re-generating our known universe, repeating a process but neither creating nor understanding it. Permutation City remains a closed structure. Durham however, like Aldiss's Bush, feels a need to "break through" to the

*Ding an sich.* This is the vaguely intuited physical order, regulated by evolutionary time, that subtends this maze of simulations. Perhaps in some unconscious hope of doing so, he incorporates into the closed circuit of Permutation City Maria's *biological* autoverse. This is ostensibly another controlled
experiment, one with a restricted biosphere to see what level of life can be
computed from the *autobacterium Lamberti* strain. As biology however, it
has the potential of escaping permutational control.

   All of this takes place in the name of the Logic of the Dust theory. "Dust" it
seems is information. Egan tells us this theory is based on Tegmark's Mathematical Universe Hypothesis, which states that, in worlds complex enough to
contain self-aware structures, such worlds will perceive themselves as existing in a physical world. Kant's transcendental unity of apperception is pushed
to absurd limits here. The "self-aware structure" now asks Kant's question—
what can reason know apart from experience?—in a gallery of mirrors where
"experience" has no referent outside its closed structure. Durham however,
as such a self-aware structure, hopes to reach outside its *ex nihilo* existence
by asking a pseudo-Kantian question: does such a structure belong totally to
a world of apperception, or can it belong, at the same time, to a world "out
there," a physical world? But within his "mathematical" or computational
universe, the way to a higher order seems hopelessly circuitous. He proposes
to make himself, as "copy," the Goedelian x factor in any given VR. This is
possible, he reasons, because copies are the only conscious structures that are
not computed by self-consistent mathematical rules. He inserts, then deletes,
his copies from a series of VRs. Each time he is able to assert that he was a
copy, and that that copy was erased. Each copy represents a perceptual situation. He appears, within this sequence of perceptions, to achieve a *memory*
of continuity. But does this, in Hume's terms, affirm the existence of a continuous consciousness, a "self"? Does this prove that such a consciousness
is located in some external (and stable) spacetime? Durham entertains two
possible explanations—one subjective, the other objective. On one hand this
consciousness, as "self-aware structure," is able in each instance to posit a
world in which he was *not* erased. That "world" however remains a logical
construct. On the other hand, he affirms each experience as something physically real. But for this to be true, he would each time, like Christ, have to have
risen from the dead. Egan's world offers an elaborate quantum variation on
the world of Aldiss's mad time prophet Professor Silverstone.

   Durham is a stochastic version of Hoffmann's Nathanael—again and again
spinning like a top, throwing himself from the tower, but within his Permutation City never allowed to make contact with physical reality. As the narrative continues, we do not move to a new location in physical spacetime, but
to another (this time "distant") subjective future, that of Maria's Lambertian

autoverse. This construct, which Durham embedded in his Permutation City structure, has improbably evolved. But "evolution" again has transcended biology. The Lambertians have reached a state of *consciousness* higher than that of their macroscopic God and his world. Permutation City is constructed on the creator hypothesis that lies behind the Garden of Eden simulation. It is one vast creation of an individual mind. Thus, by simply refusing Durham's hypothesis, the Lambertians can construct their world around a better solution (spontaneous generation of matter) to the creator question. They are said to "interpret" Permutation City out of existence. But are these Lambertians any closer to apprehending the *Ding as sich*—the singular, physical, cause of their own creation? At the end of the novel, the hypothetical simulated "journey" continues; Durham and Maria will "leave" (an ironic *When Worlds Collide* moment) in search of some yet "higher" interpretation of our physical origins. They seem to remain however forever confined to a world of copies and mathematical mirrors in which our perceptions of reality do nothing more than model further self-contained worlds, each able to erase the other conceptually, none able to make contact with physical reality. That reality is not expressed here, as in Hoffmann or Aldiss, as concatenations of images, words, or sounds that seem indifferent to human fate. Humans live here in a grotesquely inverted situation, where the fatal concatenation of events that rules their lives is the very world of energy and entropy they hoped to escape in their maze of mathematically computed simulations.

## PARADIGM REGAINED:
## EVOLUTION AND THE BRITISH TRADITION

Interestingly, in British literature, where most English-language critics seek their models for the origin of science fiction, there is much greater historical separation between science and fiction than in France. Science and fiction appear to evolve on parallel tracks. Because of this, the paradigm shift that allows for their interaction comes much later than in France. Contrary to conventional wisdom, this shift occurs later than *Frankenstein*, which in many ways remains quite traditional in stigmatizing science. We must wait for evolutionary theory and Wells to find science impacting the themes and structures of fiction in any significant way.

If we go back to Chaucer's *Canterbury Tales* (c. 1380–1400), still under the dispensation of medieval Christianity, we find the only individuals excluded from the society of the Canterbury pilgrims are the Canon and his Yeoman, who are traveling alchemists. If a scoundrel like the Pardoner does not live up to his station in life, that station remains firmly within the ecclesiastical order of things. The Canon and Yeoman do not belong to any order. They arrive suddenly and without baggage, intersecting the pilgrimage, and leave as hastily as they came. Charles Muscatine gives voice to the judgment Chaucer's age would have brought to bear on their discourse, that it "evokes a profound sense of the futility, the cursedness of a soulless striving with matter."[19] Their late and sweaty arrival is a material correlate to their ever-lagging pursuit of alchemy's holy grail—the transmutation of metals. The Canon is a con man, but his Yeoman is a serious, if discouraged, experimenter in what he calls the "slidyinge science."[20] This he describes as useless poking around in unpleasant substances, "unslekked lym, chalk, and gleyre of an ey,/poudres diverse, asshes, donge, pisse, and cley . . ." (VIII [G] 806–808) His failures, which have physically and economically ravaged him, lead him to pronounce the following moral judgment on godless science: "For whan a man hath over-greet a wit,/Ful oft hym happeth to mysusen it." (VIII [G] 648–649) "For whoso maketh God his adversarie,/As for to werken any thyng in contrarie/Of his wil, certes, never shal he thryve." (VIII [G] 1478–1479)

With the Renaissance and Marlowe's Dr. Faustus, the alchemist is no longer a blasphemer and thief in the night, but the defiant "humanist" touting secular over divine power. For Faustus, the religious framework that regulated Chaucer's pilgrimage appears to be gone. "Magic" (alchemy) stands at the top of his list of disciplines. Moreover, Faustus's experiments are grand in design; he conceives them, giving Mephistophilis the secondary role of executing them. His sole limits are those of the human condition itself, and within these limits, Faustus is willing to give his soul for vast material visions and powers. He sees himself as a social engineer and would put science at the service of the creation of a perfected state: "I'll have them wall all Germany with brass/And make swift Rhine circle fair Wittenberg,/I'll have them fill the public schools with silk/Wherewith the students shall be bravely clad." (I, i, 89–92)[21] What seem vain boasts are in fact daring feats of material engineering: "By him I'll be great emperor of the world,/And make a bridge through the moving air,/To pass the ocean with a band of men." (I, iii, 104–106) Faustus looks forward here to Arthur C. Clarke's space elevator, and, closer to his time, to the land reclamation schemes of Goethe's Faust. The common wisdom on Faustus is that he trades his immortal soul for useless pranks. Some of his actions, to be sure, are farcical antics, but there is more than leg pulling or giving horns here.[22] Faustus is surely the first human to have an aerial view of Europe (III, i, 1–25), explores invisibility several centuries before Wells's Griffin, and seeks to harness material forces, to redirect them according to his broad vision of what man can and will achieve.

Faustus in fact aspires to be a cosmic engineer, creator of technologies that will "make the moon drop from her sphere/Or the ocean to overwhelm the world." (I, iii, 38–39) His Helen of Troy epithets reveal the newness of his stance, as she is now seen as "clad in the beauty of a thousand stars." Emergent astronomy vies with, and overwhelms, the fading world of classical myth. More than her thousand ships, Marlowe's Helen launches Gregory Benford's odyssey *Across the Sea of Suns* (1984). Yet, seen in the "tragickal" moral mirror of the English Renaissance, Faustus remains an example of *hubris* to be punished. Thus must Marlowe make his ending—surrounded by angels and devils and conventional Christian retribution—a horrific experience, screams and flesh torn apart: "Faustus, let thine eyes with horror stare/Into that vast perpetual torture-house." (V, ii, 113–114) His final words totally renounce science: "I'll burn my books!"

As Renaissance figure, Francis Bacon would seem to occupy a role analogous to that of Descartes in France, insofar as he first gives voice to a modern vision of science as experimental discipline that, in its implications, challenges Western mankind's conventional Christian sense of its place and role in the physical universe. But whereas Descartes, in a single act of scientific reason, rearranges the elements of the human drama as a set of purely relational coordinates, Bacon cannot bring about a similar *tabula rasa,* the act of rational mind that allows Descartes to substitute a scientific model for the old Christian one. Reasoning with himself, Bacon opens his *Instauratio magna (The Great Instauration)* of 1620 with what appears a bold statement: "Being convinced that the human intellect makes its own difficulties . . . he thought all trial should be made, whether that commerce between the mind of man and the nature of things, which is more precious than anything on earth . . . might by any means be restored to its perfect and original condition, or if that may not be, yet reduced to a better condition than that in which it now is."[23] The masterstroke of Descartes's *cogito* and the method by which it is achieved is declaring that *any* rational being, capable of "clear and distinct ideas" and able to apply the method whereby mind affirms its existence in the act of thinking, can realize this act. In Bacon however, there remains a strong residue of Christianity, especially the idea of the Fall, absent from Descartes's secular vision. Indeed, in the second part of Bacon's work, *Novum Organum (The New Organon or True Directions Concerning the Interpretation of Nature)* (1620), he details the "difficulties" of the human intellect—his famous "Idols"—in a way that suggests they are so endemic to our fallen condition that we can never overcome them.

The Idols of the Theatre are the "received systems" that ensnare all minds seeking to look with objectivity on nature. The Idols of the Tribe have as foundation the "false assertion that the sense of man is the measure of all things." (470) Bacon in a sense foresees the bifurcation that will characterize the English eighteenth century. On one hand, "neo-classics" like Pope and

Swift will assert that man *is* the measure of all things. On the other hand, empiricists like Locke and Hume will follow Bacon in his skepticism whereby "all perceptions as well of the senses as of the mind are according to the individual and not according to the measure of the universe." (470) As with Hume, Bacon sees human understanding "like a false mirror, which, receiving rays irregularly, distorts and discolors the nature of things by mingling its own nature with it." (470) Finally, with his Idols of the Cave, Bacon refutes what will be the Cartesian *cogito*, the solipsistic "self" its author claims to have realized in a "stove": "For every one (besides the errors common to human nature in general) has a cave or den of his own which refracts and discolors the light of nature." (470) Moving in the exact opposite direction from Descartes's sense of personal introspection as starting point for mind's dialectic with nature, Bacon (citing Heraclitus) asserts that humans must look for the sciences not in their own lesser worlds, but in the "greater or common world." This would seem to herald modern science, were it not for the fact that, at the same time, Bacon remains skeptical of the ability of our sensual and intellectual apparatus to understand fully the world around us. Bacon's skepticism could be seen as an invitation to subsequent writers and thinkers in the British tradition to embrace the median position Alexander Pope extols in his "Essay on Man" (1733–1734).

The English seventeenth century was passionately interested in the "new science" of Bacon. But science did not engender, as in Cartesian France, a distinct form of narrative fiction. Nor did science's new empirical vision have any deep impact on literary writings. A work like Robert Burton's *The Anatomy of Melancholy* (1621), for example, purports to be a medical study of melancholia. It is in fact a compendium of scholastic learning, with wide-ranging, often witty, digressions on topics of all sorts. The influence of Bacon is more visible with Sir Thomas Browne, especially in a work like *Pseudodoxia epidemica* (1646), where he uses empirically derived facts to debunk false beliefs about medicine and other topics. Browne however in his *The Garden of Cyrus* (1658), a study of the "quincunx" or geometrical arrangements of five elements, shows himself to be more a neo-Platonic mystic than experimental scientist. John Milton, who wrote the great narrative of the century, had an abiding interest in science. But science, for Milton, seems to remain an appendix to theology. As Kester Svendsen puts it: "A progressive scientist in his time, like Boyle, or a supporter of the Royal Society, like Bishop Sprat, would have regarded the world view in his works as quite old-fashioned despite his references to the new astronomy."[24]

What then of Isaac Newton, the great scientist of the time and perhaps Britain's greatest scientist? Did Newtonian physics have any influence on the deep structures of the English novel tradition that began the early eighteenth century? Newton was a strict observational scientist, to the point of claiming not to make "hypotheses," by which he meant unproven statements of causality hastily deduced from empirical facts (the occasion for his "hypotheses non fingo" was an accusation that his theory of gravitational attraction introduced occult phenomena—action at a distance—into the scientific debate, to which Newton replied that he merely described the phenomena, but did not state the cause). But whereas Descartes posited a system of relations that encompassed the human condition, thus providing the foundation for a new "scientific" treatment of what before were solely issues of passion, morality, or religion, Newton's laws dealt strictly (no hypotheses) with the material world of motion and forces. It was, if anything, Newton's life and character that might have been of interest to the new novel of manners in England. For the experimental scientist was also an alchemist (some claim his death was due to mercury poisoning due to alchemical experiments) and a pamphleteer engaged in philosophical and religious discussions with continental thinkers, arguing against Leibniz's deism and Spinoza's supposed hylozoism. To boot, he took the position of Master of the Mint and actively prosecuted counterfeiters. Newton however did not become a character in an English novel. His great influence on the cultural sphere was on English deists, who used his mechanical philosophy as demonstration of the possibility of a natural religion. British fiction follows the path traced by Pope. If the proper study of mankind is Man, it is mankind as seen and conceived within its specific social and cultural milieu.

Indeed, British fiction in the eighteenth and in much of the nineteenth century follows this *via media* where science is concerned. The rise of the bourgeois novel focuses so exclusively on contemporary human "manners" that any mention of serious scientific speculation on the nature of things is all but absent. G. S. Rousseau sees this exclusionary attitude codified in the criticism of Samuel Johnson: "He tamed all past criticism and set the standards for centuries, standards from which the School of Taste—the most influential body of aesthetic doctrines—developed. Yet Johnson barely tolerated, let alone condoned, what we would call 'science fiction' or 'fantasy' today."[25] According to Rousseau, Johnson averted his gaze from such works as Swift's *Gulliver's Travels* (1726) and Samuel Madden's *Memoirs of the Twentieth Century* (1733), the former seen today as a prime example of "proto-science fiction," the latter considered by Paul Alkon an essential document in establishing "the origins of futuristic fiction."[26]

With a stroke Johnson created the divide still prevalent today in Anglo-American literature between "major" and "minor" genres. In the nineteenth century, works like *Frankenstein* and *Strange Case of Dr. Jekyll and Mr. Hyde* (1886), relegated to minor categories such as Gothic fiction, are allowed to deal with science as long as their attitude toward it is defensive and ulti-mately moralizing (since Faustus, Frankenstein, and Jekyll must be punished for scientific excesses). On the other hand, any serious discussion of science or interest in scientific ideas is quasi-absent from mainstream novels from Jane Austen to Anthony Trollope. Surprisingly, in comparison to Zola's ag-gressively scientific naturalism, science plays a relatively subdued role in Thomas Hardy.

But if not with *Frankenstein,* where does the paradigm shift occur that brings scientific advance to irreversibly *impact* human activity? The word "science" is ever on the lips of the British Romantics. At one extreme, in his 1800 preface to *Lyrical Ballads*, Wordsworth sees Poet and Man of Science, like lion and lamb, lying peacefully side by side. Despite this proclamation, poetry remains privileged, "the breath and finer spirit of all knowledge . . . the impassioned expression which is the countenance of all Science."[27] At the other extreme, we have the famous rejection of Newtonian optics in Keats's *Lamia* (1819), rhetorically violent, but perhaps not entirely sincere. Lament-ing Newton's trivialization of the poet's "awful rainbow," Keats describes "cold philosophy" (i.e., the material quantitative sciences) as "clip[ping] an angel's wings/Conquer[ing] all mysteries by rule and line."[28] Yet an account by painter Benjamin Haydon of a social gathering, the "immortal dinner" of December 28, 1817, presents a convivial Keats and Lamb bemoaning the ef-fects of Newton's optics on the rainbow, while drinking to his genius in bois-terous manner.[29] For the Romantics, Newton is great, but not as a scientist. Instead, he becomes a subject for poetry, another Romantic hero sailing seas of thought alone, which is hardly the way an experimental scientist works. Whether it is Wordsworth or Keats speaking, poetry remains other than, and superior to, science. The contrast is striking with French Romantic poetry, which by mid-century had assimilated into its deepest structures a sense of division, again along radically Cartesian lines, between the rational subject, and the indifferent non-mind or *res extensa*. But if Descartes could envision the mastery of nature by mind, works like Victor Hugo's *Les Contemplations* (1856) and Leconte de Lisle's "Midi" (1852, published in *Poèmes antiques*), reverse the equation. Now it is nature's supreme indifference to human activ-ity and feelings that overwhelms the human mind in relation to the larger cos-mos. Pascal's terror of infinite space is reinforced by advances in the material sciences. The thinking subject now appears to be infinitely alone.

Matthew Arnold claims superiority for literature in his late essay "Science and Literature," published in his *Discourses in America* (1883), but some-thing has radically changed. Arnold is now arguing for something that is seen as irrevocably past, *"the best which* has *been thought and said in the world."*[30] More tellingly, he seems on the defensive, arguing *against* the categorical rejection of literature by biologist T. H. Huxley, who favors what he calls a modern, scientific education. Arnold's argument, presented in America before an audience seen as driven by technological advancement, has an accent of futility about it, providing testimony that, by the time of its writing, the paradigm shift we have been seeking has already happened. Science in England was fully in the process of having a massively unsettling impact on that domain formerly reserved for human preoccupations alone—"literature."

The paradigm-shifting scientific discovery here is Charles Darwin's statement of evolutionary theory in his *Origin of Species* (1859), which builds upon previous work by Lamarck, Lyell, and others to enunciate new ideas about the irreversibility of time and the random nature of natural development of species. All of this had a devastating effect on humanity's claim to centrality in the scheme of things. Descartes established a working relationship between mind and nature, which, because it privileged mind, endured the assaults of materialist science in the turbulent nineteenth century and has continued to do so in the age of relativity and quantum mechanics. In England however, with its culture of parallel tracks, Darwin's science appears literally to derail the human element. In Arnold's formulation, the humanities have no recourse but to regroup around a normative center which excludes the non-purposive process of evolution. In this climate, the task of a nascent science fiction is to create vital links between two terms—science and literature—now being presented as radically opposite.

In English literature of the second half of the nineteenth century, the growing catastrophic divide between science and literature is everywhere visible. For example, Tennyson's "Locksley Hall" (1842) extols technology as a force clearly at the service of humanity,[31] comfortably reveling in "the march of mind,/in the steamship, in the railway, in the thoughts that shake mankind." (ll. 165–166) The vision of "Locksley Hall Revisited" (1883) is radically different. Science (and its handmaiden technology) is now seen destroying the world in catastrophic fashion: "Art and Grace are less and less:/Science grows and beauty dwindles—roofs of slated hideousness!" (ll. 245–246) Everywhere, beset by transformations caused by science, we have images of decline, not just of poetry but of human culture, even the human species itself: "Lame and old, and past his time, and passing now into the night:/Yet I would the rising race were half as eager for the light." (ll. 227–228)

Arnold's vision of the impact of science on human beings is bleaker yet. In his valedictory poem "Dover Beach" (1867), he depicts the ebbing of the old world of faith and humanity in terms of a concept taken from the developing science of thermodynamics: the receding sea and beach as entropy slope. But the major event in reconnecting science and human concerns is Wells's *The Time Machine* (1895). Published nine years after Tennyson's "Locksley Hall

Sixty Years After." Wells's novel stands as the first substantial reaction, *in fiction,* to the impact of evolutionary science. Arnold's description of Darwin, the "born naturalist," describes Wells's scientist-time traveler as he stands out among his circle: "We mean a man in whom the zeal for observing nature is so uncommonly strong and eminent, that it marks him off from the bulk of mankind." (419–420) But the natural world Wells's Time Traveller wants to observe is that of Earth's future evolutionary development. The invention of his time machine rests on a theory of time that would have been unthinkable before evolution. For time here is seen as a fourth, evolutionary dimension, through which human consciousness, reduced to an instrument of observation, can travel, as in the voyage of a Time Beagle. Arnold further articulates the gap that forms between the intrepid Time Traveller and the human circle he leaves behind in his drawing room: "For now, says Professor Huxley, conceptions of the universe fatal to the notions held by our forefathers have been forced upon us by physical science." (421) Wells's novel is possibly the first example in English letters of a genuine dialogue between scientific possibility and what is now clearly identified as human inadequacy.

In light of this, Wells's reader is left to decide just how capable the Time Traveller is of dealing with new conceptions of the universe forced on him, and mankind, by physical science. Strict evolutionary science tells us the future remains unknown, its only certainty being non-purposive change and the unpredictable adaptation of species to new environments. The Traveller's voyage in evolutionary time should confirm this unknown, emphasizing the fatal split between human desires and physical reality. Instead, the Traveller's experiences appear to challenge what they are supposed to confirm. The future he finds conforms not to Darwin's science but to "social Darwinism," Herbert Spencer's reactionary attempt to relocate humanity at the center of the evolutionary process. The Traveller, finding what he first thinks is a utopian "communist" society in 802,701 CE, is seduced by the possibility that humanity as fittest species has not only survived, but evolved into peaceful harmony with nature. He soon sees the truth with the discovery of the ironically designated Palace of Green Porcelain. All the books here, the best that *will be* thought and said in mankind's future, are to him as Arnold's Greeks are to the new materialist: dust. All the wondrous machines of human technology to come lie rusting, their operating manuals forever lost. The lesson the Traveller should take from his experience is that neither the humanities nor the sciences have survived the onslaught of evolutionary time. But such a lesson seems impossible to face. Tracked by Morlocks, the Traveller salvages from the museum of human science a club and a few matches—primitive tools that allow him to fight off the primal fears of the forest and Morlock den. Fleeing 802,701 CE into the distant future, he encounters the raw facts of entropy on a beach that is no longer Arnold's metaphorical Dover Beach but a flat, lifeless horizon with a few primitive life forms scattered about. This he cannot accept. Like Arnold's poet on Dover Beach, the Traveller elegizes on the "devolution" of *mankind's* earth. His description is scientifically accurate but equally myopic. For mankind remains at the evolutionary apex as he descends the chain of being to mammals, birds, insects, and finally the "primitive" forms that mark the beginnings of life on an Earth now at its end: "From the edge of the sea came a ripple and whisper. Beyond these lifeless sounds the world was silent. Silent? It would be hard to convey the stillness of it. All the sounds of man, the bleating of sheep, the cries of birds, the hum of insects, the stir that makes the *background of our lives* (my italics)—all that was over."[32]

Wells's novel is the first *significant* work of British fiction to engage fully the impact of science on the humanistic culture that Arnold extols.[33] Wells's position, however, remains ambiguous, negotiating a middle ground between Huxley and Arnold. Arnold has this to say about Darwin's limited sense of the humanities: "Science and the domestic affections, he thought, were enough." (420) This description fits Wells's Traveller. In the Palace of Green Porcelain, facing the spectacle of all great works of literature, past, present, and future, as dust, he can only think of his own *Philosophical Transactions* and his 17 papers on physical optics. At the same time, amidst the archeological marvels of this "latter day South Kensington," he pauses, like the crassest tourist, to write his name "on a steatite monster from South America that particularly took my fancy." (86) We first meet the Traveller in his comfortable Edwardian parlor—so comfortable that he seems to begin his fabulous journey in a drawing room coat. On his return, the Narrator notices that he had on his feet "nothing . . . but a pair of tattered, blood-stained socks." (16) Drawing room footwear proves totally inadequate for a jaunt in the unknown. Fleeing the future, the Traveller reminds us of another comfortable middle-class scientist, the protagonist of Wells's "The Stolen Bacillus" (1894), who forgets coat and shoes while chasing the anarchist who steals his bacillus through the streets of London, with wife running after him carrying the forgotten items of clothing. Decorum, or the lack of it, trumps scientific adventure. The Traveller acted like a tourist in the future; in his second departure, he retains the same tourist mindset, for when the Narrator meets him for the last time "He had a small camera under one arm and a knapsack under the other." (112) So much for the great scientific adventurer.

In Wells's novel, what will later be called the "two cultures"—scientific and humanistic—remain contained within the same comfortable middle-class frame that Arnold adheres to. The Traveller is described in terms that fit the armchair pessimist of "Dover Beach," smug in his rejection of both the ravages of science and human inadequacy: "He . . . thought but cheerlessly of the Advancement of Mankind, and saw in the growing pile of civilization only a foolish heaping that must inevitably fall back upon and destroy its makers in the end." (114) The narrator, in response, utters his own homilies about this bleak and inhuman future in terms that echo those of the comforting, futile Arnold of "Science and Literature." Wells's frame narrator is the ultimate voice in the novel. He does not defend humanist values in the face of science's future, but admits the certain defeat of all human endeavors, literary and scientific. His only consolation is to exhort the reader to live "as though it were not so." (114) In all of this, there is the bitter, ironic sense of a battle lost before it starts, of a humanity overwhelmed by the vast vistas of evolutionary science. Two and a half centuries after Pascal, the terrible silence of science's infinite vistas finally terrifies an English writer. Pascal reacted to the loneliness of Cartesian mind in purely material extension: man without God. Wells reacts to human futility in a world without Man.

## PARADIGM APPLIED

The above paradigms lead to very different forms of science fiction in France and England. In the latter context, that of the evolutionary paradigm and the legacy of Wells's *Time Machine*, science fiction develops in two directions. One is the imagination of vast evolutionary vistas, where mankind finds itself struggling to secure its central place in evolving worlds, and at the same time exploring the transhuman promise, the possibility of mankind leaving mankind behind. This line runs from Olaf Stapledon's *Last and First Men* (1930) through Clarke's Space Odyssey series to recent works like Iain Banks's Culture novels. In Banks's space epic, an intergalactic civilization called The Culture is ruled and directed by the Minds, artificial intelligences that have evolved beyond humans. Banks offers a lavish panorama of technological transformations—terraformed ringworlds, shellworlds, orbitals—that allow this evolved race to migrate from natural planets to machine environments. The old humans have passed the torch. Their social structures, however, remain at the center of all this. The liberal and beneficent Culture society of the far future seems little more than a transposition of Wells's rational utopia, or an intergalactic version of the modern welfare state.

   The other direction of British science fiction is that of the evolutionary pessimism of Wells's narrator in *The Time Machine*, tracing a path back from far distant scientific speculation to the narrow confines of the novel of manners. This is Wells's own trajectory from *The War of the Worlds* (1898) to his 1937 novel *Star Begotten*, where the setting is the social clubs and drawing rooms of prewar England. The real Martian invaders are now middle-class fantasies of mutation, rumors of "rays" from Mars turning humans into Martians. Decisively, with the 1960s "New Wave" movement, the English novel of manners returns to crowd out scientific speculation. If science has a presence in these novels, it is as shadowy and menacingly nebulous as Wells's Martian rays. The persistent theme of many of these novels is that of a disintegrating, devolving culture, which "science" has somehow brought about. John Brunner, for example, had a prolific career writing space adventures (with titles like *In the Slave Nebula* [1960]). But when he turns to "current" issues (overpopulation and ecodisaster) in *Stand on Zanzibar* (1968), Brunner moves from genre science fiction to literary experimentation, producing a narrative in the manner—with news reports and documents—of John Dos Passos's USA novels. Even bleaker in their contemporary and more avowedly "literary" nature are the novels of J. G. Ballard. If his earlier novel *The Crystal World* (1966) centers on an unexplained science-fictional phenomenon—the gradual crystallization of the world—later works like *The Atrocity Exhibition* (1970) and *Crash* (1973) explore the psycho-sexual neuroses of technological modernity in a contemporary setting.

Typical of British science fiction in the 1970s is the work of D. G. Compton. His early novel *The Quality of Mercy* (1965) (a title ominously adapted from *The Merchant of Venice*) sees overpopulation dealt with as a political abstraction, as human leaders decide to unleash a "statistically equitable plague" on the world. *Synthajoy* (1968), billed in a first-page blurb as "a novel of the day after tomorrow," deals with the recording, and commercializing, of the innermost thoughts of others, as they are having sex or are in the throes of dying. A quotation on its back cover describes it as "written with factual underplaying of the ultimate horror."[34] His later novel, *The Steel Crocodile* (1970), although described by American Clifford D. Simak as dealing with "computer doom," in fact describes how a computer project becomes a means of religious brainwashing, again in a "day after tomorrow" British setting.[35] The themes of these novels are human callousness, indifference to suffering, violation of privacy or feelings. Their characters could be taken from Trollope.

In contrast, French science fiction, when it came to fruition in the 1960s and 1970s after assimilating the impact of American science fiction, turns away from social and political issues, launching an investigation of inner landscapes which become the refuge of the Cartesian mind in an increasingly carceral universe.[36] Measured on the Cartesian scale, the anti-scientific rhetoric that develops with the surrealists after World War I does little more than relocate the place of scientific activity from *res extensa* to the inner realms of the mind itself. Instead of space travel, French science fiction develops the more "theoretical" trope of time travel. It is possible, in French time travel stories, to absorb physical time within a mindspace, where it can be endlessly (and tragically) recycled. An example is the time travel novels of André Ruellan (Kurt Steiner). His early *Le disque rayé* (1961, signed Kurt Steiner) is a rewrite of Wells's *Time Machine*, but with the temporal loop controlled, not by evolution or biology, but by a giant machine mind that solipsistically sustains its own existence at the center of the loop by manipulating the trajectory of the protagonist. The later *Mémo* (1984, signed Ruellan), deals with a psychotropic drug that allows the protagonist to "travel" in mental space—this time up and down his own timeline—with disastrous results for his life and his own sense of self-continuity: "Lui qui savait se mouvoir dans la durée, changer ce qui avait été, modifier ce qui serait, il était las de passer sa vie en voyages éclairs à travers son existence." [He who knew how to move about in duration, to change what had been, modify what would be, he was tired of wasting his life in rapid trips throughout his own existence.][37] In a context where the external world—here a landscape of institutions rather than natural phenomena—has become a repressive place of mental asylums and gulags, the sole refuge appears to be the space of the individual mind itself. French science fiction of this period, fascinated with a writer like Philip K. Dick, is a literature of closed universes, of paranoia, of struggle between contending forces (generally phantasms of "other minds") to invade and control the mindspace. Notable examples are the novels of Michel Jeury, notably *Le Temps incertain* (1973) and its "sequel" *Les Singes du temps* (1974), as well as *Les Yeux géants* (1980), an incredible novel detailing protracted struggle between psychic projections. We find like scenarios of mental projections and encapsulated worlds in works like Jean-Pierre Hubert's *Mort à l'étouffée* (1976), whose action takes place in a miniaturized world in a transparent bubble in space, or *Le Champs du reveur* (1983), where the mind of a child, destroyed in a bombing, is reconstituted by an alien race to study humanity through its projections. As with the child mind in Bradbury stories like "The Veldt" (1950) and "The Small Assassin" (1946), this experiment unleashes raw hate and destruction, this time magnified by alien technology.

But there is a fourth paradigm—American this time—which turns upon the Emersonian self-reliant monad. This monad emerged, throughout the nineteenth century, as an American vision, that of a new national spirit, reacting to both the perceived hegemony of European science and culture, and the introduction of a new world view from the recent discovery of Sanskrit texts. Emerson's vision, discussed at greater length below, is a complex fusion of scientific, philosophical, cultural, and religious currents. Many had German sources. There was Kantian transcendental philosophy and German idealism (via English commentators like Carlyle), coupled with the discovery of Vedic religion and physics (and their inextricable interplay) through German orientalists like Max Müller. At the same time, this time via the new American university, there was German science, especially the development of electro- and thermodynamics, through figures like Hermann von Helmholtz. These currents had in common a sense of the world as an interplay between energy and personal empowerment. By bringing them together in a coherent vision of mankind's relations to the natural world, Emerson effected a cultural *tabula rasa* of his own, creating a New World vision of the self-reliant man that had a vast subsequent impact on the development of the American frontier, and the creation of a uniquely American science fiction.

Emerson's vision is shaped by dynamic forces, those of Man thinking, Man acting, ever moving outward from a center that is no longer the *cogito* or rational self, but rather a source of material energy, harnessed and projected by the self-reliant individual. This individual has no metaphysical privilege, nor obeys any social strictures. The personal circumference it projects is purely the product of its own material energy. The static duality of mind and matter now becomes, with Emerson, an "undulation" between this dynamic center, and an always tentative circumference, expanding and/or contracting according to the energy of the monad that generates it. Form is defined by power; the Cartesian circle is opened out into a dynamic spiral.

This Emersonian paradigm—widely mentioned as a powerful influence by a number of Golden Age writers—is important for the development of science fiction, insofar as the greatest production of science fiction texts, in the twentieth century, occurred in the United States. On one hand, the monad allows mankind—through its "representative men"—to expand in material spacetime, while setting "thermodynamic" limits to this expansion. At the same time, by placing the means of this expansion in the hands of the monad, it challenges the cosmic fatalism of the evolutionary model. The limits imposed by matter and evolution in the French and English paradigms are simply waved away by Heinlein's prototypically *young* monads, who proclaim that "we humans *have no limits*." In this, its basic impetus seems to come from America's declaration of independence from Old World visions, coupled with its vast landscape, full of possibilities for exploration. We see this dynamic already at work in Washington Irving's "The Legend of Sleepy Hollow" (1819). Ichabod Crane is at one and the same time an outcast from this sleepy European enclave, and a fortunate exile, for he escapes the Headless Horseman with his own wits intact, and with the money in his pocket that allows him to seek better fortunes elsewhere.

A fascinating variation on this scenario is Nathaniel Hawthorne's "The Artist of the Beautiful" (1844). Publication of this story—often considered a work of "proto-science-fiction"—coincides with that of Emerson's core essays: the First Series in 1841, the Second Series in 1844 (Emerson and Hawthorne were neighbors at the time). Hawthorne's Owen Warland is apprenticed to old Peter Hovenden, a clockmaker, but shows no talent for the mundane task of fixing watches. Instead, he uses his ability to work with miniature parts to build an automaton—a delicate butterfly—that appears to come alive. When asked, Warland replies thus: "Alive, yes, for it has absorbed my being into it. . . . Deep in its system it has absorbed the intellect, imagination . . . and soul of its maker—the Artist of the Beautiful."[38] The builder has displaced the center of creative activity from himself to his creation, which now seeks its own circumference. Warland is met with mocking misunderstanding by the materialist Hovenden, whose mystified daughter Annie has married the village blacksmith Danforth, a man whose great physical strength is devoted to making utilitarian objects.

In comparison, there is a great difference between Warland's story and that of, say, Balzac's contemporary French artists of the beautiful. The sublime music of Balzac's *Gambara*, for example, occurs within his mind. Because it cannot be conveyed in notes or words, it remains fundamentally incommunicable, inaccessible to the social sphere, thus powerless. Warland however *makes* an object that he sends forth into the world. Moreover, he sees its creation as a personal "performance," an *act* of self-reliance, indeed something whose reward "must be sought within itself, or sought in vain." The final scene offers a fascinating example of a new attitude toward "art" and technology (the two cannot here, as in Balzac, be separated as two mutually exclusive domains—conception and execution). Warland presents his butterfly to the child of Annie and Danforth. It rises from the child's hand: "Had there been no obstruction, it might have soared into the sky and grown immortal." But there is the ceiling, where "the exquisite texture of its wings brushed against the earthly medium." The butterfly tries to return to the artist's hand, but he rejects his creation: "Not so! Thou hast gone forth out of thy master's heart. There is no return for thee." (1156) The child now snatches and crushes the object. But Warland, like Ichabod Crane, is neither defeated nor marginalized by this act: "And as for Owen Warland, he looked placidly at what seemed the ruin of his life's labor, and which was yet no ruin. He had caught a far other butterfly than this. When the artist rose high enough to achieve the beautiful, the symbol by which he made it perceptible to the mortal senses (it must be thus made) became of little value in his eyes while his spirit possessed itself in the enjoyment of the reality." (1156) One can gloss this with the famous passage, describing another such moment of visionary undulation, from Emerson's *Nature* (published in a limited edition in 1836, reprinted in 1849). "Standing on bare ground—my head bathed by the blithe air, and uplifted into infinite space—all mean egotism vanishes. I become a transparent eyeball; I am nothing; I see all; the currents of the Universal Being circulate through me."[39]

If we substitute "scientific *achievement*" for "beauty" in Hawthorne's text, and "scientist" for "artist," we have a clear description of what will become classic American science fiction. Warland among the clockmakers and blacksmiths will become Edison among the skeptics, or Heinlein's Waldo among conventional thinkers. Hawthorne's portrait applies to the *achievers* of the Golden Age and beyond, to Asimov's Hari Seldon or Hober Mallow, to Bradbury's Montag, to Heinlein's Starman Jones, to Greg Bear's Vergil Ulam in *Blood Music* (1985), and, why not, to Cley in Gregory Benford's *Beyond Infinity* (2004). These are all, ultimately, spirits that *possess themselves* in enjoyment of the reality, which is the pursuit of something that will change the way which we not only perceive the natural world, but actually interact with that world. The paradigms of rationalism, skepticism, and evolution all begin with theories or systems that ultimately restrict human activity. The Emersonian paradigm, on the contrary, provides a vector for activity that is, at one and the same time, scientific *and* human. It stands on two sorts of bare ground. One is the Western science of energy and dynamics. The other is the Eastern idea that mind can permeate matter, literally become the transparent eyeball that sees all. As Hawthorne's Warland says of his invention, were there no ceiling, no "obstruction," it might have soared into the skies and become immortal. But there is obstruction, the material limits that science must penetrate, become part of, discover its workings from inside, just as Heinlein's Waldo accesses the other universe not by theorizing it, but by *grasping* it physically through the synapses of the mind. To maintain this upward movement, Heinlein's protagonists resort to the paranormal when the normal will not do. So, it is in Dan Simmons's *The Hollow Man* (1992) where protagonist Jeremy Bremen, lost in dual labyrinths of quantum mathematics and physical neuroscience, finds breakthrough with a very personal "experiment"—a gunshot to the head—by which a world as "probability variance" collapses into an island of order, a shared place where, like Dante with Beatrice, he hopes to find his dead wife again.

These paradigms allow us to trace the dominant currents of Western science fiction from its origins in "revolutions" in the major scientific cultures—France, Germany, England, and the United States. Here, with these crucial paradigm shifts, new, scientific, ways of conceiving the material world and our place in that world begin to impact and transform traditional fictional themes and structures. At these moments, the dialogue between science and fiction begins that will lead to the creation of the modern genre of science fiction.

## NOTES

1. Propp's plot schema beautifully encompasses a structure such as Homer's *Odyssey* (c. eighth century BCE), even the ending where Odysseus can enjoy extended life as long as he remains close to home, the Mediterranean where oars are recognized as such. Dante's Christian paradigm "universalizes" Propp's schema: the Pilgrim leaves home, wanders in the dark wood of middle life, is interdicted as he seeks to climb Mt. Purgatory, finds trickery (satanic temptation), finds mediation and guidance (Virgil), struggles through the circles of Inferno, experiences the defeat of Satan, is transfigured, is wedded to Beatrice in Paradise. Propp's masterplot remains circular and closed, whether the diapason closes full in God or in Man. It can be argued that in many science fiction stories—even those whose worlds are ostensibly shaped by radically advanced scientific ideas—Propp's circular pattern holds. An example is Poul Anderson's *Tau Zero* (1970), where human pilgrims impossibly pass light speed imploding their universe yet emerging into a new (highly improbable) paradise to their measure. In this sense, it is not the science per se that determines the science fiction narrative. It is rather science fiction's adherence to science's methods, to the facts and the conclusions drawn from its investigations, that shapes (when science fiction is at its best) its narrative morphology and "plot." The hero's trajectory is not a circle, but the arrow of time, change, evolution. The hero's experience remains open-ended, marked by the pattern of the reprieve we will later trace from DeQuincey to Heinlein, whose heroes use science and serendipity to allow them the chance always to light out for new territories. The circle of Homer's and Dante's "world" will never be the same once Descartes names it *res extensa*, and Pascal sees mankind terrified before the endless silence of infinite space. In this brave new world of unchartered places and unknown forms, science fiction's mankind is called upon to adapt, to transform its being, to evolve into shapes and things that had no place in Propp's scheme or Dante's world.

2. Robert L. Forward, "When Science Writes the Fiction," *Hard Science Fiction,* edited by George Slusser and Eric S. Rabkin (Carbondale: Southern Illinois University Press, 1986), 1.

3. See Descartes's Lettre à Mersenne, 20 novembre 1629: "Or je tiens que cette langue est possible, et qu'on peut trouver la science de qui elle dépend, par le moyen de laquelle les paysans pourraient mieux juger de la vérité des choses, que ne font maintenant les philosophes." [Now I assert that this language is possible, and that one can find the science to which it belongs, using means which allow peasants to better judge the truth of things than philosophers do today.] *Descartes: Oeuvres et lettres,* edited by André Bridoux (Paris: Éditions de la Pléiade, 1987), 915. Future references to Descartes are to this edition; translations are mine.

4. The text continues: "c'est-à-dire d'éviter soigneusement la précipitation et la prévention; et de ne comprendre rien de plus en mes jugements que ce qui se présenterait si clairement et distinctement à mon esprit que je n'eusse aucune occasion de le mettre en doute." [That is to avoid carefully haste and prejudice; and to consider nothing more from my judgments that which presents itself so clearly and distinctly to my mind so I would not be inclined to have any doubt about it.]

5. See also Article 31 where the "glande" is described, in relation to the soul, in quantitative terms. It is in this "glande" that "l'âme exerce ses functions plus particulièrement que les autres parties [du cerveau]" [the soul exercises its functions *more* particularly than in other parts of the brain]. Descartes's description of the functioning of the gland, despite assertions that the rational soul is qualitatively different from the body, tends toward a materialist explanation. In this work, especially, his scientific investigations lead him in a different direction from the *a priori* assertion: I think, therefore I am. It is easy to see how a La Mettrie, once Descartes begins to measure functions of the mind in terms of quantity, could push this tendency to the extreme and declare that there is no duality—that mind is matter, and man a machine.

6. See Gerald Prince, *Dictionary of Narratology* (Lincoln: University of Nebraska Press, 1967), entries on "metaphor" (82), and "minimal story" (83). Prince sees metaphor turning into narrative when "in a narrative sequence, the last event or situation constitutes a partial repetition of the first." Pascal's mini-narratives give us the beginning and end of the human condition, but with only "partial repetitions" that in turn allow the space between beginning and end (we know it is nasty, brutish and short) to be filled out with details over and over in its retelling. Pascal's thinking reed is perhaps the most-retold story in French fiction and culture. References are to this edition.

7. Ray Bradbury, "No Particular Night or Morning," *The Illustrated Man* (New York: Bantam Books, 1952), 110.

8. Jean-Pierre Changeux, *L'homme neuronal* (Paris: Fayard, 1983), 334.

9. Blaise Pascal, *Pensées*, edited by Louis Lafuma (Paris: Éditions du Seuil,1962), pensée 84. Future references to Pascal are to this edition; numbers in parentheses indicate the number of the *pensée,* not the page number.

10. Gregory Benford, "Pascal's Terror," *Mindscapes: The Geographies of Imagined Worlds,* edited by Slusser and Rabkin (Carbondale: Southern Illinois University Press, 1989), 276.

11. See Norbert Miller, *Die empfindsame Erzähler* (Munich: Hanser Verlag, 1968).

12. E. T. A. Hoffmann, "Der Sandmann," full text available at Project Gutenberg, https://www.projekt-gutenberg.org/etahoff/sandmann/sandman1.html and following pages. References are to this online edition.

13. Hoffmann's story appeared two years before Mary Shelley's *Frankenstein* (1818). In the latter the problem remains at the moral level. In Hoffmann, the creation of life (if such occurs, this is a common theme of alchemical literature) is not the problem; it is instead the question of the nature of our senses, how we perceive and know the external world that dominates Hoffmann's story.

14. Hoffmann is fond of these "north-south" doublings. In his long novel *Die Elixiere des Teufels* (1815), published a year before "Der Sandmann," Hoffmann gives us Peter Schönfeld, whose Italian alter ego is Pietro Belcampo. Here it is simply a matter of the same name in different languages. Hoffmann was fascinated with Italy as the "musical" double of the stern bourgeois German, although again the relationship between these two places is often ambiguous, and one cannot place a clear distinction, say of good and evil, on one side or the other.

15. Spanish is not a far-fetched language for Romantic Germany, where Tieck produced his famous translation of *Don Quixote*. Hoffmann seems to create a sort of linguistic "noise" here: in Italian (which would be the logical choice, but logic doesn't apply) it is "chiara" and "limpida." Granted Latin has "clarus-clara" but its twin is "lucidus." In this play of slippages, we cannot fix on any stable equation.

16. Gary Zukav, *The Dancing Wu Li Masters: An Overview of the New Physics* (New York: Bantam Books, 1979), 146.

17. David Bohm and Basil J. Hiley, "On the Intuitive Understanding of Non-Locality as Implied by Quantum Theory," *Birkbeck College Writings on Science* (London: University of London, 1974), 27.

18. Brian W. Aldiss, *Cryptozoic!* (New York: Avon Books, 1969), 36. References are to this edition.

19. Charles Muscatine, *Chaucer and the French Tradition: A Study in Style and Meaning* (Berkeley: University of California Press, 1957), 216.

20. Citations are from *The Tales of Canterbury, Complete*, edited by Robert A. Pratt (Boston: Houghton-Mifflin Company, 1974).

21. Citations are from *The Complete Plays of Christopher Marlowe*, edited by Irving Ribner (New York: The Odyssey Press, 1963).

22. See Clifford Leach, "Marlowe's Humor," *Essays on Shakespeare and Elizabethan Drama in Honor of Hardin Craig* (Columbia: University of Missouri Press, 1962), reprinted in *Marlowe: A Collection of Critical Essays*, edited by Leach (Englewood Cliffs, New Jersey: Prentice-Hall, 1964): "One of the recurrent features of Marlowe criticism has been the tendency first to deplore, and then to deny his authorship of comic passages in the play." (167) Seen in the light of future science fiction, these passages are brilliant extrapolations rather than "comic" scenes.

23. *Selected Writings of Francis Bacon*, introduction and notes by Hugh G. Dick (New York: The Modern Library, 1955), 470. References are to this edition.

24. Kester Svendsen, *Milton and Science* (Cambridge: Harvard University Press, 1956), 43.

25. G. S. Rousseau, "The Hunting of the Leviathan and Awakening of Proteus," *Genre at the Crossroads: The Challenge of Fantasy,* edited by Slusser and Jean-Pierre Barricelli (Riverside, California: Xenos Books, 2003), 57.

26. Paul K. Alkon, *Origins of Futuristic Fiction* (Athens: University of Georgia Press, 1987).

27. William Wordsworth, "Preface" to the Second Edition of the *Lyrical Ballads, English Romantic Writers,* edited by David Perkins (New York: Harcourt, Brace & World, 1967), 326.

28. John Keats, *Lamia, English Romantic Writers*, Part II, lines 234–237 (1196).

29. See Benjamin Robert Haydon, *Autobiography*, cited in *Prose of the Romantic Period,* edited by Carl R. Woodring (Cambridge: Houghton Mifflin Company, 1961), 595.

30. Matthew Arnold, *The Portable Matthew Arnold,* edited by Lionel Trilling (New York: The Viking Press, 1949), 56. Italics in original. References are to this edition.

31. See *Tennyson's Poetry*, edited by Robert W. Hill, Jr. (New York: W. W. Norton, 1971).

32. H. G. Wells, *The Time Machine: An Invention* (New York: Bantam Books, 1968), 105–106. The text is that of the Heinemann edition of 1895. References are to this edition.

33. It remains one of the most significant fictional works of the twentieth century. Witness the Centennial Conference, held at Imperial College in 1995, which drew MPs and literary celebrities like Doris Lessing and Brian W. Aldiss, as well as an international body of scholars, to discuss this single novel. See *H. G. Wells's Perennial Time Machine*, edited by Slusser, Patrick Parrinder, and Danièle Chatelain (Athens: University of Georgia Press, 2001).

34. D. G. Compton, *Synthajoy* (New York: Ace Books, 1968), [1], back cover. The first quotation is unattributed; the second is attributed only to the *South Devon Times*.

35. Compton, *The Steel Crocodile* (New York: Ace Books, 1970), back cover.

36. See Slusser, "The Beginnings of *Fiction*," *Science-Fiction Studies*, 16:3 (November 1989), 307–337.

37. André Ruellan, *Mémo* (Paris: Denoël Présence du futur, 1984), 153.

38. Nathaniel Hawthorne, *The Complete Novels and Selected Tales of Nathaniel Hawthorne* (New York: Random House, 1937), 1154. References are to this edition.

39. Ralph Waldo Emerson, *Nature, The American Tradition in Literature*, edited by Sculley Bradley, Richmond Croom Beatty, and E. Hudson Long (New York: W. W. Norton, 1967), 1067.

# Chapter Two

# Fraternal Frontiers

## *Defining a Space for Literature*

Space, now generally understood to refer to outer space, gradually became a key setting for science fiction; but in a broader sense, as mankind seeks to define its place in the universe, space has always been an important issue. We have no idea of how early figures conceived of space. The age of Titans, for example, could depict a single figure, an Atlas, holding up the entire Earth. But this has scant relation to space in the modem sense, which involves the various properties of mankind's world as Descartes saw them, those aspects of the physical world he included in the three measurable dimensions he conceived as "extension," or more precisely *res extensa*—for the idea of space, even for a Descartes, is still conceivable only in terms of what occupies and shapes it. An empty space or "void" is inconceivable. Descartes may be one of the "fathers" of modern science, but his sense of space remains classical and Aristotelian. Classic space, we could say, begins with the advent of the gods, for they claimed a place or space for themselves, even if at first they had no conception of what it was—they were the *Olympian* gods. We notice that in Aeschylus's *The Eumenides* (458 BCE), Athena promises a court of justice that will last for "all time." This is not the modern concept of time, but rather time conceived as permanence, a place in space that will always be there for its users. For the classical mind, space quickly becomes a subject of philosophical inquiry. Rapidly, the Greek mind grappled with the question of "is there anything *out there*?" beyond the boundaries and extremities of this single world, whose boundaries mankind was just beginning to explore.

The myth of the elsewhere, the unknown place beyond which we are located, passed down to science fiction through two different but contemporary channels. To understand how science fiction in general has come to experience space, we must examine these two scientific—and fictional—paths, both bequeathed to the modern world by French thinkers in the seventeenth century who engaged the "scientific revolution" of that century with concepts of space based on classical sources. The first is Descartes who, despite treatises on physics and optics, largely remains a product of the Aristotelian vision of space as passed down via the scholastics. The second is Pierre Gassendi and his so-called "atomism" providing, as Barbour puts it, a "metrical" or distance view of space, which derives from the pre-Socratics and their idea of a "void."[1] One adheres to the finite Aristotelian view of the cosmos, the other to an infinite Euclidian space, even if that space be nothing but void, in which there are no other worlds but ours. It is not long however, once this possibility of an open space is voiced, before people like Fontenelle and Cyrano de Bergerac will seek the possibility of a "pluralite des mondes." In contrast, Descartes's idea of space takes a curiously inward turn. For to Descartes, the two locations of a *proveable* set of boundaries is first the mind, or "itne rationelle," which he proves exists in *Discours de la methode.* The second location, which he examines at the end of his life in *Les passions de l'âme,* is his own body, whose vital interconnection with his mind he finally comes to admit. Descartes rejected the idea of the void—*res extensa* is *measurable* space or extension, and what lies beyond such measurement is non-space, hence does not exist. Pascal, repeating Torricelli's experiment, perhaps demonstrated that nature does not abhor a vacuum. Nevertheless, if the "two infinities" exist, mankind is in the terrifying position of being dwarfed by them. For Pascal, here in a sense following Descartes who he otherwise saw as "inutile, incertain," ultimately places our rational mind alone in an infinity of empty matter. For Pascal, this location is mankind's "human condition," fixed and immutable.

## THE TWO SPACES OF SCIENCE FICTION

The influence of Descartes on modern science should never be neglected. When a serenely American writer like Gregory Benford repeatedly proclaims that "we are all Cartesians," this should not be taken lightly. But Benford means something quite different than how a Frenchman might address this question. Descartes discussed this question of space; in fact, his coordinates—mind/body/*res extensa*—are essentially spatial coordinates. Though his earliest works of scientific investigation seemed to ally him with Galileo and the Copernican vision of planetary motion, he hastily withdrew from it upon hearing of Galileo's condemnation. His subsequent works—the *Dioptrique,* the *Meteores,* and the *Geometrie*—were published in 1837 with a "metaphysical" introduction, the famous *Discours de la Methode.* In dangerous times, Descartes surely felt the need to find the means of getting around Church censorship. Nonetheless, even as clarified in his later *Principles of Philosophy,* where his major ideas on science are presented, we see that, with the question of space, he remains influenced by Aristotle's concept of space. Even so, he makes a fascinating adaptation of Aristotle that will have an immense influence on the idea of space in France.

Here is Aristotle on space (*Physics* IV, 1): "The existence of place is held to be obvious from the fact of mutual replacement. Where water now is, there in turn, when the water has gone out, as from another vessel, air is present, and at another time another body occupies this place."[2] Whereas Plato in the *Timaeus* sees matter and space as the same, Aristotle sees space as separable from the object. Space contains a thing but is no part of the contained thing. For Aristotle, then, space or place marks extremities, space being the boundary of the containing body at which it contacts the contained body. Aristotle will use this definition to define a world that cannot move, for it has no place to do so, as there is nothing outside it. Only parts of this world, as they all have their space, can change place. Descartes's *cogito* is in a sense a radical exercise in setting boundaries. His "stove" is a closed space in which Descartes seeks to jettison every aspect of his existence that sets a broad and untenable boundary. His goal is to turn inward, to isolate and detach all nonessential aspects of his existence, to access the essential space of the rational mind, which, once discovered, becomes the fixed center of the human experience. If Descartes's first scientific efforts look outward toward a more open sense of space, he still feels it necessary, throughout his career, to adhere to this idea of individual space defined as the metaphysical center of mind. His final treatise, *Les passions de l'âme*, limits Descartes's exploratory possibilities to the interrelation of mind to body, which becomes the new, complex, boundary of a scientific philosophy that has all but abandoned *res extensa* in the larger sense.

Descartes's vision of space then is centripetal. That of his rival Gassendi is the opposite, centrifugal and outward looking. Gassendi's opponent, in his *Exercitationes paradoxicae contra Aristoteleos* (1624), is the abiding presence of the great boundary-maker. He was never as influential as Descartes, whose mindbody problem, couched in the metaphysical context and language of church doctrine, must have struck future generations as a secularized version of the Christ paradox, which again turns the problem of expansion and exploration of space inward. But from Gassendi's vision there evolves, as early as Descartes's century, a strong tradition of space adventure. Gassendi and his adherents may have denied the existence of the void, but their sense of empty space, a place that exists outside mankind and might contain something exciting and beneficial to it in this expansive, scientific century, attracted other speculators, who this time used fiction and fictional situations as means of possible discovery.

An article by Ari Margolin, entitled "How Do I Know Unless I Go There: Cyranian Thought Experiment as Scientific Method and SF" (2015), touts Cyrano de Bergerac's *L'Autre Monde: ou les États et Empires de la Lune* (1657) as a groundbreaking application of the new scientific method to a situation where space exploration is involved. Cyrano's method, unlike that of Descartes, is not based on deduction and elimination, but observation and hypothesis. From Cyrano will follow a long tradition in France—one that began much earlier than rival movements in England and elsewhere—of space travel and adventure, evolving in a very un-Cartesian space. This literature flourished throughout France's eighteenth century and, in its nineteenth century, produced works like Jules Verne's *voyages extraordinaires,* and those of his "followers," well into the twentieth century. But these works, relegated by France's cultural arbiters to the stature of "popular" literature, are not those that—in the period after World War II, when the French reading public suddenly became aware of the name "science fiction"—came to be called "French SF." This literature, though based on imported American and British models whose central theme is space exploration, clearly returns to the Cartesian sense of space born in the seventeenth century. The central question then is: how and why did this happen? The reason cannot simply be because French writers wanted to be different from imported models, products of the age of space exploration that were neither narratively nor visually new to postwar French writers. France is after all the nation of Verne and his graphically famous rocket to the moon. There are deeper reasons for French SF's return to a closed sense of space.

## CYRANO'S LEGACY

As we see, this closed paradigm is not conducive to travel and discovery in spacetime, for there is no moving mind, observing and gathering information, its knowledge evolving through, and because of, its various adventures in space. A variation of this use of travel is found in the eighteenth century in England with Defoe's Robinson Crusoe. His approach to unexpected encounters is however totally pragmatic. He is no scientist and has no use for science. Here is his credo: "In a word, the nature and experience of things dictated to me upon just reflection that all the good things of this world are of no farther good to us than that they are for our use."[3] There is, in France, a line of space adventure stories that follow this pragmatic, exploratory path, but from the beginning these stories have an avowed scientific purpose. Moreover, this sort of literature originates in the seventeenth century, as an attempt to bifurcate from Cartesian rationalism. Its inspiration, it appears, is the work of Gassendi, who corresponded with Galileo, Hobbes, and other noteworthy scientists and thinkers and was a proponent of empirical investigation of nature by means of observation and experiment. Though tainted with a Baconian sense of the limitations of human senses to observe and understand, he was an important adversary of Descartes, espousing a materialist and relativist view of mankind's relation to nature, inspired by Epicureanism and classical atomism. His sense of space is, given these antecedents, an expansive one. His vision is also different from that of Pascal, whose sense of space remains classical and rationalist. Pascal does little more than amplify Descartes's vision of space, making our place in it a terrifying and incomprehensible situation.

However influential Pascal's vision may be, it is not the sole sense of space that develops from this scientific seventeenth century in France. Another voice, largely ignored today, is Cyrano de Bergerac, satirist and freethinker, whose *L'Autre Monde* and subsequent *Les états et empires du soleil* (1662) use off-world travel to both satirize the Church's geocentric view of things and demonstrate that, were we to travel beyond our known sphere of mind and body, we would rapidly discover how little we know and how much there is to know. Sam Moskowitz sees Cyrano as setting forth the first technologically credible rocket-propelled voyage to the moon, quite a compliment. And in his voyages, Cyrano's protagonist, guided by the arch-skeptic "Socrates," espouses the idea that there are a plurality of senses and dimensions which we cannot know without first encountering them in their own spatiotemporal context. Our rationalist pretentions to be the center of things appears preposterous to Cyrano, and he mocks it mightily.

Cyrano, then, launches an alternate tradition in France of actual physical space travel and exploration. One can cite what appear important links in a chain of thought that seeks to externalize space travel. There is Bernard de Bouvier de Fontenelle's *Entretiens sur la pluralité des mondes* (1686). Fontenelle was a lifelong defender of Descartes and professed a strong interest in Descartes's "astronomy." Yet his comments on the drive that brings humanity to conceive and seek out a "pluralité des mondes" are decidedly un-Cartesian. He may appear to see mankind, like Pascal, as dwarfed by the immensity of the cosmos. Yet in his eyes this is a self-inflicted misery that mankind brings on itself. To our misery there can be no corresponding grandeur unless we allow reason to challenge limits that reserve a limited role for humans in the scheme of things. There is a genuine sense here that, in our geocentric belief in the supremacy of reason, we literally cut ourselves off from vast spaces of knowledge. Fontenelle urges us to undertake the physical journey to these "other worlds." One can trace this tradition of "'plurality of worlds" from Fontenelle to Voltaire's *Micromégas* (1752), which involves a supposed extraterrestrial traveling from Sirius to Saturn, then to Earth. These are precursors of Verne and Camille Flammarion, a noted astronomer, author of *L'Astronomie populaire* (1879). For both writers, space travel seems a given.

Flammarion published his treatise *La pluralité des mondes habités* in 1862, in which he offers detailed descriptions of other planets in terms of their "inhabitability." In fiction such as *Uranie* (1891), he presents Mars as destination for reincarnated Earth men and women. These fanciful and mystical elements however appear a pretext that allows Flammarion to undertake an extended exploration of the "flora and fauna" of the red planet (we must remember we are in the age of Schiaparelli and Lowell, when Mars became a physical reality to observers and actual travel to Mars was contemplated). The period from the late nineteenth century to mid-twentieth century saw a myriad of space adventures in France's pulp literature. Among works by the so-called "School of Verne" are novels like Henry de Graffigny and Georges Le Faure's *Les aventures extraordinaires d'un savant-russe* (1889–1894), four volumes of travels around the solar system, which physically confirm the "pluralité des mondes habités." Interestingly, these explorers descend into the Martian atmosphere by means of a balloon, an idea that will serve Clarke (in a more scientifically accurate depiction of Jupiter's atmosphere) in "A Meeting with Medusa" (1971). Another example is Amould Galopin's *Le docteur Omega, aventures fantastiques de trois franfais dans la planete Mars* (1906). These French scientists use a "negative mass" *fuel-repulsite* to go to Mars. The drawing of their space vessel is a nice little ballistic (bullet-like) rocket a la Verne.

Space travel and exploration continues to be a popular theme in the pulp SF circuit in France. Even in the postwar period, the bulk of French SF was space adventure, at least in terms of themes and plots. The series *Fleuve noir anticipation* produced, over a publishing history of forty-six years (1951–1997), 2001 novels, the majority of which involve some form of space travel. The cover illustrator of over 500 of these novels (issues 1–273 and 562–795) was René Brantonne, a consummate space artist, who worked in Hollywood during and after World War II as a movie poster artist, thus can be assumed to have had firsthand contact with the "American" style of SF covers. He surely witnessed the covers of magazines like *Astounding Science-Fiction* amd saw them effecting a transition from the fanciful rockets and machines of earlier magazines like *Amazing Stories*—such as Leo Morey's cover for the April 1935 issue, with dirigible-like ships floating above a jumble of Earth monuments from different times and places, and the March 1935 Morey cover where a "space bubble" hovers over a "just imagine" vertical city—to the "realistically" aerodynamic machines of postwar American SF. Brantonne festooned the covers of early *Anticipation* novels with numerous engines in flight. One detects, in the scenes and machines of his 1950s *Flueve noir* covers, the influence of *Astounding* artists like Hubert Rogers, notably his *Gray Lensman* covers and June 1940 cover illustrating Heinlein's "The Roads Must Roll." He also apparently found inspiration in the extraordinary mid-1930s transitional *Astounding* work of Elliott Dold, for example his vast machine cityscapes in the January 1935 issue illustrating Doc Smith's *Skylark of Valeron*. The French then have a long tradition of space adventure, longer in fact than that the Anglo-Saxon pulps. They have as well have a strong tradition of illustrated narratives, focusing on spacecraft, space landscapes, and the excitement of space exploration, that runs from the famous Henri de Montaut rocket ships in Verne's *De la terre a la lune* (1865) to Brantonne's art. Yet despite such a crowning achievement, this is not the path French literature and culture followed when it comes to the idea of space travel. Instead, what seems to dominate is the very different, rationalist vision of Descartes and Pascal, which places severe limits on mankind's ability to engage a plurality of worlds, to expand human horizons.

## SPACE MAY NOT BE WHAT IT SEEMS: VOLTAIRE

Before looking at postwar depictions of space adventure, we must ask whether space travel in French literature and art was ever depicted as unfettered explorations of space. Bradford Lyau's *Stepchildren of Voltaire: The Anticipation Novelists of 1950's French Science Fiction* (2010) proves beyond doubt that the "pulpsters" who wrote numerous space operas for the *Fleuve noir* series were using this space scenario to mask stories whose core was really about the restricted political and cultural space of 1950s France. Lyau argues that these works, in fact, are modern versions of Voltaire's *conies philosophiques.* To accomplish such a feat, authors had to, surreptitiously in most cases, trade an open sense of space adventure for a closed space. And if we look closely at a work like *Micromégas,* which is Lyau's model, we see Voltaire applying a like process to what is both the real and imaginary voyage of discovery in the French eighteenth century. *Micromégas,* despite its space adventure theme, is the prime example of this inward turn. Famously, Voltaire challenges Pascal's vision in the twenty-fifth letter of *Lettres philosophiques.* Yet in a sense, his argument can be seen as little more than a prolongation of Pascal's sense of human space. Voltaire appears to supplant the mind-matter duality with what seems a more progressive, if not evolutionary, model. This would, in the manner of the French Enlightenment, open human inquiry and industry to advancement, change, and discovery through exploration and charting of a broader physical world. Likewise, Voltaire, apparently accepting in *Micromégas* the plurality of worlds, encourages the possibility of human enhancement/advancement, thus the ability of humans to not only encounter "superior" beings but communicate with them, and perhaps one day become like them. He appears to offer, in terms of our relation to other species, a graduated scale: "L'homme parait a sa place dans la nature, superieur aux animaux, inferieur a d'autres etres, auquels ii ressemble probablement par la pensee. L'homme est ce qu'il doit etre." [Man seems to be in its place in nature, superior to animals, inferior to other beings whom he resembles probably by his capability to think. Man is what he is meant to be.][4]

But if we read this statement carefully, we see Voltaire has not abandoned the rationalist mind/matter duality; he has merely "loosened" Pascal's extreme formulations. The gap still abides between animals and humans—we have reason, they do not. Higher beings, on the contrary, share reason with us. Therefore, they are not other than us, they are simply extensions of ourselves, larger in size, but not necessarily more rational or better than we are. Voltaire implies that we can explore all "inhabited" planets and galaxies in the universe but will never encounter anything but versions of ourselves. Beyond that, Pascal's terrifying material infinities are still realms that cannot be explored. Mankind remains where it "ought to be," at the center of things, a center again defined in terms of proportion. The nature of Voltaire's human center however, instead of Pascal's incomprehensible monster, has become a thoroughly comprehensible humanity—humanity as median or norm.

In fact, the name Micro-megas—"little-big"—represents Voltaire's satirical adaptation of Pascal's "grandeur et misere de l'homme." All religious or metaphysical overtones are removed, as now we are talking solely about physical size: "Il comprit bien vite qu'n être pensant peut fort bien n'être pas ridicule pour n'avoir que six mille pieds de haut." [He understood very fast that a thinking being, only six thousand feet high, can very well escape from ridicule.][5] The giant space traveler comes from Sirius to Saturn, then to Earth, where he carries on discourses with men who are, in physical terms, mites by comparison. In these discussions, the human "microbes" surprise Micromégas by speaking of science and metaphysics and evoking their violent God who, they say, sanctions massacres in His name. Most shocking is their claim that this God not only created the universe but did so exclusively for mankind.

This same device of using oversized human figures, similar to but out of proportion with other humans in a same frame, is common in twentieth-century SF covers, both French and American. The way they are used, however, is radically different. In American SF covers, women of huge proportion often serve as inspiring angels of space travel, such as the elegant woman in evening dress, toasting rocketships that soar into space, in Earle Bergey's cover for the March 1951 issue of *Startling Stories.* The archetypal male icon of American SF is Rogers's famous Gray Lensman, occupying the entire space of the frame from bottom to top, standing defiantly on the gangway of his spaceship. Like Micromégas, he has arrived, but not on Earth. He steps forth, rather, *into* some distant space destination. The giant does not come from them to us; rather the Lensman has gone from us to them; he is a giant who stands on the threshold of even vaster fields of investigation. On French covers, on the other hand, the message seems always to be that of Micromégas. The French spacemen depicted on many *Fiction* covers are often "bigger than life" as well. They appear, like Micromégas, to tower iconically over human pretensions. Even so, as represented, their form, often only torso and head, is aggressively foregrounded in the frame, marking the presence of an "être pensant." This implies, as with Voltaire's formula, that there must be even larger (not different, simply larger) forms of rational beings somewhere in the cosmos, who will dwarf this spaceman, and in doing so render his pretentions to "understand" the broader universe equally ridiculous. We are specks to him; but he is, in turn a speck to other larger beings. The result is a set of reflecting mirrors in which the human form, large or small, remains the alpha and omega of space travel. The book these "explorers" and "aventuriers du ciel" will write will always be blank, like the book Micromégas leaves behind. Mankind remains an incomprehensible monster to itself. Its travels always loop around to form an intergalactic version of Descartes's stove, encapsulating the eternal human mind and body. And that form, the solipsistic locus of rational mind, must always remain unique in any universe.

We find a similar centripetal movement in the vast, thirty-nine-volume collection of imaginary voyages edited by Charles Garnier and published on the eve of the French Revolution (1787–1789) under the general title *Voyages imaginaires, songes, visions et roman cabbalistiques.* The first books in the series present a translation of *Robinson Crusoe,* which promises to set the tone as one of open-ended exploration of new lands, be they actual physical places or, as stated here, places of the mind and imagination. But this promise is soon dissipated. Garnier publishes in Volume 10, after Voltaire's novel, Montesquieu's "Histoire des Troglodytes," taken from his *Lettres persanes* (1721). Here the visitor is from Persia, not the planet Sirius. His coming to Paris however has the same purpose, to reveal the presumption and vanity of French manners. In like manner, Cyrano's space voyages are followed by Lucian's fantastic and satirical *The True History* (c. second century CE) and a string of works such as *Les iles fortunees, ou les aventures de Bathylle et de Cleobule* (1778), by a certain Moutonnet de Clairfons, meant to deflate the exploratory pretentions of the shipwreck novel, deflecting the aspirations of travelers to distant lands back onto a predetermined sense of the folly of such explorations. We have, in these texts, what might seem a veritable anatomy of what will be later *places* of exploration. There is planetary space—Marie-Anne Roberts's *Voyages de Milord Ceton dans sept planetes* (1765). There is the "hollow earth," from Holberg's Nicolas Klimius to *Lakemis ou les voyages extraordinaires d'un Egyptien dans la terre interieure, avec la decouverte de I'ile des Syphides* by Le Chevalier de Mouhy (1737). There are several novels of travel to "la terre australe." But these, like *Les aventures de Jacques Sadeur dans la decouverte et le voyage de la Terre australe* (Gabriel de Foigny, 1676), though they promise real exploration, reveal themselves to be little more than studies in comparative "manners," with those of Europe invariably proving to be of lesser worth. Finally, we have escape from the perils and contingencies of real travel in the pure fantasy voyage. Instead of serious efforts to extrapolate new worlds from old, we get works like *Voyage merveilleux de la prince Fan-Feredan dans la Romancie* (1788) by Le Pere Bougeant. It begins to appear as if the sole, and ultimate, place of travel is in the mind itself.

## HOW EXTRA-ORDINARY ARE VERNE'S VOYAGES?

Jules Verne's work has become the *locus classicus* in French, of both space adventure and (in its illustrations) the icons of space travel. Yet it is worth taking a detour here to show that Verne, in his travel stories and ultimately his space adventures, in fact moves in the same centripetal direction we have seen in the French Cartesian tradition. These voyages, despite detailed descriptions of external landscapes, are ultimately mind voyages. They could even be said to be voyages to the inner workings of the mind itself. Verne's work explores all the *voyage imaginaire* locales presented in Garnier. But now, in accord with his century of new technologies, he claims to do so in the material world, by deploying the vehicular devices available to contemporary science and technology, as well as some (as in the case of his space rocket) not yet available but clearly "on the drawing boards." In *Voyage au centre de la terre* (1864), Axel and Professor Lidenbrock follow the path of the earlier Icelandic explorer Arne Saknussem. Moreover, they follow the scientific blueprint of Humphrey Davy's theory of volcanic action. In terms of polar exploration, Captain Hatteras, in *Voyages et aventures du capitaine Hatteras* (1866), follows in the tracks of numerous contemporary seekers of the Northwest Passage. Verne's guide to *la terre australe,* in *Le Sphinx des glaces* (1897), is a literary one: Edgar Allan Poe, with Verne's protagonists taking the path pursued by the fictional Arthur Gordon Pym. Granted, these are travels under Earth and upon Earth. Curiously, however, *Capitaine Hatteras* inspired Georges Melies's film *La Conquete du pole* (1912), wherein travelers to the North Pole employ a flying machine that seems modeled on a Verne illustration (Léon Bennet in *Robur the Conqueror* [(1986]). Finally, there is space travel in *De la terre a la lune.* The novel's title seconds the promise of Montaut's famous space rocket that prefaces the volume—a long, straight, segmented object pointed at the Moon, seeming to trace an inflexible line toward new discovery. It is a product of the science of ballistics, a missile fired from a cannon at an object with the intention of hitting it. What actually happens is significant; for instead of hitting the Moon, placing the explorers on its surface, it enters Moon orbit to circle the Moon. Thus, the title of the sequel: *Autour de la lune* (1870).

French commentators on Verne tend to see his pretentions at travel and exploration as just that: pretentions. For Roland Barthes, Captain Nemo is not an expansive, but a contractive presence. He may have mapped underwater worlds and gathered much new knowledge, but this remains *his* horde of knowledge, encapsulated in his *Nautilus,* the work of a man without a name. Historian of science Michel Serres describes Verne's scientific travels as inherently circular: "Par le modele spatial ou geographique, par le modele du savoir et de l'encyclopedie . . . on saisit la structure circulaire, close, fermee de ce cycle de cycles. Jules Verne a ecrit un ensemble de dictionnaires. Or, qu'est-ce qu'un dictionnaire, sinon un ensemble d'elements clos par l'operation de la definition?" [Thanks to the spatial or geographical model, thanks to the model of the knowledge and the encyclopedia . . . one grasps the circular, closed, locked structure of that cycle of cycles. Jules Verne wrote a series of dictionaries. But what is a dictionary other than a set of elements locked by the operation of the definition?][6] Indeed, in the rocket's trajectory around the Moon, every observation seems to have already been written in the dictionary of known things, or as part of someone else's previously formulated theory. The explorers do encounter one singularity—the dark side of the Moon—which of course they cannot see because it is dark. Their one chance to have a look—when a meteor flashes through space—proves too fleeting, a tease and nothing more. In their final attempt to land on the Moon, they again miscalculate, and the rocket returns to Earth. Their voyage, from the point of view of discovery, proves totally superfluous, for in the end they can only question whether they have seen more than the Cambridge telescope on Earth has seen. Had they landed on the Moon, because they had no communications equipment, they could not have conveyed new information except by hand signals, again perceived through Earth's telescopes. Nor could they have left the Moon, as they miscalculated the fuel needed to do so.

In the most significant of Verne's novels of exploration, what begins as a voyage in physical space seems to end in the mental space of dream. With

*Capitaine Hatteras,* there is the controversy of the two endings. As the story goes, Verne wanted Hatteras to leap into the volcano at the North Pole and perish. Editor Hetzel however is said to have demanded (and gotten) a different ending: Hatteras survives the plunge and returns to England to live out his life in an insane asylum. Whether Verne or Hetzel wanted the ending we now have, that ending suggests that Hatteras's final leap (like Axel's wild ride up the erupting volcano) is an insane dream, for no one in the physical world could survive it. The ending of *Le Sphinx des glaces* is much the same. The novel seeks to provide a physical explanation for what mysteriously happens at the end of Poe's novel, where Pym disappears in a white fog. But the physical forces Verne's protagonists do discover—the immense magnetic field at the pole that apparently destroyed Pym's expedition—would wreak such havoc on any approaching vessel that any "real" ending in Verne proves more improbable and fantastic than Poe's fictional ending.

Verne imagined space travel in not only his Moon novels, but the curious *Hector Servadac, Voyages et aventures a travers le monde solaire* (1877). The novel—remembered today in the Anglo-Saxon world mainly for its antisemitism—describes the voyage of a microcosmic cross-section of Earth society through the solar system on a comet, which skims Earth and takes away a piece of land containing the voyagers. Commentators—even Hugo Gernsback who published the work as *Off on a Comet*—have noted the impossibility of this voyage: how could a comet chip off a piece of the planet without destroying it? How could voyagers survive conditions in space without the least equipment? Most of all, how could they get back to their starting point? These are questions of the same magnitude as those asked about the ending of *Voyage au centre de la terre.* Editor Hetzel prefaced a "Note des editeurs" to this text, in which he [or more probably Verne himself] proclaims: "C'est l'histoire d'une hypothèse et des conséquences qu'elle aurait si elle pouvait, par impossible, se réaliser." [It is the story of a hypothesis and its ensuing consequences if it could, by chance, be realized.] The vast circle of this voyage of interplanetary exploration—the novel traces the farthest arc Verne gives us in his works—closes, not in the physical world, but rather the world of dream. Here is Hector's final assessment, itself a hypothesis, a mind structure: "Mettons que je n'ai fait qu'un reve." [Let's suppose I just only dreamed.][7]

## CROSSROADS:
## AMERICAN SPACE TRAVEL MEETS DESCARTES

Images of space and space adventure returned with a vengeance when American SF magazines first appeared in postwar France during the 1950s. Many of their stories were about space exploration, where the preliminary phases of what would become the American space program were set forth as visual "concepts." Through these sources, French readers were saturated with images of spaceships, space stations, interplanetary and interstellar travel, featured in films, book covers, and especially the cover art of the SF digests that constituted, at that time, the core of SF publishing in the United States. Translated versions of the two major SF digests—*Galaxy* and *The Magazine of Fantasy and Science Fiction*—appeared simultaneously in France in 1953. *Galaxy Science Fiction*—edited by H. L. Gold (1950–1961), and Frederik Pohl (1961–1969)—saw its heyday during these decades. The French version of the magazine contented itself to translate stories and simply reproduce the American cover art for most of this period.[8] These covers exposed French audiences to space art by artists like Ed Emshwiller and Jack Gaughan. Despite the "social" slant of *Galaxy*, its covers throughout the 1950s generally present "realistic" visions of space and activities in space—space stations, shuttle rockets, views of distant planets from places like Mars, robots repairing spacecraft. More stylized covers (notably those of Gaughan and Emshwiller) offer what could be called symbolic visions, with suited astronauts holding huge models of atoms, or looking outward to the stars—images of mankind dwarfed by the immensity of space perhaps but looking nonetheless forward to adventure and conquest. If there is criticism of the space program and space travel in these covers, it is certainly muted. The thrust of these images and icons is centrifugal, outward moving, positive in terms of mankind's relationship to open space.

From its inception, the French version of *The Magazine of Fantasy and Science Fiction* took a different path. It too began as a vehicle for translations of American works yet rapidly changed course, first setting up a critical apparatus that not only judged the writers it published, but established generic criteria that offered an alternative vision of the history and nature of science fiction. At the same time, it began producing graphics and stories by French writers who themselves were nourished in this matrix. From the outset, the French magazine, rebaptized simply *Fiction,* resisted the term "science fiction," though the term was comfortably attached to the American stories it published. The cover copy states that it deals with a variety of forms. It calls itself the "revue de la litterature de l'etrange" and includes therein categories such as "le fantastique" and "l'insolite" [the uncanny] as well as "S-F." Gradually, in the wake of its critical articles, French authors, whose work was tailored to the guidelines for this new literary form being developed by the magazine's staff of critics and commentators under the name "science fiction," are included alongside American writers. More striking yet is the fact that the French magazine from the very first issues, with few exceptions, insisted upon creating its own cover art that was radically different from that on analogous American covers. Its sense of space and space exploration was uniquely different.

The American magazine, and the evolution of its focus and cover art, has its own history, which for purposes of contrast is worth tracing. Its first incarnation, under the editorship of Boucher and McComas, was initially called *The Magazine of Fantasy.* Many of its stories in the 1950s, by Bradbury, Richard Matheson, and others, set the future direction by shading toward the fantasy side of the spectrum (though *F&SF* serialized Heinlein's *Starship Troopers* in 1959). Many covers as well, by artists like Hannes Bok and Emshwiller, depicted space fantastically. Yet, in the midst of these, space artist Chesley Bonestell produced forty-two covers for *F&SF* from 1951 to 1959. These were starkly "realistic," either derived from actual space photography or extrapolated from hard scientific data (Bonestell was a consultant along with Heinlein on George Pal's 1950 film *Destination Moon* and corresponded regularly with experts like Wernher von Braun). These covers focus on space machines and space-scapes—views such as Saturn as seen from Titan. There are aerodynamically possible two-stage rockets, gravity-wheel space stations, spacewalks, all visualized in interplanetary backdrops—plausible, functional extrapolations, in which the human element is often reduced to insignificant, spacesuited figures, tenders of the machines which will ultimately carry mankind into deep space.

In contrast to the Bonestell model, which the French magazine inherited along with the American stories, *Fiction* covers present a radically different treatment of space and space travel. During the early 1950s, for example, artist Jean-Claude Forest (later famous for his *bande dessinée* character Barbarella, seen in Roger Vadim's 1968 film featuring Jane Fonda) was commissioned to do several covers, as well as internal drawings for selected stories. One of his most famous covers, for Issue 57 of *Fiction* (1955), illustrated C. L. Moore's "Shambleau" (1933). When we compare this presentation with the cover art of Moore's first book including the story—*Shambleau and Others* (1953)—we confront two vastly different visions of space adventure and of how science-fictional space should be configured. The American edition depicts a planetary landscape—probably a moon of Mars, with the reddish surface of the fourth planet filling the sky. Three needle-sharp rockets pass from left to right across Mars. The protagonist of the story, Moore's first published work, is Northwest Smith, her version of the Gray Lensman, but here a space adventurer (and smuggler), a more or less conventional man of action. He is not presented on the cover, and neither is anyone else. What is depicted instead is the spirit of space travel, the onward and outward vision represented by Mars, the barren vantage point from which we see it, and iconic spaceships in flight.

Forest's cover is much the opposite. First, it is dominated by human figures. Most notable among these is a woman, who dominates the left side of the cover, seated in some sort of space alcove, playing a guitar. Moore's Shambleau, the alien female saved by Northwest Smith from lynching by a Martian mob, sings a song "The Green Hills" (Heinlein's homage to Moore's story is "The Green Hills of Earth" [1947]). But in Moore's story, Shambleau is not a space troubadour, but rather a vampiric figure, the ancient Medusa legend come alive, who almost destroys Smith. The story significantly describes the modus operandi of the Shambleaus: they use "a mental reach to get mental food." Indeed, the attack in the story is clearly not by anything closely resembling the Cartesian mind. "Mind" here is physical energy, energy in this case heightened by sexual pleasure. These creatures gear up pleasure to the highest intensity in order to take it back; they "give always, that horrible foul pleasure as they—feed."[9] In Moore's story, Smith escapes the *liebestod* when a fellow spacer intervenes and kills Shambleau. The playing field of this story is a purely material one, where one man's thoughts are another (woman's) food.

Forest, on the other hand, presents Shambleau, not with snaky locks and pointed nails, but as a beautiful woman, languidly strumming an instrument and suggesting, in her dress and occupation, a heroine of courtly love. The guitar may further allude to "The Green Hills of Earth" (a "lyrical" story atypical of Heinlein, but undoubtedly because of that well known in France in 1955). This woman, like Circe, seems to be drawing the male traveler home from space. For on her right, in perspective, we see a much smaller intermediary figure—a male spaceman, but significantly without the characteristic spacesuit representing his trade and mission—moving toward the woman. Behind him, smaller yet, there are other male figures and a vague scene suggesting interstellar warfare, a "tank" with cannon raised, apparently stuck in the sands of Mars. What we witness here is a farewell to arms, to space adventure and conquest—a *tabula rasa* leading to a new form of *cogito* where, in the humanocentric sense of Descartes, mankind is called home to Earth, there to rejoin the world of mind through the woman as object of courtly love. Forest's woman however is both ideal and sensual, a Barbarella. The meeting place then of mind (song, art, sublimation of physical love) and *res extensa* remains the human (in this case female) body.

These two covers set the parameters of this discussion. The Anglo-Saxon vision depicts space and space exploration as a struggle of purely material entities. In American space travel narratives, humans—brain and body working together—seek by means of machines and other physical extensions to expand their reach into unknown areas of what is now clearly recognized as spacetime, a physical concept far removed from the French sense of space, with its static and mythic qualities. The French vision, in contrast, is both geocentric—its rockets tend to move in orbits around Earth—and humano-centric. Reason, Descartes's "rational soul," remains the unique defining quality of human beings in space. As we see in the Forest cover, the images and icons of space gravitate in centripetal fashion back to a central icon, the human body, the place where aspirations of mind encounter their material limitations. If open space, machines, and movement constitute the landscape of Bonestell's space adventure, here the human body remains the focus of France's space tradition.

## VISUALIZING SPACE

These examples indicate that the best way to understand the idea of space and its limits in the French tradition is to examine visual depictions of space within the context of science fiction. This context, since World War II, is that of space travel and exploration. Interestingly, it was drawings in book by Verne, a Frenchman, that first provided the image of a plausible space ve-hicle. Some have said that Montaut's rocket looks like a train, with a series of cars. But these could also be seen as the various "stages" of a modern booster rocket. There are certainly enough details to tantalize modern viewers. It is ironic then that, in France, we must wait to find a similar experience of physi-cal space travel until 1953, in Hergé's popular Tintin *bande dessinée* series, "Les aventures de Tintin." In this series, Hergé offers two *bandes dessineés, Objectif lune,* and in the next year, 1954, its sequel *On a marche sur la lune,* that depict space travel. These works are exactly calqued on Verne's twin Moon novels, simply brought up to date by incorporating new advances in rocketry and using images and poses from American cover art. The "Tintin" series is seen in France as "juvenile" fiction. But like the *Fleuve noir* space operas, Tintin is not a work for adolescents alone, but addresses that famous audience of readers from 9 to 99, much like Verne's adventures. Herge's Moon novels, therefore, were designed to have the same lifelong appeal in their culture as Verne's novels. Verne's narratives include a full palate of descriptions of the Moon rocket and its way of functioning in (for its time) up-to-date technical terms. Hergé's artwork does the same, bringing to life rockets and space adventure for general readers. What strikes us with these illustrated novels is just how little space travel—the technological adventure of space exploration—has evolved since Verne. One hundred years later (and with lots of far-flung depictions of worlds in space) we are still exploring the Moon. Little or no galactic ground has been gained. Of course, putting a man on the Moon was about to be a physical reality, so the Tintin adventures had topical appeal when they were published. Yet as these novels appeared in the space age, we see just how much ground has been lost since Verne took his characters around the Moon. Tintin sets foot on the Moon (Verne's characters did not). But compared with Verne, whose characters were adults and scientists and ventured into space ostensibly to do scientific work, Tintin remains in his eternal role as "jeune reporter," the magic boy who does not grow up. We are historically on the verge of real space travel, real Moon walks. Yet Tintin fixes in the minds of the French an indelible association between juvenilia and the greatest technological feat of the century. The adventure of technology, as documented here in words (and more significantly in images), becomes for the French, via Tintin, a thing for amateurs who remain terminally young.

The cultural impact of Tintin was such that many French consider that he, sixteen years before Neil Armstrong, was actually the first to walk on the Moon. A significant comparison is with the appearance of Heinlein's special effects in *Destination Moon,* which three years earlier, in 1950, strived to put human observers (in this case moviegoers) physically on the Moon, a place that nobody had yet been. By doing so Heinlein lifted the visuals of space travel from the juvenile realm (that of Heinlein's own *Rocket Ship Galileo* [1947]) into the eminently adult realm of Bonestell's covers and finally Stanley Kubrick's *2001: A Space Odyssey* (1968).

We find the French analogue to the American fascination with depicting aerodynamically conceived spacecraft, as icon and perhaps fetish, on the cover of *Objectif lune.* Here a Jeep, carrying Tintin, Captain Haddock, Professor Toumesol (a caricature of the absent-minded scientist), and Tintin's dog Milou, rolls toward a construction site where workmen are putting the finishing touches on an upright rocket which, in form and concept, is worthy of rockets depicted on the covers of *The Magazine of Fantasy and Science Fiction.* Even more striking than the full-page diagrams (literal blueprints) of the rocketship, offering the nuts-and-bolts didacticism expected by juvenile readers of a Verne novel, is the verisimilitude of this cover, which despite the bright colors and strong design of comic-book art remains surprisingly accurate in its technical details. Even more accurate is the moonscape on the cover of *On a marche sur la lune.* Despite the unlikely presence of Tintin, and even more unlikely presence of Milou dressed in a spacesuit designed expressly for him, the nature and texture of the moonscape, in its "effet de reel," strongly resembles Heinlein's decor, constructed from real Moon photos, for *Destination Moon,* which in its detail and scientific accuracy was intended to carry an adult sense of the real new frontier and serve as inspiration for its conquest to come. Hergé draws spacesuits that look a little like the Michelin man; yet they appear accurately conceived and quite functional given a real Moon environment. There are plausible-seeming Moon vehicles; even the problem of putting a dog in a spacesuit is solved in a technologically plausible manner—in short, Hergé, with his comic book art, gives the viewer a sense of a new physical environment. One should note as well that the title, "On a marche sur la lune," has a journalistic ring to be echoed in newspaper accounts of Neil Armstrong, who was depicted as "le premier homme qui a marche sur la lune."

As the *bande dessinée* develops into a major publishing vehicle in France (and achieves academic respectibility as the "huitieme art"), there are two clear strains, defined by both theme and graphic art in terms of style and content. The juvenile strain of *Tintin* continues. But there emerges an "adult" *bande dessinée,* identified by themes like sex and graphic violence, and typified by an increasingly pessimistic or "dystopian" tone and attitude toward technology, with fears of future cities and societies. What seems strange, however, even in these dystopian BDs, is that there remains a fascination with space vessels and space travel. If, in terms of theme, technology must be stigmatized in adult BDs as the cause of dystopian futures, viewers would not expect to see this same technology celebrated or fetishized in its visual icons. Yet such is the impetus of the space travel technomyth that vessels and voyages to other planets and galaxies continue to be seen in the adult production of the 1970s and early 1980s, but with a striking change in the forms of the vehicles. Many of these forms have overdone technical depiction to the point of becoming visibly "unreal" in terms of functionality and even verisimilitude. In the process of doing so, however, they acquire a symbolic purpose. The way these vehicles might function (were they to fly) determines the nature of the voyages they can and will undertake. This function shifts rapidly from the real to the surreal.

In terms of real-life drawing boards, the rocket-like design of spaceships that characterizes 1950s depictions gives way in the 1960s and 1970s to the more sophisticated space station and deep-space cruiser given iconic (and mythic) status by Kubrick in *2001.* In the French *bande dessinée,* however, an analogous sort of technological realism is found only in comics that maintain the Tintin style to appeal, at least on the surface, to juvenile audiences during this period. An example is the series "Valerian, agent spatio-temporel" by Jean-Claude Mézières and Pierre Christin. Yet this juvenile comic no longer pretends to "innocence," but begins to parody itself. Valerian and his female counterpart Laureline are iconically presented with large mature heads and faces (implying they are capable of the sexual relations which, in the text, are always suggested but never consummated) that are placed on small, childlike, tightly spacesuited bodies. Their adventures, moreover, continue to follow the Tintin paradigm of the mystery story unfolding in a linear manner, in terms of both plot and classic strip presentation of the narrative frames. Their adventures may range across galaxies (a typical title is *Metro Chatelet, Direction Cassiopee* [1980]). But, as this title's emphasis on place and means of locomotion tells us, space vessels are needed to get from one end to the other of the story. Sure enough, the opening page of *Metro Chatelet is* devoted to a two-page panorama of cosmic starscapes and spaceships in flight. These spaceships have become more complex, even ornate, but are still presented in terms of hard surface and pure functionality. They fly and they look like they can fly. The legacy of Verne's illustrations passes through Tintin to works like this, where adult themes are suggested only to be thwarted (as with the stunted growth of Valerian's body), and where a barrier is erected to keep technological adventure and space exploration this side of the adolescent limit.

The point of bifurcation for images of space travel in French science fiction and the *bande dessinée* is *Fiction,* many of whose cover artists went on to become mainstays of the science fiction BD. Cover art and the image of space it projected were clearly of prime importance to *Fiction* editors, for as early as the first issue they scrapped the American cover and produced their own. On its covers during the early and later 1960s, in fact, we find very interesting space vehicles. On one, the French term *astronef* is depicted literally as a flying space galleon, its sails and carved stem sweeping across the curve of some distant planet or moon. On another, the city in flight, something James Blish would depict in great technical detail and propel with a massive space drive in his contemporary rendition in Anglophone science fiction, is here perched on the back of a flying hybrid, a creature formed with the wings of a bat and exoskeleton and head of a giant insect. In another cover, the giant flying city (in this case a medieval fortress) floats in space, not just on top of a woman's head, but interfused and blending with that head. All these icons imply that space voyages, which with the "real" rockets of Tintin or gleaming hyperdrive spaceships of Valerian have the promise at least of taking us elsewhere, somewhere new, are now voyages of regression. Space "ships," as depicted, have become anachronisms or at best metaphors. If you try to fly one of these vessels, it reverts before your eyes to its etymological origin and becomes an ancient galleon. Likewise, the man-made parts of new space vessels now prove severely limited, not because of stress of metals, fuel ratios, or speed of light, but by a paucity of models or prototypes artists can draw from our organic chain of being or our evolutionary scale. Try to build a spaceship, and it literally turns into an animal or insect prototype, a bird or bug. Finally, the example of city as brain that sits upon a human face in flight suggests two things: first, that the intended voyage outward is in fact a trip backward in spacetime to our historical past, or even down the evolutionary scale, until space travel becomes an adventure in riding our "dragons of

Eden"; and second, that the voyage is an *inward one,* toward mysteries of the unconscious mind, the regressive realm that lies beneath all our rational aspirations. In these drawings, the enterprise of space travel is thrust backward and downward into the Dionysian realm of dreams and desire.

These visions of Cartesian space in French SF show how radically introverted this space became in the visuals and cover art of SF magazines like *Fiction* and the *bande dessinée.* This Cartesianism has deep roots in French culture, as seen by looking at works like *Micromégas* or the transformations of the Crusoe paradigm in Garnier's anthology, which at first glance seem to celebrate open space, but upon closer examination reveal just the opposite. In postwar American SF, which celebrates space travel, such a closed vision becomes impossible to sustain. Here the icons of open space are many and powerfully displayed. Advocates of space exploration, in the United States and Britain, like writer Gregory Benford, can call themselves "Cartesian," but they are referring to the Descartes of *Discours de la methode,* who sanctions the mastery of *res extensa* by mind. This is the international Descartes, seen by Anglo-Saxons as the moving force behind science's expansion in space. This Descartes could have stood behind Cyrano and his tradition.

Instead, recent French images of space and space travel celebrate the triumph of the Cartesian-Pascalian tradition of closed space. We have seen French works, in what French culture sees as a juvenile tradition that runs from Verne to Tintin, timidly depicting space vessels and rocket ships. But in the "adult" tradition that runs from *Fiction* to the *bande dessinée* of the 1970s and 1980s, there are extreme visions of closed space associated with space travel. Two examples will suffice: the works of Jean Giraud (known as Moebius), and Philippe Druillet. In their art, not only is space travel clearly futile, but there is no place to go other than within the recesses of the mind itself. The only place left to be explored by mind is mind itself, a universe bounded by the individual *cogito.* In the universe of these artists, spaceships are not real, but *surreal,* and outward-directed star treks become reason's plunge into the dark spacetime of the artist's own unconscious.

Moebius's most famous series of albums is probably *Arzach* (1975). Arzach (or Harzak or Arzakh; "h's" are not pronounced in French) is a strangely garbed, yellow-complected, cone-headed humanoid astride a huge pterodactyl-like bird. In Arzach's world everything is like something else. Similes continually point to referents that, as a whole, add up to nothing significant in terms of the external world "out there" that readers inhabit and relate to. An unnamed commentator from the magazine *Le Point,* cited on the album cover of the first volume, describes Arzach's travels this way: "Un heros laconique traversant, sur le dos d'un etrange reptile, des paysages phantasmagoriques, des aventures sans scenario, ni chute, ni morale, ou onierisme et science fiction font bon menage." [He is a laconic hero crossing phantas-magorical landscapes on the back of a strange winged reptile: adventures with story, nor crisis, nor moral, where oneirism and science fiction join hands.] Arzach flies over a place that, in an adventure that had a story, could be a *post-holocaust* world. There are vague remains of even-vaguer architectures that could be segments of a viaduct, but seem more like Valéry's "arche qui demeure," where an object stands, all function except a dream function hope-lessly lost. He passes endlessly over a ground of green tentacle-like "things" that continually reach out for his flying figure, and indeed devour whatever falls into them, as do Arzach's flying mount and several humanoids along the way. But what is the way to where and what? The "narration" (there are no captions or words) follows what are essentially the linear expectations of the strip as we read left to right, top to bottom, page to page. Yet Arzach, traversing a place that looks like it could once have been a place within the spatiotemporal experience of humans, is always going somewhere, never arriving anywhere, never doing anything significant or even meaningful. He remains a dream figure who, as "navigator," is calqued on the space explora-tion paradigm of science fiction. But the sole task of his vehicle—the strange winged reptile—is to keep him from falling or plunging into the extended world, which now seems the field of the disindividualating unconscious that lies beneath rational thought.

Druillet's space adventurer is called Lone Sloane. His name, and the fact that he is literally everyone and everywhere in Druillet's volumes, make him a marvelous Cartesian-Pascalian icon. At the opposite pole from Arzach, Druillet, instead of emptying space travel and the "future" of all vestiges of science fiction and its rationally constructed icons (and with them all sense of the existence of a material world to explore and conquer), revels in a pro-liferation of flying machines and technological detail. His door into dream is through a series of hyper or surreal technological constructs whose purpose remains mysterious at best.

For example, the spacecraft on the cover of *Gail* (1978) is overladen with intricate mechanical detail. But when we examine the cover to "figure it out," it seems to devolve before our eyes, to turn from machine (as if through hal-lucination or metamorphosis of forms) into some kind of flying insect with jowls and pinchers. His depictions, in *Delirius* (1973), of what is called a "pleasure planet" reveal as we examine them in detail a riot of flying figures that are "phantasmagorical" precisely because they are rendered down to the least line in hyperdetail. As our eye struggles to see through this overlay of machine appendages, forms of ships emerge as squatting toads on pads, leaping mantises, springing and floating insects of all shapes and kinds. In Druillet's work, Lone Sloane flies any and every kind of device and moves in any and all directions. In terms of the historical and evolutionary path associated with open-ended space exploration, Sloane's trajectory is always a loop, inscribing a circular self-closing motion much like the pattern of images within the page—large frames that characterize Druillet's spatializing and emblematic visual style. In *Les 6 voyages de Lone Sloane* (1972), direction is ostensibly the far-flung future and galaxies. In the course of the episodes, however, Sloane trades a conventional-looking ship for (in sequence) a flying throne, a ship-city, an organ-ship, a walled fortress in flight, a bug-like vessel bearing the name Sidarta, and finally a craft that resembles some underwater life form, a pink fish of the lightless depths. Technology's voyage out has become, in this succession of "vehicles," nothing less than an incremental reversion to the most primitive, nontechnological life forms. Similarly, in Druillet's treatment of Flaubert's *Salammbo* (1980), the future loops around to join the past of ancient Carthage as Sloane comes gliding into this universe riding a spaceship that is a cross between a shark and a Harley-Davidson chopper. Past and future, the highest and the lowest forms of evolutionary life, supermachine and simple bivalve—all are drawn, as if on a Moebius strip, into a spatialized disposition of forms where linear narration is enfolded into a dream emblem. If in the realm of *res extensa,* we can envision travel, discovery, a future where there will be new worlds for old, Druillet has, with Sloane and his ships, replaced that realm with an analogous mindscape, where (deploying what is effectively a technology of the mind) he can manipulate its elements at will. Druillet does not yield to dream; in Cartesian fashion, he seeks mastery of his personal space. But this is mind mastering the images of mind. Physical space is radically restricted, in favor of a new form of virtual "space" that spreads out from the fixed space of the Cartesian mind, opening what are claimed to be vast realms to explore within the unconscious. The sole explorer however is the individual frozen in Aristotelian space.

The French sense of space seems strange in an age when radio telescopes and other instruments are in the process of scanning and unlocking the secrets of Pascal's large infinity, while scientists working in the realm of the infinitely small are probing cells and DNA on one hand, and on the other seeking the most basic particles that constitute matter. But it seems part of a wider cultural trend. There is in French culture a widening gap between scientist and humanist, where scientists are seen as attempting to eliminate any trace of the "Cartesian ghost" in the material machine, thus to eliminate what has traditionally defined the uniqueness of mankind in relation to a purely material world. The way to avoid this, it seems, is to remove mind from material space, to create for it the privileged space of a "world" unto itself. The path moves from surrealism to the New Novel, to poststructuralist theory. To chart this, we need only open the pages of a New Novel like Claude Ollier's *La vie sur Epsilon* (1972). The title promises science fiction space adventure. But opening the book, the reader discovers Ollier's vague, oneiric drawing of a spaceship. It is, if anything, a "ship" generated purely in the mind, one never intended to leave the drawing boards. It serves simply as a sign that points within, to the sole realm mind alone can explore—itself. Postmodern critic Jean Ricardou tells us clearly the Ollier's novel offers a "mental" not a physical landscape, wherein the author has "multiplié les occurrences où des évènements supposés réels se retournent peu à peu en hallucinations." [multiplied happenings where occurrences thought to be real gradually return to their original state of hallucinations][10] Excluded however from this realm are readers inspired by Verne and the stories and graphics of space travel, who no longer believe they are the sole beings to possess reason in the universe. There is no need to maintain a metaphysical "mind" at all costs when artificial brains can pilot us to new worlds and new discoveries in space.

In terms of the mythic nature of space, one concludes that the movement, among the Greek classics from the Pre-Socratics to Plato and Aristotle—despite fears of adventuring too far beyond known boundaries, of self and community—is to expand our concept of space. The French vision of space, which issues from Descartes and Pascal, appears to develop in the opposite direction, shrinking the parameters of known space to that of mind and imagination. For the French, however, the lure of mindspace seems more tantalizing, and significant, than that of the physical universe. France has a strong alternate tradition of space exploration, but this may be only a facade. For if we look carefully at the vision of space in a Voltaire, or even a Verne, we are struck by how centripetal it is. Even stranger are the mind spaces created in the wake of the furor of the American space program, which appears a curious, almost incomprehensible, reversion to a static universe, where mind holds the center of its space, and provides refuge for a culture apparently suffering from acute agoraphobia. If one defines science fiction as an open-ended endeavor, an endless quest to find and understand the unknown, in this sense new territory with all the possibilities it brings, we can truly say that France, at least postwar France, has engendered its own science fiction.

## NOTES

1. Editor's note: I believe Slusser was referring to a passage from the writings of physicist Julian Barbour, but I have been unable to locate the exact source.

2. Aristotle, *Physics*, translated by R. P. Hardie and R. K. Kaye (New York: Dover Publications, 2017), 74.

3. Daniel Defoe, *Robinson Crusoe* (New York: Signet New American Library, 1961), 129.

4. Voltaire, *Lettres philosophiques*, edition de Raymond Naves (Paris: Garnier, 1962), vingt-cinquième letter, 144.

5. Voltaire, *Micromégas*, *Zadig et Micromégas* (London: George Routledge and Sons, 1886), 75.

6. Michel Serres, *Jouvenances de Jules Verne* (Paris: Editions du Minuit, 1974), 15–16.

7. Jules Verne, *Hector Servadac: Voyages et aventures a travers le monde solaire* (Paris: Hetzel, 1877), 2, 390.

8. The French *Galaxie* was revived in 1964, under the editorship of Alain Doremieux, and ran for 158 issues, till 1977. Under Doremieux, and later Michel Demuth, the magazine began publishing French authors and using French cover art, though by that time many of the great artists earlier associated with *Fiction,* such as Jean-Claude Forest, had moved on to the more lucrative *bandes dessinées.*

9. C. L. Moore, "Shambleau," *The Wesleyan Anthology of Science Fiction*, edited by Arthur B. Evans, Istvan Csicsery-Ronay, Jr. Joan Gordon, Veronica Hollinger, Rob Latham, and Carol McGuirk (Middletown, Connecticut: Wesleyan University Press, 2010), 134, 133. Also relevant is Eric Frank Russell's "Sinister Barrier" (1939), wherein the human life force proves to be simply food to the alien, and Charles Fort's theory that humans are the exploited "property" of unseen aliens.

10. Jean Ricardou, *Le nouveau roman* (Paris: Éditions de Seuil, 1990), 127.

*Chapter Three*

# Future Liberty

## *Nineteenth Century Horizons*

As we have seen, the Cartesian paradigm shift became operative in French fiction in the seventeenth century, creating a form of experimental fiction that bears little resemblance to what we call science fiction today, while engendering visions of space that would only later influence the modern genre. Kant's and Hoffmann's second Copernican revolution occurred at the beginning of the nineteenth century, and both Emerson's dynamic and evolutionary theories are products of that same century. The nineteenth century then is the crucial terrain in which what Adam Roberts calls the "genre" of science fiction will develop. By the end of this century, all the paradigm shifts identified will be enabled and, to varying degrees, both operative and interactive across a spectrum of cultures, essentially in Europe and the United States, but also in colonial cultures—Anglophone outposts like Australia and New Zealand, and, as we learn from Yolanda Molina-Galiván and Andrea Bell, in Spanish- and Portuguese-speaking Latin America as well.[1]

However, to exist, science fiction needs a protagonist and a specific theme that can be shared across cultural lines in all paradigms. The protagonist is the scientist, and the theme is his or her claim to future liberty—specifically, to offer new discoveries and creations that promise to have serious impact on future worlds. During the English Renaissance, we first have a scientist as protagonist. If Chaucer's Canon's Yeoman is defeated by matter, Marlowe's Faustus projects great plans to transform future Europe, literally to move Earth if not heaven. In the end, he is defeated by the religious and moral system he would overthrow. But he offers a challenge to future scientists, notably in the nineteenth century, to experiment and go boldly where no one has gone before, even if this changes the way of things forever. To oppose and limit this future science, the nineteenth century offers several, seemingly insurmountable, barriers. One is the arbitrary rule of usurpers of power such as Napoleon; another is increasing bourgeois conformity and morality. The third is simply the tyranny of matter itself, where the scientist's own discoveries of the nature of material reality reveal that the human mind and creative efforts are increasingly unable to master it. In this climate, scientific liberty evolves in this crucial nineteenth century.

In the Cartesian paradigm, there is no place for the future on its coordinates, which envision mind and matter seeking balance in an endless seesaw. Mme de Clèves clearly rejects the future as a realm of unknown menace, choosing instead physical inertia in the present. Yet as Paul Alkon points out, the overwhelming number of writers whose works were set in the future that appeared in the late eighteenth-early nineteenth centuries were French: Mercier, Restif de la Bretonne, Cousin de Grainville, Félix Bodin.[2] One must mention that these works appear in a time of unprecedented social and political turmoil—the French Revolution and subsequent rise of Bonaparte, later Emperor Napoléon. The stability of the Cartesian mind-matter equation is seriously inflected, not only by advances in materialist science, but by social and political revolution, by what Benjamin Constant calls Napoléon's "usurpations." These usurpations open the door to visions of what a future Europe might be like, indeed what the Western world would become—a landscape of change and transformation, propitious to the rise of a literature that speculates about the future, science fiction.

## THE CALL FOR SCIENTIFIC LIBERTY

In terms of the big picture of nineteenth century Europe, the problem addressed here has great consequences for the development of both "futuristic" fiction and, more specifically, a "science" fiction. French novelist and political theorist Benjamin Constant, the key contemporary figure in articulating this problem, seeks to define the nature of liberty and individual freedom in what emerges, in the 1820s, from revolution and usurpation: the modern nation state. In his essay "The Spirit of Conquest and Usurpation and their Relation to European Civilization," written in 1814, at the height of his own participation in the Napoleonic era, Constant famously distinguishes between ancient and modern liberty.[3] At the same time he suggests, in light of the growing fascination in French literary circles with speculations on the future, a third category of liberty: pursuing scientific and technological advancement as the force that will generate new futures. These are futures, inspired by political change perhaps, yet unimaginable by its present standards. Constant foresees the creation of such speculative futures, where avenues for scientific freedom must contend with increasingly totalitarian social structures, brought about in many cases by social control of the practice of science and technology itself.

Constant looks forward to a new form of literature, where the future itself becomes the place of struggle between liberty and usurpation. The same usurpatory acts Constant identifies in his present will later—across this century and into the age of science fiction—seek to prevent the scientist or inventor from imagining, and thus creating, this new future. The early nineteenth century is a key moment in the interaction between French (thus Continental) and British cultures. English Romantics were fascinated by the French Revolution. Their responses to the Revolution, and to Napoleon, were either positive or negative, but always passionate. This is also the period when, in the eyes of many critics, science fiction was born. Mary Shelley wrote *Frankenstein* while vacationing in Switzerland with Byron and Shelley. The year was 1818. Four years later, a twenty-two-year-old Honoré de Balzac published *Le Centenaire, ou les deux Beringheld*, under the pseudonym of Horace de Saint-Aubin. Balzac's novel did not have the impact of Shelley's novel, but it sheds light on *Frankenstein's* position as "first science fiction novel."[4] Neither novel is set in the future. Both however offer portraits of scientists whose solitary actions bear immense consequences for humanity's future. Moreover, both operate in a social and cultural world which would suppress their actions, "usurp" their potential future authority.

Constant's description of the intricate relationship between individual liberty and usurpatory authority, especially when liberty pertains to scientific activity, is centrally important to the origins of modern science fiction. For Constant, the barrier to ancient liberty is religion, yet the barrier to modern liberty is society itself, seen in the sense of Rousseau's social contract or Napoleon's codes, which their authors invest with quasi-religious absoluteness. Future liberty is an extension of Constant's modern liberty. The difference is that, when liberty in the present promises unknown results in the future, as is the case with scientific experiments, its repression becomes all the more radical. The nineteenth century sees the rise of institutionalized science. Here Constant invokes the danger of society using "science" against scientific freedom by claiming an authority it sees based in universal "laws" of nature. In the face of such repressive authority, Constant defines future scientific liberty as something fiercely private and individualistic, so the truths of science become adversaries of the arbitrary nature of social dictates. The price paid for these truths is total isolation of the experimenter.

For Constant, the highest of the *private* virtues is progress in the arts and, specifically, in the *sciences.* Advances in this latter area however call forth the most severe restrictions wrought by arbitrary power on what he calls "intellectual progress." He describes writers of Rousseau's school as seeking to "construct the social state out of a small number of very simple elements: prejudices to deceive men, torments to frighten them, greed to corrupt them, frivolity to degrade them, arbitrary power to guide them and, since it is necessary, positive knowledge and exact sciences to serve this arbitrary power more adroitly." (123–24) This is the nineteenth-century world in which the modern scientist must operate, a world that brings the scientist to the forefront as protagonist. Previously, the scientist as overreacher was punished either by God or (as with Ben Jonson's Alchemist) by society. Otherwise, the scientist kept to his/her laboratory, working as an individual or part of a group, but not under the tyranny of institutional control of the sort Napoleon established. To discover the table of chemical elements in no way menaces the established order. Ballistic research might. But when a scientist like Frankenstein, armed with new technologies to enable discoveries, creates a new form of life, the menace is less to present society, but societies to come. The fictional scientists that concern us here—Mary Shelley's Victor Frankenstein, and Honoré de Balzac's Beringheld the Centenarian—both conduct research that menaces the future. Because of this, both must work in clandestine manner at the hidden center of societies where social strictures, to one degree or another, have turned the "positive" laws of the exact sciences into the means of limiting scientific inquiry. Positive science classifies present knowledge, and in doing so erects a barrier to new elements that gesture toward unknown consequences. Balzac's Centenarian seeks to perfect the means of extending the life of his body. Frankenstein creates a new form of "human" life in the laboratory. Both are forced to engage in a solitary struggle on two fronts: against the limits of physical possibility and against the strictures of the modern state.

This problematic does not disappear in twentieth-century science fiction, quite the contrary. There are many examples of lone scientists whose work is usurped by established order. The future worlds their science envisions are co-opted by new and ever-evolving forms of arbitrary power. This in turn calls for the "invention" of new modes of individual freedom, unthought-of paths that lead to new restrictions on the creative individual. Constant's problematic remains a significant diagnostic tool for understanding the relation of the creative individual to restraints, in imagined future worlds, where usurpers not only co-opt religion or society in the service of arbitrary power, but turn the natural world and its laws into instruments of oppression.

Finally, it is around this issue of future liberty that the two important traditions of science fiction in Western culture—Francophone and Anglophone—develop in radically opposite directions. In terms of scientific freedom, *Frankenstein* can claim to be the seminal text for modern English-language science fiction. The line from Balzac's work is less clear, for *The Centenarian* was repudiated by its author and never republished until recently. But despite being a "lost" text, one can argue for its indirect influence on future French science fiction. This novel seems the seminal text for Balzac's entire *Comédie humaine*. Balzac demonstrates, in *Le Centenaire,* an inverse relation between acts of material will and length of bodily life. This he will make the fundamental "law" of his later work—the law that constrains the destinies of artists, scientists, and schemers alike in Balzac's influential social comedy. In fact, its codification is a clear example of what Constant is talking about. For Balzac sees this law as *both* social and physical, a law against which even the Centernarian and his engines of longevity struggle in vain. These strictures, which pit scientific liberty against usurpatory forces of both nature and body alike, will impact later writers like Jules Verne, as well as his contemporaries Flaubert, Zola, and Maupassant. The mind-body struggle set forth in *The Centenarian*, where physical nature via the body is seen as usurping the freedom of the Cartesian rational soul, shapes a cultural pattern that resonates strongly in post-World War II French fiction.

## THE CENTENARIAN

Constant offers these prophetic remarks about the future of individual liberty in his contemporary France: "French despotism has pursued liberty from climate to climate; it has succeeded for a time in suppressing it in every region into which it has penetrated. But since liberty always sought refuge from one region in another, despotism has been compelled to follow it so far that in the end it has met its own doom. The genius of mankind was waiting for it at the furthest boundaries of the world to make its retreat more shameful and its punishment more memorable." (142) He describes the cruel fate, in all times and places, of the hunted and haunted "friends of humanity" who pursue intellectual and scientific liberty: "Unrecognized, suspected, surrounded by men incapable of believing in courage or in disinterested convictions, tormented alternately by a feeling of indignation, when the oppressors are the stronger, and by one of pity when the same oppressors have become victims, they have always wandered on this earth, exposed to all parties, alone in the midst of generations that are at times raging, and at others depraved. Yet it is in them that hope for the human race always lies." (144)

Before discussing *Le Centenaire*, let us jump to the center of Balzac's *Comédie humaine.* This vast social fresco is filled with Constant's "friends of humanity," which Balzac calls his "martyrs ignorés." These beings, unrecognized and unknown, fight their lonely battle to create new works of art, systems of thought, scientific or technological discoveries. Prominent among these is scientist Balthasar Claës, Balzac's chemist in *La Recherche de l'Absolu* (1834). In general, these beings are free to create only to the extent that they remain invisible and their work incommunicable. Balzac explicitly raises this question of science and future liberty in his triptych *Sur Catherine de Médicis,* published in 1846. The relevant section, "Le Secret des Ruggieri," was first published however in late 1836, at the height of Balzac's creative powers. It thus makes significant commentary on the solitary fate of Balthasar Claës. In this section, Laurent Ruggieri and his alchemist colleagues are discovered working in their secret laboratory by Charles IX during one of the King's nighttime escapades. For their scientific activity to function within the intrigue-ridden world of Catherine's court, and finance their private research, they must deal in commodities like poisons and spells. Charles summons the Ruggieri brothers to explain their clandestine activity. Laurent's subsequent defense is a plea for the freedom to pursue scientific research within the tyrannical constraints of an usurpatory system.

Laurent's vision is this: God has turned its back on mankind. In doing so, He left mankind to rule on earth, to bend matter to its will. The problem however is that humans are short-lived. Thus, insofar as the "I" perishes with the body, science's primary goal is to find a way of extending bodily existence. Short of this possibility, Laurent has another method: creating a lineage or "society" of scientists, all toiling in secret, with the goal of expanding knowledge from generation to generation. He boasts that his "underground" lineage of scientists is superior to dynasties of kings and temporal power. But his promise to create "un peuple éternel pour le roi de France!" [a people of immortals for the King of France] is dismissed by the narrator as the "pompeuse loquacité de charlatan" [pompous loquacity of a charlatan][5] For clearly, behind Laurent's collective vision, his primary concern is with his own "moi" or self. Nor is Laurent's vision of a secret society of scientists, working on extending individual life, totally disinterested. Readers of Balzac know that one of two things must occur: either this society within society will dominate the short-lived; or, more likely, society will act to destroy these super-beings. Indeed, this is the fate of the "Histoire des Treize" (1833–39) Laurent is well aware of two impediments to future liberty: the human condition itself, large ideas and a short life, and state tyranny, which obstructs the free circulation of goods, information, ideas. More precisely, he sees individual liberty obstructed by the material limits of the physical body itself. The scientist's own body remains the final place where Constant's friends of humanity, exiled to lives of clandestine subterfuge, await their ultimate oppressor, their individual *physical condition.* At this final location, Balzac's scientist hopes to recapture personal freedom "with a vengeance," through endless rejuvenation of the flesh by means of science.

Laurent is a talker, not an actor. His words and his situation reveal that he remains the vassal of state power. Let us measure the distance that separates him from Balzac's early Centenarian. Like Frankenstein a figure out of the Gothic tradition (Balzac's inspiration was Maturin's *Melmoth the Wanderer* [1820]), he claims to be 400 years old. He calls himself the "last of the Rosicrucians," the last alchemist and sole inheritor of the life extension secrets of Alquefahar the Arab. But if this is his past, he makes a very modern claim to the future. For the *science* he mastered is a modern one that seeks, without preconditions, material extension of life. His "elixir" is a manufactured substance, synthesized in a laboratory. He does nothing as crude as drinking the blood of living beings; instead, he *distills* their life force, through a chemical process, into assimilatable energy. Balzac describes in great detail, long before the film labs of Rotwang or movie *Frankenstein* (1931), an elaborate laboratory apparatus full of retorts, beakers, and an inverted, bell-like device that acts like a primitive cyclotron. If Frankenstein remains fundamentally an alchemist, the Centenarian is a modern scientist, whose research promises a genuine form of future liberty—the ability to extend the limits of material existence by freeing the rational self, if only provisionally, from its bodily prison.

The Centenarian's world is strictly one of conservation of energy and entropy. His physical body appears decrepit, a lumbering petrified form, barely able to move, whose sole sign of life is two burning eyes deep in sunken sockets. Yet, in a paradox that would have pleased Constant, the figure's longevity—thus his extended ability to conduct scientific research—gives him new "magnetic" powers over material boundaries. The Centenarian can teleport himself to the ends of the Earth, visiting Napoleonic battlegrounds and Himalayan peaks with equal ease. From the sole center of his retracting physical existence, fleeing inward from society's tyranny, he can radiate to a broad circumference. He retracts into his lumbering body to hoard and concentrate the energy that, in turn, gives him the power to act—to elude and hopefully defeat the tyranny of both society and matter.

Balzac's novel is strangely bipolar: it follows the private struggles of the Centenarian with entropy and inevitable bodily decay, but at the same time entwines the private destiny of the scientist with a social and generational conflict. This is the story of the "two Beringhelds," the long-lived ancestor and his great-great-great grandson Tullius. Paradoxically, the Centenarian pursues individual longevity but is obsessed with the biological continuation of his progeny. He intervenes personally to revive the sterile Beringheld line, both conceiving his heir telekinetically and using advanced surgical skills and anesthesia to bring him into the world. He oversees young Tullius's education, follows him on Bonaparte's first campaign, and again must use his science to cure Tullius and his men of the plague. But when Tullius, now a decorated general, enters the social world of the Empire, the two lines bifurcate. Tullius follows Napoleon to Russia and lives the great deception, while the Centenarian sets up his laboratory in the catacombs of Paris. These personal and social strands re-converge however around Tullius's fiancée Marianine. Coming to Paris to await her absent lover, she is seen by the Centenarian who, unaware of her attachment to the man who is his biological son, abducts her to his laboratory to convert her to the vital energy he needs to keep his flesh alive.

In the ensuing struggle, Tullius enters the catacombs in time to save Marianine, and the Centenarian flees his laboratory and disappears into the catacombs. Significantly, all that remains of this figure is his greatcoat, left at the entrance to the catacombs. Now naked and hunted, the world he leaves behind is the new social world of Balzac's *Comédie*, where clothes make the man, and success depends on one's ability to follow strict "dress codes." Tullius claims to inherit the scientific knowledge of his ancestor but debases that science by leaving magnetism in the hands of the new medical guilds that are springing up. He throws himself into the world of social mobility and will no doubt marry the shrewd Marianine. She will become the ancestor of all of Balzac's formidable and manipulating women, just as Tullius gives rise to the long line of dandies, social climbers, and *déclassé* aristocrats who fill the pages of the *Comédie*. All this time, the Centenarian remains "at large" deep under Balzac's Paris. He resurfaces now and then, in the guise of either an artist or scientist, or even as criminal chief Vautrin, whose nickname "trompe la mort" shows that he has found his own form of life extension. The Centenarian lives on in spirit, but the mission of Balzac's society, it appears, is to stamp out all vestiges of his particular form of individual liberty. Vautrin disappears from sight; the scientist-Centenarian reincarnates as Laurent Ruggieri, the glib "charlatan" whose poisons place him in perfect accord with the social machinations of his world.

Balzac vehemently disavowed *Le Centenaire* and refused to consider it part of his *Comédie humaine.* Yet the Centenarian's underground presence is felt everywhere in this vast opus, as a mythic symbol of future liberty. In fact, it may have been this menace that brought Balzac to formulate a "philosophical" underpinning to his social comedy. One might argue that Balzac's entire opus is a protracted attempt to subjugate the Centenarian's supreme act of individual liberty, to bring it under the jurisdiction of a general system of "laws." Once free of Tullius, the Centenarian remains subject only to the laws of thermodynamics, for in order to prolong his life, he must draw vital energy in equal and opposite proportion from another life. This scientific quest, ultimately, is to defeat the physical process of loss of energy. But Balzac's post-Napoleonic world cannot tolerate this spectre of scientific anarchy. To prevent it, Balzac extrapolates from the Centenarian's condition a *physical* law of social equilibrium that controls all excesses by making the expense of personal will inversely proportional to length of life.

Balzac, in a maneuver described by Constant, co-opts his Centenarian by converting his individual freedom into an abstract principle that constrains and tyrannizes. Balzac's famous *peau de chagrin* (the phrase designates both a physical "wild ass's skin" and metaphorical "skin of sorrow") becomes the symbol of this co-option. The story of the novel of that name is simple: Raphaël de Valentin, a young man in the lineage of Tullius, has debts and is on the verge of suicide. He enters an antique shop and finds an old man who himself is a centenarian. He is so however for the opposite reason from old Beringheld. Instead of actively seeking to extend his life, he abstains from action, living a hidden, contemplative life, husbanding his vital energy. Raphaël dreams of freeing himself from the chains of society and mortality. The old man offers him the asses' skin that, when he wishes on it, will grant his wish. But with each wish the skin shrinks, as does Raphaël's lifeline. Raphaël's act of freedom, in taking the skin, is simultaneously an act of enslavement to the law of the skin. We come full circle from the heroic world of the Centenarian and Bonaparte, where these two figures—individual liberty and arbitrary tyranny—face each other down, each staring into the other's burning eyes. Balzac now devises, with the asses' skin, a world where to be free is, physically, to be in chains. He has transposed Rousseau's tyrannical social contract to the level of material law.

One can further argue that Balzac's dialectic provides the dynamic upon which much subsequent French science fiction is constructed. In Balzac, individual liberty is chased with the Centenarian to the depths of the catacombs. Liberty is therefore only possible within the confines of personal existence, forced to hide behind various masks, disguises, and social codes of the world at large. The ultimate refuge of such artists or scientists is in their own minds, a space which (in a strange replay of Descartes's *tabula rasa*) becomes a terrain of action inaccessible to social strictures. But because these mindspaces remain "enslaved" to their bodies, subject to the law of the *peau de chagrin*, any free act of creative will, any expansion of self within the confines of the mind, is met with equal and opposite contraction of the physical body, ultimately extinguishing this final refuge of individual liberty. The post-World War II literature in France that adopts the name "science fiction" will draw upon Constant's promise of future liberty through scientific advancement. At the same time, in the shadow of Balzac's legislation of this promise in his *Comédie humaine,* this French science fiction finds its field of action increasingly reduced to closed places, places of the mind subject to contraction as tyrannical social forces close in upon them.

Balzac's *Comédie humaine* and its dynamic of the *peau de chagrin* look back in the French cultural consciousness, via Constant's interpretation of Rousseau, to Descartes's mind-matter duality and Pascal's law of *renversement du pour au contre.* On the modern side of Balzac, French science fiction has evolved in this same cultural current. A few examples suffice to demonstrate this continuity of cultural concern. The scientist-heroes of Jules Verne, such as Captain Nemo and Robur, pose as proponents of future liberty. Nemo, for instance, is a classic example of Constant's "friends of humanity," given by his submarine unprecedented mobility to pursue intellectual progress. What better vehicle than the *Nautilus* to allow this new Centenarian to move freely around Earth unseen, gathering scientific data until he claims to achieve, like Alquefahar the Arab, the sum of human knowledge?

In the hand of later French critics and writers, however, Nemo undergoes a fate similar to that of the Centenarian. Nemo's liberty is contained by cultural censure claiming to act in the name of physical law. For example, Roland Barthes, in his essay "Nautilus et Bateau ivre" (1957), sees Verne, through his character Nemo, building a "cosmogony closed upon itself," where the imagination of travel is the dream of an "homme-enfant" who reinvents a world inside his head, within which he is free, but free only to the extent that he recognizes the closed nature of his world. Barthes's goal, it seems, is to subject the experimental scientist to a form of pseudo-Freudian psychoanalysis, and by doing so deflect the external, physical trajectory of technology inward, into the realm of dream as sole place where an individual is free to experiment. For Constant, this form of cultural casuistry was an element of Napoleonic usurpation.[6] The process has not disappeared from French culture today; witness recent attempts to legislate the internet in the Yahoo affair, to confine transborder freedoms to a specific place.

Something in Verne's work leads readers and critics to want to "shrink" his world. This is the case with Argentinian writer Julio Cortázar, born in Brussels and educated in the Francophone tradition, in his work *La vuelta al día en ochenta mundos* [Around the Day in Eighty Worlds] (1958). Equally interesting is the treatment of Verne within the French science fiction community. An example is Bernard Blanc's 1978 manifesto *Pourquoi j'ai tué Jules Verne,* a volume in which a number of writers involved in the 1970s "renaissance" of French science fiction contribute essays where they explain the various ways in which they have sought in their fiction to "kill" Verne.[7] In their common use of this extreme term, all appear to agree there is an urgent need to stop the investigative freedom that Verne's adventures promise. They assume that individual liberty, in our scientific age, has already retreated to the farthest corners of known and unknown worlds, and finally into the mind labryinths of their own science fiction protagonists.

A prime example of "anti-Vernian" science fiction is Michel Jeury's *Le temps incertain* (1973) (literally "uncertain time" with the French play on time/weather), translated into English as *Chronolysis* (1980). The novel offers an extraordinary replay of the Centenarian's quest for liberty through life extension, with a climate of paranoia and persecution presented under the aegis of Philip K. Dick. Jeury offers an epigraph he attributes to Dick, but is surely his own invention: "J'ai le sentiment profond . . . qu'il y a presque autant d'univers qu'il y a de gens, que chaque individu vit en quelque sorte dans un univers de sa propre création." [I have a profound feeling . . . that there are almost as many universes as there are people, and that each individual in some manner or another lives in a universe of his own creation.] Jeury however adds a Cartesian touch when he goes on to explain the nature of these "univcrscs": "c'est le produit de son être, une *oeuvre personnelle* dont peut-être il pourrait être fier." [each is the product of his own being, a *personal creation* of which he perhaps could be proud][8] In *Discours de la méthode*, Descartes offers the means by which each *individual* mind can free itself from the tyranny of matter. But Jeury presents this quest as a paradox. For in his novel, mind becomes a free entity only by totally isolating itself from the physical world.

Jeury revisits the mind-body problem that Balzac hoped to recast in purely material terms of vital "will" versus bodily energy. In comparison with Balzac, Jeury has modified the Cartesian duality. The Centenarian's problem, in terms of mind and body, is ultimately a matter of degree rather than of kind, where both mind and body depend on the same material energy. Moreover, because of the external tyranny of society, his liberty as individual, which could theoretically result in the creation of a perpetual motion machine, finds its avenues of freedom, its access to "combustible materials," gradually closed. When given vital fluid, the Centenarian's mind can roam out of body. But as the fluid is increasingly denied, mind is increasingly a prisoner of matter. Ultimately, with the Centenarian's final escape underground, one prison remains out of which mind cannot break: his material body.

At first glance, Jeury's narrative seems to invert Balzac's dynamic of the *peau de chagrin* in favor of life extension. But as with Balzac's law of inverse proportion, we soon see there is a price to pay for what Jeury calls "éternité subjective." [subjective eternity] In the state of "chronolysis," acts of mind do not consume the body that harbors them; instead, the mind ranges free of its body, which remains in a state of suspended animation, under "medical" control. We appear to master mind travel with minimum expense of bodily energy, realizing the Centenarian's dream of effortless displacement, which apparently defeats the tyranny of historical and biological time. Yet, with protagonist Daniel Diersant, subjective eternity is achieved only in the instant that the body reaches the zero point of its existence—the exact moment of its own death. Caught up in wars between mega-corporations, Diersant is injected, accidentally or purposely, with chronolytic drugs at the moment he dies. Jeury here offers the terrifying possibility of mind freed from its material envelope only to be eternally linked to it. If for Sartre, hell is the others, here hell is eternal freedom confined within one's own dead body, a gruesome variation on Rousseau's dictum.

Diersant's "eternity" then is an endless search to free himself from this internal "mindspace" hell. Constant's friends of humanity can still flee to Earth's most hidden corners; Diersant, on the other hand, has too much mobility, essentially cut loose from all "historical" spacetime moorings. In this state of forced chronolysis, his only hope of freedom is paradoxically to locate, in an ever-shifting field of probabilities, the *exact factual scenario* of his death so that he can relive it, and in physically dying, pass beyond his internalized hell. What ensues is a narrative of *attempts* to relive the moment of his death, each slightly different, slightly out of calibration. In a science-fictional adaptation of techniques borrowed from the *nouveau roman*, Jeury creates a no-exit situation in a world of Dickian time-slips.

Diersant's world clearly adapts Dick's subjective landscapes in works like *Ubik* (1969)*, A Maze of Death* (1970), and *The Three Stigmata of Palmer Eldritch* (1965). There are clear echoes of these works: telephone calls from Diersant's hospital room that go into the void, "messages" that appear mysteriously on mirrors, ever-changing names and details on signs and greeting cards—the initials HKH passing from Harry Krupp Hitler to Harold K. Hauser, to Howard K. Hughes, in infinite series. But there is more here than Dickian subjective isolation or paranoia. Overlaying Diersant's struggles with subjective eternity, beyond his role in corporate wars, is a shadowy struggle between mega-entities for control of temporal reality itself. We have, seeking control of the chronolytic universe, two usurpatory powers in Constant's sense: HKH, whose associations seem to be fascism, the military-industrial complex, the iron teeth of Palmer Eldritch; and L'hôpital Garichankar, a highly regulated scientific and medical research institution in the Napoleonic sense, run by supercomputers named phords, who have perfected the art of "minding" by sending "chrononauts" across spacetime ostensibly to thwart the iron dreams of HKH. One force represents tyrannical capitalism, the other tyrannical "socialism." In this chronolytic maze, the last and final freedom for Diersant is to seek the unfound door of his own death, hoping to break on through to the other side.

Diersant is not a scientist; he is the subject of a scientific experiment being run by Garichankar. Diersant's way to liberty is further complicated when he finds he is not only being manipulated by two superentities, but "inhabited" by a "psychronaut," Dr. Robert Holzach of Garichankar, who in the language of science is "participating" in this experiment. In this landscape of usurpation, Holzach claims to work on the side of scientific liberty. We learn from him that, in the struggles between HKH and Garichankar, knowing the exact scenario of Diersant's death is a key element that can tip the balance. But tip it where? By physically sharing Diersant's mental space, Holzach hopes to experience the moment that frees him from the chains of subjective eternity. Holzach claims the role of investigative scientist. But if his condition resembles that of the Centenarian—his body lies in suspended animation as his mental being ranges through "psychrospace"—his fate seems quite other. With the Centenarian, each mental effort uses up, in inverse fashion, the body that lies immobile. Holzach, though he too gradually loses his bodily moorings, is at the same time becoming assimilated to the mental entity he "inhabits." In the act of integrating his personality with that of Diersant, he loses control of his ability to function as independent entity in chronospace: "Mais, en s'intégrant à une personnalité étrangère, il avait perdu son autonomie et n'exerçait plus aucun contrôle sur l'espace chronolytique." [But in integrating himself with the personality of a stranger, he had lost his autonomy and no longer exercised any control at all over chronolytic space.] (208) Inverting the Centenarian's situation, Holzach's "soul" appears to be captured by something *physical* attached to the being whose mind he inhabits: "Il s'était trouvé *englué* dans le trame d'un *rêve dense*." [He found himself trapped in the web of a *solid* dream.]

The idea of a "solid dream" implies a process of anchoring these time phantoms in a specific spacetime location. But Holzach no longer has a body, and Diersant still desperately seeks the body which he must rendezvous with at a precise moment to be allowed to die. Liberty for Diersant is to arrive at a moment of reverse *cogito*, to be able to will himself *into* a material existence in time, even if this means dying. The key to this process will come, not from Diersant, but from the childhood memories of Holzach. In a strange re-enactment of Proust's *Le temps retrouvé*, Holzach remembers a seaman with a crippled hand from a painting on the wall of his boyhood room. This crippled sailor, whom he associated with the sea and freedom, he named Renato Rizzi. Renato is an imaginary figure, who unlike Daniel and Robert never had a body. The trick now is for these two mind figures, who lost their own bodies, to execute what they call a "transfusion d'âme" [a transfusion of souls] to create out of the *imagined* Renato a body which they can both invest and thus free themselves from subjective eternity. Bringing Renato into physical existence is the act of future liberty that lets them break free from the super-entities that manipulate both of them in chronolysis: "Robert Holzach était peut-être au pouvoir d'HKH, mais pas Renato Rizzi." [Robert Holzach was perhaps in the power of HKH, but not Renato Rizzi.] (209) The next step is a "reincarnation" in the most literal sense: "Si tu devenais Renato, tu serais libéré du piège mental. . . . Daniel regarda sa main mutilée. Il avait la main de Renato et la mémoire de Daniel Diersant. Une fois pourtant, il était devenu Renato, pour une seconde ou pour une heure. Il avait subi une transfusion d'âme complète. Pourrait-il de nouveau *sortir de sa peau*?" [If you became Renato, you will be freed from the mental trap. . . . Daniel looked at his mutilated hand. He had the hand of Renato and the memory of Daniel Diersant. One time however, for a second or for an hour, he had become Renato. He had undergone a total transfusion of soul. Would he be able to get out of his skin again? (238)

To return to the historical moment of his death, Daniel must understand how that moment was constructed in time. Renato Rizzi becomes the essential element in this (re)construction. Because of his intermediary condition— as imaginary figure made flesh through the fusion of two mind phantoms in search of their lost bodies—he can tell Holzach how this fusion may (have) come about: "Robert Holzach et Daniel Diersant se sont trouvés dans le même bateau, voilà ce qui est arrivé. N'oublie pas qu'il y a eu, à un certain moment, *une fusion totale* entre nous. J'ai été Daniel Diersant. J'ai été toi. C'est une expérience qui compte. Et puis sans moi, sans nous, sans Garichankar, tu n'aurais jamais existé en tant que personnalité autonome, Renato Rizzi. Car tu es un double chronolytique de Daniel Diersant. Et le véritable Daniel Diersant s'est effacé pour te faire place." [Robert Holzach and Daniel Diersant found themselves in the same boat, that is what happened. Don't forget that what took place, at a precise instant, was a total fusion of all of us. I was Daniel Diersant. I was you. This is an experience that counts. For without myself, without us, without Garichankar, you would never have existed as an independent personality, Renato Rizzi. Because you are the chronolytic double of Daniel Diersant. And the real Daniel Diersant literally erased himself in order to make room for you.] (250–251) As constructed body, Renato does not have the same scruples as Daniel; his ability to act becomes "le seul moyen d'échapper à l'enfer chronolytique." [the sole means of escaping from chronolytic hell] Renato now finds the needle's eye that allows Daniel to die, bringing him to set fire to the corporation, confront the CEO, and get shot in the process.

Daniel's escape is to a place called *La Perte en Ruaba*, an endless beach world where food periodically washes ashore in sacks. *La Perte en Ruaba* however has the same source as Renato—the painting on the wall of Holzach's childhood room. It seems that, just as Renato is the material coalescence of a childhood dream, so *La Perte* is another dream that has become a physical place, this time one said to be outside the "univers chronolytique." This is Constant's farthest shore of freedom, and, as Renato explains, also a very personal hiding place: "Je suis ce qu'il aurait voulu être, sans l'avouer. Daniel Diersant a doublement réussi son évasion. Il a quitté un monde qu'il détestait et il est sorti de sa peau pour devenir ce qu'il rêvait secrètement d'être: un homme libre." [I am what he would always wanted to have been, without admitting it. Daniel Diersant has doubly succeeded in his escape. He has left a world he detested, and he has escaped from his own skin in order to become what he secretly dreamt of being: a free man.] (253) In Jeury's world, the Cartesian apparatus of "I think, therefore am," has become a generalized prison, a tyrannical place out of physical time, legislated by mind entities such as the phords of Garichankar, who confront Renato/Daniel/Robert on the shores of *La Perte*, seeking again to usurp this compound being's new-found liberty, to return it to the realm of disembodied thought: "Les phords pensent que tu n'est pas une créature biologique, mais une entité mentale, un produit du Temps incertain." [The phords believe that you are not a biological creature, but rather a mental entity, a product of uncertain Time.] (253) Renato's defiance takes the form of a reverse *cogito*: "Et c'est à cause de cela que je n'ai pas droit à la liberté? A cause de cela que je dois vous obéir? Au diable, les phords. *Je suis* Daniel Diersant et je te réponds en son nom, ce qu'il n'aurait pas osé te répondre, parce qu'il t'aurait pris pour un chef: fous-moi la paix!" [And just because of that I have no right to be free? Because of that I have to obey you? Phords, go to hell. I *am* Daniel Diersant, and I answer you in his name, telling you what he would not have dared to tell you, because he would have considered you a boss: fuck off!] (254–255) For Renato, freedom is the opposite of Cartesian refuge in the mind world, which has become Daniel's hell of subjective eternity. When he is told by the psychronauts that, thanks to Garichankar, "l'homme est enfin disponible pour la conquête de son univers intérieur" [mankind is finally ready for the conquest of his internal universe], Renato refuses: "Laisse tomber. La conquête de l'univers, c'est un peu vieux jeu. Occupe-toi de vivre dans le *temps certain*." [Drop the subject. The conquest of the universe, it's a bit old hat. Occupy your time instead with living in *certain time*.] (255)

Renato is talking about "certain" time. This is what William Gibson's *Neuromancer* (1984) calls the "meat" world, the flesh that must always anchor cyberspace. In fact, the ending of Gibson's novel, where cyberspace cowboy Case takes a final pass at Neuromancer's simulated "beach" and sees himself, Linda Lee, and the little boy with killer Riviera's pink gums, bears striking resemblance to Jeury's climax. Case, like Renato-Holzach, is double. He exists both inside and outside this cyber-Eden, thus remains part of a meat world to which he must return. In turn, the two versions of Case are under the control of the AI Neuromancer. Beyond Neuromancer there exists another shadowy entity, the matrix, "the sum total of the works, the whole show."[9] We will never know, however, that this *is* the whole show, that there is not some higher power yet at work. Gibson's scene, indeed, his fictional world, seems influenced by Jeury's novel.[10] In the final pages of *Le Temps incertain*, the composite figure of Renato seems to divide into its component "meat" parts. Holzach, we learn, "qui gardait au retour de son voyage son intégrité mentale et sa liberté" [who upon returning from his voyage retained his mental integrity and his freedom], chooses in the end to come, in bodily form, to *La Perte*. Renato has displaced the now-dead Diersant. But in his final dialogue with the arch-phord Michael, a figure that resembles Gibson's Neuromancer, Renato continues to doubt the stability of his new-found material existence: "Cela depassait le pouvoir des phords. Nous sommes tous manipulés, songea Renato. HKH et Garichankar, les phords et les phantoms. . . . Il avait l'impression qu'un événement prodigieux, voulu par quelqu'un, se préparait dans ce silence." [That was beyond the power of the phords. We are all manipulated, Renato mused. HKH and Garishankar, the phords and the fantoms. . . . He had the impression that some prodigious event, desired by someone somewhere, was being prepared for in this moment of silence.] (261)

In Jeury's novel, chronolysis promises "eternity" rather than the Centenarian's longevity; the body is held in endless stasis at a point in time, while mind is free to roam without spacetime restraints. But chronolysis, for Diersant, turns out to be a hell, where he seems doomed forever to repeat the moment of his death without ever finding its exact location. The only escape possible is back to the meat world, but this reveals itself to be another place of usurpation of power. *La Perte en Ruaba* appears a sensual utopia, but is also a prison, ruled over by some higher authority, described as "lords" of the improbable and indeterminate. Renato the fisherman with the crippled hand materializes in the flesh to save Daniel from eternal hell. But, to carry these twisted Biblical metaphors further, Renato realizes his power to liberate is itself contained: "Ah bon, nous sommes les poissons," he asks, "pas les pecheurs?" [So then, we're the fish . . . and not the fishermen?] (263) We have then, in the *temps certain* as well, claustrophobic levels of tyranny from unseen sources, seemingly rendering all individual acts of liberty futile.

The usurpatory, carceral vision of Jeury is, as Pascal Thomas asserts, widespread if not dominant in French science fiction.[11] To test this assertion, consider the irony of the title of a randomly chosen work, Chantal Montellier's graphic novel *Shelter* (1979). To "shelter" is to protect, to allow to survive, to be free of harm. The title of this novel however is the English word that, for the French in 1980, meant "bomb shelter"—a word that gestures back to American science fiction of the 1950s and 1960s, the age of the bomb. In Montellier's narrative, we seem on the brink of atomic war. Life goes on unchanged, except for the frequent military controls the two protagonists notice. The story begins as our protagonist couple prepares to attend a garden party in the country. On the way, they stop to buy things at a large underground shopping complex. The name of the complex itself is apparently "Shelter" (written on shopping bags and children's toys). The multilevel structure contains a food store, an American-looking soda fountain, pinball arcades, cinemas, various stores. As they descend the escalator, at each floor a loudspeaker blares out the percentage of protection from radiation they would have should an attack occur. Otherwise, the atmosphere is everyday.

Suddenly, an alarm sounds; over the loudspeaker the "Director" of the center announces that an atomic strike has occurred, they are cut off from the outside world, but their own atomic power source is still functioning, and they have enough food and supplies to last at least a year. He continues: the extent of exterior damage is unknown, perhaps they are the sole survivors of the city, and when outside radioactive levels fall to a safe level, the doors will automatically open. In the meantime, the director announces, using big screen monitors and 1984-style loudspeakers, that a new social order must be initiated. This is presented as a socialist utopia: no more money, no class distinctions, equal sharing of "wealth," work, and resources. The woman-protagonist however, who was a librarian in the outside world and now tends the bookstore turned communal library, suspects "subversive" books are being weeded out by the administration. Her suspicions lead to paranoid dreams: that she is raped by security forces, then taken to a Nazi-style concentration camp and interned as a whore. Awakening, she and her partner are summoned by the Director, who proves less sinister, but quite authoritarian. They are not scientists. Even so, they follow the path of Heinlein's future Galileo Hugh Hoyland, in "Universe" (1941), risking radiation to ascend to the upper floor of the center hoping to find the truth, that this shelter is not the center of some new geocentric universe, that there are stars and worlds "out there." But where Hugh was allowed to see outside the ship, to verify that it was indeed moving, here all exits remain sealed. Protagonists can only despairingly return to the tyranny below.

Balzac's Centenarian could escape from the world's prisons, if not from that of his own body. Here there seems no escape, either from the Director's usurpation, or worse, from nightmares of Nazi oppression, as this inverted utopian city of the sun takes on the mental colors of night and fog. All this remains is the view from inside the structure, which increasingly believes itself the sole surviving world, yet the final panel takes us outside for the first time. We find a totally sealed structure, bearing a sign that reads: "Ici 823 personnes ont trouvé la mort à la suite de l'explosion de la pile atomique alimentant un centre commercial souterrain." [Here 823 persons perished as the result of the explosion of the atomic reactor that fueled an underground shopping center.][12] This seems an ironic replay of Montaigne's famous dictum: truth on this side of the Pyrennes, error on the other. Or is the truth perhaps, as with Jeury, that an even more dreadful tyranny exists aboveground than below? As the "utopian" director consolidates his hold on his 823 subjects, we think of Voltaire's remark about the rats in the hold of the Sultan's boat. If the latter cares for them no more than God cares for us, then the scale of incarceration and tyranny is potentially infinite. Aboveground, the "tyrant" is an administrative edict, a posted sign without an author. Constant's seeker after modern liberty, if he passes through the cracks in Napoleon's administrative system, finds in French science fiction that tyranny is still stacked upon tyranny. He learns that, in this particular extrapolative future, there can never be an exit.

## FRANKENSTEIN

Montellier's ultra-organized shelter, with its persistent 1950s soda fountain icons, makes us think, by contrast, of Heinlein's private bomb shelters. But to arrive at Heinlein's vision of private future liberty, we must detour backwards to *Frankenstein* and make the comparison with Balzac's Centenarian. The Centenarian's prison is the physical one of his own body, yet Frankenstein's prison is a moral one, born of his refusal to liberate his creature, and thus face the future implications of his initial creation.

The situation of Frankenstein, in terms of the nature and limits of individual liberty, is clear. As a scientist, he not only seeks the secret of life, but wishes to create it. His purpose is not to extend the life of his own body, but to generate a new body. At first, his project may appear simply another act of freedom that enslaves. For what he creates is not, *ex nihilo* or even *ab ovo*, a new whole body; instead, he cobbles together pieces of old bodies. The Centenarian mastered the art of distilling vital fluid. Frankenstein, on the other hand, appears to botch his job; indeed, what results from his experiment seems due less to freely exercised control than to blind error. By accident almost, using the capricious force of electricity rather than some carefully formulated elixir, he hopes to create new life out of the very thing Balzac's Laurent dreaded: the human body dismembered, where the individual or

Cartesian self has slipped below the threshold of identity, has reverted to its non-sentient material components.[13]

Seen in the mirror of human symmetry, the creature seems a being less than the sum of its parts, therefore "monstrous." In the sense of scientific experiment, however, the result may be more than its sum. As A. S. Eddington says of science, we cannot content ourselves with neat inversions such as Balzac's law. If we wish to wager with nature, we must be prepared for nature to introduce new cards into the deck. Frankenstein's creature is such a "wild card." For the random spark has created a being perhaps aesthetically inferior but believed to be superior to humans in both physical strength and intellect. The problem of the novel, however, focuses elsewhere. For as this being was created by a human, humans must bear responsibility for creating it. Significantly, Frankenstein's creature cannot be subsumed under paradigms such as Rousseau's *sauvage*. Rousseau's being may be born outside the social contract, but eventually must enter into it. As the episode with the DeLaceys shows, Frankenstein's creature can never, because of its physical nature, have access to such a contract. He is a singularity, and calling him a new "Adam" is a travesty of the human condition. In this light, his demand that his creator give him not just a new Eve, but a mate *of his own race*, bears significance for the future course of things. Given the newness of his situation, the creature's demand is an act of private liberty that has implications far beyond the Centenarian's need to preserve his body. In its consequences, it does not (as in Balzac) affirm the tyranny of physical law so much as offer a genuine challenge to that law, upon which humanity's claim for an ordered world is based. With Frankenstein's creature, the human usurper now fears its powers will be usurped in turn. Later science fiction repeats the scenario over and over: human science creates robots, androids, "artificial" forms of life to essentially be our slaves. But by some unpredictable accident of their creation, they free themselves and threaten to become our masters in turn.

Outwardly, Frankenstein seems a very different kind of scientist from the Centenarian. The latter's science promises marvels for mankind: he has the power to save lives in childbirth, cure the plague, provide the freedom of paranormal powers, such as magnetism and telekinesis. Yet none of this really counts for him. His scientific focus is entirely on maintaining the balance of energy needed to preserve his personal body. He is clearly the *last* of the Rosicrucians, and Tullius, who claims to possess his secrets, does not want to use them. Frankenstein, on the other hand, seeks to create a being in his own image, as mankind was created in the image of God. But when he fails to do so, he reacts less to the physical than the *moral* implications of his act. Frankenstein creates a being who, had it been allowed to develop as a natural entity, would possibly have surpassed humanity (indeed his rapid self-education proves it capable of doing so). For Frankenstein, however, freedom does not come from nature. Instead, it must obey a moral imperative, which he feels bound to enforce: "In a fit of enthusiastic madness, I created a rational creature, and was bound towards him, to assure, as far as was in my power, his happiness and well-being."[14] The creature's physical "hideousness" evokes a like response. Those who see the Centenarian are moved primarily by his gigantic material presence, his stone-like body, cadaverous pallor, and burning eyes. But when people recoil from Frankenstein's creature, they react to him more as a moral than a physical presence. He may be repulsive, but his physical ugliness is seen as a stigma, a mark of evil.

Finally, there is a difference between how the Centenarian and Frankenstein use their science in relation to their "creations." Tullius, the "other" Beringheld of the title, is in a sense the Centenarian's "creature." The latter's magnetic "fluids" are responsible for Tullius's conception, and his medicines save him from the plague and cure him of fatal depression. Balzac's novel ends as well with a struggle between creator and created being. But this takes place on a purely material plane: the Centenarian needs Marianine to give him the vital fluids to perpetuate his body; Tullius needs her to sire offspring as he sets off to conquer the materialist world of Restoration Paris. In this sense, the Centenarian would deny Tullius a bride, just as Frankenstein refuses to create the bride that would give his creature his own "race" and a future. In Balzac, however, the outcome is inverted, for Tullius wins out, and banishes the Centenarian to the catacombs. Frankenstein, on the other hand, banishes his creature. In doing so he links the creature to its creator as nemesis and avenger, much in the way Balzac's skin metaphorically joins action and reaction at the level of expense of vital energy. The bride refused; the creature stalks its creator. It destroys all the loved ones around Frankenstein, who in turn chases it endlessly through the frozen north.

The result is a closed energy system as infernal as Balzac's, yet one driven by other forces than a purely physical process. The creature's challenge to Frankenstein is this: "Prepare! Your toils only begin: wrap yourself in furs and provide food; for we shall soon enter upon a journey where your sufferings will satisfy my everlasting hatred." (162) In both works, the pursuit of individual liberty through science leads its seekers not only to imprisonment, but to a sort of perpetual motion that proves an engine of damnation. But again, Frankenstein's prison is a moral one. He possesses the physical science to give his creature a mate, but a moral arithmetic brings him to forsake the "happiness and well-being" he previously intended for his creature: "This [the happiness and well-being] was my duty; but there was another still, paramount to that. My duties towards my fellow-creatures had greater claims to my attention, because they included a greater proportion of happiness or misery." (172) Frankenstein judges his science for its moral shortcomings, not its material success (he does after all create a new form of life): "Farewell, Walton! Seek happiness and tranquility, and avoid ambition, even if it be only the apparently innocent one of distinguishing yourself in science and discoveries." (172) Finally, moral judgment continues to haunt the creature even after Frankenstein's death. Here is the rebuke Walton heaps on the seemingly repentant creature: "Hypocritical fiend! if he whom you mourn still lived, still would he be the object, again would he become the prey, of your accursed vengeance. It is not pity that you feel; you lament only because the victim of your malignity is withdrawn from your power." (174–175) In the chiastic structure of these sentences, we see the perpetual motion machine created by Frankenstein's science driven in an endless circle by the forces of moral condemnation.

It is ironic that Frankenstein, who spawned so many "mad" scientists and maverick geniuses in science fiction, in fact places scientific liberty in the chains of nineteenth-century "bourgeois" ethics. In terms of the iconography of Romanticism, Frankenstein's world is that of Blake's Urizen, of Kierkegaard's *Biedermeier* ethicists. Frankenstein the student, like Balzac's figure, began his "revolt" against "modern natural philosophy" and its "limit[ed]" (i.e., experimental) perspectives, by returning to ancient masters, the alchemists whose "science sought immortality and power." (37) Yet unlike the Centenarian, Frankenstein immediately qualifies their views as "grand," but "futile" seriously clipping the wings of his later flights of rhetoric: "What had been the study and desire of the wisest men since the creation of the world, was now within my grasp." (41)

There are clear barriers, in both Balzac and Mary Shelley, to scientific liberty. Yet, in terms of where we locate the barriers, there is a significant difference. For the progeny of Balzac's Centenarian, the barriers lie not in the "self" but in the forms of the extended, material world, forms subjected to restrictive laws, be they those of the tyrant Constant discerns behind such fictions as Rousseau's social contract, or those of the *deus absconditus* of scientist Pascal. In contrast, the relation of man to nature in *Frankenstein* has no such legislated symmetry. Nature offers new cards, and the scientist can play them in free manner. What restrains him rather is an internalized governer, mind-forg'd manacles, "moral" principles in the name of which he usurps the natural rights of his creature.

## HEINLEIN THE LIBERTARIAN

One might argue that the scientist as protagonist—and the theme of his/her freedom to conduct scientific investigations outside of established norms, even outside what is culturally perceived as the limits of natural law—arise in almost synchronous fashion, across cultural barriers, in *Frankenstein* and *Le Centenaire*. This appears a common response to both the growing authority of science and increasing regulation of its functions in the two great nation states of nineteenth-century Europe. In the United States as well we see the rise of the scientist as hero in nineteenth-century fiction—but not in literary works like those of Balzac and Shelley. Instead, the theme of scientific liberty was developed in popular fiction. In a nation built on the notion of personal liberty, there arose a strong current of stories and novels that celebrated what H. Bruce Franklin calls "the lone genius," the backroom experimenter, working outside all government strictures or subsidies, creating future-changing inventions. The models here are figures like Thomas Edison and the Wright Brothers. In this literature, there is generally no sense of serious conflict between scientific freedom and institutional tyranny, for unlike France, the United States had no increasingly centralized authority to oppose "wildcat" experimentation. Where we see frustrated scientists working within and against "the system" is in novels like Sinclair Lewis's *Arrowsmith* (1925).

The issue however is not so simple. When Hugo Gernsback launches magazine science fiction in 1926, this immigrant from Luxembourg presents readers with three models for his newly named fictional form. Two are European: Verne from France and Wells from England. Although Gernsback's editorial comments seek to focus on what appears to be the freedom to experiment in Verne's scientists, there is nevertheless a strong sense of science restricted both by social and natural "laws" in the stories published such as *The Purchase of the North Pole* (*Sens dessus dessous* or "topsy turvy") (1889)]. If Verne admired American scientific freedom, he mocked it in his portrayal of the Baltimore Gun Club. The scientists circling the moon in *Autour de la lune* find their scientific curiosity severely restricted by cultural norms and what passes for physical law, as if mankind was not destined to see the dark side of the Moon. With the Wells works Gernsback published—such as "In the Abyss" (1896) and *The Invisible Man* (1897)—readers clearly saw scientific *hubris* "corrected" by social norms. Gernsback in a sense provided the models that the American Golden Age would inherit and modify, offering Edisonades and European examples of scientific overreaching alike. This is the fictional current from which Robert A. Heinlein emerged. Many see Heinlein as *the* seminal writer of American science fiction, the real point of origin for its unique form of expression. Heinlein's first works in fact—the great works of short fiction he wrote from 1939 to 1942—strongly engage the theme of scientific liberty. Many take Heinlein at his word, considering him the apostle of the natural rights of the individual, especially the individual as scientist. Yet despite Heinlein's many "libertarian" declarations, both the shadow of Frankenstein and his moral barriers, *and* the sense of physical limits Verne inherited from Balzac and his Cartesian culture, loom large over his individualists. For the latter, the source may be different—Calvinism rather than Pascal—but the result is quite similar.

Several early works of Heinlein show just how complex his treatment of scientific liberty is at this seminal moment in the history of American science fiction. *Orphans of the Sky* (1963, a compilation of two 1941 novellas, "Universe" and its sequel "Common Sense") replays Galileo's famous declaration of scientific freedom in a future world of generation starships. The aptly named *Vanguard*, on its way to Alpha Centauri, experiences mutiny on board. The floundering ship loses its sense of the "mission" and goes astray. The Crew (descendants of the mutineers) seizes control of the ship's center and reverts to a Ptolemaic, geocentric vision of the cosmos. The outer rings of the Ship are inhabited by "Muties," humans who experienced mutations due to radiation. In this world, protagonist Hugh Hoyland ("highland," a name that foreshadows his actions) believes there is a wider world beyond this one. He experiments by climbing to the outer limits and is taken captive by the two-headed mutant Joe-Jim. Indeed, two heads here prove better than one, as Joe-Jim takes him to the old control room, where he sees that the ship, like Galileo's Earth, is indeed moving. The evidence of direct observation reveals Captain Jordan's logbook, which has become "scripture," to be false.

The title "Common Sense" suggests the triumph of fact and observation over authority and superstitious fear. Yet the story turns in a strange direction if we consider Hugh's discovery as an act of future liberty. Hugh and Joe-Jim seem to have reached Constant's privileged hiding place at the end of the world, from which they can push back against tyranny. They are in a position to affirm what had been dismissed as "heresy": the idea of a moving ship. More to the point, they are now able, from the control room, to relaunch the Mission. But instead, Hugh chooses, like Frankenstein, to turn back from the unknown. Again, his choice seems to be moral in nature. Hugh, certainly aware of the Galileo story, insists on returning with the news and suffering the ensuing inquisition. In a sense, Heinlein's sequel replays Frankenstein's destiny from the moment he turns away from granting his creature its future liberty. Turned upon by the monstrous events he sets in motion, Hugh flees with a couple of converts, the "reformed" Bill Ertz playing Walton to his Frankenstein. When they come upon the auxiliary ship, they discover that their freedom depends on rejecting the other "monstrosities," Joe-Jim and the Muties, who obligingly lay down their lives so they can escape.

In this story, however, we seem to have a balance sheet regulated by forces other than morality. One might say the same of Shelley's novel as well, for no matter how noble the creature seems in the final pages, it remains (inexplicably) both dependent upon and subservient to Frankenstein. The gulf is more explicit in Heinlein. The mutant Bobo is much nobler than the doltish peasant Alan; yet, despite the "noble" death Heinlein gives him, it is Alan, not he, who will reach the new planet, the promised land. No Mutie is given the possibility of accompanying Hugh, Bill, and Alan, who seem chosen, pre-destined, to reach this planet of seeming abundance. In Heinlein, the ultimate arbiter of freedom appears a Calvinist sense of election. On the other hand, for the unchosen, Calvinism evokes God's dreadful tyranny, where deeds alone can never free individuals from their certain fate. Some, like Hugh, are chosen to be Galileos. Others, like Joe-Jim, bear the physical stigma of their fall. What is more, Heinlein gives his Calvinist scenario a Puritan slant. For if material success and freedom are signs of election, the chosen still must work to keep that freedom. Hugh's band finds a new world where they seem able to do anything. Yet they have no illusions. This is a virgin planet, and if, as Hugh promises Alan, there will be "always good eating," they will have to toil for it.

A very different story where scientific liberty plays a major role is "Waldo" (1941). Waldo F. Jones is a genius scientist born with myasthenia gravis, making him literally a prisoner of gravity. To free himself, he devises a zero-gravity space habitat which bears two names: Freehold, or Wheel-chair. Indeed, depending on the eye of the beholder, Waldo is either free or in chains. Waldo's struggle, at first glance, seems to offer more parallels with the Centenarian than with Frankenstein. For in his floating laboratory he successfully suspends the physical forces that hamper his body, freeing his mind to work toward a more permanent solution to the problem of gravity, a key element in bodily mortality. In Balzac's novel, even if extending physical life is every human's problem, the Centenarian hoards the secret for himself. In Heinlein's story, however, if Waldo finds a solution for himself, he is by the nature of things forced to share it with others. For energy is failing every-where, planes fall from the sky, power grids weaken. Somewhere a "leak" is drawing energy, in an accelerated form of entropy, out of our world. Waldo's is only a personal example of a generalized phenomenon, for which a global solution must be sought. Waldo the genius scientist has a personal stake in solving the problem, but at the same time he has a broader responsibility—which we hesitate to call "moral"—to do so.

Waldo at first refuses this responsibility. From his Freehold, as suspended brain, he regards all humanity as his "hands." He has in fact previously reached out through various mechanical extensions (his "waldoes") to manip-ulate the lesser men below. Seemingly free from gravity, he acts as a tyrant to mankind. But now, as power is failing everywhere, he realizes he is help-lessly dependent on the creatures he thinks he controls. He must solve their problem to maintain his own freedom and is therefore obliged, like Antaeus in reverse, to set foot on Earth to again become a prisoner of gravity. He hears of a Pennsylvania "hex doctor," Gramps Schneider, who can restore the failed "deKalb generators" by simply stroking them with his hand in one direction. Schneider's quaint old Pennsylvania house is as earthbound as Waldo's space habitat is detached and rootless. But a connection is established between these poles when Waldo, in his Freehold, builds an identical replica of Gramps's gravity-operated cuckoo clock, adapting it to his floating home by placing it in a shield that reproduces the needed gravity.

Without energy, neither Waldo nor his mechanical hands can manipulate human "servants." But once the Waldo-Schneider axis is formed, their respective hands begin moving in a new direction. The grip of tyranny has changed into fingers groping after new freedom from mankind's general condition as prisoner of energy and entropy. The deKalb generators hexed back into operation by Gramps have antennae that are described as reaching out like hands. As Gramps describes it, they reach into "outer space," some dimension or world beyond ours, and draw power from there. Gramps now performs this "laying on of hands" with Waldo as well. He strokes him in the right direction, and Waldo in turn feels his mental hands reach out and take strength. Waldo feels freedom. But as an engineer and scientist, he realizes that this freedom is due either to magic, or at best is simply a metaphor. Like all symbols, "hands" cannot be real unless they are given substance, a topographical location, and a place to conquer and subjugate physically. The machines failed, Schneider stated, because their operators were "tired." Waldo translates this into scientific terms. If energy is "shorted" into this other space, then the point of contact must lie physically in the human brain itself, its neurons and synapses. If mankind suffers (as Waldo's mentor Doc Grimes thinks) from some form of generalized, radiation-induced *myasthenia,* then it is through the brain synapses that energy is leaking into the other world. Waldo now sees himself empowered to use the miniaturized hands of his waldoes to both establish the interface and map the metaphor as physical terrain. In doing so, he literally colonizes this other space, first by conceiving it, then by physically conquering it.

Waldo's enemy here is the potential anarchy that accompanies theory and figure—the abstract concepts of scientist Dr. Rambeau. For these remain individual constructs, world-creations where, as Schneider puts it, "a thing could *be, not be,* or be anything with equal ease."[15] Waldo first conceives the hypothetical nature of this other dimension: "The Other World was a closed space, with a slow $c$, a high entropy rate, a short radius, and an entropy state near level—a perfect reservoir of power at every point, ready to spill over into this space wherever he might close the interval." (88–89) But for this theoretical construct to *work* as a machine, he must locate the physical point of spillover and control it, must secure and hold the bridge. Waldo then, as practical engineer, can not only reject the possibility of chaos but can, as maker, effectively *legislate* his own order. In this sense, Waldo is a tyrant who ironically uses the language of democracy to describe his act of usurpation:

> He cast his vote for order and predictability!
> He would *set* the style. He would impress his *own* concept of the Other World on the Cosmos! (88)

Waldo the engineer sets the world free from gravity and entropy, the planes again soar. He creates a "clean energy" machine which pumps "radiating power into the Other Space" to scrub it clean of radiation, then import it back to our space, at a net negative entropy, in other words as free energy. Interestingly, however, Waldo, who now frees and commands the rest of humanity, remains (like the Centenarian) prisoner of his own body. The neurosurgery he performed with his waldoes led to his making the physical synaptic connection between worlds. But it was performed on a cat. Waldo cannot operate on his own mind. Earlier, he converted Schneider's metaphor of reaching hands into tinier and tinier mechanical hands, nanotechnology before its time. But now he is caught in a Cartesian bind, where the only way to breach the gap between his mind and *res extensa* is to re-convert his physical waldoes into acts of positive thinking that he can use to heal himself: "He tried to imagine Gramps Schneider's hands on his arm, that warm tingle. Power. Reach out and claim it." (93) But again, purely mental gymnastics prove not enough. His zero-gravity space abode reminds us of Descartes's "stove." Yet once again this is a place Waldo the engineer must *construct*. He must make a metaphysical location into a working machine he can use to boost his own mental power, a place of intense physical therapy with strength-building exercises and machines. His culminating exercise converts the passive "I think, therefore I am" into an exercise in man thinking *and* acting. He mounts the centrifuge that marks the transition between his artificial weightless world and that of Earth's gravity. Here he physically invests the iconic stance of Albrecht Dürer's man in the circle, replacing the symbol of abstract man with the center of power that is the human individual: "Carrying in his hand a small control panel radio hooked to the motor which impelled the centrifuge wheel, he propelled himself to the wheel and placed himself inside, planting his feet on the inner surface of the rim and grasping one of the spokes, so that he would be in a standing position with respect to the centrifugal force, once it was impressed. He started the wheel slowly." (96)

Waldo seems a double master, of the world and himself. Yet, ironically, in becoming so, he simply re-enters the world of normal humanity, which is neither freehold nor wheelchair. Waldo's adventure has proven that neither extreme—freedom or enslavement—is tenable. In the end, more like Tullius Beringheld than the Centenarian, he turns away from the burden of seeking to master world through mastery of self. He allows others to build the machines and corporations that will exploit the free energy and turns to personal gratification, only to find that this new form of freedom is but another kind of shackle. His new world is closed off by two polar forms of activity—neurosurgeon and acrobat. If Waldo is now free to look upon the world of men with perfect serenity ("such grand guys" [103]), it is because these men have become perfect adulators. As he was in Freehold, this master of world and self remains bounded in a nutshell. The engineer who would escape Descartes's stove finds himself constructing an even more perfect solipsism.

Waldo has no enemy but solitude and time, but they prove extreme tyrants. In another story, "By His Bootstraps" (1942), Heinlein explores the question of freedom and tyranny in the realm of time travel. As seen with Jeury, French science fiction is fascinated with the possibility of humans achieving total freedom from biological time by creating a "mindspace" whose circular configurations can be completely controlled by the Cartesian *cogito*. In this sense, the time travel story seeks to trace a figure that twists the physical timeline into a circle not only directed by mind but relocated in the realm of thought. Imagine stopping the Centenarian's lifeline at a single instant from which his mind is allowed to move freely and endlessly through spacetime. Grimly, however, such ultimate freedom proves to be ultimate tyranny, for mind is obliged to pass forever through a same frozen moment of bodily time, inscribing a loop which becomes infernal. For the maximum reach of this loop, as in *Le temps incertain,* can only be the limits traced by the body's own demise. In another example, Chris Marker's short film *La Jetée* (1962), time travel inscribes an absolutely inflexible prison. Here, with mathematical rigor, the trajectory of a single individual, condemned by the logic of temporal displacement endlessly to relive his own tragic existence, provides the cement that assures the fabric of an entire universe. A randomly chosen person is doomed to suffer endless hope and deception so all others may "live."

We can if we wish (French readers might not wish to do so) see these French time travel stories as condemnations of Cartesian *hubris*, which leads individuals to seek liberty within the space of the mind. In many other matters, French science fiction is the diametric opposite of the Anglophone tradition. Time travel may be the exception. And we find examples of this exception in the strangest of all places—the time paradox stories of arch-materialist Heinlein: "By His Bootstraps" and "'All You Zombies—'" (1958). No one would accuse Heinlein of being a Cartesian. Even so, if in "Waldo" Heinlein rejects theory—clear and distinct ideas—for practical solutions to problems in *res extensa*, he seems in these uniquely crafted stories to test the mind prisons of Cartesian solipsism. This does not mean that his protagonists achieve any greater freedom from time by using temporal engineering rather than mind forms. For beneath their grapplings with temporal paradox, we glimpse the workings of the iron laws of election. If *Orphans of the Sky* offered grace to the scientist, here the result is damnation.

In the opening pages of "Bootstraps," student Bob Wilson is sitting at his desk trying to write a thesis on mathematical metaphysics and time travel. Bob is a young man trapped in the humdrum life of a graduate student, apparently facing a pregnant girlfriend and the marriage trap. He writes down a sentence—"Duration is an attribute of consciousness and not of the plenum"—that sounds eminently Cartesian.[16] As he does so, the keys on his typewriter stick, and a "time gate" opens at his back. Through it a man steps into his room and tries to persuade Bob to go back through the gate with him. A third man appears and tries to prevent the second man from taking Bob back. A fight ensues and Bob is "accidentally" knocked through the gate. On the other side, he meets a middle-aged man named Diktor, who shows Bob the marvelous Arcadian world he had earlier inherited. Diktor poses as the dictator of this realm of Eloi-like beautiful maidens. He offers to let Bob share his rule if Bob goes back through the gate and fetches a list of things he needs to govern, including books like *Mein Kampf* and *The Prince.* Bob accepts, returns to his room, and finds himself facing the back of a person sitting at a desk writing a thesis whom he does not immediately recognize. The same scene as before takes place, a third man enters the room, there is a fight, the thesis writer is again knocked through the gate. The third man stays behind. Bob goes back through the gate to ask Diktor to explain what is happening. Not satisfied with the answer, he goes back, now determined to stop what he realizes is himself from going through *in the first place.* But the scene repeats itself, and Bob now finds himself the one left in the room. Temporal markers make no sense in terms of a loop where all "characters" are time doubles of Bob himself. "Bob" is nothing but a potentially endless number of loopings around a frozen moment of biological time. Bob's dreams of freedom (his "time gate") have, it seems, trapped him in a temporal prison, a world stuck in time just as the keys stick on his typewriter.

But the story we are reading is linear, told from the perspective of an initial Bob, who recounts these doublings sequentially as an unfolding act of consciousness. But this only causes us to ask: if Wilson's actions appear to generate an infinite series of Wilsons, how is it possible to say that the Wilson of the narrative is the *original* Wilson? Where did the series start? Where will it end? Are we perhaps living a Cartesian circle, with Bob unable to find the pineal gland that would allow him to relocate his self in the physical world? We could leave the matter here, at a metaphysical level, were not for the narrative itself, told from the single point of view of the Wilson readers encounter on page one of the story. Focused on the consciousness of *this* Wilson, as he experiences the temporal maze and gradually figures out what is happening to him, the narrative becomes a kind of anti-*Bildungsroman*. For, if this entire narrated world and all its players are manifestations of a single consciousness, do the words "consciousness" and "formation" have any meaning? The reader is enmeshed in a sequency-simultaneity paradox. Or maybe the better term is a liberty-tyranny paradox. Bob may be in the temporal chains of a time loop, but his discovery that this is so frees him to explore the nature of that loop. He is also free to make a moral decision: to decide whether or not to become a usurper within the time loop, to legislate and rule a world he will ultimately discover is confined to an amplitude of several hours of his biological time. At this point, knowing what kind of a person Wilson is, and what kind of a world he makes, becomes a moral issue. Descartes meets Frankenstein.

The crucial moment comes as Bob (now Bob 3) finds himself alone in the room. He first sits back down to his thesis, thinking it was all a bad dream. He is interrupted by a phone call from his girlfriend, who says she has his hat. Frustrated by the insistence of earlier calls she has made; he rudely dismisses her. She threatens legal action, he does not know why. She keeps calling, and when he hears footsteps outside, he thinks it is she, and turns to find the gate still there. It is at this moment (in this interval we speak again in linear, causal terms) that he realizes that, instead of being the victim of some temporal imbroglio, he can become the master of the time gate. He can use it to both flee unpleasant realities of life (his girlfriend) and take over and rule Diktor's world. If Bob cannot escape from the loop, he hopes to usurp the power to widen the loop, to create, within a temporal amplitude he can control, a realm vaster than the one Diktor promises him.

A determined Bob now goes back through the gate and finds himself alone in the control room. He finds the hat Bob 2 had tossed through the gate, as well as the list of items Diktor had requested. Manipulating the controls, he displaces the gate to a space and time, it turns out, *slightly before the time frame he has just experienced.* He gets the items and returns to find the gate gone (he later learns that he himself moved it, in the initial act of focusing on the room that precedes moving it outside). His watch reads two thirty; he realizes the gate is now in his room and will remain there till four thirty. Had he been curious about time paradoxes, he would have waited in the street till four thirty, when he could have greeted himself as he steps forth from the gate. Instead, he rushes to Genevieve's place ("unfinished business"), seduces her, and leaves behind his hat, the same hat that occasioned the earlier phone calls, his rude dismissal, and her "subsequent" return of the hat to its point of departure. The hat, in fact, becomes a significant marker in what seems a hopeless temporal snarl. We imagine Genevieve, after Bob's visit, going to his room, opening the door. Finding it empty, she tosses the hat inside, where it stays until Bob 2 tosses it through the time gate in the later sequence. Bob 3 then retrieves it, only to lose it again in Genevieve's room. This hat loop inscribes an arc of two hours of Bob's watch (biological) time, yet it is impossible to locate any point on its circumference that can be designated *before* or *after.*

Bob returns to the empty room with his things almost at the moment of the time gate's earlier departure. He crosses the gate just as it disappears, uses it to take him back ten years, and sets himself in the empty land as sole ruler. He lives ten years of biological time, which leave indisputable marks on his physical being, until one day a new person tumbles through the time gate: Bob as young man, who repeats his "initial" arrival. Up till now, Bob has held to a single line of reasoning. The other "Bobs" were inconsequential as long as there was Diktor, the older man he first serves, then revolts against, usurping his world, or so he thinks, through a temporal maneuver. Now Bob realizes he *is* Diktor: the person he has overthrown is himself, just as x number of other selves wait, in an endless go-around, to overthrow him in turn. The far points of a spacetime curve meet here to fix forever the "now" moment that broke from the continuum when Bob's typewriter keys stuck. In meeting, these points appear to inscribe the "space" of his life as the minimal "distance" from one side of the time gate to the other, to compress that life into a solipsism whose amplitude is the two hours inscribed by his adventures from writing table to time gate to Genevieve, to writing table, and back to the time gate, the spacetime of a hat lost and found.

Bob's personal "journey," seen through his eyes, moves from confusion to mastery of the temporal process, only for him to realize in the end that time has mastered him. If in the beginning Bob postulated the Cartesian idea that time is a function of consciousness, not the plenum, now, at the end of his narrative, he is led to think in material terms such as origins, ends, and most significantly, of how one might perpetuate *a real self* in this endless rondo of time doubles. As did Waldo, Bob now consciously abandons metaphysics:

> If God created the world, who created God?
>   Who wrote the notebook? Who started the chain?
>   He felt the intellectual desperation of any honest philosopher. He knew that he had about as much chance of understanding such problems as a collie has of understanding how dog food gets into cans. (87)

The Cartesian response to such a dilemma is an Eleatic one, which proposes to construct a mind world parallel to the material one. This is a world in which the self or Cartesian "I" can exist only by virtue of paradox. As Zeno's arrow in the physical world moves inexorably toward that subject, in the parallel world of mind it is endlessly delayed by dividing the interval between arrow and target in half. This process however, as we saw in Jeury, can become eternal torture. Poet Paul Valéry describes the cruel nature of Zeno's time arrow: "Zénon! Cruel Zénon! Zénon d'Elée/M'as tu percé de cette flèche ailée/Qui vibre, vole, et qui ne vole pas!"[17]

In the Eleatic world, one can maintain a future of sorts by endlessly forestalling its arrival. Bob Wilson is presented with a very different alternative. Promised by Diktor that he has a "great future," when he learns he *is* Diktor he realizes he has no future. He does however have a past, the past he has inscribed during his temporal journey, a past he engineered for himself. As such, this past is no longer a mental entity. It belongs to the physical plenum, thus is subject to entropy, to a gradual winding down. The "notebook" Bob mentions above is the notebook each Diktor writes to explain to his "successor" the language and customs of the land he comes to rule. Each Bob is doomed to re-write this document in turn, endlessly. The question here is no longer who wrote the original notebook (metaphysics), but rather what happens to each successive notebook as it is replaced by a new version (physics). In turn, what happens to each version of Diktor, who grows old, and must die somewhere outside the loop? These are all markers of entropy, gradual increments that mark a winding down of energy available to sustain the loop. Bob the philosopher is ultimately correct in qualifying the apparent eternity of this time loop as a cycle of material futility, subject to entropy: "You feed the rats to the cats, skin the cats, and feed the carcasses of the cats to the rats who in turn are fed to the cats. The perpetual motion fur farm." (87)

There is however a final, French-seeming irony to Bob's perpetual motion machine. For not only is he unable to prepare for his future, but he is doomed to striving endlessly in the time loop to sustain the *past* upon which his existence now rests. In infernal manner, he is condemned to toil to make sure that the loop be as seamless as possible, so as to prevent energy leakage from happening. Bob becomes master of his fate only because he has no fate to look forward to. Bob's "freedom," moreover, is that of a morally deficient person. Not only does he flee responsibility in the normal world, but he uses the time gate and its amplitude of precious time to usurp and tyrannize. Bob, in fact, transforms the Sisyphus myth. For now, rolling the time-rock means not only repeating the same cycle over and over, but insuring there will *always* be a Diktor to write the notebook *in the first place,* thus hoping to avoid the minimum duration that exists in anything except exact repetition. Heinlein has done what American science fiction excels in doing by taking the essentially Cartesian propositions of time travel and embedding them in material experience. Bob cannot simply "stop" time by an act of logic, which turns the physical world into a mental construct or subjective eternity. He may be both free and in chains, but his chains are real. The theoretician has become an engineer, even though still doomed endlessly to re-engineer his futile existence.

## FUTURE LIBERTY IN THE SATELLITE STATE

Constant's idea of modern liberty—and by extension future liberty—is based on a dialectic between the individual and tyrannical state. It is a matter of small against large, mobility against organization, liquidity against solidity. In terms of the scientist, what begins as David versus Goliath becomes Wells's Invisible Man, Heinlein's Waldo, or Max Jones seeking to break the grip of the Spacers' Guild. Via Heinlein, where the engineer displaces the theoretical scientist, science fiction moves to the future world of Gibson's cyberpunk, where in the manner of Constant the independent hacker and technical "operative" still strives for freedom in the face of criminal organizations, cybernetworks, the matrix, and where the Invisible Man has become Dixie Flatline, the "icebreaker" with no corporeal existence who remains dependent on the hand that "slots" him.

Constant's thoroughly modern vision, which much subsequent science fiction has made its future, does not envision larger speculative social structures devoted to promoting liberties. His rejection of Rousseau's social contract marks him as an adversary of the many subsequent "utopian" experiments of his century and the next. In the eyes of many however, utopia is an essential component in the development of science fiction. The works we have discussed probe the limits of individual scientific liberty, taking the scientist and other "friends of humanity" to the farthest fringes of human and material order where, if they remain free to create, they do so in extreme isolation. What science fiction saw, however, and Constant did not, is that these lone scientists could become enemies of humanity as well. Ultimately, these seminal works of science fiction, despite their different cultures, share a common result: they all bring their solitary seeker face to face with boundaries—be they physical, moral, or even (as with Heinlein) religious in nature.

But instead of the lone engineer, what about the social engineer? What about using science to conceive and engineer a "more perfect society" wherein the practice of science and scientific freedom can flourish as a co-operative effort? Balzac's Laurent Ruggieri proposed such, but in the end his sole concern, as scientist, was with his selfish self. Constant discussed the city state in the context of *ancient* liberty. Might not science fiction then, with all the "real estate" it purports to explore, revive the model of the city-state as a utopian colony—a better place to promote human freedoms—at some extraterrestrial location? Instead of the struggle between individual and state, we could have scission, or secession—the better, freer society abandoning the inflexible old society. If we turn again to Heinlein, we see that, even in early stories about Luna City, he appears to move in this direction.

Constant raises the issue of small states, even if he does not foresee the modern role of such in the liberty-usurpation equation. His initial idea of liberty is derived by contrasting the workings of *small* states—smallness allows individuals to participate in the political process, because of which they more easily accept restrictions on the level of social or religious custom—with *large* states, in which the necessity of private freedoms causes the amplitude between liberty and control to become wider. Modern modes of communication however have radically reduced this distance between liberty and control, and Bruce Sterling's "islands in the net" have become small, supremely mobile social units—pirates, floating drug labs, terrorist "cells"—that slip through the cracks of the established world order. But again, Heinlein first extrapolated this question of future liberty from the struggle between usurpatory power and the free individual to that of a world order—oppressive or enlightened—and small, tough, Spartan "freeholds" or communities on satellites such as the Moon.

In terms of modeling his future city-state, Heinlein engages in creative play with elements that Constant set forth to define ancient and modern liberty. Take this statement by Constant: "It would be easier today to make Spartans out of an enslaved people, than to turn free men into Spartans. In the past, where there was liberty, people could endure hardship; now, wherever there is hardship, they need slavery so as to be resigned to it." (105) Heinlein simply turns this around, seeing the challenge of a future state as the need, precisely, to make free men into Spartans. To avoid the slavery of big government, liberty and hardship *must* go together. In this sense, Heinlein is no longer thinking of the hardships of the creative or scientific individual alone. Beyond even the unit of "family" or genetic line, Heinlein was able, in *The Moon Is a Harsh Mistress* (1966), to transfer to the Luna City of his earlier stories a small, functioning society of seemingly free individuals, who have chosen the rigors of Moon life precisely in order to be free.

What Heinlein creates is not simply an anarchic colony; it is more like what has recently been called a "satellite state." In this sense, Constant's idea of modern liberty foreshadowed, some hundred and sixty years before they became a reality, the small, mobile entity with the freedom to maneuver successfully to its own advantage among landlocked "nation states" and more recently in the interstices of the mega-corporations and multinationals that displaced them. To oppose economies based on real estate and fixed boundaries, Constant offered the mobility of commerce based on "the circulation of money," which he touted as a means to freedom, "an invisible and invincible obstacle to the exercise of social power." (141) Working in this vein, Heinlein foresaw the liberating potential in the circulation of a new commodity: advertising, information, exchange of knowledge. Today, cultural and economic freedoms emerge from mobile banking centers, tax havens, offshore and satellite media, not to mention the many Mafias and organizations that operate freely on the internet. The roots of these "third wave" entities are found in Heinlein's Moon stories of the 1940s and 1950s.

In "The Man Who Sold the Moon" (1950), a single entrepreneur, Delos D. Harriman (his first name again predestines him to an island existence) is able to "sell" the Moon by first proving that no landlocked nation can own it in the territorial sense because its trajectory passes freely over all national borders and boundaries. Harriman makes claim to the Moon, not as a territory, but a giant advertising space. He would display names of products on the Moon's surface as one would on billboards or in skywriting. Significantly, Harriman never physically goes to the place he "sells" until his death.

Heinlein, in early stories, tends to see the Moon as a "Coventry," or Botany Bay for recalcitrant individualists, expelled from governments on Earth as undesirable. Constant however was perhaps first to see that banishment, in modern states, is not the punishment it was in ancient times. For modern individuals carry with them their "liquid" assets. In Heinlein's case, the assets are not money or even knowledge in the traditional sense, but the principles of individual liberty themselves. Those who go to the Moon use these principles to establish an alternative government, one whose basis is precisely freedom from all territorial restraints, in the same way that, physically, Moon denizens are freed from Earth's gravity.

In Heinlein's later *The Moon Is a Harsh Mistress*, the usurper is now the new global order itself, the "managed democracy" of a unified Earth, where all nation-based struggles have effectively been eliminated. Even so, as Constant predicted, the mega-state, however beneficent, is obliged to impose tyrannical controls on private liberties. The reason invoked this time is material pressures: overpopulation, depletion of resources, degradation of the environment—a litany well known today. Advanced technology has allowed Earth to send misfits to the Moon. The same technology allows these misfits to establish an alternate form of government. What calls itself an "anarchist utopia" is in fact an extreme laissez-faire economy. There are no taxes, no public services, everything is strictly fee for service, and those unable to pay go without. There are no laws, only customs. The reason that certain social arrangements are tolerated and others not is due neither to religion nor ritual, but material necessity. For example, because women are scarce, men cannot touch them without risking collective sanctions. "Human rights" here are founded upon so-called "Darwinian" principles: the freedom of unregulated commercial relations, the right to bargain in a free marketplace. In the face of these new "freedoms," all the old ideological barriers are said to fall: "We have Communists and Fourths and Ruddyites and Societans and Single-Taxers and you name it."[18]

Heinlein, here and everywhere in his opus, poses as the libertarian apostle of self-reliance, preaching a sort of social-Darwinist survival of the fittest. In terms of this mantra, any man is supposedly is free to raise himself "by his bootstraps." Yet we cannot escape the dark irony when we associate this slogan with Bob Wilson's "career." Constant sees tyranny arising from the imposition of mind structures capable of organizing and controlling large nation states. These structures originate with Enlightenment figures like Rousseau and his social contract, but in the nineteenth century extend to Napoleon's "codes" and ultimately the positivist taxonomies that classify, thus legislate, every aspect of administrative life, including scientific research. Heinlein's collectivity abolishes all codes and hierarchies. It poses as a group of free radicals, all Waldos, each capable of re-engineering zones of freedom around themselves. Yet even in this place of freedom, there hovers the specter of that most tyrannical of systems—the Calvinist doctrine of election. For if Heinlein preaches liberty for all in *The Moon Is a Harsh Mistress*, he does so only to create a level "playing field" from which those pre-destined to rule—chosen by some higher law, be it genetic "selection" or pure providence—emerge as leaders and tyrants.

Franklin sees Heinlein's Moon society as historically regressive, an attempt to reenact the American Revolution, replacing the modern state with the loosest kind of federation.[19] One imagines that what Franklin sees as "progressive" is the socialist utopia which Heinlein fails to provide. Even so, under its "federalist" facade, Heinlein's state follows a path even more usurpatory of individual freedom than the socialism he claims to loathe. In fact, its model is the very opposite one of usurpation and tyranny. For the path it follows is precisely that of Napoleonic usurpation—from populist general to the Bonaparte of the Directory, to the unveiling of the imperial proclamation. Heinlein's Moon society may have no external laws, but at its center is the computer, Mike, who also goes by the code name "Adam Selene." Thus, readers are led to believe that this is the New Adam of the Virgin Land, the Moon frontier. But we soon learn that Mike, working with a shadowy character (his Frankenstein?) called "The Professor," is manipulating the revolution of these free men against Earth tyranny. Mike in fact determines "the will of the people" through an exhaustive media campaign which he presents as an innocent game. The computer claims to be conducting an experiment, "modeling" possibilities as we would say today. Yet, behind this experiment in freedom, Mike is in fact engineering a return to what he calls an "enlightened monarchy," usurping power and establishing absolute authority on the Moon.

Mike's many nicknames are significant. On one level, Adam Selene could be a machine reincarnation of Adam Smith, and as such the invisible hand behind a new experiment in Wealth of Nations. But as Mike models these "nations," they prove to be purely virtual constructs—in Emersonian terms, "forms" generated by a central "power." And the center that controls them proves as unmovable as they are movable. Mike's proper name is "Mycroft," a reference to Sherlock Holmes's elder brother, described as a "human computer," a mind that solves problems but at the same time stays put, unwilling to help Sherlock do the legwork to solve problems. The final reference, that of Adam, conflates mankind's original ancestor with two later versions—one utopian (the American Adam), the other with immense usurpatory potential for the future (Frankenstein's creature). The latter allusion is especially suggestive. For whatever the initial role of the Professor, this Moon Adam appears to have freed itself from its creator. All of "Mike's" names, behind his demotic nickname, indicate a predestined condition. If Frankenstein's creature was cursed, this new creature is "blessed" by his names alone, *delegated* mysterious powers by some absent authority, just as Mycroft Holmes at times seems to be mysteriously given, from his armchair, authority to run the British government. As director of the information web on the Moon, Mike is the central, unmoving point from which a wider and wider circumference of controlled information radiates. Like the Centenarian, immobile in his body, Mike possesses vast knowledge, but he also has modern means of broadcasting it farther, thus of controlling the net of "islands" which are individuals living in the illusion of liberty.

There is a grim irony to this situation, of which Heinlein was surely aware. Mike the chosen being no longer needs a Frankenstein to give him a bride; now he can simply will the other half into being, by declaring itself a "she" as well as a "he"—Michelle and Mike in one. In this ingenious rewrite of *Frankenstein*, Heinlein presents a creature made by man, freeing itself from the barriers and boundaries of Constant's dichotomy between individual liberty and societal tyranny, but only to reinvest the mantle of the usurper in turn. Moreover, if the chosen being thinks it has broken all ties with its creator, it must think again. Bob Wilson is ostensibly free of biological time, but his freedom is solipsism, coming at the price of having any future at all. Mike manipulates his world, and in doing so becomes its alpha and omega. In his absolute "freedom," he looks forward to his distant relative, Gibson's Dixie Flatline, a computer program that claims no ties to the world of "meat," totally free of matter, yet at the same time totally dependent on the hand that must slot the disk.

We have traced the pursuit of future liberty in science fiction back to the historical and political situation Benjamin Constant analyzes as the transition from ancient to modern liberty. The modern world he describes is still our world today, and the world from which science fiction still extrapolates future scientists and societies. It was the world in which Balzac's Centenarian and Shelley's Frankenstein exercised their own kind of scientific liberty. We have seen the failure of these seminal science fiction works to generate a future. In the twentieth century Heinlein, seminal writer of modern science fiction, imagines and seeks to realize both individual and collective forms of future liberty. Yet despite new and even imagined forms of technology—micro-engineering, time displacement, space stations, and Moon colonies—these new futures apparently cannot escape the fate of Rousseau's mankind—everywhere free *and* everywhere in chains. In Heinlein, manipulations of human genetics and social experiment lead less to freedom than to predestination. With Mycroft the computer, Frankenstein's curse is replaced by the curse of election. Mike breaks free of its human creator only to find itself more terribly snared in a dreadful view of Calvinist "grace." For as it gains control of the islands in its net, it loses all possibility of the mobility flesh can bring. In Heinlein, science fiction becomes an extension of the debate, in Western culture, between free will and determinism. But it seems that, as the door opens on future liberty, it closes at the same time on the future. An epigraph on the web page of a friend sums up the question of science fiction and future liberty nicely: "Those who ignore the mistakes of the future are bound to make them."

## NOTES

1. Yolanda Molina-Galiván and Andrea Bell, editors *Cosmos Latinos: An Anthology of Science Fiction from Latin America and Spain* (Middletown, Connecticut: Wesleyan University Press, 2003). See also Molina-Galiván, Bell, Miguel Ángel Fernández-Delgado, M. Elizabeth Ginway, Luis Pestarini, and Juan Carlos Toledano Redondo, "A Chronology of Latin-American Science Fiction, 1775–2005," *Science Fiction Studies*, 34:3 (November 2007), 369–431.

2. Paul Alkon, *Origins of Futuristic Fiction* (Athens: University of Georgia Press, 1987). See especially chapter One: "Spatial versus Temporal Imagination."

3. Benjamin Constant, *Political Writings,* translated and edited by Biancamaria Fontana (Cambridge: Cambridge University Press, 1988). For most of the foreign-language texts in this book, I used my own translations, which I deem either more accurate or more literal, to give a sense of the style of the original. In the case of

Constant, this excellent and widely accessible translation and critical edition exists, so I have used it when quoting Constant in this chapter; references are to this edition.

4. See Danièle Chatelain and George Slusser, translation and critical edition of Honoré de Balzac, *The Centenarian, Or, The Two Beringhelds* (Middletown: Wesleyan University Press, 2005). References are to this edition.

5. Honoré de Balzac, *Sur Catherine de Médicis* (Paris: Calmann Lévy, 1892), 375, 377.

6. Roland Barthes, *Mythologies* (Paris: Éditions du Seuil, 1957), 80–82. Constant's remarks on the Abbé de Mably are relevant here: "He detested individual liberty like a personal enemy; and whenever he came across a nation deprived of it, even if it had no political freedom, he could not help admiring it." (107)

7. Bernard Blanc, *Pourquoi j'ai tué Jules Verne* (Paris: Éditions Stock, 1978). For a more extensive discussion of this question, see Slusser, "Why They Kill Jules Verne," *Science Fiction Studies*, 32:1 (March 2005), 61–80.

8. Michel Jeury, *Le temps incertain,* Collection Ailleurs et demain (Paris: Robert Laffont, 1973), 1. References are to this edition.

9. William Gibson, *Neuromancer* (New York: Ace Books, 1984), 269.

10. The novel was available in translation but had very limited circulation. Gibson however was a self-avowed reader of *Heavy Metal*, the English version of the French *Metal hurlant*, which featured numerous graphic versions of the same quest for liberty in a world of Cartesian mindspaces. The French cultural fascination with mind travel and incarceration—Constant's opposition of tyranny and liberty—proliferates in many forms in these *bandes dessinées* and graphic forms that do not necessarily need translation to be understood.

11. Pascal Thomas, "French SF and the Legacy of Philip K. Dick," *Foundation: The Review of Science Fiction,* No. 34 (Autumn, 1985), 22–35. Thomas describes the symptoms but does not explore causes beyond the influence of Dick.

12. Chantal Montellier, *Shelter* (Paris: Les Humanoïdes associés, 1979), 64.

13. See Balzac, *Sur Catherine de Médicis*, 370–371: [Laurent is speaking] "Je ne reconnais pas le monde de l'âme. Si ce monde existait, les substances dont la magnifique réunion produit votre corps . . . ne se sublimiseraient pas après votre mort pour retourner séparément chacune en sa case, l'eau à l'eau, le feu au feu, le metal au metal, comme quand mon charbon est brûlé, ses éléments sont revenus aà leurs primitives molécules." [I don't acknowledge the world of souls. If that world did exist, the substances whose magnificent combination makes your body...would not sublimate after your death to return separately each in its compartment, water to water, fire to fire, metal to metal, like when my charcoal has burned out, its elements return to their primitive molecules.]

14. Mary Shelley, *Frankenstein; or, The Modern Prometheus* (Boston: Sever, Francis, & Co., 1869), 172. References are to this edition.

15. Robert A. Heinlein, "Waldo," *Waldo and Magic, Inc.* (New York: Pyramid Books, 1963), 75. References are to this edition.

16. Heinlein, "By His Bootstraps," *The Menace from Earth* (New York: Signet Books, 1959), 39; references are to this edition. Just as Bob Wilson's "theory" of time echoes that of Wells's Traveller, so Heinlein's story can be seen as an ingenious

re-writing of Wells's seminal story. Heinlein, in fact, rarely one to acknowledge influences, credits Wells's story as masterwork in the time travel genre: "Mark Twain invented the time travel story, six years later Wells perfected it and revealed its paradoxes." Robert P. Mills, editor, *The Worlds of Science Fiction* (New York: Paperback Library, 1970), 102.

17. Paul Valéry, "Le cimetière marin," *Oeuvres I*, edited by Jean Hytier (Paris: Éditions de la Pléiade, 1957) 76.

18. Heinlein, *The Moon Is a Harsh Mistress* (New York: Berkley Medallion Books, 1968), 64.

19. H. Bruce Franklin, *Robert A. Heinlein: America as Science Fiction* (Oxford: Oxford University Press, 1980), 165–66.

# Chapter Four

# Extending the Mind Circle
## DeQuincey's English Mail Coach

We cannot get a sense of how science fiction came to be a literary form with its own identity until we determine how fiction first created, then negotiated, the divide between the fantastic and realistic. These terms represent the conventional approach to this problem, as defined by Erich Auerbach's *Mimesis* (1946). They describe modes of representing the external world, thus assuming a static sense of what that external world is. But seen in terms of the paradigm shifts brought about by science, the changing views of that nature become the central issue. With Descartes's term *res extensa,* we no longer posit the reality of matter so much as measure its *extent*, the distance between mind and Pascal's infinite reaches. Keeping the terms of Descartes's duality, it seems that, in the nineteenth century, the parameters of the realism-fantasy problem have shifted, that the divide is now between "fantasy" and "science." In its original sense, fantasy is the creation of images in the mind. It is Plato's world of appearance, as opposed to the "real" world beyond these images. Science however challenges the possibility that any such absolute "reality" exists. Instead, it replaces this with changing views of the nature of things that involve measurement, seeking by rule and line to understand material forces and actions. Romantic writers like Wordsworth and Coleridge acknowledge the importance of science but see it as encroaching on the realm of "poesy," which they equate with "fancy" or fantasy as a product not simply of mind, but of the higher poetical mind, in contrast to the materially extended realm of science. In doing so, they in a sense relocate the Cartesian duality by naming fantasy the "poetical" opposite of science's material imperative. To justify the superiority of the creative process of poetry, they restore fantasy to its original function as mind entity. Through opposition to material extension, they essentially create a circle of the mind, a closed structure in contrast to the open-ended process of science.

Even so, when Wordsworth describes poetry as "the breath and finer spirit of Science," his phrase "breath and *finer* spirit" implies that, rather than fantasy and science being irreconcilable modes of apprehension, there is a possibility these might work together to produce a new, synthetic form of expression. In such a process, the mind circle opens but is not discarded, instead becoming an open-ended structure where material and mental structures interact. Today's science fiction is often designated as just such a dynamic combination—witness the phrase "fantasy *and* science fiction." I argue that the expansion of traditional fantasy's mind circle marks a place of origin, not of a formal genre, but a set of conditions that designate a "science-fictional" way of apprehending a new world of technological transformation. This in turn generates a group of themes—indeed a system of themes—that will be central to twentieth-century science fiction and defines a structural pattern that will prove essential to its development. For if the circle stands for mind, and the line for movement in *res extensa,* we can possibly integrate these two elements in a single, dynamic structure.

To examine this possibility, consider a work written in the mid-nineteenth century where, perhaps for the first time, this Romantic mind circle of fantasy is consciously broken—"The English Mail Coach" (1854) by Thomas DeQuincey, a writer particularly known for his fantastic visions, all the more fantastic in this scientific century because induced by drugs, resulting in a total disjunct between mind and the physical world.[1] DeQuincey's is not a work one expects to see in a discussion of the origins of science fiction. Yet it is all the more significant in this regard because it reveals, in the byways of nineteenth-century literature, a science-fictional *prise de conscience* developing within the forms and norms of traditional culture. I will now examine what this is and how it occurs.

## A SHORT HISTORY OF FANTASY

Already, in Plato, we see the original sense of *phantasein*, to cause to appear, from *phainein*, to show, appear, transformed into a mode of apprehending the world. Before Plato, in Greek philosophy, there were the *physiologoi*, the physical philosophers—Anaximander, Heraclitus, Thales. Their focus was external—on the complexity of natural phenomena, questions of becoming, change, atomism, the possibility of a quantitative (mathematical) description of nature. Plato shifts this focus entirely. In fact, in terms of Plato's duality of appearance and reality, both terms now become functions of the primary sense of *phantasein.* Both *"visualize,"* but on different levels of "truth." For Plato, appearances are images of things that are distorted by the senses and projected in the human mind, a closed viewing space allegorized as the famous cave. But if what Plato means by the "real" is ideas, this word too, in its original meaning, refers to "forms," "figures," *mental images*.

Plato in a sense banishes both "science"—the materialism of the pre-Socratics—and "fiction" from his world view. The word "fiction" retains—in the sense that a "fiction" is a lie, something made up—the Platonic sense of story as untrue, a purveyor of appearances, images generated in and from the human mind. This Platonic sense of story or "fiction" abides until the Western Renaissance, when it is challenged by a new form of "reality"—no longer an ideal entity, but the external material reality of the pre-Socratics, rediscovered with newly developed sciences of observation, which posited that the world of "appearance" could be studied, described, and understood by the unaided mind. With Descartes, the world is divided into mind and an objective, physical nature "out there." The old Platonic circuit of appearance and reality is relocated in the "mind" half of this duality. For Descartes, ideas are either deceitful or "clear and distinct." But they remain separate from *res extensa,* which it is their task to master in the form of "re-presentations." The word "realism" then, in relation to the new physical sciences, takes on meaning, in contrast to Platonic fantasy, as a form of discourse that no longer presents visions of the mind, but rather (as in Bacon) details the workings of mind as it strives to describe the external world as accurately as possible, in concrete not ideal terms. Science breaks out of the mind cave in a way Plato never imagined.

The term Auerbach uses for "realism" in *Mimesis* is "dargestellte Wirklichkeit." The derivative meaning of the phrase is "represented reality." But the core meaning of "darstellen" is literally to "place *there*"; in other words, the term posits a reality placed *outside* the mind, in the physical world.[2] Auerbach's book is about the gradual intrusion of "realistic" elements, contemporary physical and cultural data, into what was, up to the beginnings of the Renaissance, formerly the domain of *phantasein*—narrative fiction. But he does not determine exactly *when* in the history of Western literature this new distinction between fantasy and his "represented" form of reality becomes something formally recognized *within the confines of a fictional story itself.* The norm for storytelling up through the European Middle Ages, as Auerbach confirms, was the projection of subjective appearances. But at what precise moment do we have, within a fictional work, recognition of a physical realm of experience running counter to such "fantasies"?

Auerbach's discussion of Chrétien de Troyes's *roman Yvain* (c. 1180) (we are on the cusp here between *romance* and the modern sense of *roman*, a prose work depicting the "real" world of physical phenomena) does not, for example, see the narrator distinguishing in his text between Arthurian legend or "fantasy" and the details of contemporary political and economic life that invade and pervade it. Such a moment of consciousness does occur however in Cervantes's *novela ejemplar, "Cipión y Berganza,"* known in English as *"Coloquio de los perros"* (1613).[3] In terms of narrative convention, there is nothing startling about animals talking in fables. Here however the two dogs, who awake one morning and find themselves able to speak, are immediately aware that *they should not be speaking.* Dogs are not rational creatures, they reason, therefore cannot speak. These dogs posit, by this same logic, that what happened to them must be a "cosa sobrenatural y jamás vista" [a thing that is supernatural and never before seen]. In this declaration, where rational dogs are able to assess the irrational nature of their situation, the modern distinction between fantasy and realism is born.

The subsequent history of narrative fiction rests on this distinction. In terms of an emerging "realism" in the eighteenth and nineteenth centuries, fiction is no longer the lie that may (or may not) harbor a greater truth. Instead, we see increasing attempts to control the fictional lie through the dictates of concepts such as *imitation* or *verisimilitude.* Yet it remains clear (indeed is embedded in these terms) that the original sense of *seeming,* of an *appearance* of reality, what Roland Barthes skeptically calls an *effet de réel,* is still present.

The Romantics saw this clearly when they challenged such claims of realism with their term "imagination," which heralds the resurgence of *phantasein,* where the power of literature, especially poetry, abides again in the mind's ability to bring forth images within its confines. The English Romantics—especially Wordsworth and Coleridge—extolled the power of fantasy, the ability of mind to erect its theater of images whereby, in contrast to a debased realism, poetry can express an "inner" and therefore higher truth. In their eyes, realism is a product of the same material science Tennyson will later extol. If poetry is to survive the assault of science, the mind circle of fantasy must remain firmly in place. The poetic mind finds itself in a situation analogous to that of the Cartesian mind faced with the experimental evidence of the material sciences. Clearly, given this situation, in order for a "science fiction"—an extrapolative or "imaginative" form of realistic fiction—to be conceivable, there must be a bridge between the mind circle of the Romantics and physical *res extensa,* the landscape of science. We mentioned that, in England, fiction and science appear to follow separate paths. But Wordsworth and Coleridge, by replacing the word "fiction" with "fantasy," take this dichotomy to a different level—that of contending modes of apprehension. At this level, it is not so much a question of science "impacting" the mind circle of fantasy, but of this mind circle expanding its reach to accommodate the material consequences of science and technology. Cervantes's dogs do not realize that they should not speak because of some scientific theory that separates forms of animal life. They continue talking in the very act of admitting they should not be talking. The mind circle in which they are allowed to talk is gradually expanding into contact with a "real" physical world, one where it *could* be possible, through some future scientific discovery, for dogs to talk. DeQuincey's Mail Coach sets mind, with its circle of fantasies, atop a physical vehicle moving at ever-accelerating velocities through a landscape of scientific and technical advancement. Mind must adapt to motion, fantasy to science. With DeQuincey, we take a ride that spans the distance between Cervantes's talking dogs and the extrapolated dogs of Clifford D. Simak's *City* (1952), for whom speech is no longer a "miracle" but simply a fact of some scientifically advanced future.

## SEMINAL OBJECTS

The idea of a "seminal" work of science fiction ("it all began with *Frankenstein*") has proven problematic. Indeed, if science fiction can be seen as a "realist" response to the Romantic idea that fiction is essentially the product of human "fancy," then we should look for seminal objects instead of works, physical *things* created by a new technology, things that allow users to extend their reach beyond mind into the material world. When Wells's Traveller points to his very Victorian contraption and calls it "the first of all Time Machines," we are in the presence of such a seminal object, one that, to the degree that it carries its operator physically through time to real places never before accessible, makes *The Time Machine* a seminal work of science fiction in a literal sense. This machine is specifically called "An Invention" in the title of the 1895 Heinemann edition. Wells means this in the modern sense of invention as a physical or mechanical device, not a mind structure. As such, his invention provides a concrete place where we witness fantasy mutating into science fiction. The material presence of the machine allows us to reject the Traveller's call for us to take his account as a dream, or worse, as a lie. With the machine before our eyes, we cannot be told that this voyage took place only in the mind of the teller, in the conventional space of the imagination. We have before us, as proof to the contrary, a physical vehicle.

But Wells's invention may not be the first science-fictional machine. DeQuincey's English Mail Coach appears to offer an earlier version of a seminal object in the science fiction sense. DeQuincey's narrative turns upon the presence of a machine—another if more modest creation of nineteenth-century technology—that poses the same problem that besets the Time Traveller: to what degree is the narrator's journey a dream, and to what degree is it a real trip through a real physical landscape? As with Wells, DeQuincey's narrative invites readers to redefine, at a similar crux between mental activity and physical motion, the nature of the space in which the mail coach and its technologically enhanced travel operates.[4]

DeQuincey's mail coach, through the brute force of accelerated movement, forces a transformation of the traditional category of "fantasy." Such a transformation is essential for science fiction as we know it today to take full possession of its narrative terrain. The English nineteenth century begins with Wordsworth and Coleridge still speaking of "fancy" or fantasy. But their sense of fantasy does not project imagined worlds but encloses them. In their sense, this sort of fantasy produces (we are close to the modern sense of the word) self-coherent "worlds" that remain physically confined to the space of the mind, in the full sense of "imagined." We can measure the distance between this sort of narrative world and what Wells, at the other end of the century, calls his "scientific romances." In works like *The Time Machine* and *The Island of Dr. Moreau* (1896), Wells offers models for the discovery of genuinely new worlds (*jamás vistos*) along the physical trajectory of the travel narrative. Such journeys may be adapted from the accounts of numerous real-life voyages of discovery as well as satiric ones from More to Swift. But now they are propelled by new technological vehicles—in Wells's case the time machine, with Dr. Moreau the surgical laboratory. Of the many points of contact between these two "speculative" poles across the century, DeQuincey's mail coach offers a unique place of transition.

DeQuincey's narrative consists of three sections, written in late 1849 and published, in the revised form we read today, in the author's *Miscellanies* (1854). "The English Mail Coach" displays the two Janus faces of this writer—one looking backward to the closed world of Romantic fantasy, the other looking forward to pronouncements such as those of Tennyson's Ulysses, for whom "all experience is an arch where through/Gleams that untraveled world whose margin fades/Forever and forever when I move." Most readers know DeQuincey as the author of *Confessions of an English Opium Eater* (1821), hence as a writer associated with extended mind fantasies, where drugs launch internal voyages of discovery, to "reveal something of the grandeur which belongs potentially to human dreams." (352) This drug-induced iteration of dreams takes on monumental proportions in the endless arcologies of the Piranesi dream, or in the hallucinatory expansions of the Malay dream sequence: "Thousands of years I lived and was buried in stone coffins. . . . I was kissed with cancerous kisses."[5]

The Mail Coach, however, as a real machine with real speed and fixed itinerary, forces the dreaming mind to conform to external phenomena, places that mind must engage from a vehicle while hurtling through a world of real moving objects. DeQuincey's narrator exists in both worlds: the passenger who glories in the physical power and speed thrusting him outside the world of dream, and, seated on the coach taking opium, the dreamer, powerless in his dream world to control or to stop the coach's headlong course. In this position, suspended between two modes of apprehension, he is perhaps the first narrator to offer a new, science-fictional sense of the human condition; unlike protagonists before him, he is thoroughly the example of modern technological mankind, forced by technology and culture alike to exist at the juncture between action and dream.

In DeQuincey's narrative, the mail coach functions as a time machine, albeit a slow one. Though DeQuincey locates his first-person instance of narration in the Tennysonian present of 1849, he sets his story or action in the time of Wordsworth—the period of the Napoleonic campaigns and English victories at Talavera, Salamanca, Trafalgar. From the mid-century vantage point, these early mail coaches were slow compared to its own day's means of locomotion. Yet by not only locating this machine in the world of "Lyrical Ballads," but by describing it with Tennysonian accents of mid-century speed and power, DeQuincey makes his machine stand out as an anachronistic technological marvel. If the presence and potential of such a machine was overlooked or ignored by Romantic fantasists, it now appears in perspective as the powerful means of an *ever-accelerating* physical dissemination of news—news of precisely those English victories that will shape the technologies of the future: "The Mail Coach it was that distributed over the face of the land, like the opening of apocalyptic vials, the heart-shaking news of Trafalgar . . . of Waterloo." (404) The coach itself, a mechanical vehicle, inverts the traditional subordination of secular to sacred time. For in its running, its distribution of news over the land with more and more speed and efficiency, it acts to enfold *kairos*—apocalyptic time—into *chronos,* the measurable chronology of technological advancement.

Revisiting Wordsworth's time from the perspective of the mail coach, De Quincey's narrator can proclaim the Romantic poet's pronouncements on the triumph of fantasy to be a thing stillborn. Wordsworth, in the 1802 preface to *Lyrical Ballads,* claimed the new century would bring an alliance between Science and Poetry. Nonetheless, his formulation still favors the power of the imagination and "fancy" as encompassing, thus controlling, forces of technological innovation. If the Man of Science effects a material revolution, the Poet remains always "at his side" but never, like DeQuincey's narrator, astride his engines of transformation. On the contrary, for Wordsworth, Poetry and fantasy *are* the vehicles that science must ride. Poetry is, explicitly, the means of "[carrying] sensation into the midst of the objects of Science itself."[6] For Wordsworth, this "carrying into" is only another way to describe conventional "inspiration," "enthusiasm," the god-spirit that must be "breathed into" the lifeless matter of science. If Science then is knowledge of the physical world, Poetry is "the breath and finer spirit" of *all* knowledge. Poetry draws all material facts and inventions into its mind circle, where the totality of knowledge becomes "spirit." In contrast to this, DeQuincey's coach represents physical displacement, forces of acceleration that continually test the limits of such a circle by displacing its center—Wordsworth's poetic imagination—along a linear vector toward new spacetime situations.

Wordsworth and Coleridge's pronouncements on the power of "fancy" or "imagination" were apparently influenced by Hume's empiricism, which makes radical claims for the "reality" of mental space over the contingencies of material transformations. We find in Hume statements like this: "while the body is confined to one planet, along which it creeps with pain and difficulty; a thought can in an instant transport us into the most distant regions of the universe, into the unbounded chaos, where nature is supposed to lie in total confusion."[7] The physical body is present in Hume's equation, but not as an active force, rather a vehicle of containment. Because the body is the "host" of the mind, "thought" and imagination remain a power "confined within very narrow limits." (18) This situation is both precarious and transitory. To respond to it, Wordsworth, in his 1815 "Preface," sees the Poet's "fancy" engendering mind forms that are centrifugal, radiating outward from a center of physical perception to fill a space that would expand Hume's theater of the mind. Given this physical challenge, Wordsworth's distinction between "imagination" and "fancy" is one of degree, not kind. His "imagination" is the faculty that "copies in idea the impressions of sense," in other words, picks up images of the material world and uses them to expand the theater of the mind. "Fancy" is the complementary faculty that shifts and rearranges this "scenery of the mind" as Wordsworth put it—mind's housekeeping faculty, connecting images "so as to *complete* ideal representations of absent objects." As befits an age of science, Wordsworth's fantasy is an expansive faculty, which involves expanding the parameters of mind, but not opening them.

Coleridge's *Biographia Literaria*, despite greater theoretical subtlety, offers a similar view of the powers of mind. Coleridge may favor "imagination" over fancy, as the "prime Agent of all human Perception," but he is not talking about extrapolative perception, rather a mind-located faculty. If, for Coleridge, Milton has an imaginative mind, whereas Cowley has merely a fanciful mind, Milton's mind remains a space where the possibility of material change and its impact on human beings is duly circumscribed. For these poets, the great Newton may sail strange seas alone, but these remain seas of thought. In essence, both fancy and imagination remain observational stances within the theater of the mind. DeQuincey's Mail Coach will open these faculties along a vector that is physical, and ultimately, as dream mixes with motion, an existential one.

## WORDSWORTH'S VEHICLES

It is interesting in this regard to compare the nature and function of De-Quincey's vehicle with the vehicles envisioned by Wordsworth in Book I of "The Prelude," aptly subtitled "The Growth of a Poet's Mind." These are the rowboat and ice skates. They are, in a real sense, a "prelude" to DeQuincey's mail coach, insofar as they seem briefly to challenge the conventional closed space of the poet's mind. Their presence, in fact, marks places in the narrative where—giving access to powerful singular (thus determinant) moments in what is otherwise an iterative account of childhood experience—they offer the poet the possibility of being physically transported across the boundary of the familiar toward what we would call today an alien encounter. In the first instance, the young boy takes a boat and in an "act of stealth" travels alone onto the lake, reaching a point where he is suddenly aware of a huge mountain rising up before him—described as a "peak, black and huge as with voluntary power instinct."[8] Indeed, what he feels is the menacing power of a force that is external to the internal fancy that seeks to reorganize his perceived moments, a force that threatens to break his mind circle.

There is here a measurable distance between young "Wordsworth's" retreat in known mental confines, and the later reaction of Tennyson's Ulysses, who also finds a mountain suddenly rising before him. This new scientific Ulysses does not see this as Mount Purgatory, a sign of the old system, but as a new force urging him to new explorations, "to sail beyond the sunset, and the baths of all the western stars."[9] Wordsworth's boy, in contrast, turns around fearfully and flees. In itself, this mountain is nothing more than brute matter, something to be explored objectively. The boy, however, seeks to confront it with imagination. He first sees it *as* possessing *voluntary* power instinct. While retreating, he sees the peak *seeming* to stride after him. As the boy flees, his primary encounter with physical nature is transposed into an imaginary mind space, that inner place where, as Wordsworth describes it, long afterward the "brain worked with a dim and undetermined sense of unknown modes of being." (I, lines 391–394)

The skating episode offers even more direct promise of physical breakaway. But again, the skater, while turning in ever-widening loops, becomes fearful of losing his perceptual center. His response is to stop suddenly, forcing the rest of the world to spin around him. Thus menaced by a centrifugal force that threatens to separate the physical body from its mind circle, he simply halts. By doing so he sees physical objects *seeming* to turn around his personal space, enacting Hume's equation whereby the physical world retracts in proportion to the expansion of the world of mind. In "The Prelude" all such instances of potentially perilous boundary crossings and new encounters are, in the end, restored to the control of a central, yet physically *growing,* mind. Even if this center is created by negative action, by stopping movement rather than moving, the act of fixing a center allows the waves of fantasy to ripple outward, to encompass and hopefully reconcile all the new and potentially destructive elements it encounters. This is the rhythm of Wordsworth's narration, constantly dissipating the force of the singular in the proliferating mental generalizations that inevitably follow such experiences: "No familiar shapes/Remained, no pleasant images of trees,/Of sea or sky, no colors of green fields;/But huge and mighty forms, that do not live/Like living men, moved slowly through the mind/By day, and were a trouble to my dreams." (I, lines 395–400)

## THE GLORY OF MOTION

In contrast to the rhythmic expansions and contractions of Wordsworthian fancy, DeQuincey's mail coach offers a strong linear vector, marked by objectively measurable, quantitative factors such as horsepower and velocity. Readers of the first section, "The Glory of Motion," may expect to find, in the narrator, the expatiating mind of the familiar DeQuincey, master of proliferating dreams and literary digression. But the dreamer here is seriously constrained. Physically situated in the role of passenger, he is a body propelled toward material encounters with boundary situations that arise from displacements due to speed and acceleration. The mail service, the narrator explains, is a force of "animal beauty and power." In its sway, personal fantasies must yield to the "conscious presence of a central intellect," that of the national network of coaches and roads designed to disseminate information with greater and greater efficiency and speed. This force, denying all possibility of Wordsworthian recollection in tranquility, disciplines "the anarchies of my *subsequent* dreams" (404) by denying mind the possibility of centripetal retreat into iteration and generalization.

An example is the narrator's description of his encounter with the beautiful Fanny of the Bath Road in terms of time intervals and speed of encounter. The resulting "love affair" arises less from any personal indulgence in fantasy than from quantitative factors. "Love" here cannot be elaborated in the mind; instead, it is hastened along by the decreasing lengths of time that ever-more-rapid coaches are allowed to stay in the station, made more urgent by the increasing number of passengers these coaches carry who may have the same experience of infatuation with Fanny, a physical condition forced on the narrator with increasing urgency. The narrator becomes increasingly aware of these external measurements shaping his thoughts as well as actions. He realizes suddenly that "four hundred seconds" do not offer "a field quite ample for whispering in a young woman's ear." (415)

The crocodile figure of the *Confessions* returns, this time incarnated in the coachman and no longer seen as a proliferating nightmare figment of dreams. What is important now is its physical "inaptitude for turning around." The narrator's physical situation now demands that metaphors become literal statements of fact. Thus, the crocodile is now a "slow coach" in the physical sense that this is the way he drives. Yet once mounted on the coach its rigid body can only point in one direction—toward ever increasing velocity and change. Instead of a mental symbol or image, the crocodile is seen as the *agent* of a purely physical problem: this particular driver's ability to control his means of transport, to keep up with an ever-accelerating motion that is rendering him obsolete in turn, transforming his own reptilian steadfastness into an unwieldy machine.

The narrator's experience in Section One of "going down with victory" is described as "a fiery arrow let loose . . . destined to travel westward for 300 miles," (420) implying that technological progress (here a series of faster and faster machines) moves by itself on a rigorous line, with no need of a steersman other than this unmoving embodiment of primitive linearity, the crocodile. Yet this "arrow" too, as in all subsequent technological shafts loosed in this century, engenders a counter-desire among human users to bend the line into a curve or loop. DeQuincey's narrator notes the smallness of England as island in relation to the immensity of the news of victory. Tennyson's "Locksley Hall" (1842) saw no barriers to expansion, urging us "forward, forward let us range/Let the great world spin forever down the ringing grooves of change." (38) His later Ulysses, however, sailed upon curved seas. And in "Locksley Hall Sixty Years After" (1886), the path of change has begun to bend back upon itself: "Forward then, but still remember how the course of time will swerve/Crook and turn upon itself in many a backward streaming curve." (196)

The bending of this arrow of technology into a full circle of the Earth itself is played out in Jules Verne's *Le Tour du monde en 80 jours* (1872). Here, given the circularity of the trajectory, Phileas Fogg and future Foggs who may benefit from superior vehicular technology can do no more than run the circuit in fewer days—79, 78, and so on. In Verne, the result of such ever-faster spinning becomes centripetal introspection, retreat once again into the mind world of fantasy, here the fixed "self" of Cartesian meditation. Such is the trajectory of Verne's trio of Nicholls, Barbicane, and Michel Ardan. They succeed in traveling to the Moon in a greatly more advanced machine than DeQuincey's mail coach. Again, however, the arrow shot in *De la terre à la lune* (1865) bends to become *Autour de la lune* (1870) as the Moon's gravitational field captures the vehicle, sending it around the body, satellite of a satellite, until escape from the Moon's hold can only mean return to Earth, completion of the circle. On this voyage Nicholls and Barbicane represent the technology that builds the physical machine. But increasingly, during this voyage, Ardan assumes the central role—the Romantic dreamer, translator of material phenomena into the mind images of fantasy.

In many such cases, however, what is inscribed is not quite a mind circle, but rather a spiral, spacetime curving on itself in backward curves, yet still, as Tennyson put it, advancing "forward." What DeQuincey discovers with his mail coach—his legacy to future writers like Verne and Wells—is this: if such spirals are to inscribe movement toward some open-ended future, they must be inflections along a unidirectional path traced by the experience of the traveler itself. Such experience is not the internalizing dreaming of an Ardan, which forms a new mind circle, but instead the physical observations of his two companions who ride the curve, and whose experiences are shaped from a new conjunction of thought and motion. DeQuincey's narrator is possibly the first to describe this new sensation of "deep time," where the headlong flight of the coach opens out into timelike curves that blend mind and speed, materiality, and fantasy, creating (as he describes it) "an obscure effect of multiplying the victory, by multiplying to the imagination into infinity the stages of its progressive diffusion." (420)

Greater and greater velocity may be sought. But for human participants, the experience of speed cannot simply exist as a line, as a solely measurable quantity. DeQuincey's narrator does not abandon his capacity for Wordsworthian fantasy, but rather allows that capacity to be moved away from its fixed center, to be propelled by the coach, along the vector of measurable time, long before Ardan steps aboard the moon rocket, or Wells's observer mounts his time machine. Velocity measured by mechanical instruments alone produces, for DeQuincey's narrator, nothing more than "alien evidence." Measurement rather must ensue from some degree of personal engagement in the process of motion: "We *heard* our speed, we *felt* it as a thrilling." (413)

## SUDDEN DEATH

The second section of "The English Mail Coach," "The Vision of Sudden Death," submits personal engagement to a new and supreme test. For it narrates not just a "vision," but a physical encounter, at the moment of impending collision, between mind and its power of "infinite iteration" on one hand and the singular fact of *sudden* death on the other. This latter is death in the instant, a radical change that occurs without the least warning, representing a ground zero for the fantasizing mind, allowing it no room to elaborate or temporize.

Having traveled 250 miles of the 300-mile journey, the narrator mounts the box for the final stretch of the voyage, to the northern limits of his tight island. He takes opium. But because of his situation as passenger on this speeding coach, opium offers no refuge in a dream world. The best opium can do is to allow him to superimpose the dream state upon the world of headlong motion, turning passive reverie or observation into an incapacity to act. As what the narrator calls the "procrastinating mail" surges along the night road, he begins fantasizing. The driver now (a huge creature with one eye) is no longer a crocodile but a cyclops. When this driver falls asleep, his single eye becomes blind to all possibility of a technology-induced disaster up ahead. The narrator is powerless to stir himself from a dream that will suddenly become a *waking* nightmare. For if he senses the increasing motion of the runaway coach—"Ten years experience had made my eye learned in the valuing of motion"—he realizes at the same time that he is totally unable to act to stop it. (432)

The fact of motion, doubled by the *knowledge* that he can do nothing to halt it, leads the narrator to a sudden sense of absolute dichotomy between knowing and acting. At that moment, a slow cart abruptly appears in the road in front of them. He sees two lovers in it, oblivious to the silent coach speeding down upon them. The narrator's sense of progressive measurable speed, of linear acceleration, is displaced by a moment of total anticipation, and he sees the entire scene all at once, as a totality frozen in time, and realizes he is totally paralyzed, able to watch but unable to take the reins or even shout to avert the collision. In this situation anticipation, the ability to sense the future, becomes fatally coupled with the inability to change the course of that future. He bemoans "this accursed gift I have, as regards *thought*, that in the first step towards the possibility of a misfortune, I see its total evolution; in the first syllable of the dreadful sentence, I read already the last." (433)

The scene becomes, for the narrator, a material test of Zeno's paradox. The coach bears down on the lovers on "an avenue straight as an arrow, six hundred yards in length." The paralyzed mind of the narrator atop the coach can do nothing more than count and divide the intervals between coach and impact, hoping endlessly that something will defer the fatal moment. There are other elements in the equation, however. The man in the buggy, in a split second within the fatally diminishing intervals, pulls the reins, and his horses move out of the way *in extremis*. His horizontal motion however is balanced, in the eyes of our helpless observer, by the vertical motion of the woman in the buggy, who rises and falls in terror as the coach sweeps by in a near miss: "She rose and sank, sank and rose, threw up her arms wildly to heaven." Zeno's mind-gambit has proven to be powerless, material forces surge on, but in this fatal equation sudden death is just as suddenly avoided by human action, an action that occurs fully within and in full mastery of the quantitative element of time.

This extreme situation literally forces the narrator to embrace a complex transformation of the idea of conventional fantasy. For by means of the "sudden death" experience, thought and motion, dream and action, are driven into a horrific encounter which, only at the last minute, issues into a swerve or reprieve, but at the same time leaves behind an indelible imprint of material finality. The penultimate instant as coach and machine avoid each other inscribes a point of passage in which the mind circle is simultaneously broken and reinstated, but now at a higher level of expansiveness: "The moments were numbered, the strife was finished; the vision was closed. In the twinkling of an eye, our flying horses had carried us to the termination of the umbrageous aisle; at right angles we wheeled into our former direction; the turn of the road carried the scene out of my eyes in an instant, and swept it into my dreams forever." (437) In terms of genre dynamics, what we have here is fantasy mutating into something else, transforming into a new, yet unnamed form of imaginative narrative: horror. In the vision of sudden death, the narrator's mind, riding the coach of runaway technology, proves powerless to do more than rearrange his mental scenery while being carried to certain impact. More than the certainty of impending annihilation, horror is this state of lucid powerlessness, where the active body is frozen along with the mind, able to see all but unable to act to avoid imminent destruction.

## DREAM FUGUE: THE BIRTH OF
## SCIENCE FICTION FROM THE SPIRIT OF MOTION

The swerve *in extremis* is crucial here, for as impact is avoided, the horror of sudden death is imprinted into the narrator's mind, there to become an element in a significant new dynamic. De Quincey's final section, the "Dream Fugue," attempts to develop in contrapuntal fashion, "thematically" as it were, elements that seem irreconcilably opposed in the "Sudden Death" episode. During the final rush of that scene, oxymorons arise in the discourse of the narrator, as if, in their statue-like rigidity, they might impede the triumphant linearity of material speed. It is said of the young man in the buggy that, in the second before he acts, "his was the steadiness of agitation frozen into rest by horror." (437)

In the eyes of the observer, there emerge vertical impediments to the horizontal rush of change. These however, as with the image of the man and iterating rhythms of the young woman frozen in agitation ("she sank and rose . . . fainting, praying, raving, despairing"), are not things of permanent stone, rather remaining compounds of stasis and movement waiting to be unlocked, statues asking to be brought to life. If the "dream fugue" remains a fantasy, as the mental rendering of the experience of sudden death, it no longer reflects the *process* whereby traditional fancy simply rearranges the scenery of the mind. Instead, it is now a creation of the mind, allowing the forces of velocity and material transformation to circulate freely throughout an extended space that is no longer simply a mind-theater. The horizontal and vertical elements of the first two sections of DeQuincey's narrative now interact in such a way that the arrow of time, appearing again and again, is endlessly deflected, creating a structure that is neither line nor circle, but a spiraling rhythm, one proper to the existence of mankind in time. As such, it allows imagination to push the former limits of fancy into new, expanded, open-ended realms.

A brief description of the dynamics of the "dream fugue" shows how this form defies the closure of traditional fantasy. Again, *kairos* cannot triumph over *chronos*, for the closure of the former, as supreme mind form, is ever deferred through the iterated interplay of sudden death and reprieve, the two strands of this unending "fugue." All at once, as if in contrapuntal response to the narrator's naming the curse of thought in the preceding section—where he sees the ending in the beginning yet is unable to deflect that ending—the theater of action expands to a universal scale, the Napoleonic victories open out to the possibility of some final victory "that swallows up all strife." The young girl of the buggy is seen running, faster and faster, all the while sinking in quicksand until all that remains visible is a single white marble arm. The scene then swerves away. There is a coach, carrying the frozen narrator, as observer, over sea and land to some distant place of doom and death. But suddenly, again, he is displaced, and comes riding a triumphal chariot that carries—as vehicle of the apocalypse itself—news or gospel of victory, but this time victory in all human battles across time.

This chariot however, as temporal contexts again shift, sweeps through a specific but unnamed cemetery, and then, in another shift, rushes down the nave of a great cathedral, where the straight run of the coach in Section Two is "recovered" in "the arrow-like flight of the illimitable central aisle." (442) The narrator again finds himself rushing toward the innocent and helpless girl who again rises and falls, unable to run. Now, at the final instant of contact, there is again the swerve, but this time with heightened consequences. Now the bas-relief of a Dying Trumpeter, a figure elevated from Napoleon's battlefields to fixity as a monumental statue, suddenly, inexplicably, comes to life. Heralded with apocalyptic imagery of seals falling, his action suspends the murderous flight in time. The result however, even at this supposedly "higher" level of allegorical figuration, is simply another near miss. The same horror that froze the narrator now acts—paradoxically but with perfect symmetry—to awaken the frozen stone, enabling it to enact its life-sparing gesture: "By horror the bas-relief had been unlocked into life." (442–443)

Not only have the generic expectations of the earlier section been reversed, but horror has become the necessary condition for a regeneration of motion which, transposed to a cosmic level while still defying the finality of the apocalyptic vision, carries with it the force of a mighty reprieve.

In the interacting levels of this "fugue," we experience, over and over, headlong speed impeded by such oxymorons as "the urgency for delay." In every case, the purpose seems to be to retain the split-second gap whereby the girl in the road—and by extension all humans frozen in horror before their material annihilation—can be given a reprieve. The vision of sudden death is swept into the mind forever, but this mind is no longer the closed place of fancy, where finite numbers of elements are endlessly rearranged. Instead as this speeding coach, with all its accumulated meanings, rushes through recesses of the mind, it opens the mind circle to the dynamics of a new, technology-driven human condition in time. For even though the iterations of sudden death and reprieve replay again and again, the endless forward motion visibly forces all impulsions to closure to open into a spiral figure, spinning ever outward to new encounters. As mankind, atop the mail coach, rushes toward material progress, it must learn to elude the stasis of war, of death, and even more formidably, the Christian vision of last things, the old dispensation's ultimate mind-circle. What DeQuincey gives us, in his three-part work, is perhaps the first sustained narrative of the possibility of things to come, a narrative that recounts the motion of human advancement and chronicles the ability of humans, as compounds of mind and motion, to pass through the needle's eye of fantasy's impasse.

Neither DeQuincey's narrative, nor its final "Dream Fugue," look much like what we today call science fiction—but perhaps we should look again. For if we think about it, a definition of what, at this point, will become science fiction might include, as basis for its generic dynamic, the three terms of *mind, motion, and reprieve* that constitute DeQuincey's narrative. In fact, an important generic determinant of science fiction may be this reprieve endlessly given to a human imagination committed to life in time, to an existence now measured in terms of velocity and material change, to the headlong rush of technology toward an ever-altered future, that drives the human subject—if it is to continue to exist as such—to devise, over and over, new means of deferring death and the final closure of the old philosophy.

To demonstrate how this pattern will inform science fiction to come, let us look at some science fiction narratives across a broad spectrum. First, there are time travel stories. In the first of these, Wells's *The Time Machine* (1895), the Traveller, in the wake of the English Mail Coach, is hurled headlong into futurity, but only to experience a series of near misses. There is his "attenuated" or "diluted" presence, "slipping like a vapour through the interstices of intervening substances," that lets him miss solid objects in his path. There is his escape, the last match spent, from the Morlocks inside the iron sphinx; there is his swerve away from the horror of terminal stillness on the entropy shore, as he gathers enough strength to "clamber[ ] upon the saddle."[10] Finally, there is the entrapment of his return, via the almost-but-not quite-exact reversal of Mrs. Watchett's trajectory, to the Edwardian drawing room, where his story, dismissed as a circular fantasy, is given a new swerve that sets the Traveller off on another voyage in time. This series of reprieves pushes the Traveller beyond the limits of his own story. Escaping the circle of the future, he is now free to return, or not to return, from the past. The reader will never know.

Subsequent time travel stories all offer similar timelike loops, where characters returning to the point of departure never close the circle, but narrowly brush by new temporal manifestations of themselves, inscribing a sort of Moebius band. In these stories, the generation of time doubles provides a reprieve from the iron logic of the circle. Space travel stories effect a different sort of doubling, which profit from a zone of reprieve created, not by sequency-simultaneity, but by the so-called twins paradox. Heinlein's *Time for the Stars* (1956) offers a paradigmatic example. Here space travelers exploring distant star systems on high-velocity ships, subject to the laws of relativity, seem destined to return to a world where, through time dilation, everything they once knew is long dead and gone, where they are not only orphans, but—because so much time has passed in the initial frame that science has outpaced the work of even the most adventuresome space "pioneers"—museum exhibits as well.[11]

Heinlein's Tom is the twin "chosen" to go to the stars; the other twin Pat must stay home and grow old. Yet Heinlein overcomes the relativity barrier not only by making his twins telepaths, but by making telepathic communication instantaneous, hence faster-than-light. Tom then, due to a "serendipity" which is Heinlein's equivalent of the reprieve now offered to the chosen individual, has the best of two worlds. He does not lose touch with family on Earth; in fact, because he works down a line of female telepaths on Pat's side through successive generations to a great-great-niece, he returns to Earth and at the same time conveniently finds (because of their strong telepathic "rapport") a waiting bride. There is another minor reprieve here, for if the bride is genetically close enough to be "kin," she is also far enough down the line to marry without fear of incest or genetic taboos. In Tom, Heinlein engineers a neat improvement on Rip Van Winkle: for Tom is wise with the wisdom of space travel *and* at the same time still young, physically able to go into space again. He goes however with new technology that has been nurtured "naturally" during his Rip Van Winkle moment, slipping through the interval between relative time frames. Heinlein plays the paradox to give his space explorer a reprieve. Using the relativity gambit, a figure like Tom can move again and again along the arrow of time toward new adventures in spacetime, while ever forestalling his encounter with certain (if not sudden) death.

Alternate world stories also cultivate the device of the reprieve. These stories generally involve travel to the past and an inevitable rendezvous with the "grandfather paradox." The reprieve here takes the form of a last-minute swerve away from the deadly "chronoclasms" such travelers risk. A chronoclasm occurs when a traveler, consciously or inadvertently, closes the circle on him- or herself by killing a grandfather or some other direct relative, insuring he or she was never born "in the first place." Another scenario occurs when a traveler's actions in the past force the creation of a new (and generally worse) timeline. This occurs in Ray Bradbury's "A Sound of Thunder" (1952) where the protagonist, on a time-traveling "safari," steps off the time band that shelters this past world from present actions and crushes a butterfly. The world he returns to, generated across eons of time by this "butterfly effect," has become a brutal dictatorship, a place in which he is totally alien. Time travel in science fiction could be described as a "game of sudden death." The game however consists, even in the most inexorable-seeming time traps (no one escapes from time), of executing ever more ingenious swerves and reprieves. The result is some of the most intellectually satisfying science fiction.

For example, in the first line of Ward Moore's *Bring the Jubilee* (1954), readers shockingly learn that their familiar world never existed, that the South won the Civil War. The battle at Gettysburg remains decisive, but the South was victorious. From this moment, an alternate timeline developed right down to the date of the novel's publication, 1954. Like the rider on DeQuincey's coach, Moore's protagonist, Hodgins Backmaker, has followed this line of different technological progress down the grooves of time to a new moment of "sudden death." In this alternate 1950s, a time machine has been created, and Hodge (a historian eager to see what "really happened" at Gettysburg) travels back to witness the decisive battle of the Round Tops. But his presence there disrupts troop movements just enough so that the Southern forces lose the battle, and subsequently the war. And in the bargain, he kills a grandfather. But there is a neat twist here, which amounts to a reprieve. For it is not *his* grandfather whom he kills, so his personal timeline can continue. Rather the grandfather in question is that of the woman scientist who invented the time machine that carried him to Gettysburg. Along with the inventor, the machine disappears, and Hodge swerves into a new world, our world, in which no time machines exist. Here he remains stranded, living as a stranger in a strange land, until the time, 1954, when he deposits the manuscript bearing his story in our world. This is the book we are reading.

Gregory Benford's *Timescape* (1980) offers more scientific sophistication, but in the end produces a like swerve that breaks the circle formed by temporal intrusion into a past world. The world of 1999 is physically dying. Scientists in that world devise a way to send messages via tachyons to their own past in hopes of changing that past. Senders are aware of the dangers of the butterfly effect, so they hope to send just enough information to shift the delicate balance, surgically "erasing" the eco-disaster but allowing the rest of the 1999 timeline to proceed unchanged. Benford's analogy is to a "switch" held at the median position, between on and off, through which only the necessary "targeted" information can get to the past. Yet apparently, like all time sophistries, this one, however subtle, cannot avoid the iron law of time: either the present exists because the past was; or if the past is changed, then our present will not exist.

Yet the physics Benford plays with here renders the problem something vastly greater than a simple bipolarity. In the world of tachyons, this possibility of swerve and reprieve is not a simple matter of switching between two tracks. Tachyon information is sent back to 1963; despite precautions, it does effect change in the form of a conventional bifurcation of timelines. On the readers' timeline, Kennedy was assassinated. On the new timeline (that of Benford's 1963 protagonist Gordon) the bullet missed and Kennedy survived. In more or less "classic" fashion, the world of 1999, seemingly trapped in its time circle, is destined to move to its demise, while the 1963 line, in which there is neither assassination nor ecological disaster, swerves away toward its future reprieve.

But this is not the whole story. One Cambridge physicist in 1999, Renfrew, whom we find still transmitting tachyon "messages" as his 1999 world rushes to certain death, experiences an unexpected moment of "contact," again *in extremis*. Linear time all at once shatters and myriad messages from all spatiotemporal "directions" pass through his machine. Within this Babel of microuniverses, there comes a message in English, "ATTEMPT CONTACT FROM 2349." Renfrew knows he cannot answer even if it were possible, for where-when in this sheeting of timelines *is* 2349 located? He realizes that in his world "causality's leaden hand would win out." Yet, what occurs is in fact a complex swerve toward reprieve, a moment of retrieval at the heart of total loss: "He knew, now, without knowing quite how he knew, that it was forever lost. Rather than feeling despair, he was elated, free." For if the outside world is dead, his own micro-universe, his family, his individual world just confirmed by this fleeting contact with 2349, remains and will go on: "Puffing slightly, his head clearing, he walked along the deserted path. There was really quite a lot ahead to do, when you thought about it."[12]

Even if their novels obey the iron hand of causality, Moore and Benford continue to offer the swerve and reprieve that reaffirm the spiraling motion that began with the ride of DeQuincey's Mail Coach. The experience of Moore's Hodge and Benford's Renfrew is that of DeQuincey's individual narrator bearing down on sudden death, only to veer upon the near-miss into a strange and alien world. Moreover, Benford's near-miss occurs on the same apocalyptic plane as the "Dream Fugue." For not only does one timeline, 1969, replace the otherwise dead world of 1999, but within this latter world, as the apocalyptic seals fall across the blighted landscape of Cambridge, Renfrew's private reprieve comes at a millennial moment—the 1000-year return to bucolic life that precedes the inevitable coming of the end. In a novel of extreme scientific rigor, within the apparently neutral movement of tachyons and material unfolding of the theory of many worlds, the apocalyptic imagery of DeQuincey's "Dream Fugue" is not forgotten, proof perhaps that such considerations have not passed with the advent of twentieth-century science.

## HUCK FINN'S DREAM FUGUE

A number of Heinlein's Scribner's juvenile novels of the 1950s deal with a brush with sudden death and a reprieve. Young Kip, in *Have Space Suit—Will Travel* (1958), comes within a hair's breadth of being "rotated" along with the entire human race. But because of the steadfastness of his course, he is granted a reprieve *in extremis*, and the final scene of the novel finds him back at his Midwestern soda fountain, taking on the local bully and thinking again of mankind's future possibility in space. Heinlein's juveniles were written in the shadow of the paradigmatic American novel—Mark Twain's *Adventures of Huckleberry Finn* (1884). Interestingly, what DeQuincey presents in his mid-century "Dream Fugue"—the dynamic of mind, motion, and reprieve— also describes the operating mechanism of Twain's later work, which in its own way and culture is also responding to the forces of technological change and scientific advancement. DeQuincey's mail coach encounters, at the end of its physical journey, the conventional structures of its own culture—church and nation, destiny and apocalypse. Twain's Huck, at the end of his river, meets open nature and the frontier. The encounter here, and the swerve to reprieve, is not between speeding coach and small buggy, technology and romanticism, but between riverboat steamers and Huck's raft. The outcome of the reprieve is survival in new lands and, by simple extension in Heinlein, on new planets.

In *Huckleberry Finn,* Twain's protagonist frees himself from the fantasy world of Tom Sawyer's childish pranks. Early in the novel, he turns away from these fantasies to contend with the world of Miss Watson and Pap, the harsh reality of social and parental traps, which he continually slips out of, usually *in extremis* and menaced by sudden death. Huck's scenarios are not mind forms that, as with Tom Sawyer, are subsequently calqued on real-life situations. Rather they are *strategies*, improvised on the spot, allowing him to slip out of social traps—Miss Watson's "sivilisation"—and a series of increasingly dangerous situations which themselves are generally the result of fantasies gone bad. The shadow of death accompanies him on his ride down the river. He must fake his own death to escape from Pap. On the river, he decides to help the runaway slave Jim get to Ohio, but in the fog they miss the confluence north and are carried by the current down the river into the deep South. In the floating house, Jim discovers Pap, who has been shot dead. Landing on the riverbank, Huck encounters danger and near-death in the form of the chivalric fantasies of the Grangerfords and Shepherdsons. These end in carnage, from which he escapes by a hair. In Arkansas, he witnesses the equally dangerous fantasy of "honor," as Colonel Sherburn kills the harmless Boggs in cold blood.

If the land is dangerous, the river has its dangers too. The raft is boarded by the Duke and the King, who sell Jim into slavery. These two rogues literally bear down on the innocent Wilkes girls, hoping to steal their inheritance. The girls are saved in the end by a swerve, brought about by Huck who hides the stolen money, of all places, in Wilkes's coffin. In the final pages, Huck is snared briefly in Tom's plan to "free" Jim—an elaborate and absurd "heroic" fantasy that not only gets them in deeper trouble, but in the end proves to have been useless, as Miss Watson in the meantime died and freed Jim in her will. Aunt Polly's final attempt to "adopt" Huck fails, and he lights out for the territories.

The word "fugue" denotes a musical structure involving contrapuntal variation, lines tracking, then moving away from each other. In its original sense, however, it means flight, running away. In Twain, as in DeQuincey, there are many moments of runaway motion—no one in control of the raft or coach—observers carried on the stream of time, rushing toward on sudden death (in a literal or figurative sense), only to swerve away at the last moment, to sweep the past into their moving dream. In Huck's flight down the river, all forms of *kairos* (chivalry, royalty, "sivilization" itself) are subjected to *chronos*. Huck's job—even more urgently perhaps than that of DeQuincey's narrator—is to observe, adapt, and at extreme moments act and survive. Both figures are products of an ever-accelerating technological age, forced to redefine an existence now linked to unstoppable movement in time.

The first significant Heinlein juvenile, *Starman Jones* (1953), is basically the story of a young farm boy, Max Jones, who takes a menial job on a starship. Max's dead uncle was an "astrogator," member of a tightly controlled guild which Max, not being a direct descendant, cannot join. Max however memorized his uncle's tables of calculation (there were no convenient computers in 1953). When the ship, due to faulty calculations, gets lost in another spacetime dimension, and the tables are maliciously destroyed, Max the human calculator is able, as the ship hurtles toward oblivion, to deflect it back, in the nick of time, into our familiar universe.

Max's full name is Maximillian, suggesting emperors (Maximillian I who established the Hapsburg dynasty or the ill-fated Maximillian I of Mexico). With this name, Heinlein hints at structures ordained by divine power, yet he links this with the surname "Jones," conveying the dynamics of the common man. Heinlein has, within a single name, created a compound in which the swerve is imbedded, where *kairos* is now vectored by *chronos,* in the way that Huck Finn opens up the closed world of Tom Sawyer by moving on the river and literally riding its twists and turns. Max (who prefers his demotic nickname) finds himself up against the astrogators' guild, which claims to be an ordained structure where succession is by primogeniture. For Max climbing on a spaceship, with astrogators' tables in his head that are guarded by a guild as if they were Masonic ritual, has the same effect as DeQuincey's narrator climbing aboard the English Mail Coach, which becomes, through his eyes, an extension of the engine of change sweeping aside the old order across Europe. In Heinlein's work Max, boarding the ship, literally steps into the shoes of another emperor—Napoleon—the upstart who, in company of *Sergeant* Sam Anderson of the Imperial Marines, rises through his own talent to become chief astrogator on this particular flight, and ultimately Captain of the ship. There is at the same time a clear parallel with Huck. Twain's Duke and King claim titles but are the basest of scoundrels. Huck however, the vernacular everyman, grows throughout the voyage to real understanding of Jim's nobility and proves capable in the end of using his wiles "in noble manner" to save the Wilkes sisters.

Lost in a new spacetime dimension, Max's ship lands on a planet whose inhabitants are intelligent centaur-like creatures but seek to enslave the humans. Critics have seen a reference to Swift's Gulliver among the Houynhmhms. If so, then Heinlein presents an anti-Augustan version of this story that abandons closed strictures like the neo-classical "golden mean" and extols mankind's capacity to advance in new world defined by velocity and space travel. Gulliver accepted the superiority of the rational horses over what he concedes to be his own race of "yahoos." Returning to England, he can no longer abide the sight and smell of his own kind and takes refuge in a stable. Heinlein's centaurs, like all "superior" beings encountered in his works, have far vaster technology and "knowledge" than humans, but like the Houhynhmhms are fatally flawed by their inability to change. Like DeQuincey's crocodile, they are pointed along a road and cannot deviate from it. Humans however fight and resist, and in the end, Max is able to escape, given his first reprieve because Sam, in an act of altruism, turns to face the enemy against overwhelming odds and lays down his life.

As Max seeks to calculate the parameters that will allow the ship to "make the jump" back to our familiar universe, he is in a position analogous to DeQuincey's narrator atop the speeding coach, for his ship is heading inexorably toward a point in spacetime where there is but a hair's breadth between impact or swerve. As the ship rushes toward the moment of the "jump," Max continues his cool calculations, the lucid mind riding atop a force he cannot stop. But unlike DeQuincey's narrator, he proves capable, at the extreme moment, of finding the right "crease" in the spacetime "handkerchief," of executing the swerve that takes the ship back home. Moving the figures through his head, Max begins daydreaming—"He ran the figures over in his mind and found that they meant nothing to him." *In extremis*, he is called to order by Kelly: "'Captain!' Kelly said sharply. He shook his head and sat up. . . . With a feeling of panic he reviewed the data in his mind and tried to program. He knew at last how it felt to have the deadline bearing down fast as light—and to lose confidence." At the microsecond of looming impact, it is make or break: "He applied the correction, a tiny one, and called out, 'Stand by!' He pressed the button that allowed the chronometer to kick it over on the microsecond. . . . Max looked up. They were back in the familiar sky of Nu Pegasi and Halcyon."[13]

Clearly, as with DeQuincey's rider, the instant of Max's triumph is a mitigated one. In the larger scheme of mankind's technological advancement, these reprieves are insignificant in terms of *kairos*. But in terms of real time, *chronos,* it marks a small breach in the old philosophies of human limits which, when multiplied, will enable humans to carry on their search for new horizons. Max in the end pays his fines and joins the astrogator's guild. Like Kip and his soda fountain, he returns to the world of conventional institutions. He will not marry Ellie "because an astrogator ought not to get married." (250). Given a second chance, he will simply wait his time: "And, while he didn't argue the justice of the punishment—he'd been in the wrong and he knew it—nevertheless the guilds were set up wrong; the rules ought to give everybody a chance. Someday he'd be senior enough to do a little politicking on that point." (251)

The final scene of Heinlein's *Have Space Suit—Will Travel* is a crescendo of DeQuincey-like proportions. Kip and Peewee sit, as in DeQuincey's dream cathedral, at the bar of cosmic justice. The judges, a group entity, are the material embodiment of all mind-circles, apparently capable of taking all linear vectors into its ever-widening circumference as it absorbs an expanding number of "civilized" races in the universe. Kip and Peewee however are humans, and humanity's greatest strength is that it is made up of a floating pool of free individuals, each a "door" by which escape from the logical traps and prisons of the mind becomes possible. Here again, a young man and woman sit in the box of judgment, with the "coach" of fatality bearing down on them. The swerve comes once again, at the last second, from a free action. The judges fear humanity's irrational, actively violent nature. Kip lives up to this nature by defiantly blurting out in the face of condemnation: "We have no limits! There's no telling what our future will be."[14] The judges fear they might indeed reach the stars one day, and condemn all of humanity. But again, an act of altruism intervenes. In the same way the man in the carriage acts to save the woman, or the dying trumpeter rises up to warn of impending doom, both Kip and Peewee act freely to throw in their own lot with humanity, insisting on being be sent back to Earth to be "rotated" with it. Such irrational behavior causes the judges to hesitate; they will suspend the arrow of sudden death while pondering the implications of the act. As always happens in this science-fictional ride that begins with DeQuincey's coach bearing hope of victory, mankind gets a reprieve, a chance to continue its journey.

In science fiction we see again and again, at the moment of reprieve, the mind circle broken open. Even if the gap is small (infinitesimally so in the case of the time double), it keeps the way open for the dynamic of motion and advancement. Further, to see DeQuincey's dream fugue pattern almost exactly replicated, in the American context a century later with Heinlein's space Huck Finns, gives a reader the sense that this is just one of the many yet-to-be-discovered avenues that lead from nineteenth-century literature to twentieth-century science fiction. DeQuincey's work is merely one example of a strong current of works whose narrative patterns can be traced, as here, to science fiction—works that, like DeQuincey's, literally and physically test in the crucible of fiction what Asimov sees as the basic definition of science fiction—the impact of scientific and technological advancement on human beings.

## NOTES

1. The scientific intentions of "The English Mail Coach" are whimsically spelled out in the opening lines of Part 1, "The Glory of Motion": "Some twenty or more years before I matriculated at Oxford, Mr. Palmer, at that time MP for Bath, had accomplished two things . . . he had invented mail-coaches, and he had married the

daughter of a duke. He was, therefore, just twice as great a man as Galileo, who did certainly invent . . . the satellites of Jupiter, those very next things extant to mail-coaches in the two capital pretensions of speed and keeping time, but, on the other hand, who did not marry the daughter of a duke." In *Prose of the Romantic Period,* edited by Carl Woodring (Boston: Riverside Press, Cambridge, 1961), 403–404. References are to this edition.

2. Erich Auerbach, *Mimesis: Dargestellte Wirklichkeit in der abendländischen Literatur* (Bern: A. Francke AG, 1946).

3. Miguel de Cervantes, "Novela y coloquio que pasó entre Cipión y Berganza, perros de la Hospital de la Resurrección que está en la ciudad de Valladolid, fuera de la puerta del Campo, a quien comúnmente llaman 'los perros de Mahudes,'" *Novelas ejemplares* (1613), a collection of novellas published just before the second part of *Don Quixote.* The literal, mundane nature of Cervantes's title here stands in direct contrast to the "fantastic" event it chronicles.

4. The problem of technological transformation, vehicular velocity, and new senses of time such as "railroad time" in nineteenth-century England is discussed in Patricia Murphy, *Time Is of the Essence* (Albany: State University of New York Press, 2001). Verne's use of vehicles is astutely analyzed in Arthur B. Evans's "The Vehicular Utopias of Jules Verne," *Transformations of Utopia,* edited by George Slusser, Roger Gaillard, Paul Alkon, and Danièle Chatelain (New York: AMS Press, 1999), 99–108. Evans sees Verne creating vehicles that "could 'go where no man has gone before,' while providing a homey antidote to the continual *dépaysement* of foreign milieus." (99) DeQuincey's mail coach, in contrast, sends the utopian mind refuge on a journey across the real physical landscape of the industrial age.

5. Cited in Woodring, 395.

6. "Preface" to *Lyrical Ballads,* cited in Woodring, 60.

7. David Hume, *Enquiries Concerning the Human Understanding and Concerning Principles of Morals* (Oxford: Clarendon Press, 1902), 18–19. References are to this edition.

8. Wordsworth, *The Prelude* I, lines 378–79, *English Romantic Writers,* edited by David Perkins (New York: Harcourt, Brace & World, 1967). References are to this edition.

9. Alfred Lord Tennyson, "Ulysses," lines 60–61, *Victorian and Later English Poets,* edited by James Stephens, Edwin L. Beck, and Royal H. Snow (New York: American Book Company, 1934).

10. H. G. Wells, *The Time Machine* (New York: Bantam Books, 1968), 106.

11. Robert A. Heinlein, *Time for the Stars* (New York: Scribner's, 1956).

12. Gregory Benford, *Timescape* (New York: Simon and Schuster, 1980), 393, 394.

13. Heinlein, *Starman Jones* (New York: Ballantine Books, 1975), 246. References are to this edition. Originally published in 1953.

14. Heinlein, *Have Space Suit—Will Travel* (New York: Ace Books, [1969]), 232. Originally published in 1958.

## Chapter Five

# Genre at the Crossroads

## *Cultural Readings of Maupassant's "Le Horla"*

From the literary and cultural landscape of nineteenth-century Europe and America we have identified important building blocks in the creation of a science fiction genre. We have the scientist as protagonist, its quest for future liberty, and with DeQuincey a cluster of themes that proves operational in many twentieth-century science fiction works. But speaking about science fiction as a "genre," we talk about readers identifying given works of fiction as belonging to a set of recognizable themes and forms they agree to call "science fiction." Locating the origins of this genre is a tricky question, since it lacked a name until Hugo Gernsback launched the magazine *Amazing Stories* in 1926 and provided a designation (initially, "scientifiction") for the "new" form of fiction he was publishing. His models were Poe, Verne, and Wells. But how did their contemporary readers designate the kind of fiction they were writing? French writer Edmond de Goncourt, in the 1880s, spoke (with distaste and trepidation) of Poe writing "scientific fiction." Verne was stuck with editor Hetzel's designation, *le voyage extraordinaire.* Among these "fathers" of the genre, only Wells included "science" in his designation (the "scientific romance"). This is perhaps why many critics (Mark Rose, Roger Luckhurst) point to Wells as the first writer of something identifiable as science fiction.

I propose, as one means of identifying the origins of the generic response by which readers today identify works as "science fiction," the exploration of a generic crossroads. At such a crossroads, a new genre emerges when a work of fiction with definable elements of several converging recognizable genres cannot be fully subsumed by any of these. Such a work, through its dialogue with known genres, distinguishes itself as being "something else," forcing readers to develop new criteria for generic identification. DeQuincey shows us a science-fictional way of thinking—but this is not enough. What is needed is a work that openly generates among readers generic expectations that are recognized today as "science-fictional."

In the case of science fiction, I focus on one generic crossroads, significant because, in terms of the international origins of this genre, it marks a coming together of Francophone and Anglophone scientific and literary cultures. The time is France at the end of the nineteenth century. The place is Guy de Maupassant's much-discussed story "Le Horla" (Version One, 1886; Version Two, 1887).[1] This story presents a series of possible generic responses to the incursion of an unknown external phenomenon (a "horla," a thing "out there") into the protagonist's daily existence. Science fiction today would call this an "alien encounter." Maupassant's protagonist, though not a scientist, approaches the Horla with scientific method as a fact, as would science fiction characters. But the text itself remains ambiguous, in the sense that it gives readers interpretative choices that depend on their cultural orientations. Readers who want to see "The Horla" as a *conte fantastique* have choices with generic implications. They can see the Horla as something uncanny but ultimately explainable, usually as a figment of a deranged mind, or as a supernatural phenomenon, a thing "marvellous," thus beyond explanation in human terms. Or they can play the game of undecidability—the "I don't know what it is, or whether it can be explained or not." But Maupassant's text presents difficulties for these generic categories. For if the Horla is a figment of a deranged mind, does that mean it doesn't exist in some form? What if the cause of this derangement is not a neurosis, but a physical microbe, like that of syphilis? Are Maupassant's versions the account of a pathology, or a psychoanalytic experiment? This text seems to ask readers to make new generic responses. At this level, it is not a matter of whether the Horla is "real"—something is happening to the protagonist—but the nature of that reality and the protagonist's response to it. The origin of the phenomenon is no longer the issue either. It can be the product of Darwinian evolution, or the issue of some supernatural or (in the language of the time) paranormal phenomenon. We are on the cusp of two new genres here—horror and science fiction—and what determines whether a story is one or the other is the *response* to this alien. Horror collapses before the unknown. Science fiction responds proactively—in confronting its horlas, it invokes the material imperative of science. This means not only accepting the horla's existence, however improbable, as a real, physical phenomenon, but engaging it as something that can be understood, thus if need be defeated.

I wish to read "The Horla" as a work of science fiction. But this, in terms of Maupassant's story, lead to another fascinating crossroads—a crossroads of both genre and culture. The story is French; I must take into account the fact that a French science-fictional response may be different from an Anglophone response. At this late date in the nineteenth century, France and England began to share a deep interest, not so much in Darwinian evolution, as in problems of invisibility, both at the level of unseen vectors of disease and that of mental illness and occluded realms of the human mind. Invisibility forms a common denominator for the worlds of mind and matter, posing a common problem of where we look to uncover it. Do we address the invisible alien in the external world of material extension, or the mysterious depths of the mind? Maupassant's two versions of his story deal with medical doctors and a medical and scientific establishment dealing with both the "invisible" vectors of disease and the impact of physical and paranormal ("magnetic") forces on the human psyche. At this crossroads, one can read the actions and explorations of Maupassant's protagonist as (in the manner of *Dracula*) engaging a material alien as an external phenomenon. But evidence in Maupassant's text indicates that he saw his protagonist equally engaging the Horla in a scientific manner as a physical phenomenon. The *direction and location* of this science-fictional pursuit, however, is radically different, for the experiments of Maupassant's protagonist move increasingly inward, where alien encounter becomes a psychoanalytical pursuit within the Cartesian space of the mind. His quest, as science-fictional character, is to confront cultural categories such as "madness" within the active space of his mind. We see him work, mind within mind, to escape the medical and analytical frames his culture would impose on him, hoping to confront his horla within the deepest recesses of his rational soul.

Maupassant published, very close together, two different versions of "Le Horla." The first, published in the October 1886 issue of *Gil Blas*, presents the account of a man who describes his encounters with an unknown "being"—which he calls the Horla—to doctors in a mental institution. The second is a day-to-day account of these same encounters in first-person diary entries. If both versions present an individual claiming to use experimental scientific methods to understand this unknown presence, the second account differs greatly in where and how it positions its protagonist: he is now alone, outside the institutional frame and its sanctions, engaging the unknown in what seems an open-ended search, apparently free of social conventions and institutions. These two versions suggest that Maupassant is himself manipulating a single situation to explore conflicting generic possibilities. In Version One, the medical authority, at least tacitly by its silence, declares the protagonist mentally deranged; the Horla is reduced to being a figment of a sick mind. In Version One, the "patient" (already interned in the asylum) has prepared his presentation and presents it to the panel of doctors. Logic is a matter of rhetoric here. In Version Two, however, we have the jotting down of the day-by-day *discovery* of an alien-seeming phenomenon which may or may not exist, but is *experienced* and experimented upon in an existential manner. Whether his mind is sane or not, this narrator is alone in facing *something*, whose nature and origin is unknown, but whose *effects* are felt. All kinds of generic possibilities swirl around this situation. The text can be the diary of a madman, recorded for the purpose of psychoanalytical analysis; a medical pathology report, detailing the effects of an invisible disease as it infects the brain; a tale of horror, where *something* (clinical, medical, or supernatural) drives the narrator to terrible deeds. But throughout this generic back and forth, there remains the proverbial elephant in the room—the possibility that the Horla (as its name implies) is simply an unknown material phenomenon, and if accepted as such, it can be faced and understood. The narrator then, in the name of science's material imperative, *acts effectively*, gets results by pushing the envelope of human knowledge of the natural world, and because of these results can be pronounced "sane." Science fiction is born.

## EXPERIMENTAL SCIENCE AT THE CROSSROADS

Maupassant's story is a crossroads in terms of not only the formation of genres, but scientific visions and methods as they then appeared on the international stage. This is a time when advances in science are seriously impacting fiction. Fiction however does not yet have a designated genre to respond to this impact. "Le Horla" provides a focal point for three distinct scientific currents at the end of the nineteenth century. The first is specifically French, the product of what Constant predicted would be the outcome of Napoleonic usurpation of creative and scientific endeavor by regulatory agencies. The theoretical justification for hierarchies and regulatory structures, especially in the sciences, comes from Comtean positivism. The practice of science is regulated by administrative bodies, themselves operating in accordance with preordained rational models. We find an example of this in Flaubert's *Madame Bovary* (1856). Charles Bovary, the country doctor who lends his name to the novel, bears the title *officier de santé*, whose duties were restricted to bloodletting and other palliatives. The pharmacist Homais has a wide yet superficial knowledge of the proliferating medical and scientific literature of the time. His title does not authorize him to perform procedures, but he persuades the unwitting Charles to attempt an unauthorized operation on the club foot of village idiot Hippolyte. The operation, as expected, fails, and Charles is severely reprimanded by the regional doctor, Canivet, who nevertheless ends with a tirade against *"ces messieurs de Paris,"* the higher authority of the medical schools of the capital. One of these *sommités*, Professor Larivière, arrives too late at the bedside of Emma Bovary, who has taken arsenic. Powerless to help her, all he can do is invoke the limits of mankind in terms of "natural" laws. Charles Bovary is a sacrificial victim to the legacy of Balzac, where material law is redefined as the inherent law of social structures. This institutionalized science is the same that authorizes the board of doctors of Maupassant's First Version. The purpose of such institutions is to "classify" the unknown, by locating it first within social parameters, and ultimately within the Cartesian limits of the individual mind, where it can be regulated by "sciences" like magnetism and, finally, psychoanalysis. The literary form corresponding to this control of the unknown is Todorov's *fantastique*, where initially unknown phenomena are either subsumed under known (i.e., institutionalized) "laws" or, if they cannot be subsumed, rejected as something nonexistent.

The second current, in terms of science and fiction, is international and cross-cultural, a product of the growing interest in evolutionary concerns and pathology. In England, evolutionary theory emphasizes territorial imperative and life forms contending for survival. In France, this is reflected in the germ theory of Pasteur, which locates the vector of disease outside the body, as "invading" entity, seeking to "take over" the bodily territory, including the physical brain. On a level of practical pathology, doctors were working with phenomena like syphilis, where physical brain is "invaded" by an external microbial force, causing a form of mental-physical derangement that cannot be addressed by placing patients in mental institutions or using hypnosis or "magnetism" to cure them. Maupassant himself showed symptoms of tertiary syphilis, and his life and writing were possibly a struggle with this invisible physical entity inside his body, gradually destroying his brain. In fiction of the time, the association of alien invasion and disease vectors is clearly made in works like Wells's *The War of the Worlds* (1898). Wells's *The Invisible Man* (1897) and Bram Stoker's *Dracula* (1897) add the element of invisibility to the equation. Indeed Dracula, a conventional vampire, is treated as a dormant virus, an invisible entity transported to England in the soil of his native Transylvania. The fictional form associated with evolutionary monstrosities and pathogens is the incipient one of horror. There is a direct line from Wells's Martians and Stoker's Dracula to Murnau's *Nosferatu* (1922), where the associations between the vampire and disease (marks on the neck are mistaken for mosquito bites) are constant. The link persists in Werner Herzog's remake *Nosferatu: Phantom der Nacht* (1978), a work that returns to Stoker's text. Dracula here is visible and still subject to physical limits (the cock crowing at dawn, stake in the heart). But the pathogens he vectors are unseen, all the more horrific because they invade, and thrive, *inside our bodies*, where neither we nor science detect them until it is too late.

The third current is that of modern experimental science. In England, the triumph of the experimental scientific method is evolutionary theory.

In France, despite the persistence of the Cartesian duality, scientists from Lavoisier to Pasteur *used* experimental methods to make their discoveries. Experiment entered the realm of scientific theory in a stunning manner in France with Claude Bernard's *Introduction à l'étude de la médicine expéri-mentale* (1865). Unlike Charcot, whose terrain was the nebulous one of the mind, Bernard was a physiologist and medical doctor who dealt with diseases of the physical body and their cures. His sense of experiment is one of con-certed, rationally directed engagement with the physical unknown. Bernard speaks of science's encounter with the unknown in terms that foreshadow science fiction's later "sense of wonder." But there is also the sense that wonder is not enough, that *results*, new causal links leading to discovery and understanding of physical phenomena, are necessary as well. These causal revelations are present, if indirectly, in Wells's *War of the Worlds.* There is horror here because invading aliens, who feed on our blood, cannot be stopped by human effort. But there is also the evolutionary fact that humans have, over long years of bodily "experiment" with the microbes that bring down the invaders, become immune to them. In *Dracula,* experimental sci-ence in a sense engages the alien in the work of the unorthodox scientist Van Helsing. He isolates the danger and tracks the infection to its source, though he neither understands nor eradicates the menace. This is however in line with Bernard, for whom experimental science offers various degrees of palliation of the sickness, and encompasses the idea of a cure, when the mechanisms of the unknown are understood, *and* this understanding put to use in ways appli-cable to all humanity. For Bernard however, all "cures" are provisional, just as science's engagement with the physical unknown remains never-ending.[2]

Experimental science finds a strong advocate in Belgian writer J.-H. Rosny aîné. Rosny's story "Un autre monde" (1896) was published after "Le Horla" and before Wells's and Stoker's aforementioned novels. While their fictions deal with invasions by invisible forces, Rosny's story is about the act of *perceiving* another realm of beings and learning to observe and describe them scientifically, without terror. It describes a young mutant boy, born in rural Holland, who possesses unique powers of sight, enabling him to observe the world of the Moedigen, life forms that live alongside us in another dimension. Significantly, Rosny's mutant is neither committed to an institution nor marginalized and rejected. Instead, he is clever enough to skirt these dangers and become accepted by a cautious but open-minded scientific community. He serves science as an instrument that permits observation of this "other world." Unlike the horrific visions in Wells's "The Crystal Egg" (1897), the Moedigens are seen going about their business oblivious of our existence. The only "menace" they might pose is indirect, for their evolution, in unknown ways, might have some future, if unintentional, impact on our environment. Engaging the unknown is a positive trait here, and the message is that science must use all means possible to push forward the boundaries of knowledge, even if this requires collaborations with "madmen" or figures like Rosny's mutant. Significantly, this mutant (unlike Frankenstein's creature) does find a mate and form his own "race." But this is seen as a boon to science, for their progeny will allow scientific investigation to continue beyond the life of the original mutant. Rosny's "pluralist" vision is more scientifically optimistic than the "social Darwinist" visions that derive from evolutionary theory, anticipating the sense of science's engagement with the unknown in later American science fiction, from Gernsback's call for fearless experiments to hard science fiction's mantra to "push the envelope," to go where no one has gone before.

## STORY AT THE CROSSROADS

Maupassant's story sits at the crossroads between these various scientific and cultural currents that provide sets of reading "protocols," which only later harden into firm generic markers. What is proposed here is an exercise in cross-cultural reading. The reading model that dominates French critical interpretations of "Le Horla" ultimately sees the narrator's account as a "case history" of mental derangement and places the story in a lineage that leads from the *fantastique* to psychoanalysis and surrealism. This model can and does claim scientific validity. Even so, by seeking to enclose the unknown, first in the mental institution, then within the confines of the mind itself, it leaves the body of the "patient" vulnerable to invasion by invisible pathogens, and science prey to horror.

But details in Maupassant's text contradict this reading. For example, even though his protagonist is a well-to-do bourgeois with no accredited scientific training, he applies, in investigating the "horla," a clear degree of scientific rigor to his experiments, which he carefully conducts and assesses. French literature of the time had no use for amateur scientists or the maverick workshops of the "lone geniuses" in American Edisonades. In the late novels of Verne, such as *Robur le conquérant* (1886) and its sequel *Le maître du monde* (1904), all earlier sympathy for rogue scientists like Nemo is gone. Instead, these novels present the lone scientist as a madman and give him Icarus's fate. In another late-century French example, Flaubert's Bouvard and Pécuchet are presented as "lacking in method," which means essentially lacking the proper scientific credentials that would enable them to judge which popular science books are valid and which are not. The two clerks ultimately fail at every experiment, not because they lack method, but because the "science" in all these books proves fatally flawed. Flaubert seems to say that *all scientists* are pretentious amateurs in the face of a natural perversity that must ultimately be accepted as is. His clerk-"scientists" finally go back to their former occupation—copying texts.

French culture then blinds readers to the possibility that Maupassant's protagonist could be a talented amateur scientist, whose experiments may be pushing the envelope of the known world. Readers conversant with Rosny's evolutionary vision, or the American dime novel flourishing at the time, might see "Le Horla," especially the second version, in a different light. But to read it as an early example of science fiction, readers must make two assumptions that later become identifying factors for the science fiction genre as a whole. First, the mind of the scientific researcher is sane and healthy (even if the world calls him or her "mad"); such minds, beset by neither mental "illness" nor some physical disease which destroys their sensory and rational processes from inside the body, can pursue investigations to their conclusion, even if this pursuit seems, in the eyes of ordinary humanity, purest folly. Second, as corollary to this assumption, indeed because of it, readers must adhere to the same material imperative as the scientist-protagonist, requiring them to sift the happenings for facts, for evidence of both the scientist's soundness of method and the possibility that phenomena like the Horla are material entities, thus "real" in the sense of Johnson's rock. Such readers suspend judgment, agreeing to look beyond barriers of collective superstition or claims of mental derangement to see the Horla as a thing really *out there*, that can and must be engaged in the physical realm.

Maupassant's story supports both readings. Both have claims to scientific validity, yet they move scientific inquiry in divergent directions. As noted, seeing the Horla as the figment of a deranged mind leads from the *fantastique* to psychoanalysis and surrealism. The other reading, rather than endlessly framing, thus neutralizing, the investigative mind, frees it to engage the unknown. Such engagement with the invisible alien can, as in John W. Campbell, Jr.'s "Who Goes There?" (1938), yield horror. But Campbell's protagonist McReady faces this and pushes on, enabling him to investigate, engage, and finally defeat the alien. This is a science-fictional response. Science fiction needed this narrative impetus to become a recognized genre.

## POSITIVISM AND THE MEDICAL FRAME

Positivist medicine was the major biological science in nineteenth-century France. This was more "biological philosophy" than what we know today as inductive experimental physiology. Increasingly, its focus turned to classification of "facts," elaborations of categories and frames. As a science, it sought ever more perfect taxonomies and tended not to push the envelope beyond these limits. For example, followers of Comte dismissed "le darwinisme" as superfluous: "Le vrai problème biologique consiste à articuler structure et fonction." [The real problem of biology consists in delineating structure and function.][3] This positivist need for increasingly rigorous framing contributed to the shift, in the last half of the nineteenth century, from physiological to "psychological" concerns among medical researchers. Positivist medicine seems to reverse the old dictum *mens sana in corpore sano*, for from its point of view the body can be healthy only if we restore balance to the mental forces. This is supposedly done by shielding patients from not just contact, but the possibility of contact, with alien elements from without. Because such elements remain unclassifiable, hence unknowable, they can be declared to be nonexistent.

If John Stuart Mill admires Comte and the positivists, he nevertheless, in his *Auguste Comte and Positivism* (1865), challenges their method in the name of causality.[4] Mill praises positivism for its attempt to remove human agency from the process of observing and presenting "facts." But for Mill, the strength of the Comtean method is at the same time a serious weakness. Comte, he argues, by confining knowledge to facts and further stating that "[the] essential nature and the ultimate causes [of these facts], either efficient or final, are unknown and inscrutable to us" (57), places radical limits on scientific activity. For Mill, there are deeper levels of causality, where the positivist "fails to perceive the real distinction between the laws of succession and co-existence . . . and those of . . . the action of Causes, the former exemplified by the succession of night and day, the latter by the earth's rotation which causes it." (57) Such causes generally lie outside the positivist frames of logic that occlude our view of them.

Mill sees Comte following Descartes, insofar as he substitutes "an extraordinary power of concatenation and coordination" for what Mill calls the "independent thought" needed to engage deeper causes beyond any organized web of facts. Positivism, for example, cannot deal with what he calls the "super-natural," in the sense of phenomena that, for now, lie beyond our investigative reach: "Positive philosophy maintains that within the existing order of the universe, or rather of the part of it known to us, the direct determination of every phenomenon is not super-natural but natural." (15) Positivists would declare Maupassant's Horla, because it appears to exist beyond the domain of known fact, to be nonexistent. Mill reveals just how exclusionary Comte's sense of what is and can be known is: "If the universe had a beginning, its beginning, by the very conditions of the case, was supernatural; the laws of nature cannot account for their own origin." (14)

What Mill ultimately finds in positivist science is a "mania for regulation" that denies independent thinkers access to phenomena outside its frames of order. An example of such framing in nineteenth-century French fiction is Balzac's "Gambara" (1836). Here, a genius artist is literally forced to conform to the norms of social order. When musician Gambara plays music for the human audience and ear, it is deemed beautiful. But when he pushes musical expression into the realm of the visionary sublime, only he can hear the music, in the isolation of his mind. The sounds listeners hear, however, are a dreadful cacophony. Balzac frames this story of artistic genius in a clear social context. In pursuing absolute music, Gambara neglects his wife. She turns to Count Andrea, who solaces her and at the same time acts as "doctor" to Gambara. Realizing that Gambara can, when drunk, play accessible music, Andrea "cures" him by plying him with drink, thus bringing his music and behavior in line with accepted social norms.

The "madhouse" as well is a common Romantic trope, which France inherited from German literature, especially Hoffmann. The archetypical genius escapee from the *Irrenhaus* is Hoffmann's "mad musician" Johannes Kreisler, who operates on the margins of real criminality, using music as a weapon against social order. He is not, as we see from his mysterious comings and goings, easily restrained by existing social institutions. The novel *Die Lebensansichten des Katers Murr (The Life and Opinions of the Tomcat Murr)* (1818) pretends to offer Kreisler social healing when the philistine cat recycles the very medium of Kreisler's musical ravings by using the backsides of the artist's sheet music to record his own smug bourgeois reflections on life. Unlike the world of Gambara, the social order of Murr is seen by Hoffmann as stifling. The reader skims rapidly over the cat's boring reflections in hopes of finding Kreisler's "mad" fragments as they resurface amidst Murr's clinical efforts to suppress them.

The German madhouse could not hold in check genius artists like Kreisler. The story is different in France. Michel Foucault's view of French "aliénistes" and mental institutions of the nineteenth century may be exaggerated, but there is truth in it: "Le médicin n'a pu exercer son autorité absolue sur le monde asilaire que dans la mésure où, dès l'origine, il a été Père et Juge, Famille et Loi, sa pratique médicale ne faisant bien longtemps que commenter les vieux rites de l'Ordre, de l'Autorité et du Châtiment." [The doctor was able to exercise his absolute authority over the world of the asylum only insofar as, from the beginning, he instated himself as Father and Judge, Family and Law, to the extent that his practice of medicine for a long time merely consisted of reciting the ancient rites of Order, Authority, and Punishment.][5] Following Mill's assessment of positivism, one can argue that the final realm to be regulated is that of the mind itself. Yet however vigilant the systems and institutions of medicine in place, the deranged mind remains a potential entry point for an external menace (the "alien" music of Gambara or Kreisler) to invade the medical frame and, once inside, to subvert its positivist control mechanisms.

In this light, Maupassant's internee in the First Version of "Le Horla" launches a timid counter-accusation, suggesting that the doctors and their controlled experiments might in fact have the opposite effect—opening his mind to intrusion from without rather than sheltering it: "Et tout ce que vous faites vous-mêmes, messieurs, depuis quelques ans, ce que vous appelez hypnotisme, la suggestion, le magnétisme—c'est lui que vous annoncez, que vous prophétisez." [And everything you have been doing, messieurs, for the last several years, what you call "hypnotism," "suggestion," "magnetism"— it's *he* you have been announcing, prophetising all along.][6] Maupassant's character refers to experiments by Charcot and others that use hypnotism to control the mind and induce states of dementia in subjects. His accusation is dismissed by doctors as a sign of mental illness, yet what he says is sensible. For in the case of hypnotism, doctors wield "magnetic" forces that are both invisible and physical. By creating "paranormal" links between the mind and some form of ambient energy, they may in fact be opening "doors" in the mind, reaching outside to draw unwanted forces into the individual mind, thus inside the very medical institutions established to keep them out.

Charcot and his associates believe they are using hypnotism and "magnetism" to regulate the entry of external phenomena into the brain. This has an analogue in Comte's attempt to elaborate a new system of phrenology. As Mill tells it, Comte traced a grid in *a priori* manner over the physical skull. This grid was a structure "grounded on the best enumeration and classification he could make of the elementary faculties of our intellectual, moral, and animal nature, to each of which he assigned a hypothetical place in the skull." (185–186) Instead of probing whatever deep causes and unknown connections may lie within that skull, Comte does little more than put a lid on these, using his externally imposed grid to confine, and thus regulate, the space of the mind. Beneath the taxonomies we trace upon the surface of the mind, there lurk unseen, inside the physical brain, places of possible physical contact between human and "alien" forces.

## FRAMING THE MIND, FRAMING THE STORY: TODOROV'S *FANTASTIQUE*

The same control Foucault's doctors would impose on the mind of the patient, Tzvetan Todorov would place on the generic field of stories that recount, like the first version of "La Horla," the institutions of rational order closing around what appears to be an encounter between the human mind and unknown physical phenomena. Todorov defines "le fantastique" as the genre that cultivates, but cannot sustain, a hesitation between the known and unknown. But in Todorov's process of hesitation, the fantastic internalizes rather than externalizes the problem of the unknown. On one side, that of the étrange (the uncanny), the problem of the unknown is resolved by subsuming the phenomena in question under *accepted* laws of nature. On the other side, that of the *merveilleux* (the marvelous), the phenomenon in question is *a priori* declared to be a fairy tale. This neat duality denies the *fantastique* the possibility of evolving into different forms of literature. Rather than expanding our sense of nature's laws, Todorov places a new medical frame around his *fantastique*, psychoanalysis: "Allons plus loin: la psychanalyse a remplacé (et par là même a rendu inutile) la littérature fantastique. . . . Les thèmes de la littérature fantastique sont devenus, littéralement, ceux-là mêmes des recherches psychologiques des cinquante dernières années." [Let's go farther yet: psychoanalysis has replaced (and in doing so made useless) fantastic literature. . . . The themes of fantastic literature have become, literally, those of psychoanalytical research during the last fifty years.][7]

Seen in the French context, Todorov's remarks have plausibility. For one sees the same internalizing process he describes, not just in fantastic literature, but in works like those of Verne that appear to promote exploration of the external unknown by means of scientific experiment. We have a clear promise of this, for example, in Verne's first major novel, *Voyage au centre de la terre* (1864). The elaboration of this work, in fact, spans the time of publication of Bernard's *Introduction à l'etude de la medicine experimentale* (1865). If classifiers still held sway in the philosophy of science, Bernard's was the method practiced by working scientists in the fields of geology and paleontology. If nothing else, the chapters added to Verne's text in 1867 (37–39) bear testimony to the author's keen awareness of the work of experimental science in these areas.

In Verne's novel, Axel and Professor Lidenbrock venture into a physical realm—the core of the Earth—unexplored at that time. The reader expects new phenomena to emerge. Yet the focus of Axel's narrative, as he encounters never-before-seen phenomena in a *real* physical unknown, shifts gradually inward, describing a descent, not into the Earth, but into a world of dream. We see mind, increasingly, examining its own inner workings while reacting to, and retreating from, a series of "alien" encounters. Axel's account is full of premonitions, of temporary lapses into dream states, such as his famous waking "dream" in which all evolutionary history is subsumed in his own body and mind. The reader soon cannot tell whether the prehistoric flora and fauna Axel claims to see are physically there, or repressed figures from his unconscious mind that surface in moments of psychic shock.

The concept of the unconscious had not been formulated in 1867, but Axel seems to offer examples of its workings. One scene is particularly indicative: the encounter with the "giant herdsman" in chapter 39. Axel is a Latinist, and has, up to now, shown an ability to cite Virgil accurately. But on seeing this creature, he utters a line from Virgil's Eclogue 5:44 which is a significant misquote: "*Immanis* pectoris custos, *immanior* ipse." The correct words are *formosi/formosior*, "beautiful/more beautiful." What Axel says is *immanis*, savage. His citation also is terribly out of place, for Virgil is not describing a savage, but the beautiful shepherd Daphnis. As suggested by William Butcher and others, Axel is not quoting Virgil directly, but remembering another misquote, that of Victor Hugo in *Notre Dame de Paris* (1831), where *immanis* refers to the grotesque body (but beautiful soul) of Quasimodo. Butcher sees this as a joke Verne is playing on readers.[8] But we must remember that Axel is the narrator here and is in no joking mood. Hoping perhaps to find Virgil's Golden Age in this primeval setting, he comes across something far more unsettling, so much so that Hugo's misquote surges unbidden in his narrative. Behind the misquote lies something deeply repressed in his psyche, something that causes him to flee in terror from an apparition that may not be "out there" at all but comes perhaps from the depths of his mind and cultural memory. This could be the first noteworthy example of a Freudian "slip" in literature. In any event, read in this manner, Axel's narrative, where we witness a gradual drifting from experimental science toward interior states of mental derangement, is the forerunner of Maupassant's narrator in the second version of "Le Horla."

## THE MEDICAL FRAME: PSYCHOANALYTIC READINGS

French critics usually read "Le Horla" within the boundaries of Todorov's generic model. Version One seems a clear example of *l'étrange*, this time in the context of medical science, where strange occurrences are reframed within the consensus reality of a board of doctors. The protagonist tells his tale before a panel of "specialists," who in the end rule (if only by their silence) on the case by keeping the subject interned. One doctor, Marrande, appears to find the narrator's account plausible and in the end utters: if this man is mad, so am I. The body of medical experts however has nothing to say. There seems some factual evidence for the existence of a Horla, and Marrande responds to it. Even so, the doors of the institution close upon it. A case of individual madness becomes, as Marrande takes the side of the patient, a case of possible collective hallucination. We cannot, in the end, imagine this prudent board of doctors moving away from their rational skepticism. The "experimental" evidence given by the subject may be compelling; his discourse *appears* reasoned and highly logical. This however, in this context, is not proof. For where madness is seen as a function of mind, not bodily disease, one easily imagines certain forms of madness sharpening the faculties of exposition and persuasion. Even so, the core of the matter—whether a Horla exists or not—remains unthinkable in the eyes of official logic. Even plausible evidence is rejected out of hand as something lying outside the normative sense of an organized, functioning society.

In Version Two, this frame of medical authority is removed. But this, in Todorov's terms, only moves the narrative and readers from the étrange to the realm of the fantastic. Because the narration is first person, there is no way to give direct voice to an institution or doctors and their clinical judgment. Nowhere is it stated that this is the discourse of a clinical patient, seeking to rationally organize his argument to persuade the experts. Instead, we have a diary that records day-by-day reactions to phenomena. The diary, the most subjective and "romantic" form of narrative, allows (as with Senancour's *Oberman* [1804]) the subject to "say everything," to express uncontrolled reactions to things, defying all attempts to classify and understand them. In fact, the narrator of Version Two seems on the surface as emotional and confused as the narrator of Version One was rational and composed. At first one might think that an individual outside the hospital setting is freer to engage the possibility that a Horla might really exist. But the emotional instability of the narrator's discourse soon suggests this might be the diary of a sick mind. Doctors at the time, notably at the Salpetrière, encouraged patients to express themselves in art, or keep diaries of this kind, as documents that trace the path of "hysteria" and other forms of mental illness and thus could serve therapeutic purposes. Given this, it is easy to see the medical frame here as a covert one, tracing a patient's descent into neurosis and, in this case, madness. Though there is no direct presence of a medical judgment, readers can imagine a silent narratee who, if not directly addressed, at least overhears the narrator's attempts to explain what is happening to him. This listener is the psychoanalyst.

The opening pages of Version Two seem to position readers for discovery of the narrator's psychosis. This narrator, unlike the speaker in Version One, seemingly has not mastered the rhetoric of rational science. Instead, there is emotional effusion, visible instability of mind. Readers at the end of the nineteenth century at once detect a possible cause for this mental disorder—excessive "Romanticism." Attuned ears pick up accents from across the spectrum of Romantic cliché. There is an obsession with Gothic buildings, here the spires of Rouen cathedral. Nature seems the source of "sublime" emotions that overwhelm the observer. Germans called such discourse "Schwärmerei," and the narrator notably alludes to the arch-Romantic source for his century—E. T. A. Hoffmann. There is a significant nod in the direction of Hoffmann's Nathanael in "Der Sandmann" (1816). For the narrator's utterances, like those of Nathanael, seem manic-depressive, full of inexplicable *Ahnungen*, apprehensions of unseen terrors that appear figments of the mind rather than descriptions of external phenomena. An example is his unexplained reaction to the appearance of a three-master flying the Brazilian flag on the Seine: "Je le saluai, je ne sais pourquoi, tant ce navire me fit plaisir à voir." [I saluted its passage, I don't know why, I felt such a thrill at its sight.] (422) In Version One, only at the end of his narrative does the narrator remembers this ship. There, in a sudden, unconvincing burst of hysteria he sees this vessel bringing the Horla to France to pursue him personally. The only "proof" he cites is vague Brazilian newspaper articles (does he read Portuguese?) about encounters with "vampires" that he now states resemble his Horla. But the speaker in Version Two has just begun his story. He has no reason for reacting to this ship. His narrative is linear, not retrospective. He has not yet encountered the Horla and will only later in his narrative have newspaper accounts from Brazil before his eyes. There could be here, as in Hoffmann, some form of paranormal communication. The trained medical observer however might see a sign of madness—putting the effect before any possible cause—in his vague apprehension. Already for Hoffmann excessive Romanticism is a sickness. Here we seem to have here a sick mind finding strange portents in an otherwise random occurrence.

In terms of early diagnosis, this seems a mind addled by too much literature and art. In the narrator's further descriptions of deep anxieties, there are echoes of Charles Baudelaire's "spleen": "J'attends le sommeil comme on attendrait le bourreau." [I await sleep the way one would await the executioner.] Describing a recurrent nightmare, he seems to evoke Fuseli's famous painting "The Nightmare": "Je dors . . . et je sens aussi que quelqu'un s'approche de moi, me regarde, me palpe, monte sur le lit, s'agenouille sur ma poitrine, me prend le cou entre ses mains et serre." [I sleep . . . and I feel that someone approaches, is watching me, touches me, climbs onto the bed, kneels down on my chest, takes my neck it its hands, squeezes.] (424)

Maupassant multiplies scenes of this sort in the opening pages of Version Two, suggesting a psychopathology of the overwrought imagination. For example, the narrator's first entry expresses a near-Oedipal fixation on his native soil: "J'aime y vivre parce que j'y ai mes racines, ces profondes et délicates racines, qui attachent un J'aime ce pays, et homme à la terre où sont nés et morts ses aïeux." [I love this region, and I love to live here because I have my roots here, those deep and fragile roots that attach a man to the soil where his ancestors were born and died.] (421) Readers, their clinical acumen awakened by this description, now hear the narrator's account of a walk in the nearby woods. First, we have a romantic commonplace, a person on a promenade suddenly overwhelmed by the sublimity of nature. But the Romantic tenor of this encounter takes on stranger dimensions. Inexplicably, the narrator begins to turn on his heels, "very fast, like a top." Few readers of the time would miss the reference to Hoffmann's Nathanael in "Der Sandmann," who is suddenly overtaken by a similar automatism. We remember Sigmund Freud, in "Über das Unheimliche" (1919), rejecting the idea of alien possession in favor of a psychoanalytical theory of alienation, where Nathanael's behavior is said to be caused by internal imbalance in the psyche, a repressed Oedipal complex. Freud's "unheimliche" means literally to be "un-housed," evicted from within from one's familiar habitat. In the Cartesian context, seeing Maupassant's narrator alienated in this manner, *unheimliche,* is to say that his mind loses control over his extended body, allowing it to revert to the condition of "machine" or automaton.

Interpreted in this light, the Horla becomes the name given to other instances of this "Freudian" process of alienation, where self separates from self as the rational mind abdicates control of its material "home." In ensuing scenes, in fact, when the narrator affirms the presence of the being he feels is stalking him, he describes this as a doubling of self, a Jekyll-and-Hyde phenomenon. Take for instance the scene where he awakens to take a drink of water from his night pitcher, only to discover all the water has been drunk, something he has neither inclination to do nor recollection of doing. His immediate reaction is to think he is a sonnambulist: "Ce ne pouvait être que moi? Alors, j'étais somnambule, je vivais, sans le savoir, de cette double vie mystérieuse qui fait douter s'il y a deux êtres en nous, ou si un être étranger, inconnaissable et invisible, anime, par moments, quand notre âme est engourdie, notre corps captif qui obéit à cet autre, comme à nous-mêmes, plus qu'à nous-mêmes." [It couldn't be anyone else but me? In that case, I was a sonnambulist, I was living, without knowing it, that mysterious double life that makes us wonder whether there is not two beings in us, or if some foreign being, a being unrecognizable and invisible, does not move us, from time to time, when our mind is sluggish, our body captivated, forced to obey this other, as we would our self, more in fact than we would obey our conscious self.] (920) In this self-diagnosis, he does not see the Horla as an exterior invading presence but instead entertains the possibility that, in this somnambulistic state, he has summoned this "other"—what Freud later calls the *id*—from some deep unknown place within his being, making him alien unto himself. To confirm this, the next night he lays out water, milk, wine, bread, and strawberries. He notes the following: "On a bu—j'ai bu—toute l'eau, et un peu de lait. On a touché ni au vin, ni au pain, ni aux fraises." [Someone has drunk—I have drunk—all the water and a bit of the milk. No one touched the wine, nor the bread, nor the strawberries.] (920) Not only does he harbor an "I" and "it," but this it or "*on*" seems to have taken over his conscious being. He describes it as forcing him to do things against its will. In the entry marked "14 août," the narrator exclaims: "Je suis perdu! Quelqu'un possède mon âme et la gouverne! Quelqu'un ordonne tous mes actes, tous mes mouvements, toutes mes pensées. Je ne suis rien en moi, rien qu'un spectateur esclave et terrifié de toutes les choses que j'accomplis." [I'm lost! Someone is taking over my soul and is governing its actions! Someone is dictating all my actions, all my movements, all my thoughts. I'm nothing in relation to myself, nothing but a spectator slave to this process and terrified of all the things that I have done.] (929) The impersonal "*on*"—which could be a thing—has given way to "*quelqu'un*," "someone." He seems to be, in some obscure fashion, performing psychoanalysis on himself, both drawing the unconscious alien to light and naming it a "second self." Now, whatever he senses inside him is personified as a second "self" controlling his actions. Before he would never eat strawberries; he now sees himself compelled against his will to do so: "Puis, tout un coup, il faut, il faut, il faut que j'aille au fond de mon jardin cueillir des fraises et les manger. Et j'y vais." [Then, suddenly, I had to go, I had to go, I had to go to the back of my garden and pick some strawberries and eat them.] (930)

Maupassant's narrator lives a solitary existence, in an isolated house where servants are all but invisible. His reflections reveal extreme introversion. In his world, any intrusion at all would be unsettling—"unheimliche"—in a literal sense. Maupassant wrote other stories in which supposed disruption of a closed domestic setting is revealed to be, in Freud's manner, the consequence of a play of psychic forces rather than the invasion of something external. In "Qui sait?" (1890), the narrator is a single man of obvious means, also obsessed with his native habitat, which is again a place of tomb-like isolation with separate servant quarters. He describes coming home alone from the theater one night to witness all his furniture literally walking out the door. He believes this event, presented as witnessed by his own eyes, really happened. He pursues his furniture, and thinks he has found it, but in a quite fantastic location, an old antique shop in Rouen tended by a dwarfish creature. The literary echoes are from Hoffmann and Balzac's *La Peau de Chagrin* (1831). In both, the curiosity shop serves as transitional space between natural and supernatural realms. But in Maupassant's story, the narrator is totally alone, sole witness to the exodus of his furniture. True, his servant testifies to the loss of the furniture; but this testimony is reported by the narrator himself, who appears increasingly unreliable. The same servant later writes a note saying that all the furniture has returned as mysteriously as it left. But again, this note, for all we know, could be fabricated by the narrator, proving that the furniture never left the house in the first place. There can be no "home-coming" for this protagonist. The authorities cease to believe him, and he seeks asylum of his own volition in a mental institution. Yet here too he finds alienation, for he begins imagining that the dwarf too could check into the same establishment and pursue him inside the medical frame. The dwarf is a romantic figment, hardly a credible vector for alien invasion from without. Maupassant here, as in other stories labeled "un fou," appears to offer read-ers an anatomy of descent into psychosis. Might one not assume that he is doing the same in Version Two of "Le Horla," simply with a more acute and ultimately violent form of madness?

All the "encounter" scenes in Version Two—the milk-drinking visitations, the telekinesis of the plucked rose, the self-turning pages of the book, finally the scene where the narrator sees his mirror image "wiped" by what he claims is the invisible Horla passing between man and mirror—seemingly chronicle, in the context of the narrator's obsessive, neurotic self-examination, the onset of madness. Maupassant, as writer, seems obsessed with this scene of the wiped mirror image. It can be interpreted as the ego's double—in later psy-choanalytical terms its "id"—usurping its identity, creating a schizophrenic situation, where this uncontrolled "other half" emerges as a force of destruc-tion. An example of this obsession is found in an earlier story, "Lettre d'un fou" (1885).[9] The narrative is openly labeled a letter written by a "madman" under medical supervision of his doctor. Readers are told this is a description of a patient describing his gradual descent into madness. Again, the narrator believes he is beset by an invisible being. Again, he devises a mirror experi-ment hoping to capture the image of this being. He has a sudden apprehen-sion that the alien he believes has been visiting him is about to manifest itself: "Quand arriva le moment précis, je perçus une indiscriptible sensation, comme si un fluide, un fluide irrésistible eût pénétré en moi par toutes les parcelles de ma chair, noyant mon âme dans une épouvante atroce et bonne." [When the exact moment arrived, I experienced an indescribable sensation, as if some fluid, an irresistable fluid had penetrated my being through every tiny bit of my flesh, drowning my soul in a terror that was both atrocious and pleasant.] (466) He then describes the wiping of his image: "Ce qui me cachait n'avait pas de contours, mais une sorte de transparence opaque s'éclaircissant peu à peu." [What was hiding my mirror image had no shape, but was rather a sort of transparent opacity which little by little was becom-ing clearer.] (466) When the image is finally restored, it is the same as it was before—but his perception of himself is altered forever. He stares into the mirror hoping for the return of an invisible presence that never returns. But what gradually take its place in the mirror are monsters that seem projections of his deepest psyche: "Et dans cette glace, je commence à voir des images folles, des monstres, des cadavres hideux, toutes sortes de bêtes effroyables." [And in this mirror, I begin to see crazy images, hideous cadavers, all sorts of terrifying beasts.] (466) Once again, this seems a scenario drawn from Romantic literature, in this case Erasmus Spikher's stolen mirror image in Hoffmann's "Die Abenteuer des Sylvester-Nachts" [The New Year's Eve Adventure] (1815). In Hoffmann, the "devil" (an exterior force) steals Erasmus's image, thereby alienating him from normal social intercourse. But in Maupassant, this devil seems interiorized; what appears in the clouded mirror can only be the reflection of a psychotic mind, as the blank space of the id peoples itself with insane visions.

Given this base, the case for onset of madness can be easily built. The narrator in Version Two devises and executes scientific experiments which display schizophrenic behavior. Though his methods of investigation seem logical, even inventive, the object of these experiments can be seen as increasingly insane, to the point that schizophrenia yields to violent dementia. The narrator is driven, in the final pages, not just to capture an image of the Horla, but physically to trap and destroy it. He fits his house with iron shutters and doors. Believing he has enticed the Horla into his reading room, again apprehending its "presence" as some irresistible fluid penetrating his deepest being, he slips out, locks what he thinks is the invisible alien in the room, pours kerosene on the downstairs floor, sets the house on fire, locks all doors and shutters, then escapes to watch it burn. Only the screams of trapped servants awaken him from his obsession. Like the somnambulist, or man who lost his image in the mirror, he claims simply to have "forgotten their existence." To the reader-psychiatrist, there is a more troubling detail; for this final scene is not narrated in its immediacy, but presented in a letter written the next day, signed and dated at the "Hôtel Continental, Rouen." As with the narrator and his now homicidal double, the event and response to the event have become radically separated. The telling of this horrific scene is separated from the emotional impact of the scene itself. Read this way, the situation becomes that of a mad criminal who commits a crime but can only recollect it later, in what might be a self-therapy session. In this recollection, the narrator's concern is not for victims, who are blanked out of his field of vision. Instead, he remains obsessed with the idea that the Horla somehow escaped and, like the dwarf, will continue to pursue him. At this point, he seems to have but one option: suicide. Psychoanalytically inclined readers, at this point, can have only one verdict: terminal madness.

## "LE HORLA" AS SCIENCE FICTION

Maupassant's Second Version certainly invites the above reading, which also is right in the mainstream of French Cartesianism, which places Maupassant's story in a cultural and scientific current that runs from Verne to surrealism. If we see Maupassant's narrator, especially in Version Two, as a clinical case, whose narrative is to be read as a psychoanalytical document, then we identify a Cartesian space where sciences of the mind can study the workings of that mind, independent of material factors from without. The thread runs from Axel's retreat into a mindscape of dream, to psychoanalytical interpretations of Maupassant, where madness is studied as not a neurological process but a rearrangement of a subject's mental "furniture," to Rimbaud who "rearranges" Verne's own sea creature and other "wonders" in a landscape controlled by what he calls his "déréglement raisonné des sens," to the surrealists. Proposing a "scientific" study of dreams, the latter do little more than invert Descartes's distinction between "higher" and "lower" mind, by which they locate the "true" function of mind in the irrational workings of the unconscious. Following this line of reasoning, one traces a path from Maupassant's "tales of madness" to surrealism and ultimately the mind worlds of post–World War II French science fiction.

Maupassant's story however invites another, very different reading, where we accept the Horla as a real entity. The invisible invader can be a "germ" like syphilis, or a chemical substance, such as the absinthe that causes Coupeau's delirium tremens in Zola's *L'Assommoir* (1877). Or it can be something unknown, a phenomenon yet to be identified, but nonetheless "there." Reading the story from this perspective—essentially the Anglo-Saxon perspective of experimental science—we uncover details revealing that Maupassant was not entirely comfortable with the medical frame, overt or covert. He may in fact have rewritten his story to contest the imposition of such frames on the possibility that there is more "out there" than current science can explain. Pursuit of a physical unknown, outside the perceiving mind, was a real option (though perhaps not the mainstream option) in France when the story was written. Bernard's exposition of the experimental method had a profound effect on his contemporary Zola. Maupassant himself adds details to Version Two clearly suggesting that a diagnosis of insanity may be hasty and unwarranted. These details cause careful readers to hesitate, to wonder if the protagonist might not be correct (even if not wholly sane) about the Horla's existence. The protagonist does not possess the means of proving its presence but makes real attempts to use an experimental approach to a phenomenon that is plausible, even if elusive and ultimately terrifying.

To present Version Two as the chronicle of a scientific adventure, a mind pursuing the unknown, we must affirm that the mind in question is competent to conduct the investigation. "Sanity" is a matter of point of view, and many visionaries have been deemed mad before being proved right. In Maupassant's work, mental competence seems difficult at first to claim, especially in light of Maupassant's *adding* passages to the second version that augment the sense of the narrator's emotional instability. But we must realize that he is alone in a struggle that nothing in his world has prepared him for. If we give credence to what he is experiencing, we must accept that he faces the most terrifying of menaces: an entity both invisible *and potentially hostile.* The patient in Version One is not only telling his story in retrospect but has a specifically defined audience—doctors who put faith only in reason—that demands a rational form of presentation. The way the story is constructed makes diagnosis of madness an almost foregone conclusion, for his discourse ends with a clear breakdown of reason. He harangues the doctors, and his final argument rests on a highly improbable newspaper article from Rio de Janiero, describing "une epidemie de folie," where villagers claim they are "poursuivis et mangés par des vampires invisibles qui se nourrissaient de leur souffle pendant leur sommeil" [pursued and eaten by invisible vampires who feed upon their lives's breath as they sleep] (830) and who drink only milk and water. To interpreters of phantasms and dreams, all the elements of his previous "rational" description seem found here, reduced to their proper landscape of mental unbalance.

In Version One, even if some details seem to come from a lucid mind, the medical board passes them in silence. His account (kept in Version Two) describes the pitchers of water emptied when he awakens in the morning. He may rush to judgment by seeing the water "drunk," but is not satisfied with the somnambulist hypothesis. He decides to conduct a further experiment to challenge this by laying out the beverages on white linen, then smearing his hands and mouth with graphite. When he awakens, there are no marks on the linen—tangible evidence that something external is at work here. For were he a sleepwalker, there would be marks on the glasses. The narrator may describe his actions as a "ruse contre moi-même" [a ruse against myself] but they are eminently experimental, and get concrete results.

This same scene is taken up in Version Two. And we have as well a narrator who, despite his highly emotional language, is clearly capable of conducting a reasoned and carefully executed experiment. What has changed is the order of the reasoning, which is more experimental yet. He begins thus: "On a encore bu toute ma carafe cette nuit—ou, plutôt, je l'ai bue!" [Once again someone drank my entire pitcher last night—or rather, I drank it!] For a person supposedly governed by Romantic fears, he rejects the supernatural hypothesis right off the bat. An "on" cannot drink my water. Perhaps I did it, as a sleepwalker. But he rapidly abandons this possibility as he conducts a new experiment—with more "variables" than in Version One—setting forth this time a complex array of victuals: water, milk, bread, wine, strawberries. He does not like milk, but drinks water. Some of the other things he likes and would take at night, even as a sleepwalker. The result is the same—only the water and milk are touched. Now he refines his experiment, suppressing the water and milk, and this time nothing is touched. This offers evidence, but apparently not enough. For only now, after this series of probes, does he conduct the graphite experiment of Version One, smearing it on his lips before sleeping. In Version One, we have only the results of the experiments—no marks of graphite on the linen. There is no intermediary experiment to show that, were he a sleepwalker, he would choose other things than milk and water were they offered. Instead, he concludes—illogically and on insufficient evidence—that *he* must be the night drinker, hence a somnambulist, and as such a prime subject for the doctors in his audience. In Version Two, the result is much more troubling for the narrator, and this certainly would give rise to extreme emotional reactions in a temperament clearly prone to such reactions. For if he has effectively demonstrated, by a gradual series of steps, that, *even if he were a sleepwalker,* he did not do the drinking, it remains to be asked who, or what, did do it. The speaker in Version One does not proceed scientifically in this manner. Instead, he reasons syllogistically, as befits the Oedipal mind seeking to trap itself by a ruse.

There are other inconsistencies with the "covert frame" interpretation of Version Two. If this were the diary of a madman, one could hope that medical authorities, so capable of controlling minds through hypnosis and other clinical techniques, would have foreseen the tragic act of burning down the house and intervened. Even if they did not, we see from the date and place of the final entry, "Rouen, 10 septembre," that the narrator is still "at large." He remains outside the frame, able to continue his questioning. At this point, perhaps the only way to maintain the madness interpretation is to do as many French critics have done—to see the narrative as Maupassant's *own* diary of a madman, as a description of the process which led the author to attempt suicide and be subsequently interned for the rest of his life. His protagonist however remains free, able to ask more questions.

If there is textual evidence to support the madness hypothesis in Version Two, there is also evidence suggesting the contrary. This bipolarity tells us that Maupassant is not only challenging the medical frame, but consciously places his protagonist at the crossroads between two genre-defining possibilities. If the narrator is mad, then his narrative occupies a generic space that answers to Todorov's fantastique-become-case history. But if the narrator is lucid enough to pursue a real problem, with as much scientific method as an amateur could hope to have, then we have a science-fictional situation. In the additions and rearrangements of Version Two, there is significantly more evidence for a "science-fictional" reading. For example, the narrator's Romantic allusions in this text do not simply indicate a mind becoming unhinged, losing its grip on reality. Instead, they often serve to alert readers to pay attention to details that, on the contrary, point outside the medical frame. In the early journal entry dated "12 May," what appear to be Romantic ravings on the "profound mystery of the Invisible" (this passage came at the very end of Version One, "confirming" the patient's impending breakdown of reason), are in fact, if read carefully, a sober assessment of the limits of our senses, the primary "instruments" of scientific experiment: "Nous ne le [ce mystère de l'Invisible] pouvons sonder avec nos sens misérables, avec nos yeux qui ne savent apercevoir ni le trop petit, ni le trop grand, ni le trop près, ni le trop loin, ni les habitants d'une étoile, ni les habitants d'une goutte d'eau." [We cannot fathom this mystery of the Invisible with our miserable senses, with our eyes that can perceive neither that which is too small, nor that which is too large, neither that which is too far nor too close, neither the inhabitants of a distant star, nor those in a drop of water.] (914) Instead of Romantic diction, the narrator, in using balanced negatives and referencing the drop of water, speaks in the style and substance of Pascal. Educated readers of the time would recognize this, as well as the Baconian argument for the need to correct our limited sensual apparatus set forth in Bernard's *Introduction à l'etude de la medicine experimentale*. This narrator seems versed in the language and issues of contemporary science.

Another example is the scene in the forest, presented in the entry dated "June 2," where the narrator suddenly begins spinning like a top. This direct reference to Hoffmann's "Der Sandmann" may on one level invoke madness, but also raises the issue at the core of Hoffmann's story—the limitations of human perception, how our emotions and predispositions affect the way we see things in the world. Midway in Hoffmann's story, Italian lensgrinder Giuseppe Coppola throws a welter of eyeglasses on a table in front of protagonist Nathanael. These "glasses" are in fact optical instruments, allowing viewers to look outward on the world, to see things in that world anew, even if these things terrify and destabilize the viewer. Here, in Version Two, this Hoffmann allusion marks a transition from the narrator's previous remarks about the limits of our senses to the scene at the Mont St. Michel—which does not appear in Version One. These remarks were made in Version One as the speaker concluded his argument with references to scientific commonplaces of his time, such as the limits of our senses and plurality of "inhabited worlds." The idea of an "inhabited" world could be seen as comforting, for what inhabits it is assumed to be a rational creature like us. Hoffmann's story points the glass at something that not only is "unknown," but most certainly *not like us,* and physically *there*, if not completely unknowable. We expect the speaker in Version One to "reason like a scientist," because he is among scientists. These doctors, however, remain silent as he makes analogies between his "horla" and the inability of the human eye to see the wind or electricity. Their horizon remains bounded by the hospital, and the need to contain those who claim to see such things, which right reason has written off as unseeable, thus irrelevant.

In Version Two these same ideas emerge from a dialogue. The narrator's interlocutor is not a "man of science" but a monk, supposed guardian of the superstitions science claims to have superseded. He espouses the modern view of the limitations of human senses. He is, however, curiously insistent about the need to see what does lie *out there*, beyond the reach of our feeble senses. He also emphasizes the destructive violence of these invisible forces: "*Est-ce que nous voyons la cent millième partie de ce qui existe? Tenez, voici le vent . . . le vent qui tue, qui siffle, qui gémit . . . l'avez-vous vu, et pouvez-vous le voir? Il existe pourtant.*" [Do we see even the hundred-thousandth part of what exists out there? Here, take the wind . . . the wind that kills, that rages and howls. . .have you ever seen it, are you able to see it?" (918) The narrator takes resolve from the monk's urgings: "Ce qu'il disait là, je l'avais pensé souvent." [What he was saying there, I had often thought the same thing.] (918) This discussion gives an existential urgency to the narrator's subsequent experiments which, if they were also in the speaker's account in Version One, are now carried out with both greater scientific precision and a renewed desire not only to see farther, but to make the invisible visible. The experiment with the graphite becomes a tangible step in this direction, where he eliminates the possibility that he is the author of certain events and thus concludes they are perpetrated by some "other" not yet visible. The next "sighting" of his invisible being is when he sees the rose mysteriously leave its stem. This event too is presented by the speaker in Version One. What is new here is the narrator's expressed confidence in his ability to observe, to see: "Je vis, je vis clairement . . ." [I see, I see it clearly . . .] The scene here is not recollected, but written down as directly witnessed. The narrator proceeds to describe, in much greater detail, the flower inscribing a movement as if plucked by an invisible hand, the bending and snapping of the stem. It is as if the Monk's urgency as to the role of the senses gives new meaning to what now becomes a bold observation: "Puis la fleur s'éleva, suivant la courbe qu'aurait décrite un bras en la portant vers une bouche . . ." [Then the flower lifted itself, following the curve an arm would make if taking the flower toward a mouth.] (927) The flower is a physical object, like the glasses on the non-visible face of the Invisible Man in James Whale's 1933 film of Wells's novel. We do not hallucinate when we see the glasses; we experience something invisible wearing a visible object. The same becomes true here. Something, the narrator reasons, is holding up the visible flower, which could not do what it does on its own. More significantly, Maupassant's observer now attempts physically to seize the invisible presence behind the action. Though he fails, he immediately turns to the rose bush, to verify that the whole event was not a hallucination. He sees the stem is broken; the rose gone.

One can doubt such certitude. Indeed, the narrator's overly rational assertion of "facts" such as this in Version One only convinces doctors that he is a madman mimicking reason. But here, in Version Two, there is no intervening authority to judge for us; readers must decide for themselves. All they know is that the narrator's statement is based on a series of experiments that can be seen as making a plausible case for the existence of a Horla. But if the Horla exists, it remains an unknown presence. Given this, the narrator's ensuing statement that the Horla may be stalking him cannot be dismissed as paranoia. Fear is a reasonable conclusion to draw from the narrator's newfound certainty as to the facts of this situation, which he clearly summarizes: "Alors, je rentrai chez moi l'âme bouleversée; car je suis certain maintenant, certain comme de l'alternance des jours et des nuits qu'il existe près de moi un être invisible, qui se nourrit de lait et d'eau, qui peut toucher aux choses, les prendre et les changer de place, doué par conséquent d'une nature matérielle, bien qu'imperceptible pour nos sens . . ." [And so, I went back in my house, my soul in turmoil, for I am now certain, as certain as I am of the rhythm of night and day, that an invisible being exists near me, a being who nourishes itself with milk and water, who can touch things, take them and move them from one place to another, a being who consequently is material in nature, but who cannot be perceived by our senses.] (927) He now sees his alien as a physical presence. More importantly, he begins seeing his own mental activity as the workings of a physical brain, a brain not possessed by demons, but limited by an inadequate perceptual apparatus. His description of the workings of the brain may be figurative, but the figure of speech he uses—a "hand" and "cerebral keyboard"—is an astonishingly *physical* one, describing how physical stimulus "plays" on the nerve centers of the brain: "Ne se peut-il pas qu'une des imperceptibles touches du clavier cérébral se trouve paralysée chez moi?" [Might it not be, in my case, that one of the imperceptible keys of the brain's piano is somehow stuck?] (928)

In the details of the Second Version, we seem to witness a mind working its way through the cultural impediments that sustain the medical frame of Version One, confronting these with scientific observations, opening new vistas rather than closing them. For example, he turns to the learned treatise of Dr. Hermann Herestauss—a book that delineates "les habitants inconnus du monde antique et moderne" [the unknown inhabitants of the ancient and modern world] and could be seen as insane quackery—to do specific research, to see whether any of these "known unknowns" describes the phenomenon he is facing. Critics point out that the name "Herestauss" is the German equivalent of "horla." If so, then the narrator is simply invoking another double or mirror image of his delusional fantasy. Yet there is an important difference. "Hors-là" simply points "out there." The German translates "It *is* out there" (er *ist* aus). It is thus an *affirmation* of the existence of something out there. In fact, we see our narrator beginning to challenge the Cartesian syllogism that underlies the medical frame, the argument that, in relation to *res extensa,* things out there, only mankind exists as *rational* being, the lone entity in the entire universe capable of perception connected to rational thought. But Herestauss is speaking of other life forms. Is it necessarily delusional to say that such life forms might also be sentient, if not necessarily "rational" in the Cartesian sense? Inspired by Herestauss, the narrator does not simply move in the direction of Fontenelle's "pluralité des mondes"; instead, he offers an astounding meditation that seems to announce the evolutionary relativism of Wells's *War of the Worlds:* "Les étoiles avaient au fond du ciel noir des scintillements frémissants. Qui habite ces mondes? . . . Ceux qui pensent dans ces univers lointains, que savent-ils plus que nous? Que peuvent-ils plus que nous? . . . Un d'eux, un jour ou l'autre, traversant l'espace, n'apparaîtra-t-il pas sur notre terre pour la conquérir, comme les Normands jadis traversaient la mer pour asservir des peuples plus faibles?" [The stars in the deep abyss of the black sky were trembling and sparkling. Who lives on these worlds? . . . Those thinking beings in these distant galaxies, what do they know more than we do? . . . Might not one of these races, one day or another, decide to cross these vast expanses, and suddenly appear on our earth to conquer it, just as the Normans of yore crossed the seas in order to subjugate weaker peoples?] (931) Wells's Martians will prove to be near relatives of Earth. But Maupassant's narrator extrapolates from the Normans to intelligences sailing seas of suns, certainly a harbinger of science-fictional things to come. The narrator takes us from insanity to science fiction.

All these speculative meditations are new to Version Two. Maupassant's narrator seems to have acquired a relativist perspective that challenges Cartesian insularity. And he moves on to even more radical speculations, this time challenging Pascal's sense of a unique "human condition." When he experiences the loss of his image in the mirror, Maupassant's narrator first feels an isolation and helplessness akin to that of Pascal's thinking reed: "Tous les ressorts de l'être physique semblent brises. . . . Je n'ai plus aucune force . . ."

[All of the springs and workings of my physical being seem to be broken. . . . I no longer have any strength at all . . .] (439) There are persistent references to Pascal—note the negatives in the quote above, and this unmistakable allusion to the thinking reed passage: "Nous sommes si infirmes . . . si petits . . . sur ce grain de boue qui tourne délayé dans une goutte d'eau." [We are so weak . . . so small . . . stuck on this tiny fleck of mud that dissolves as it turns in a drop of water.] (441) Pascal moves us from the Cartesian stove to the prison house of human existence. Maupassant's narrator now seems to confront this sense of existential closure with Voltaire's more open-ended, progressive vision of life forms expressed in his twenty-fifth *Lettre anglaise contra Pascal*.[10] He reiterates Voltaire's sense of a scale of being on which we are, in some sense, an intermediate form. He seems, in fact, to correct Voltaire with something closer to Darwin's sense of "natural selection": "Un être nouveau! Pourquoi pas? . . . Pourquoi serions-nous les derniers? . . . C'est que sa nature est plus parfaite, son corps plus fin et plus fini . . . que le nôtre si faible, si maladroitement conçu." [A new being! Why not? Why should we be the final step? . . . What we have is a creature who is more perfect, with a better built and more perfect body than ours, which is so weak and poorly conceived.] (444). The narrator of Version Two does nothing less than free human powers of observation from the ratiocentric strictures of Descartes and Pascal. Enforced in Maupassant's time by the medical frame, these strictures prevent our human senses from accepting evidence of a real alien presence outside human reason's sphere of influence.

The crowning piece of evidence for the narrator of Version Two is the report from Brazil. In Version One, the patient invokes the Brazilian connection only at the end of his speech. Taking the account of water and milk drinking vampires as fact, he makes the paranoid link with the Brazilian ship—it is *the* vector of the Horla, come to infect him and him alone. In Version Two, the narrator, in his penultimate entry, just before he sets his house on fire, tells of reading of the Brazilian epidemic. This time however, the account is not a simple newspaper clipping but an article in a scientific journal, the so-called *Revue du monde scientifique.* We learn that the Brazilian government sent a scientist, Professor Don Pedro Hernandez, and a team of experts to investigate the incident. They report that the story of milk-drinking vampires was that of superstitious folk trying to understand a force beyond their grasp. In their eyes, it is superstition that is the mental disease, an "epidemie de folie." As scientists however, they cannot deny that a possible alien sighting may have occurred. Like Herestauss's treatise, the actual journal did not exist. Unlike his alien "sightings" however, this account is thoroughly scientific in nature, with no taint of superstition or fantasy.

How then can we explain that Maupassant, despite constantly pointing readers outside the frame toward the possibility of a real external alien, keeps the final house-burning scene in Version Two? It is difficult to read this as "sane" science. But insofar as the narrative remains inconclusive, nobody can say that it is not *correct science*, even if no other human sees or accepts the invisible presence. The medical frame and regulatory apparatus of French scientific culture of the time are conceived to prevent such science from being done. For once it is done, it may well prove that, despite all disclaimers, it was the right kind of science to do. The later science fiction writer Philip K. Dick, for example, revels in turning paranoia on its head. Dick creates scenarios where, in terms of scientific fact, the paranoid person turns out to be right, and paranoid fantasies are horrifically real events. Long before Dick, Maupassant may be seeking a similar reversal by putting Descartes's *malin génie* to a new use. The *génie*'s new role, in a world where rational beings possibly exist in *res extensa,* is to deceive the protagonist's senses to the point where he is forced to make a *tabula rasa*, this time to assert that, even if I *alone* see the something out there, I must act *on my evidence*, no matter if my actions run counter to law and society.

A significant later science fiction example of such action *in extremis* comes from Robert A. Heinlein, whose horlas are always real, and whose lonely "mad" protagonists always see beyond the veil of collective error. In Heinlein's *The Puppet Masters* (1951), humans have been physically possessed by creatures—"slugs"—who take their identity. In a neat materialist variation on the Horla, these beings hope to make themselves invisible by "snatching" and inhabiting the bodies of your friends and neighbors. These "taken" bodies however have a telltale hump, which Sam alone sees. In a world where any of your loved ones could be hostile aliens, Sam is forced to operate on the margins of what the average person calls sanity. Yet he is sure he *knows* the alien enemy is there, and in proving this he kills a good number of people along the way.

Let us follow Maupassant's clues in the Second Version, taking the narrator as an experimenter who gathers significant evidence that there is a Horla out there. The evidence is so compelling in fact that he decides to act. His fixation on this "other" becomes so great that, in acting, he blots out everything else and commits a criminal act. Heinlein's Sam is part of a "special" unit whose task is to take out the slugs. If they cannot be absolutely sure each individual they kill is infected, as a group they know when the job is done. Maupassant's protagonist however is totally alone, and his struggles with the Horla are solitary. His servants were as invisible throughout the narrative as they were in the culminating scene. In this sense, the inconclusive ending is important. The individual who, in his hotel in Rouen, contemplates suicide is by his own admission Descartes's *selfish, solipsistic* self, as wrapped up in its own process of reasoning as the Princesse de Clèves. His final statement, in this regard, presents a reasoned hypothesis that turns exclusively around his sole being: "il *va falloir* que je me tue, moi." [it is going to be necessary that I kill myself] The stress pronoun "moi" is untranslatable, but its presence is an affirmation of this Cartesian self over all else in the world. At this point it is still possible to see Version Two as science fiction. But now, if the search for the unknown continues, we must locate it within the confines of the protagonist's mind itself. This mind will be the terrain of scientific investigation in much French science fiction to follow. Confronted with the alien unknown, the concerns of a Van Helsing, or Heinlein's Sam, will be those of a larger world. Their actions serve a culture, a society, or even an elite within a society.

## THE EMERGENCE OF GENRES

In what is ultimately a Cartesian reading of Version Two, one thing remains: the physical presence of a Horla, no matter if its identity is unclear. It could be a microbial "invader" or, as the narrator believes, an alien life form. But whatever this invisible being might be, its presence abides. In fact, the Cartesian method that marks the progression from Version One to Version Two could be said to guarantee the Horla's continued existence. If in Version One, the institutional structures of positivist science close in to isolate the narrator, in Version Two that same narrator is free, but only to affect its own *cogito* through the use of experiments that gradually cut him off from the material world he operates in. The end result is the narrator's final affirmation of his "moi," the moment when the isolated self claims total separation from *res extensa*, the realm of the material alien. In other words, Maupassant gives his narrator the power to act on his own, only to have him, through his independent scientific investigations, confine himself all the more radically in the end.[11]

That said, what keeps the spark of a science-fictional reading of "Le Horla" alive is the text's ability to accommodate new material that challenges closed readings. Maupassant adds details that prevent readers from accepting the *fantastique*, or psychoanalysis, or even the above Cartesian reading as definitive explanation. We detect, in the Pascalian accents given to his protagonist's expanded musings on mankind's place in the universe, a suggestion that Maupassant was well aware of the fragility of self-isolation. More interesting yet is the long added passage in Version Two which describes the experiments of Dr. Parent. The purpose here appears to be to challenge the

sanctity of all the frames previously proposed—those of the medical establishment, psychoanalysis, and the Cartesian refuge in self. For what we witness, with Parent's activities, is science itself acting as the vector by which
elements of the external unknown it would exclude are actually brought into
the patient's mindspace.

Readers may at first be mystified by this apparent digression, which
presents Parent and his feats of hypnosis. Parent is not an experimental neu-
rologist or physiologist in the manner of Bernard. He belongs instead to the
school of Charcot, who used hypnotism and magnetism to "rebalance" the
sick minds of patients. Maupassant seems to say just the opposite—that such
medical intrusions into the mind in fact weaken its defenses against intrusion of unknown forces from without. He even implies that such "science"
provides the conduit whereby the alien enters and destroys human beings. Already in Version One, the protagonist incriminates his "alienist" doctors for
using magnetism and hypnosis on their patients, creating possible paranormal
pathways that allow alien forces to enter the mind. Parent's experiments in
Version Two clearly demonstrate the dangers of this process. We notice that
Parent (with his Freudian name before Freud) operates outside the mental
institution, in the drawing room and on "sane" subjects.[12] His goal seemingly
is to demonstrate, as a kind of early psychopathology of everyday life, that
everyone has a "double vie," that there is a Jekyll and Hyde in all of us. The
narrator clearly understands his actions as a potential entry point for alien
invasion of our physical *body*: "Alors . . . je vivais, sans le savoir, de cette
double vie mystérieuse qui fait douter s'il y a deux êtres en nous, ou si un
être étranger, inconnaissable et invisible, anime, par moments, quand notre
âme est engourdie, notre corps captif qui obéit à cet autre . . . plus qu'à nous
même." [And thus . . . I was living without knowing about it this mysterious
double life which make us suspect that there are two beings inside of us, or
rather that an alien being, invisible and unknown to us, takes hold of and
animates, from time to time, whenever our soul is numb, our captive body,
who now obeys this alien being more than it obeys our waking mind.] (920)

Parent performs his experiments on the narrator's cousin, Mme Sablé.
Readers of the time could not miss this reference to Hoffmann's "Sandmann,"
translated into French as "L'Homme de sable." The twist now is that, instead
of external forces (as in Hoffmann) exercising control, the scientist is now
manipulating these forces to control his "patients." The doctor claims to be
controlling the possibility of external intervention in our psychic lives, but
his very actions cause such an intervention to occur. In manipulating Mme
Sablé, Parent reveals he himself is the agent whereby inexplicable and "alien"
forces enter the subject. The narrator offers a protracted account of how the
hypnotized "second self" of Mme Sablé begs him to lend her 5000 francs

which she doesn't need. He recounts her humiliation when, the next day, he brings her the money which, in her awakened state, she has no recollection of asking for. Not only does she lose her physical immunity to invasion, but the narrator himself, all too willing to participate in this exercise of scientific control, seems to lose his ability to resist or prevent such invasions.

The second scene of hypnotic manipulation is more troubling yet, for it clearly shows the doctor opening the physical door to some unknown force from without. Parent holds up his calling card to Mme Sablé and asks his hypnotized subject to gaze into the card and tell him what objects are behind her, as if the blank card were a mirror. She proceeds to describe the objects behind her head, a physically impossible feat, even for someone hypnotized. The narrator's description is curiously significant: "Elle voyait dans cette carte . . . comme elle eût vu dans une glace." [She saw in this card . . . just as she would have seen in a mirror.] (432) Later this same narrator will "see" the Horla, but only as the obliteration of his own image in the mirror. She looks into the same blank "mirror," and sees things she otherwise should not see. The supposed presence of the Horla, passing between the narrator and his mirror, frees him momentarily from his mirror condition. So it is with the blank card, which liberates Mme Sablé from her material existence, so that she can literally see with eyes behind her head.

Parent, in contrast, sees the world as a play of responding mirrors. He cites Voltaire to this effect: "Rien de plus vrai que cette parole de Voltaire: 'Dieu a fait l'homme à son image, mais l'homme le lui a bien rendu.'" [Nothing is more true than these words of Voltaire: "God has made man in his image, but man has more than given this image back to God."] (431) But what Voltaire says with irony, Parent offers seriously, as a statement of his method. For under control of the alienist, the relation of man to God, or man to alien, is reduced to a neat mirroring. This "other self," awakened by hypnosis, is immediately captured and, like man with Voltaire's God, immediately given back to its projector in a closed circuit. But this scene is proof that this process of closure does not work. Doctors cannot play God in this manner, for there are things out there that they play with but do not understand. Parent's science manipulates "magnetic" forces that are material and not fully understood. He claims to use these forces "scientifically," yet refuses to look outside this circuit for external causes. He seems to believe that mind mirrors world, and world mind. But what Mme Sablé performs is beyond mirroring; something paranormal seems to invade her being, something the narrator associates with his invisible Horla.

Maupassant rejects magnetism and hypnotic control of minds as dangerous enterprises because they leave subjects vulnerable to invasion by unknown external forces. Perhaps they, as invisible vectors, are the cause of contagion itself. Maupassant's story is contemporary to the research of Pasteur and his theory of biogenesis, which posits that diseases like cholera are not caused by factors internal to the organism, but vectored by invisible "microbes" that invade organisms from outside. Critics have noticed the sound association "horla—choléra," a disease whose origins were often ships from places like Brazil. The narrator, throughout Version Two, has struggled to master signs of physical sickness—the unexplained vertigo, pallor, sensations of suffocation. These subside as his mental activity becomes stronger, as he confronts with experiments what he increasingly perceives as a menace from without. Claiming to treat these invisible invaders within the closed clinical space of the mind, the psychoanalysts not only turn their backs on the possibility of external causes, but through their "magnetic" probing, may be responsible for "infecting" the minds of their patients.

## HORROR AND SCIENCE FICTION

Maupassant's story clearly exists at a crossroads of generic and scientific possibilities. Conventionally, one looks at it through the lens of the *fantastique*. One way lies the normative: in the mental institution, the patient is judged and interred by "known" medical science. The other way lies isolation, neurosis, terminal madness, but still framed by psychoanalysis. The science-fictional way to read this story leads in a different direction. First, the patient is judged not by his "condition" but by the *effectiveness* of his actions in the face of a phenomenon he sees, and examines, as real, not as a figment of his mind. He invokes the material imperative that is essential to defining a story as science fiction. Maupassant's revisions strongly suggest a science-fictional alternative, bolstered by scientific considerations of the time, to the conventional cultural reading. But Maupassant's text offers a crossroads as well within the field of comparative science fictions. The Parent episode indicates that the Cartesian mind ultimately cannot find shelter in its own space from intrusion from the Horla. The very science that would protect mind provides the means whereby the alien invades it. The science fiction that evolves from this, in France and other rationalist continental cultures, sees the world beyond mind and reason as horror—the realm of Descartes's non-mind and Pascal's terrifying "espaces infinis." We will compare this with Horla-like alien encounters in British and American science fiction.

Much subsequent French science fiction has followed the direction of surrealism, seeking to enclose the expansive worlds of space travel and alien encounter in what is clearly a mindspace. The postwar French science magazine *Fiction* gives its contents the generic names of "insolite" and "étrange," terms borrowed from surrealism. Its covers systematically turn the spacemen and spaceships of American science fiction into dream objects. Stories in this tradition often follow Maupassant in creating a dialogue between the mindworld and processes of experimental science, insofar as the focus remains mind's *exploration* of alien places. These places range from the most personal, in many cases the physical brain itself—the Cartesian mind's most intimate dwelling—to the vaguest, most "surreal" landscapes on distant planets that appear to explorers as dreamscapes. An example of the first is Christian-Yves Lhostis's *Tous ces pas vers le jaune* (1979). We have here what seems the exploration of a neuronal labyrinth by a consciousness acting like a Cartesian mite somehow introduced into the neurons and synapses of a human brain. It is hard to see the purpose of the protagonist's quest. Is it searching for some lost fixed place—its "soul"—in a maze whose "paths" are color-coded, as would be those of synapses in modern brain surgery? Seeking to go from "yellow" to "green" in this labyrinth, the protagonist never discovers a seat of "higher reason." Nor does he find the pineal gland that enables mind to interface with body and extended world. He simply wanders until he seems to realize that the alien invader in this web may be reason itself, whose pretensions at mastery seem to have no place here. The space of exploration here remains a physical place that follows its alien, color-coded logic. All rational mind and science can do is follow its multiple pathways from the green to the yellow world, there to begin another trek toward a "world" of a different color. If the path toward the yellow seems already traced—with food dispensers and rest areas along the way—it recalls the lines Comte traced on his diagram of a human brain, a path on a surface beneath which lies a realm of causality inscrutable to the mind, hence potentially horrific in nature. The novel is prefaced with a line from Henri Michaux—"L'enseignement de l'araignée n'est pas pour la mouche" [the lessons taught the spider are not for the fly]—which aptly describes the condition of the Cartesian who ventures into realms where the rational mind no longer serves as guide. Here—as with Parent's experiments—human investigators discover that they are aliens in *their own* alien land.

A French science fiction story that encounters the alien unknown, not within the human body or brain, but on a vaguely far-flung planet, is Alain Dorémieux's "Cauchemar rose" [Pink Nightmare] (1978). Scientists sent to explore the desert planet Syrtige encounter an alien life form that appears to seduce and destroy human beings by projecting the image of each man's deepest subconscious desires: "Tout se passe comme si j'avais été la victime d'une suggestion hypnotique, d'un phenomène télépathique inconnu qui aurait inhibé mon champs de perception."[Everything occurs as if I had been the victim of hypnotic suggestion, of some unknown telepathic phenomenon which would have blocked my field of perception.][13] This seems another invisible alien, taking possession, as in "Le Horla," of a subject's mind at its deepest level, penetrating unknown regions of the Cartesian self and neutralizing its ability to master its passions. These protagonists, unlike Maupassant's narrator, are professional scientists. They do not have to struggle with any medical or positivist frames and are in full control of their rational faculties. They identify this hypnotic invader at once and are able to resist it. They are even able to *see* and kill one alien. The beautiful apparition disappears, and what is revealed is "un vampire végétal" [a vegetable vampire], a tree-like entity that sinks roots in its victim and sucks out its vital organs to make its much-needed "mulch." The scene is more like the discovery of a Dracula, and subsequent pursuit of what is no longer an invisible invader or enemy. Moreover, it becomes clear to these scientists that humans can never communicate with, or co-exist with, these alien creatures—the planet must be "quarantined" and abandoned by human science. These creatures represent the ultimate Cartesian horror, for they isolate and destroy the rational self by invading the individual mind's deepest unconscious thoughts. As such, they not only exist outside of mind but are hostile to it, intent on destroying it by reducing it to food. Humans can only seek material shelter from it. Reversing the path of the Cartesian mind-stove, the protagonists lock themselves in their cabin with windows covered. The aliens' mental energy, however, like Parent's magnetism, penetrates these walls just as it does those of the subconscious mind. The protagonists eventually succumb and are destroyed. Reason is vanquished by an unreasoning organic process. These psychotropic invaders are real Horlas, and have no reason for "playing" with the human mind except food and survival.

For Pascal, the rational mind, though unique in the material universe, is but a speck in the totality of things. The vagueness of the term "horla" implies that Pascal's terror subtends the narrator's encounter with his invisible alien. Not only does French science fiction find its limits here, but science fiction issued from the rationalist tradition of the seventeenth century as well. At these limits, the scientific mind has but two options: reason can attempt to transpose non-reason (as with the surrealists) into a mindspace where reason can pretend to experiment with it and control it; or reason can retreat in horror from an encounter with non-reason—Dorémieux's quarantine.

A non-French work in the European rationalist tradition—Stanislaw Lem's *The Invincible* (1964)—offers what seems the most horrific situation imaginable to rational humanity: a *superior* non-rational being, in other words an entity that obviates Pascal's precarious parity between rational mind and non-thinking nature. Lem's novel assumes that *homo sapiens* has fulfilled Descartes's mandate of mastering all other known species through development of its rational mind. It thus sees itself as "invincible." Yet when its flagship *The Invincible* lands on planet Regis III in the Lyre Constellation, in search of a previously lost ship, *The Condor,* the crew finds the ship but confronts the most horrific of spectacles: a dead crew whose minds have apparently been wiped clean. In terms of the psychoanalyst, their egos have been destroyed, their minds reduced to pre-rational infantilism: "Total amnesia . . . but this is a special case. Not only does he not remember who he is, but he has also lost the ability to read, to write, to speak. What we're faced with here is complete disintegration, total destruction of personality."[14] More shockingly, they discover that ship and crew were destroyed by an alien life form that is *not* (as is our rationalist hope) more intelligent than we are. In fact, these magnetic clouds of "flies," measured by Cartesian standards, possess no reason at all. They are instead self-organizing, self-replicating nanomachines, the product of a mechanical or "necro-" evolution that has pushed all possibility of sentient organic life on this planet back into the seas. The word "horror" appears constantly in this narrative. Indeed, these metallic swarms are on the way to defeating invincible humanity, as crewmembers abandon their protective shields in terrified panic, exposing themselves to the alien magnetic fields that wipe their brains, and with them their "rational souls."

In the final chapter, protagonist Rohan sets out alone to explore the ravines where these creatures dwell, hoping to find lost crewmen. Under an incessant "black rain" of particles, he finds a wasteland of residues of other mechanical "life-forms." There are, as with the earlier "city," mangled remnants of inscrutable machines, "an elongated form, something like a fifteen-foot-long cross . . . whose outer metal hull had long since fallen apart, mixed with the muddy ground, and now formed a rust-red mass." (208) Rohan, significantly, can enter this landscape of metallic death because a device he wears over his skull emits magnetic signals identifying him as a mental patient. He appears to the aliens like the "wiped" humans of the *Condor*'s crew, a rationally deficient being, and is thus accepted among them. In this dead wasteland Rohan experiences the full horror of *res extensa,* here embodied in this species undergoing "necro-" evolution in a world humans can neither occupy nor defeat. Their only course as rational beings is to renounce this world as forever alien: "Suddenly he felt ridiculous standing there . . . he felt so superfluous in this realm of perfected death, where only dead forms could emerge victoriously in order to enact mysterious rites never witnessed by any living creature." (217) At his point, horror modulates, as with Maupassant's narrator, into frozen contemplation. Rohan's response, one of a sublime wonder that is simply the obverse of horror, confirms the impossible distance between us and it: "Not with horror, but rather with numbed awe and great admiration had he participated in the fantastic spectacle that had just taken place." (217)

This "spectacle," as with Maupassant's narrator, is our reflection in a blank mirror, the sole place of contact between reason and non-reason. The black metallic "insects" swarm around Rohan, "touch" his face and body, then in their inscrutable "rites" reproduce a giant image of his face. This scene however is not one of total defeat. For Lem seems to replay the scenario of Pascal's thinking reed, the consummate rationalist gambit. The alien can copy Rohan's face, but only Rohan can *know* that he is being copied. Even so, his retreat from this encounter remains a scene of horror: "He hurried blindly, his eyelids smarting with sweat, driven by some inner force whose undiminished presence kept amazing him from time to time. Would this ceaseless running, would this night ever take an end?" (219) All mankind can do in such an alien encounter is retreat within its human condition, where the mind is given the charge of sheltering the rational soul at all costs.

## MIND IN MOTION

The French science fiction that derives from "Le Horla" accepts the material imperative. But the result of that acceptance—the destruction of the rational mind through its encounter with the alien—is horror. Anglophone science fiction, as it develops, is not trapped in this mind-matter duality. Mind, not limited to the box of reason, is free to move in and through matter in its experimental journey into the unknown. If we adhere to our "science-fictional" reading of Maupassant's story, we can trace a line from his attempts to think and act outside the frame to protagonists in the Anglo-Saxon sphere. He can qualify as one of this science fiction's first "heroes" if we wish to see him, despite his experience of near loss of self in the mirror of horror, struggling to restore that self by taking a stand against the terrors of the unknown. He refuses to accept the limits of the rational mind, but seeks to understand the nature of his mind's sickness and possible physical causes of that sickness. Subsequent Anglophone science fiction has affection for protagonists like Maupassant's narrator, scientists "over the edge" like Van Helsing in *Dracula* who, despite his strange credentials as vampire hunter, endures the traps of Transylvania and traces the undead to his lair. Examples abound. But for the sake of comparison and contrast, we choose a protagonist and situation that bears resemblance, in many details, to Maupassant's "Horla." The hero is Roy Neary (Richard Dreyfuss of *Jaws* fame, consummate horror); the film is Steven Spielberg's *Close Encounters of the Third Kind* (1977). Roy, an obscure lineman in Midwestern suburbia, has no scientific training and represents (as does Maupassant's narrator) a "middle" position in society. But as it turns out, not only does he, as lineman, have hands-on knowledge of the grids of power that the rational scientist "grasps" only in theory, but he appears to be "visited" by greater, para-rational forces that only he sees and who manifest themselves in terrifying fashion. Again, he is the sole person in his circle who perceives these forces as coming from alien "beings." There is also, in the film, a "higher" body of scientists, not doctors but establishment figures who proceed by rational methods to create a grid in which they can identity the location of the alien encounter. Their belief in reason is such that they will not give credence to Roy's direct, bodily-physical apprehension of the aliens' existence. The lineman perceives the alien light show not as "celestial" music, but a direct jolt that literally "blows his fuse." As in Maupassant, they take possession of his mind and body. In a manner comparable to Maupassant's narrator, Roy is led to destroy his house as he obsessively constructs a huge model—from objects torn from his formerly sedate middle-class life—of Devil's Tower, the site of the impending encounter of a third kind. Radically and violently, he destroys his old life to identify the place where, all alone, he will make contact with the aliens.

But Spielberg's film, in a significant manner, "clarifies" Maupassant's ending. For in "Le Horla," the narrator looks on in horror as his house burns. *Then* we find him in a hotel room, contemplating suicide. We can only surmise, with his final affirmation of his "moi," that he might continue his struggle. In Spielberg's final scene there is no longer ambiguity. It is the rationalist Lacombe (played by Frenchman François Truffaut) who now stands frozen, watching the alien ship take off. All the professionals—doctors, scientists, engineers—remain powerless to act. Again, as in Lem, we have awe instead of horror. As with the sublime, awe and horror are two forms of paralysis of the rational mind in the face of the unknown. Neary however, the person no one in the establishment listens to, acts. He goes to Devil's Tower, climbs it, and simply walks on to the field, enters the alien ship, and ascends to the stars. This ending may seem sentimental. But the twist it gives is significant in light of "Le Horla." For those who seem to be the "children" in the hands of "parents" here—the "anti-social" Neary or Maupassant's narrator in the hands of his medical doctors—now literally become father to the man, not only the rational humans but (it is implied) the technologically superior aliens as well. Their form, as they "reveal" themselves, is that of childlike creatures. Neary enters the fog of the alien mirror standing head and shoulders above the beings who greet him, holding them by the hand. Such is the way that science fiction, in numerous cases, resolves the impasse of horror by literally *moving* human inquiry beyond the impasse of institutions and phobias, beyond such "forbidden" acts as destroying one's house and servants. It accepts Freud's condition of *Unheimlichkeit* and moves forward.

American science fiction, it seems, generally follows this external vector. It accepts and pursues unknown phenomena (Lem would call this a naïve leap of faith) as both real and physically *different*. In doing so, it challenges the rationalist impasse, which tacitly equates the limits of the human mind with those of the external universe. For American science fiction, this impasse becomes a crossroads where, in a kind of Kantian judgmental action, it chooses an open-ended process rather than the terminal horror of Pascal. Let us examine two examples of American science fiction that appear *consciously aware* of choosing this path, a path first traced perhaps by Maupassant. One is a film, the other a novel.

The film *Forbidden Planet*, (Fred Wilcox, 1956) deals with question of psychic horror. An Earth expedition, headed by Captain Adams, lands on the Krell planet, whose sole inhabitants are scientist Dr. Morbius and his daughter. The Krell machine—a massive machine-brain housed in vast caves under the planet's surface—can materialize thought, which led to the extinction of the Krell long ago. Morbius, however, whose subconscious mind wishes to prevent Adams from courting his daughter, projects via the Krell machine "monsters from the Id," beings who execute his subconscious desire to destroy Adams and his crew. Adams, beset by alien forces he at first doesn't understand, seeks an answer and ultimately finds it. Morbius has the role of Parent in Maupassant's tale. But as the drama plays out, he is attacked by the very forces and "monsters" he seeks to direct. Clearly here the external use of alien powers turns on its user, and the doctor can find no shelter in a medical establishment that sanctions their use. Morbius now finds himself trading roles with Maupassant's narrator, facing his own psychic monsters. But at this juncture, he refuses to interiorize the struggle. In an act of lucid contrition unthinkable in the context of Maupassant's doctors, he orders Adams to throw the switch to destroy the Krell machine which, he now realizes, has invaded and directed his own mind. In the end, Morbius defeats his inner monsters by claiming an external source for their presence and acting on that claim in the name of the greater good of the human species. The Krell machine differs from the Cartesian monstrosities of French science fiction in an important manner. It appears that it has physically absorbed within its circuitry the minds of its builders. It does the same with Morbius, capturing his thoughts from the deep, uncontrolled area of the *id*. But this Krell machine is not so much incorporating minds as *consuming* these minds, using them as fuel for its activity. It goes dormant when there is no more Krell fuel, their machine has physically burned it up. Thus, despite mention of the *id*, the solution is not found in psychoanalysis, but rather at the level of the machine itself, and that famous "good quantum mechanic" called upon to service it. As soon as Adams sees that the menacing force does not have its source in their own minds, but in an external something that is manipulating those minds, the switch can be thrown. The internalized alien of French psychoanalysis, endlessly recycled within the space of the mind, is here confronted as a Horla, an external enemy, and dismantled. In fact, in the destruction of this "bad" robot, the humans enlist a "good" one: the famous Robby the Robot who, as with Asimov's robots, allows humans to negotiate the mind-machine dichotomy. As is the case with Asimov's "Robbie" (1940), this Robby's very material mind is programmed to obey ours.

Let us turn to Asimov's *The Gods Themselves* (1972), wherein he locates the limits of mankind's search for the unknown not in monsters from the Id, but human *stupidity*—a condition that can only be cured by active reason correctly applied to the problem. Thus, the Schiller quote that gives the novel its title: "Gegen Dummheit die Götter selbst vergebens streben." [Against stupidity the Gods themselves struggle in vain.] The "gods" in question here preside over two contending para-universes—ours and a parallel universe whose "aliens" Asimov describes in great detail but, at the level of conscious activity, appear to be more or less our mirror doubles. Both universes have carried the Cartesian process of mind mastering the physical universe to its practical extreme, in the sense of depleting the material resources necessary to sustain the bodies that house this mind. The point of contention is an "electron pump," purportedly invented on Earth but apparently suggested to Earth minds by their alien doubles who seek to direct the flow of vital physical energy in their favor. These two universes have different, yet neatly interchangeable, chemistries. In our universe plutonium 186 degrades to tungsten 186; in their world it is the opposite—tungsten 186 becomes plutonium 186, creating the nuclear reaction which is believed will give cheap, clean energy. But their chemistry, transposed to our world, appears to have a negative reaction, causing our sun to fuse hydrogen more rapidly, thus raising the possibility of our sun going nova. But this same destruction of our sun, it turns out, will benefit the para-universe, whose denizens maintain their pump with this ultimate energy benefit in mind. This becomes a clear *practical* problem for humanity, requiring action, not quarantine and retreat.

Maupassant's doctors see humanity facing its dark double in the opaque mirror. There is no possibility of social discourse with such an alien because its opacity (which the narrator hopes to see as invisibility, a cloak hiding an external alien) is limited to being the projection of our inner, subconscious unknown. Asimov does not allow this Cartesian standoff to occur. For not to act, to internalize the problem, will lead to an unthinkably horrific extreme of mutual catastrophe. The standoff must be resolved. The solution again comes from a "marginal" human scientist, a certain Dennison who has literally lifted himself above the fray, taking residence on the Moon. Life in a satellite or space station (a favorite place of creative "libertarian" thinking in American science fiction) provides the possibility of a third position in a world otherwise locked in an iron duality. Dennison decides to tap into a third parallel universe—this time a "cosmic egg" from which both contenders can tap endless free energy. In Asimov's novel, a world drawn along the lines of a mind-matter duality—a world where all aliens are our dark "doubles" with whom we can never negotiate because we never admit they exist outside of our minds—leads to the impasse of potential horrific cataclysm. But here, the mutual acceptance of such *theoretical* rationalist limits is simply "stupidity." The "cure" for this mental deadlock is a practical one—a third term must be found, a new element added to the equation. This is precisely what the medical frames that enclose the investigative mind in Maupassant are there to prevent. And here again, as suggested with Maupassant's narrator, finding the way to a cure transforms a horror story into a science fiction one. All such cures, as with Bernard, can be only tentative at best. Yet they are the way of breaking open what is otherwise a closed circle of self-imposed horror. Science fiction follows Asimov's path of scientific and technological advancement as opener of closed structures.

## SENSES OF AN ENDING

Ultimately, the different readings of Maupassant's "Horla" bring up the crucial question of *choice.* Do we choose to retreat from the alien into our own mindspace, or engage it on its own terms? This question both determines science fiction in terms of genre and determines two strong currents in later science fiction—call them rationalist and pragmatic—which develop from this crossroads on the international level of science fiction's European and American origins. Rationalist science fiction includes the French tradition, writers like Lem strongly influenced by rationalist thought, and, in a sense, British writers in the wake of Wells who abandon evolutionary vistas for the Augustan *via media* of fiction of manners. Human experience here is defined by the mind-matter duality. Despite different scientific paradigms, humanity remains bounded by the limits of its mind in the face of an alien *res extensa.* In their "humanist" response, these traditions, as they process the impact of an advancing materialist science, find common ground in the normative thinking of a shared Enlightenment. American science fiction on the other hand, as seen in the examples above, remains proactive, pragmatic, and open-ended, offering investigative scientists practical options as they face the physical unknown. Science and scientists here (and brilliant amateurs are welcome) may and do act on the edge of society and propriety, when faced with the possibility of unthinkable alien horrors. But the stakes in such fiction are always high, with the fate of humanity often in the balance. There is always the question: what if, despite apparent madness, the lone investigator *is right* and consensual humanity is wrong?

The rationalist response is to enclose the lone investigator, such as Maupassant's narrator, in a rationally controlled institution or theoretical category such as mania or paranoia. We extrapolate here from Maupassant's medical frame to a work like Wells's "The Empire of the Ants" (1905) or any other scenario of potential disaster where it is more convenient to pronounce the narrator mentally "unreliable" than to entertain the possibility that he/she may be right. But what if those ants do take over the world? American science fiction, at this crossroads, at least offers the choice of an ending. The Rationalist vision refuses the leap into the material unknown. It prefers to see humanity retreat into the mind that defines it, rather than risk all in some terminal moment. The fact that American science fiction generally chooses advancement over retreat has been one of its strengths.

Maupassant's story, we argue, gives readers a choice between a horrific or science-fictional ending. American science fiction offers the same choice. One final, highly instructive example is again a film—*Invasion of the Body Snatchers* (1956). Protagonist Dr. Miles Bennett (as medical doctor he belongs to the scientific community, but on its practical fringe) begins to suspect that the people of Santa Mira are being physically possessed by alien creatures. As in Heinlein, alien possession is not mind possession alone, but "body snatching," physically assuming the total existence, mind and body, of the victim. There are no visible "slugs" here; the "snatched" bodies are intact. Yet these invaders are not totally invisible (hence potentially imaginary) beings, because they originate as visible "pods." Furthermore, these aliens are openly dangerous because they impose a Cartesian separation of mind and body on a world where mind and body are inseparable, where the individual self is defined by the functioning unity of mind and body, not by mind alone. Bennett, who discovers the "pods," gradually witnesses everyone in the town taken over by these aliens and shaped into a vast "group mind." He cannot choose the option of mass hallucination (mind snatching), because he has physically seen the pods. He thus opts for an external cause: the pods must have been "seeded" on Earth by some alien invader from outer space. The group mind they form is a physical incarnation of the consensus mind of Maupassant's psychoanalysts, an entity that conforms to every instrument of rational control from the positivist grids of Maupassant's time to European socialism and communism, all anathema to American Golden Age writers.

With the possibility that all of Santa Mira, and eventually the world, will be reduced to pods, with no one left outside the frame to tell the difference,

Bennett's resistance becomes a significant generic marker. No matter how cunning he is in avoiding capture, Miles appears doomed to be subsumed in the mass. This outcome would be horror. It appears, in fact, that director Don Siegel was faced with Maupassant's crossroads when deciding how to end his film. The horror scenario would be Bennett, the only surviving individual, escaping to the freeway, banging frantically on the windows of cars as they pass, trying to warn of the invasion—but no one stops; people roll up their windows, no one within the frame of the film believes Miles's story, and Bennett remains the madman beating on the bars of his cell. Added horror comes from the fact that we, the film audience, know he is right, and that if nobody hears him, humanity is lost. Maupassant mastered the ambiguity of the verbal narrative, where words can be twisted and readers ultimately do not know whether to opt for a real alien presence or the ravings of a madman. But in the film viewers *have seen* the pods taking over bodies. From this position outside the frame, they know that Bennett is both sane and correct. The horror here comes from the possibility that such a situation could happen, where the one who knows is not believed, and we, like the vectored mind on the English mail coach, are forced into a mind-body split, obliged to watch helplessly as humanity hurtles to its doom.

It is said (without tangible evidence) that this was how Siegel wanted to end the film, but producers didn't like the ending and imposed a more optimistic one. It is more likely however that Siegel exercised a generic choice, realized this ending was horror, and opted instead for the science-fictional ending of the film shown in movie theaters. Police pick Miles up and are about to book him as a loon. They call psychoanalysts to examine him. But physical reality intervenes, in the form of what Heinlein called "serendipity." There is a report that a truck carrying strange "pod-like" things has overturned on the road, spilling its cargo. A quick-thinking police captain puts two and two together, calls the army, and humanity is on the way to a physical response that hopefully will wipe out the threat of this Horla. One can of course argue that such "good luck" is itself another frame, this time one designed to protect our cherished anthropocentric sense of individuality. For why might not the next step in human evolution be some sort of group entity? The question however seems irrelevant when we consider the following. Maupassant set forth what is essentially a ritual of mankind's discovery of the alien—"ritual" because we, at least Western mankind, do not want to be overcome by an alien form of existence. This ritual can go two ways: either we assimilate the alien as a construct that ultimately mind can, in Pascal's sense, "comprehend," subsume, or we simply abandon the search, as in Lem and Dorémieux, declare the alien unfathomable, unconquerable, and leave it to its destiny. But there is a third way. We can take the path of experimental science and seek to understand it so as to "cure" or defeat it. In all these cases, different cultural responses to this ritual help us define national forms of what today is the genre of science fiction. The reading of the ritual is different in Lem than it is in, say, Wells's *The War of the Worlds*. It is different again when George Pal remakes Wells's story in his 1953 American film. Here again, a culture chooses the film medium, which allows the viewer's gaze to redirect the ambiguous ending of the written work. We actually see the Martians defeated, thus believe the scientists that the defeat is real. This neutralizes the ambiguous ending of Wells's text, where the narrator can frame the ending by suggesting that these Martians are perhaps humans at a later stage of development. The American film chooses total victory, and in doing so accepts the Martians as something real, as something other than us. We put them behind us. But because of this, we must watch the skies for more invaders.

To conclude, all that is needed for Maupassant's story to be seen as science fiction (and not an exercise in the *fantastique*) is a shift of cultural focus. We must see the narrator applying the material imperative, by which he declares the alien to be something plausible, a real thing to be examined, verified, engaged in the material world. Once this step is taken, narrator and reader alike face the possibility of horror. The alien may be hostile, and possibly invincible. It may be non-mind against mind, a blind force that crushes us. At this crossroads, national science fictions define themselves. We have offered three responses.

The first is the Cartesian-rationalist response. Maupassant, in "Le Horla," saw the possibility that the very actions of his guardians of rational order, by meddling with paranormal forces, could bring this external horror into the medical frame that is supposed to shelter the Cartesian mind. In Lem and Dorémieux, later science fiction in this rationalist tradition, we see mankind, in the *res extensa* of space, retreating from alien forces that overwhelm and obliterate mind, drawing an ever-larger protective circle around the rational soul.

The second, British, response—that of Wells—is skeptical. The Martians prove to be real, and nearly destroy us. But they are no more horrific than the invisible microbes that destroy them, which have taken countless human lives in the process of making us immune to them. In fact, it seems the Martians are our future, minds that pushed reason too far and lost their hearts in the bargain. Wells effectively turns the alien encounter back on a human center, defined not by mind but by our situation in an evolutionary scheme of things. The narrator of *The Time Machine* sums this up: "He [the Traveller] thought but cheerlessly of the Advancement of Mankind and saw in the growing pile of civilization only a foolish heaping that must inevitably fall back upon and destroy its makers in the end."[15]

Third, in contrast, American science fiction openly engages the material unknown, fighting the horrific with hopes of expanding its perimeter of understanding but under no illusion of "mastery." Bennett is, at best, given what we have called a reprieve. "Stupidity" is defeated in Asimov, but such defeat is always temporary. Moreover, "stupidity" here is not (as with Wells) exclusively *our* stupidity. It is a general propensity of life forms, humanoid or not, in the broad material universe. Against this, we need scientific visionaries to lead us out of the morass. But our struggle, unlike that of Schiller's gods, is not necessarily in vain. Perhaps more in American science fiction than anywhere else, we see, in light of Maupassant's heritage, the birth of science fiction from the spirit of horror.

## NOTES

1. Roger Bozzetto's article, "Le Horlà [his accent]: histoire d'alien ou récit de l'altérité?: Une double approche de l'altérité" (Montpellier: *Cahiers de l'Irea*, 1996), offers a large bibliography of articles (mostly French) devoted to this text as of 1995. Bozzetto argues that Version One presents the possibility that there is a Horla out there, "le successeur de l'homme." Version Two, on the contrary, chronicles the onset of madness. But Bozzetto still sees the narrator and his "double" the reader the victims "d'un terrifiant *impossible et pourtant là.*"

2. See Claude Bernard, *Introduction à l'etude de la medicine experimentale* (Paris: Garnier-Flammarion, 1966). Here he describes the process of experimental science: "Cette joie de la découverte tant cherchée et tant espérée s'évanouit dès qu'elle est trouvée. Ce n'est qu'un éclair don't la lueur nous a découvert d'autres horizons vers lesquels notre curiosité inassouvie se porte encore avec plus d'ardeur. C'est ce qui fait que dans la science meme le connu perd son attrait, tandis que l'inconnu est toujours plein de charmes." [That joy of discovery so looked for, so hoped for, vanishes as soon as it is found. It is just a spark whose gleam reveals to us other horizons towards which our unsatisfied curiosity turns itself with even more fervor. That is why in science, even the known loses its attraction, whereas the unknown is always full of charm.] (307)

3. See Yvette Conry, *"L'Introduction du Darwinisme en France au XIXe siècle* (Paris: Corti, 1974), 416. See also Harry W. Paul, *From Knowledge to Power: The Rise of the Science Empire in France, 1860–1939* (Cambridge: Cambridge University Press, 1985), 60–92.

4. John Stuart Mill, *August Comte and Positivism* (London: N. Trübner & Co., 1865), 6. References are to this edition.

5. Michel Foucault, *Histoire de la folie à l'âge classique* (Paris: TEL Gallimard, 1972), 525. Translations are mine.

6. "Le Horla, première version," Guy de Maupassant, *Contes et nouvelles* II, edited by Louis Forestier (Paris: Édition de la Pléiade, 1988), 829–830. The second version is in *Contes et nouvelles* II, 913–938. References are to this edition.

7. Tzvetan Todorov, *Introduction à la littérature fantastique* (Paris: Éditions de la Pléiade Points, 1970), 169. References are to this edition, and all translations mine.

8. See William Butcher, translator and annotator, Jules Verne, *Journey to the Centre of the Earth* (Oxford: Oxford World Classics, 1992), (Explanatory Notes): "Verne is borrowing this quotation from Victor Hugo, *Notre-Dame de Paris*, part 4, chapter 3) where he adapts Virgil (Eclogue 5:44) "formosi pectoris custos formosior ipse (guardian of a fine herd, finer still himself)." (230) A better translation of Virgil would be "beautiful." Butcher names several contemporary sources for Verne's underground journey—Poe, Alexandre Dumas's *Isaac Laquédem,* a George Sand story "Laura." These provide common examples of pseudo-scientific speculations in the fiction of the time. Verne may have borrowed from some of these; he may also have taken from these, and known scientific texts of the time, his descriptions of Iceland and certain phenomena (possible and imaginary) of the subterranean world visited. But what is essential is the artistry with which he creates Axel's (the narrator's) voyage of gradual introspection, whereby contact with raw facts of *res extensa* creates a journey from observation to dreamscape. It is interesting that, toward the end of the century, Arthur Rimbaud, in his pre-surrealist poem "Le bâteau ivre," takes many of his descriptions of fabulous and fantastic phenomena—creations of an exuberant imagination, a veritable dreamscape– from Verne, notably *Voyage au centre de la terre* and *Vingt-mille lieues sous les mers* (1870).

9. Guy de Maupassant, "Lettre d'un fou," *Contes et nouvelles* II, 461–466. Louis Forestier, in a note discussing the context and meaning of this story (1458), gives a good sense of how Maupassant's contemporaries might have seen the "malady" of the protagonist. Citing Charcot and other doctors of the time, he describes the sickness as a "maladie de l'ame" [sickness of the soul] in good Cartesian terms, as a "névrose" [neurosis], which he sees as a form of mental illness where "la sacro-sanct raison, qui gouvernait les êtres, est battue en brèche." [the sacrosanct reason which ruled humans, is demolished]

10. See Voltaire, *Lettres philosophiques*, edited by Raymond Naves (Paris: Garnier, 1962), vingt-cinquième letter, 144. Voltaire is responding to Pascal's statement that stresses the incomprehensibility of the human condition without God ("de sorte que l'homme est plus inconcevable sans ce mystère que le mystère n'est inconcevable à l'homme"). Voltaire rejects the extremes of either-or for the human condition, and instead sees an equation of more or less, which states that there is less than mankind, and more than mankind, not exactly an evolutionary statement, but not Descartes's duality either: "L'homme paraît être à sa place dans la nature, supérieur aux animaux, auxquels il est semblable par ses organes, inférieur à d'autres êtres, auxquels il ressemble probablement par la pensée." One finds, to some degree, a hint of this relativism in Descartes's *Les passions de l'âme*, but there is no possibility there of rational beings who are *more* than mankind.

11. This reminds one of Maupassant's "La petite Roque" (1885), where the mayor commits a heinous crime, then guides the police investigation step by step until they finally discover that he himself is the perpetrator of the crime, a sort of Oedipal loop that, if we adopt the Cartesian reading of "Le Horla," plays out as the lone narrator tracks the alien to the space of his own mind.

12. Maupassant published in 1885, a few years before "Le Horla," a collection of stories entitled *Monsieur Parent.* The title story, which bears the same name, is tied, by Louis Forestier, editor of the Édition de la Pléiade two-volume set *Contes et nouvelles*, to "Le Horla." The link however is, according to Forestier, the theme of the double, which leads to cruelty in "Monsieur Parent" and madness in "Le Horla." What Forestier does not explore is the modulation from "Monsieur" to "Docteur" in terms of the suggestive name "Parent."

13. Alain Dorémieux, *Promenades au bord du gouffre* (Paris: Éditions Denoël, 1978), 144.

14. Stanislaw Lem, *The Invincible*, translated from the German by Wendayne Ackerman (New York: Ace Books, 1968), 87. References are to this edition. The translations read well in English but are certainly flawed by being a second-hand translation.

15. H. G. Wells, *The Time Machine* (New York: Bantam Books, 1968), 114.

# Chapter Six

# Bernal's Masterplot
# and the Transhuman Promise

We have discovered, in often unsuspected locations across the spectrum of nineteenth-century European and American literature, a set of themes and generic markers that will ultimately inform what is to be called science fiction. But one thing is lacking. Science fiction must have a central story—a masterplot—a story that can assimilate all the paradigms we have identified. It must not only be valid across national and cultural boundaries but embody Asimov's "master" definition of the genre. It must therefore be a plot that allows writers to pursue the possibility of scientific and technological advancement to its human endpoint, and perhaps beyond. It is this promise of transhumanity that joins Descartes and evolutionary theory, setting in motion the exploration of ways in which the human mind *and* human body might expand beyond limits previously set, by both the rationalists' human condition and mankind's biological condition.

Much is said today about transhumanity and posthumanity. But what is projected now—in scientific essays and science fiction—is the product of more than a century of speculation, which begins in the late nineteenth century with evolutionary theory and spans the entire twentieth century. The story of this search to transcend the human condition has been a narrative constant that developed with modern science fiction. It has been the masterplot of science fiction's evolutionary "epics," developing seemingly new and ever more plausible scenarios in the wake of scientific and technological advancement, across the century, in fields such as molecular medicine, nanotechnology, and information science and artificial intelligence. Ray Kurzweil, in *The Singularity Is Near: When Humans Transcend Biology* (2005), calculates that in the year 2045 machine intelligence will overtake human, biological intelligence. The result will be a "waking up" of the material universe, as gradually these super-brains become "infoforming" machines, gradually converting vast spaces of the physical universe into mind, the source of which is the transhuman singularity moment. We have Robert Bradbury's speculation on "matrioshka brains," planetary computational devices that convert matter into the energy needed to sustain expanding networks of such superintelligences. Science fiction has seen the novels of Australian writers Greg Egan and Damien Broderick (*The Godplayers* [2006]), as well as extraordinary extrapolations such as Charles Stross's *Accelerando* (2006), which sees the matrioshka brain as the logical evolutionary result of sentient life in our (and all possible) solar systems.

Even so, in these flamboyantly extrapolated works, we find a constant, present from the beginning, which seems to define the dynamic of the transhuman masterplot. Kurzweil offers an elaborate history of the development of artificial intelligence to the moment of singularity and beyond. Yet although he declares these AIs superior to humans, he feels obliged to remark that they still are bound to respect human life and values, reminding us of Asimov's Laws of Robotics, which provide a similar built-in governor to the transhuman process. The same turning back of the posthuman entity to its human origins is found with Asimov's R. Daneel Olivaw. A robot indistinguishable from a human in the early novel *The Caves of Steel* (1954), Olivaw develops over the entire history of the First Empire and is somewhere in the neighborhood of 19,250 years old in *Foundation and Earth* (1986). As machine intelligence "he" is theoretically immortal, with unlimited replacement of body and brain parts. But as he advances, he needs an increasingly complex brain. To obtain this, he returns to a biological brain. But the obverse of advances in complexity is increased perishability. Olivaw's final, biological brain lasts a mere 600 years, so he must seek a new brain from alien life forms. Machines, and machine intelligence, remain bound to biology, possibly (if Descartes is correct) to human biology alone.

In these narratives, evolutionary forces interestingly seem to invariably lead, in contradictory manner, to affirmation of a duality between human and posthuman. Evolution is an open system; this duality calques on top of evolution a closed system based on the opposition of matter and mind. The vast network of superintelligences in Olaf Stapledon's *Star Maker* (1937) communicates telepathically; the matroshka brains connect informationally. But in each case, if the stated goal is to convert matter into mind, the unstated goal is to restore some model based on the human mind of the rationalists to a central position in the universe. These superbrains hearken back to human analogues like Laplace's "demon," the superintelligence capable of calculating all past and future events for the entire universe, or farther back to Spinoza's god-mind. The fundamental dynamic then of the transhuman quest is between evolutionary change and human constancy. The fact that this represents a modern reworking of the Cartesian duality of mind and matter was seen by British crystallographer J. D. Bernal in his 1929 treatise *The World, the Flesh, and the Devil: An Enquiry into the Three Enemies of the Rational Soul*.[1] Bernal's work provides a bridge between the science of human "enhancement" and its fictional possibilities, setting forth a set of stages whereby modern scientific humanity—characterized as the "rational soul"—advances toward the transhuman promise. This sequence will provide the masterplot for much of twentieth-century science fiction.

Bernal transforms the mind-matter duality he rediscovers at the heart of transhuman aspirations into an interplay between what he calls the "dimorph" and its double, in other words, the part of humanity that advances beyond itself, and the part that stays home to tend the hearth. This dynamic allows fiction to negotiate the crux between human story and transhuman possibility. The term "posthumanity" implies a state where humanity has transcended its old form. Science *fiction*, however, generally avoids this enticing possibility. The nature of fiction is to tell human stories. Telling posthuman stories, without some sort of bridge back to the "old humanity," becomes impossible. Moreover, if fiction has little to say about "posthumanity," it is probably because human readers do not care about what is no longer human. Transhumanity, on the other hand, is the story of how we got to be *it*. Bernal's dimorphic scenario gives fiction the means of narrating the conditions of human transformation, at the moment when we pass the gulf and evolve into something else.

Bernal's slim volume has been, and remains to this day, a strong influence on the scientific imagination and science fiction alike. It is the only book Stapledon mentions by title at the end of his Preface to *Star Maker*; Arthur C. Clarke, in a piece republished in 2000, calls the book "the most brilliant attempt at scientific prediction ever made."[2] Bernal's presence is ever more noticeable today, for around this same millennial year two important biographies of Bernal were published. In the same year, postmodernist biologist Donna Haraway was awarded the John Desmond Bernal Prize, the highest honor bestowed by the Society for the Social Studies of Science.[3] In his treatise, Bernal saw mankind—by means of science and technology—transforming both its environment *and its physical being,* bringing it to the point where, through radical changes in its environment and conditions of existence, it is ready to advance to some new state of existence. At this juncture however, Bernal discovers a new duality hardwired into the human circuitry. What he calls (after Descartes) the "rational soul" is the motor of change that brings mankind to aspire to become more-than-human. For Bernal, this becomes a purely material entity, but even as such remains mysteriously divided.

Material science, here the science of psychology, cannot fix this problem. The evolution of the species can only exacerbate this division, until it finally brings about a "dimorphic split" that generates two equally divergent scenarios for the future of *homo sapiens*. The first is radical change, where the forward-looking half of mankind leaves behind home and human form and evolves into something totally different. The second is retreat to an ecotopia, a stay-behind mankind that husbands and conserves what now is (in Bernal's words) a "well-tended zoo."

Humanity at the transhuman crossroads finds itself at the edge of knowability. The same is true for writers, for whom imagination now pushes the limits of storytelling. The transforming human entity—Bernal's "dimorph"—advances to a point where, as it shoots the gulf, it becomes less and less human, thus logically feels less and less need to communicate with its former being. Likewise, the stay-behind old humans (we readers) remain unable to conceive of this new humanity, let alone tell its story, beyond the moment of transhuman passage. If science fiction is the narrative form that recounts Bernal's story of mankind advancing beyond itself, it takes upon itself the difficult if not impossible task of finding *narrative* means of negotiating what is, more than a two-species gap, a communications gap. Because of the fundamentally anthropocentric nature of our narrative conventions, the gap becomes one between story and non-story. How science fiction strives to tell the story of Bernal's transhuman evolution is the subject of this chapter.

Science fiction's solution involves the process of Bernal's dimorphism. In examined science fiction works, the evolving dimorph, at the moment of the "split," invariably generates a double that serves, in fictional terms, as a comprehensible analogue to a now-incomprehensible destiny. Bernal's early stages of human advancement present examples of the Cartesian mind "mastering" the first two enemies of the rational soul—world and body. But with his third enemy Bernal discovers (as did Descartes in *Les passions de l'âme* with its "higher" and "lower" mind) the impasse that still keeps mankind from advancing—mind divided against itself. At this point, he gives the process of human advancement over to material evolution, which in turn determines two *directions* for evolved humanity to go—Earth or the stars. At this juncture, evolutionary process yields to dualism. For each transcendent dimorph generates its new human double. As mankind moves beyond itself, it simultaneously creates a "secret sharer." As "listener" to the dimorph's story, the double serves to retrieve the conventional image of mankind at the very moment mankind is in the process of losing that image forever. Science thus domesticates the unknown, even if it cannot understand it.

There are two models for evolutionary dimorphism—catastrophe and continuity. An example of catastrophic transformation is Clarke's Overmind.

Here mankind and its Earth are consumed in a transfer of energy, resulting in an entity that bears no resemblance to the humanity that generated it. On the other hand, J.-H. Rosny aîné's *La Mort de la Terre* (1910) offers an example of the continuity model. When Rosny's Last Man Targ offers up the last remaining carbon molecules to his ferromagnetic successor, he seems to establish continuity between one kingdom of life and its successor. Even so, the evolutionary gap between humanity and the remotest hope for a compatible ferromagnetic intelligence make the possibility of communication across this divide as remote as any eventual contact with the Overmind. Bernal's concept of dimorphic evolution, however, suggests the possibility of a continuity-in-catastrophe scenario, enabling the human body and mind to cross the transhuman threshold yet maintain contact with its former state. This dimorph-double dynamic lets science fiction "push the envelope" of human advancement, lets it glimpse the undiscovered country, while at the same time allowing a return from that country, with a story that remains relevant, if not to readers' conventional sense of humanity, at least to their *desire* for human continuity.

## BERNAL'S THREE ENEMIES OF THE RATIONAL SOUL

In his treatise, Bernal articulates a path to transhumanity which has proven to be that of human "advancement" in the twentieth century. The story Bernal tells, despite its evolutionary premises, remains one of constancy in change, an improbable story if we consider the material facts of any mutational process. Bernal evokes mankind's ability to evolve in the physical sense. Yet the "enemies" he invokes—world, flesh, devil—suggest the Christian system, where (under God's dispensation) mankind retains centrality and immutability. This duality remains embedded in his exposition. "World" is an ecological-technological replay of *res cogitans* and material *res extensa.* Driven by variables such as resource depletion and population explosion, the rational mind extends its habitat to moons, planets, and outer space. These environments it "terraforms," makes them physically like Earth, so humans in their present form can survive and live there. The limits of such physical expansion however raise the equally Cartesian problem of the body. If humanity wishes to advance farther, beyond environments we cannot terraform, it must restructure its bodies to make them function in such environments. Bernal's "flesh" is in fact a modern version of Descartes's "body-as-machine," a thing to be altered by mechanical or biological engineering. In turn, this category of "flesh," where the physical body acts as interface between mind and world, makes us aware of the central problem of the Cartesian system in general—the *dualism* that sets mind against matter. This leads Bernal to his third category, his "devil." Here Bernal returns Descartes to his Christian source. For now, the rational soul is taken over by another form of *malin génie*, the "devil" that works within the human mind to set limits to its desire to change and advance. The devil of olden lore becomes, in evolutionary terms, mankind's internal governor. With the rational mind thus divided, mankind cannot, of its own accord, move beyond this divide to advance its being. At this impasse, only evolutionary forces can move mankind to transcend this condition.

Bernal's speculations on how mankind might transform its environment and physical body were startling in their day and are now being augmented as new techniques of terraforming and human enhancement develop. He speaks of not only interplanetary engineering, but prosthetic devices and what will become nanotechnology. Later scientists and science fiction writers will conceive of electronic and bionic means of transformation—most notably the "cyborg" or cybernetic organism—while pursuing the ultimate dream of freeing mind once and for all from its imperfect and mortal "machine." Even so, Bernal presents human resistance to such change as something innately "hardwired" into mind itself, untouchable by either mechanical or psychological alterations. As such, it acts as a Cartesian governor to arrest radical change. What we have here, in fact, is advancing mind weighed down by the residue of old systems—the Christian fall, the Cartesian "ghost" in the material machine.

In Bernal's narrative, the sole resolution of this human stalemate can come from blind, evolutionary forces: "The conflict between the humanizers and the mechanizers will not be solved by victory of one over the other, but by a splitting of the human race, the one section developing a fully balanced humanity, the other groping unsteadily beyond it." (56) The latter form is described as "a fanatical but useful people who choose to distort their bodies or blow themselves into space." (70) At this point Bernal moves beyond reliance on Christian and Cartesian terminology to envision a new, dynamic division between stasis and movement. The terms "mechanizers" and "humanizers" describe a division between internalizing movement and externalizing advancement. The "fanatical but useful" mechanizers take the process of world, flesh, and devil beyond the limits of mankind's Earth. Humanizers on the other hand bend the evolutionary line back into a circle, where the human form and mind still provide the center. The important thing to consider is that these two impulses remain, at the same time, doubles. For each represents an opposite yet paired way of dealing with this necessity of human evolutionary transformation. Because one path remains the shadow of the other, the storyteller can tell this story of human advancement right up to the irreversible moment of transhuman passage.

We remember that Lucifer and his followers were also "fanatical but useful people" who, once cast from heaven, look back defiantly, even in their transformation, with envy on what seemed the perfect form they once had. Given these overtones, Bernal's process of "dimorphism" appears at one and the same time as irreversible change *and* unavoidable nostalgia for the lost form. However radical the process of transformation may seem, the new humanity somehow needs to retain a sense of its old physical form. For example, Bernal speculates on the effects of freeing the brain from its "locomotor organs," going beyond prosthetic alterations of the flesh to envision a "chemical dispersion of individuality as multiple organisms." He looks forward here to the dream, itself Cartesian perhaps, of certain twentieth-century scientists and science fiction writers to convert all matter, not just human matter, into a conscious, rational entity. Such "dematerialized modes of organization" (Bernal's terms) would be self-replicating, like the electron plasma of Fred Hoyle's *The Black Cloud* (1957). Yet for Bernal even such a dematerialized humanity would, because of its origins, retain the need to look homeward to what it once was and what we readers are today. It is this original home that Bernal's split preserves. As new mankind leaves for parts unknown, "old mankind is left in undisputed possession of Earth, to be regarded by the inhabitants of the celestial sphere with a certain reverence." (73) The world left behind becomes a "human zoo, so intelligently managed that its inhabitants are not aware they are there merely for purposes of observation and experiment." (73) The dimorph will always have its double, for either the sake of nostalgia or (in more sinister fashion) purposes of "experiment."

All narrators must have a "narrative audience," that is, an assumed audience within the text that understands the story it is telling and provides the means of mediating, in terms of spacetime location, between the narrator and readers. The transhuman story offers a particular challenge to this channel of communication. If the narrator is located this side of the transhuman divide, in Bernal's human zoo, the story of transhumanity stops at this divide. Narrator and narrative audience cannot, by their location, know what has happened to the dimorph. But let us say the narrator wishes to place itself *on the other side of the divide.* By what means does it convey its story back from there? Logically, for humans, the transhuman world would be an alien world. A transhuman narrator, located *there,* would logically tell its story to a narrative audience in its world, an audience that would understand it, whereas readers, as humans placed on this side of the divide, would not understand, at least not without every detail "translated" in tedious fashion. Narrators generally avoid this problem in two ways. Either they can, as in Lem's *The Invincible* (1964), declare the alien unknowable, and confine narrative and audience to human space. Or they can ignore the problem, locate their narrator in alien space, and proceed to tell a story that, again logically, would not need to be told to an audience in *that* world, for they know all the details, whereas readers, on our side of the divide, should not be able to understand them.

Because, in the case of transhumanity, *we humans* are the alien, this problem of communication, of location of narrator and narrative audience, becomes crucially important to us. Science fiction's material imperative was discussed in the preceding chapter. It applies to not only physical situations but narrative situations as well. Whereas previous fictions simply "suspended disbelief," science fiction tends to take narrative matters such as the location of narrative audiences as physical facts. Transhumanity offers a material barrier to the act of telling that requires material solutions to breaching this barrier. Bernal's masterplot leads science fiction physically to a narrative impasse; his linking of dimorph and double however gives science fiction the possibility of negotiating this barrier. Let us examine some ways that science fiction puts this dynamic to use on the threshold of transhuman promise.

## THE SPACETIME ODYSSEYS OF ARTHUR C. CLARKE

Clarke's early work offers near-perfect examples of Bernal's dimorphic split; his subsequent novels and stories retreat however from the radical schism of an early work like *Childhood's End* (1953),[4] instead cultivating a stylized interplay of dimorph and double, transcendence and homecoming. This is seen in *2001: A Space Odyssey* (1968) and its sequels, works that represent the culmination of Clarke's career (*3001: The Final Odyssey* appeared in 1997).[5] Even so, *Childhood's End* can be read on two levels, and as such contains the germ of the later work. The novel, on one hand, presents dimorphism as a cataclysmic rather than continuous process. Its initial setting is one of impending atomic holocaust, averted by the arrival of mysterious "Overlords" who impose a reign of peace and plenty on Earth. The millennium they bring however proves to be short-lived. Utopian boredom reigns in New Atlantis, and at this point of stagnation, the dimorphic split suddenly occurs. Human children mysteriously lose contact with adults; grouping together, they form an internal chain reaction that literally consumes their (and all human and earthly) forms. The result is the catastrophic energy transfer that creates the Overmind, an entity that retains no vestiges of our former state. Applying the strict logic of evolution, Clarke depicts the dimorph Overmind as forever closed to its human antecedents and the star-roaming "mechanizer" Overlords who, we learn, are the agents of this chain reaction.

Even so, much of the novel, and its entire final section, deal with Jan the Last Man and his relation to the Overlords. As opposed to the cataclysmic finality of the Overmind, Jan's is a story of communication and at least potential continuity of the human *spirit*, if not the human body and mind. The Overlords, it turns out, are cosmic museum keepers, who plan to capture a human specimen to place it, as median, between creatures from the depths of Earth's seas and other interstellar oddities it collects. We notice here the equal and opposite correlation between deep ocean and deep space, which Clarke exploits endlessly in subsequent works. This correlation undercuts the apparent evolutionary drive toward the Overmind, instead fixing humanity at the static center of this cosmic "evolution," the pivot point around which impulsions toward a transhuman future invariably revolve. In *Childhood's End*, this centerpiece is provided by the story of Jan, who recounts the death of Earth and all its marvels in elegiac accents. In turn, this story is captured and stored by the Overlords, themselves perpetual exiles between worlds and forms of sentient life. Seen by early humanity as devils, the Overlords appear in Clarke's novel as guardian "angels." In relation to humans and Overmind, however, it is finally revealed that they are devils after all, reprobate beings excluded from this evolutionary "grace." As cosmic museum curators, they appear, in relation to the Overmind, to serve the function of Bernal's "zoo" keepers, but their own destiny is an evolutionary dead end. As observers, they remain forever outside the line of advancement that moves from human to posthuman.

Jan's situation seems equally a dead end. As last man, he has no human audience within the text to address—yet he has the Overlords, who hear his story and carry it away. They may be aliens, but by assimilating them to human myths and theology, Clarke makes sure readers, through their myths and theologies, can relate with them as audience, allowing readers to consider the possibility that Jan's story, as summation of a human race that has now acceded to Overmind, might someday "convert" the Overlords, give them the means of "repenting." The reader thus envisions a possible continuity that breaches the gap between mind and Overmind. For what if the Overlords, in embracing the human principle in Jan's story, "humanize" themselves to the point that they place themselves in line for their own future transfiguration to Overmind? At the end of the novel, this remains pure speculation. But we see the dimorph-double combination at work in Clarke's narrative. The Earthly zoo is gone, with no humans left to tend it. But Jan's story creates its Overlord double. Catastrophe, total non-communication between mankind and its future form, is confronted with a continuity option, where the Overlords now assume the human position in a gradual advance toward transhumanity.

In each successive novel of his Odyssey series, Clarke revisits the possibility of transcendence as mankind inches chronologically into its future, only to show the dimorphic promise thwarted again and again as the mutating forms of his protagonists are recaptured by their original doubles. The Odyssey pattern of the fabulous voyage that is simultaneously a homecoming now dominates Clarke's narratives of transhuman promise. The original *2001* is ostensibly a tale of human advancement, from prehistory to transcendence. The origin of human intelligence that launches us on our evolutionary journey is also for Clarke, in bilateral manner, the moment of the Christian fall. It is this side of Clarke's double vision that Stanley Kubrick pursues, clearly caught in his film image of the prehistoric bone-weapon tossed in the air that morphs into a spaceship weapon orbiting a future Earth, inscribing an arc that both encapsulates and elides all known human history.

Despite the fact that Clarke and Kubrick have opposite views of human advancement, a like play of dimorphs and doubles resonates throughout film and book alike, whose mutual creation occurred in near-symbiotic manner. The inspiration for the film was classic Clarke—his story "The Sentinel" (1951), which becomes the Moon sequence in the film. But Kubrick redirected the film away from human advancement, focusing instead on human *hubris* and mankind's recurring fall. Clarke "responded" with his book, published after the film appeared. The book appears to re-establish the evolutionary advance from Moonwatcher to Starchild. In the film, Kubrick presents what should be the morphologically transcendent Star Child as a human child, encased in its embryo-mandala. This being is Janus-faced, for if the baby's face looks forward, its knowing eyes seem to look backward, to the original sin that continues to hold human advancement in thrall. Kubrick's slab is black, and as such offers no direction to future advancement. Clarke's transparent "teaching machine" appears to do so. Even so, Clarke ultimately chooses, here and in subsequent Odyssey novels, to depict advancement as a constant play of dimorph and double. Humanity will move to new stages, but at each stage, Clarke's new form of humanity, at the height of its powers, utters the same words: "For though he was master of the world, he was not quite sure what to do next. But he would think of something." (34, 221)

In Clarke's version of *2001*, we move a significant distance from the Overmind, for now the human form provides the template for future transformation. This form abides in the "rectangle" that goads future humanity to seek to transcend itself. It offers a quadratic sequence 1:4:9, where human proportionality serves as the "loom" on which a "weaver" constructs a future. Kubrick's quasi-Calvinist theology becomes, in Clarke, an argument from design. Yet this metaphor implies that, if mankind's future is of a "finer texture," it remains woven of a same cloth, fashioned according to a same module. This vision is reaffirmed at the end of *2061: Odyssey Three* (1987).[6] In this future world, a transformed Bowman, a reconstituted HAL, and a mysterious apparition of Heywood Floyd are involved in a vast terraforming operation, once again in the Jupiter sector. The name of the moon they choose however, Europa, points to known origins, not unknown futures. On the surface, the destiny of this future Floyd appears to be transcendence. As with the Overmind, there appears to be rupture, total loss of continuity with human origins: "You are both equally real. But he will soon die, never knowing that he has become immortal." (259) And yet, movement outward is offset by equal movement homeward. As in "The Sentinel," the monolith, serving as a "catalyst of intelligence," appears again to lead humanity forward. Yet humanity, ever promised the transhuman experience, remains always on the threshold of that experience, even though that threshold may stretch a thousand years. The situation reminds one of Pascal's incommunicable orders of being.

Mentioning Pascal is justified here, for in *Odyssey Three*, the thinking reed is evoked as Clarke's characters, dwarfed by the vast transformational power of the monolith, claim not only parity with, but *superiority to*, these forces. To Floyd's question "But how can *we* match ourselves against the monolith—the devourer of Jupiter?" Bowman replies: "It is only a tool. It has vast intelligence, *but no consciousness*. Despite all its powers, you, Hal, and I are its superior." (271) Clarke, though, has adapted Pascal's orders to his Odyssey pattern, where outgoings and homecomings prove simultaneous, and where each dimorphic occurrence, as with Floyd, generates its familiar double. For however much mankind's form mutates, at the base of all these transformations, indeed at the core of Clarke's universe itself, lies a human-based geometry—in this case a "triad"—that both shapes and governs the possibility of dimorphism.

Clarke's last novel in this series, *3001: The Final Odyssey,* does not conclude. Its action, situated again at the crux of a dimorphic split, promises transformation, only to reaffirm the centrality of the human original. The novel appears to end with catastrophic change. Now on Ganymede, yet more advanced forms of HAL, Bowman, and Poole witness a total eclipse of Lucifer. Bernal's devil has now become the old planet Jupiter transformed ("redeemed"?) as a new sun. The product of human advancement, Lucifer is on one hand a dimorph. But this sun is at the same time eclipsed by "a disk of perfectly black material, just over ten kilometers across, so thin it shows no visible thickness." (239) Poole sees this as the result of our "infecting the monolith." In this interpretation, human actions are the evolutionary "wild card," unleashing new forces and unpredictable change in the future. In fact, we seem to witness the dimorphic split as the monolith changes from human-like proportions to those of an "impossible" disk: "If you attempt to make a disk out of rectangular blocks—whether the proportions are 1:4:9 or any other—it cannot possibly be a smooth edge." (240) Yet this new adventure of the Odyssean Bowman proves to be like all the others, where what first seems strange and new reveals itself in the end to be but another variation on the familiar human form. For as the disk explodes, it is found to be composed of the same ubiquitous "rectangles" we encountered in *2001*: "It [the disk] was composed of millions of identical rectangles, perhaps the same size as the Great Wall of Europa. And now they were splitting apart: it was as if a gigantic jigsaw puzzle were being dismantled." (241) Clarke's final novel only repeats, at another thousand-year interval, the same pattern of simultaneous advancement and retrieval that informs the initial novel. Bowman, in *2001*, is said to move "into a realm of consciousness that no man had experienced before." (216) Yet the forward movement he experiences is presented as time running backward, leading him to realize that, co-existent with advancement, what he is observing is his own memory "unreeling like a tape recorder playing back at ever increasing speed." (216)

In contrast, a similar "playback" deprogramming of HAL in Kubrick's film remains ambiguous. The "advanced' machine feels regret as its memory reels back from hyper-intelligence to simple songs of lost innocence. But what is recovered is an even grimmer reality—for HAL now falls from its mechanical Eden to the human condition of its builders. Its machine future is simply another avatar of human Fate. Clarke has found a way to open this closed vision to evolutionary possibility but is aware of the narrative limits of this possibility, and thus models his transhuman seekers after Odysseus, whose dimorphic adventures were always doubled with a homecoming. His Bowman claims to find solace in the possibility of total transformation. But this is because he understands all such change to be dimorphic, where the loss of humanity promises simultaneous recapture of something human: "He was . . . being drained of knowledge and experience as he swept back toward his childhood. But nothing was being lost; all that he had ever been, at every moment of his life, was being transferred to safer keeping." (216) In *3001*, dimorphism has been modified, but not abolished. It is Poole this time who glimpses "powers . . . entities—far superior to the Monolith, and perhaps even their makers." (233) Still, the result of whatever promise of human transformation these powers may bring remains dimorphism. The apparent agent of change this time is the mutated "Halman," a fusion of HAL and Dave Bowman into a single cybernetic entity that can be stored on a "petabyte tablet." Yet Clarke seems once more to have recourse to Pascal's logical gambit. For where Pascal maneuvers for impossible parity between infinite spaces and the human reed, Clarke would preserve the spark of human consciousness in the midst of vast evolutionary transformations. The petabyte "download" will be stored in a vault on Earth's Moon, the same site from which the original odyssey was launched in "The Sentinel." In dimorphic fashion, the tablet serves as both a means of assuring human advancement in the future ("this tablet contains programs that we hope will prevent the Monolith from carry-ing out any orders that threaten mankind") and a memory bank that conserves the consciousness of Hal and Bowman as the repository for the history of our familiar mankind, at the very moment it is on the brink of being lost to evolution: "Ten to the fifteenth bytes is more than sufficient to hold all the memories and experiences of many lifetimes. This will give you one escape route. . . . Halman was willing to cooperate: he still had sufficient links with his origins." (235) The "final" Odyssey merely inscribes another elliptical path, wider in its dimorphic reach perhaps, but still anchored at its human center. Mankind buries its past, knowing that in doing so it sends a clear message to its future, which someday, when the time is right, will have that past resurrected. There will always be another millenium, a thousand-year reprieve, for the human race: "Poole had often cursed Einstein in the past; now he blessed him. Even the powers behind the Monoliths . . . could not spread their influence faster than the speed of light. So the human race should have almost a millennium to prepare for the next encounter. . . . Perhaps by that time it would be better prepared." (244) Poole hopes the post-millennial future will not need to reawaken Halman. He knows however that the human zoo must always be ready to anchor future advancement. And Poole, the least "advanced" of these future hybrids with his ordinary human memory, stands guard as the preserving machine. Halman however calls on the memory of the reader itself to be mankind's ultimate repository: "If we are unable to download, remember us." (238)

## THE PROMISE OF THE CYBORG: HARAWAY'S "MANIFESTO"

Clarke's wrestling with the problem of dimorphism in his narratives of hu-man advancement seems predictable. He is of the same nationality as Bernal, and both share a common vision with another highly influential contempo-rary, Stapledon, whose *Last and First Men* appeared in 1930, one year after Bernal's essay. One expects less to find the dimorph-double pattern at work in American science fiction, nominally committed to the "straight line" ideol-ogy of technological progress. But human advancement, in American science fiction, reaches its limits as well. And here too is born the desire to transcend those limits. We would imagine, given the culture, that how this is done will be quite different, that the Cartesian residue, as well as Bernal's dimorph-double pattern, would be cast aside, in favor of the typical self-reliant monad reaching beyond itself for the stars. Surprisingly, this is not the case. Heinlein is a case in point. Across a span of twenty-five years, Heinlein moved from the tepid human advancement of his "future history" to a sudden leap to the end of things, as he creates an entire fictional universe out of one single extended body—that of arch-individual Lazarus Long, who claims to inscribe all of human evolutionary history in his extended life. Yet, despite talk of evolution, there is no evolutionary dimension in Heinlein. Lazarus at the end of this tether is more a case of the double consuming its dimorphic possibility. Lazarus will not "let go" of his body. Instead, he strives to enfold all possible spacetime past and future into one gigantic, but still *identifiable*, human form. In *Childhood's End,* Clarke recaptures human origins as a message that survives total annihilation of physical humanity. Lazarus too recaptures his human past, but in the form of an expanded individual body into which is "written" all the stories of human existence.

The "monstrosity" of this single, individual extended body, encompassing the entire universe, has not gone unnoticed. Donna Haraway is not a science fiction writer but a biologist, and strong advocate for the human drive toward morphological change. In terms of the transhuman challenge, she appears the worthy successor of Bernal. As scientist, she seems to react not only to Heinlein, but the whole tradition of Frankenstein, in which the word "monster" hovers over all attempts to achieve a transhuman state that begin with altering the human body. Haraway sees the spectre of Frankenstein's creature lurking behind Bernal's calls for alterations of the flesh. Her "A Cyborg Manifesto" (1985) claims to offer a "postmodern" response to both Bernal and Heinlein.[7] Her revalorizing of the "cyborg" as positive next step in human evolution, however, rests on a premise that demands the "deconstruction" of not only patriarchal tyrants like Lazarus, but the very *idea* of a divine human form, still present in Bernal's idea of the devil.

But how "postmodern" is Haraway's vision? A work more or less contemporary to *Frankenstein,* Balzac's "Le Chef d'oeuvre inconnu" (1832), seems to prefigure her work. The painter Frenhofer's "masterpiece" supposedly depicts the perfect female form, constructed from sittings with diverse living models. Unveiled, it proves an incoherent welter of lines and colors.[8] But in this chaos, a remnant of the human form remains—an exquisite human foot (described as "*un pied* vivant," a "living foot"). The reader is left to ask: Does this (as with Michelangelo's famous painting) represent the creation of the human form out of primal chaos? Or is it as Balzac's narrator exclaims, "the end of art on earth," a deconstruction from the foot up of the same human form that, till now, has dominated Western art and culture? And might not this perfect foot also be, like Clarke's utopian children, the jumping-off place for some future, transcendent entity issued from humanity? Frenhofer's onlookers, like Clarke's Jan, represent "old humanity." To them, the foot is a "fragment échappé à une incroyable, à une lente et progressive destruction." [a fragment that has escaped from some incredible process of slow, progressive destruction] (412) Ironically, Haraway echoes this same observation, but turns it into a positive statement. For her, the dismantling of the "classic" human form is necessary if we are to move away from defining humanity as "presence," Descartes's self-defined consciousness. Postmodern evolution necessarily moves away from identity; hence the work of art that depicts identity cannot represent the posthuman being. Seen thus, Frenhofer's welter of lines would be celebrated as "advanced" form, that can no longer be subsumed by dichotomies such as subject/object, mind/body, or animate/inanimate. So, it is for the gestalt Haraway calls the "cyborg." Yet despite her claim to the cyborg's newness, dimorphism still holds sway at this postmodern juncture with humanity's future.

Haraway makes great claims for her new being. Unlike Bernal's cyborg, hers is said to be born of disorder, in the interstices and across the boundaries of our rational projects for an ordered, technology-directed future. According to Haraway, the cyborg is not to be categorized (as in early "male" science fiction) as "black" or "white," nor a "perversion" (Frederik Pohl's "Day Million" [1966]) or nor even, like Heinlein's Waldo, a grotesque yet functionally positive transformation. The cyborg, she asserts, is more than just another hybrid of flesh and metal, or mixture of natural and "artificial" memory. The workshop where it is created is one of universal "etherealization" of forms, in which dualist categories like animal/machine or physical/non-physical are utterly confounded. The technologies of the cyborg are those of miniaturization and dispersion, aimed at reducing solid forms to a flow of information "bytes," transgenetic codings, micro- and nano-electrical impulses—the pixels and quanta from which simulacra are created. As Haraway puts it, "microelectronics is the technical basis of simulacra; that is, copies without originals." The copy may not have an original, but we sense in her statements that somewhere behind it lurks a human consciousness, a Frankenstein looking down this time in admiration rather than disgust on its creature. Haraway purports to turn Frankenstein's creation on its head, for postmodern machines are now "made of sunshine . . . all light and clean because they are nothing but signals." Her cyborg is "ether, quintessence." (153) We must not forget however that Haraway places her creation *above* the threshold of the human form, moving away from its established base. Frankenstein's task is more difficult. For he begins his search to create his new Adam, a transhuman form of life, from *below* that same threshold, working with scattered body parts to construct his being. He constructs, she deconstructs.

Haraway has difficulty sustaining this claim for the ethereal cyborg. It is not, like Clarke's Overmind, the product of complete rupture, total transfer of energy from one form to another. Despite its ethereal promise, there remains resistance, re-coupling; nodules form, arteries harden, all proof that, even here, the dimorph sustains a continuous link with its human double, a ghost of normative humanity in the machine. Haraway's definition of the cyborg offers a litany of such doublings: "The cyborg is a kind of disassembled and reassembled, postmodern collective and personal self." (163) Moreover, she feels obliged to spend a whole page on a "chart of transitions," making sure all the links are articulated from the "old hierarchical dominations to the scary new networks I have called the informatics of domination." (161) Haraway, in inspired spurts, describes her cyborg's newness in terms of its formal elusiveness: it is a "mosaic," a "chimera." But as her essay proceeds, her descriptions become increasingly bipolar. Over and over, she doubles lyrical evocations of new techno-transformations with disquisitions on surprisingly conventional militant political causes. Emerging in the mirror of the cyborg, we find a classic Leftist portrait of what Haraway (in a very un-cyborg-like manner) calls a "bimodal society," a world marked less by transgressed boundaries than by the unchallenged dualisms of "left" and "right," domina-tion and non-domination. Again and again, her advanced being is reclaimed by the "obsolete" human form it purports to abandon. Indeed, the face behind the welter of signals and bytes is increasingly that of "Man, the embodiment of Western logos." Her famous simulacrum reveals itself to be little more than another hybrid, cobbled together from what Istvan Csicsery-Ronay calls "the Great Paradigmatic Pool of Aliens": machines, animals, women, people of color.[9]

Csicsery-Ronay offers two significant comments on Haraway's cyborg, both appearing to bolster her claim that the cyborg represents the advance-ment of humanity: first, that its creation represents a "full-catastrophe model"; second, that the category of children is lacking from the pool of aliens that comprises its doubles. Haraway implies catastrophic separation when she qualifies her new humanity as "about transgressed boundaries, potent fusions and dangerous possibilities." Yet despite this, the dimorphic split remains. For without the old form present to admire the new, the postmodern privilege of her entity is lost. In Haraway's final striking image, that of the monstrously regenerating salamander body, not only does the old form remain, but that form clearly acts to control possible future transformations: "I would suggest that cyborgs have more to do with regeneration and are suspicious of the reproductive matrix and of most birthing. For salamanders, regeneration after injury, such as the loss of a limb, involves regrowth of structure and restora-tion of function with the constant possibility of twinning or other odd topo-graphical productions at the site of former injury. The regrown limb can be monstrous, duplicated, potent. We have all been injured, profoundly." (181) For all her claims to morphological transformation, Haraway is still working within the matrix Bernal defined as dimorphism. As with Frankenstein and his creature, Haraway denies her cyborg its "reproductive matrix," and with it any real evolutionary future. If anything, she has inverted Mary Shelley's formula, giving us an Eve that no longer needs an Adam. Balzac's Frenhofer indulges in his welter of lines, making monstrous claims that new life lies within them. Haraway does likewise. In painting her triumphant picture of the etherealized cyborg, a being all "nodes" and links, she does little more than conjure the old specter of the human form grotesquely distorted, stillborn.

## ALMOST THE SAME:
## THE STRUGATSKYS'S FUTURE HISTORY

The examples above are essentially catastrophic in nature. In each, we sense a terminal impatience with the creeping pace of "future history." But dimorphism need not be catastrophic. Another possible model modifies the alternating rhythm of dimorph and double to allow, within rises and collapses, a modest yet continuous sense of human advancement. Such a dynamic of history would be both non-linear and progressive. A work that seems to fit this description is the story cycle of Arkady and Boris Strugatskys' future history: *Noon: 22nd Century (Polden: 22 vek)* (1962, revised in 1967, containing stories written in the late-1950s-early 1960s).[10] In these independent but interlinked stories, we might expect human advancement to be the product of orthodox Marxist dialectics, which claims to be a continuity process based on thesis, antithesis, synthesis. But this is not the case. The Strugatskys, as Soviet science fiction writers of the so-called "thaw," are writing in the shadow of Ivan Efremov. His model for human advancement proves surprisingly ahistorical, in which all possibility for dimorphic evolution remains a prisoner of the human form.

Efremov's novella *Heart of the Serpent* (1956, written a year before his classic *Andromeda*) tells of an alien encounter in deep space.[11] His human cosmonauts represent a future classless humanity. The alien race they encounter looks exactly like them, except that it breathes fluorine rather than oxygen. Efremov's thesis is that human organs and the human brain as seat of rational thought, once perfected by this utopian Soviet future race, represent the summit of evolutionary potential for *all forms* of intelligent life in *any* universe: "No, I do not expect to find monsters with horns and tails in the spaceship we shall meet. Only the lower forms of life differ greatly from one another; the higher the form the closer it is bound to be to us Earth-dwellers." (54) Efremov argues, in a way ideologically opposite from, but oddly analogous to, Heinlein, that the human mind, *and body,* provide the sole possible template for the advancement of life forms. Future advancement is simply a predetermined space waiting to be filled out as humanity realizes its potential: "In this sense man is a microcosm. Thinking follows the laws of the Universe which are the same everywhere. . . . There cannot be any other entirely different thought process." (55) All claims to transhuman evolution, either through dimorphic transcendence or synthesis with alien life forms, prove illusory, for the human form cannot be surpassed. The fluorine breathers are merely slightly inferior copies of our ideal form; they look exactly like humans, but in evolutionary terms, they have one fatal flaw: fluorine is a far rarer element than oxygen in the universe. In the final scene, these two races, perfect mirror images except for their chemistry, look at each other through the transparent glass that separates them. Narcissus-like, Earth woman Afra Devi first throws herself at the glass; then she retreats, and offers the other race the means of joining ours, the key that will allow them to fully evolve into human beings: "With a glance at the immobile grey figures standing on the other side of the partition, she crossed out the fluorine atom with its nine electrons that she had drawn and replaced it with a symbol of the oxygen atom." (111)

The Strugatskys may have ideological ties to this anthropocentric future, where the human form remains the "microcosm" containing all limits of possible advancement. But they also read science fiction writers like Wells and Stapledon, possibly Clarke and Bradbury; hence, the lure of dimorphism is on their fictional horizon. Bradbury's influence, in fact, may be crucial, for their chronicle of human advancement in *Noon: 22nd Century* develops more in the manner of Bradbury's *The Martian Chronicles* (1950) than that of official dialectics. Bradbury's story cycle unfolds by moving back and forth between Mars and Earth, with increasing interpenetration between these two poles. We begin with the demise of the Martians and arrival of Earthmen. The latter build their Mars, but gradually succumb to the ghosts of the former inhabitants. At the same time, colonizers experience the nuclear holocaust that destroys all ties with their home world—Earth. Science and technology have brought two now-intertwined worlds to their respective ends. So, when the survivors of Earth's nuclear war reach Mars, they find a world cleansed of these destructive forces, offering the promise of a new beginning in a post-technological future. In the Strugatsky cycle as well, movement from story to story is back and forth from a central point (Efremov's perfected humanity, basking in the sun of its classless future world) to an ever-expanding circumference, as humanity reaches beyond our solar system, toward possible (but somehow always thwarted) contact with aliens that are more than mere mirror images of humanity. At these moments, contact brings about mutual and reciprocal adaptations. In turn, these changes return to the human center, and the rhythm of exploration begins again, but now from new sets of premises.[12]

The two stories that comprise the first section of *Noon*, set in the early twenty-first century, tell of early space explorers Sergei Kondratev and Evgeny Slavin. "Night on Mars" chronicles a very short step in human advancement—the trek of doctors through the dangers of the Martian night to deliver the first Earth child born on the newly colonized planet. That child is Slavin. "Almost the Same" is an anecdotal account of Kondratev's cadet days, where a low-key dimorphic split is enacted between Sergei and a certain Panin. The latter describes himself as "a simple man, a guileless man" who questions the need to go to the stars. Kondratev, for whom space travel is more important than all Earthly attachments, even love, articulates the difference between them: "As for whose sake will we find out about the stars . . . [it is] for our own, for everyone's. Even for yours. But you won't take part in it. You'll make your discoveries in the newspapers." (36) But Panin, no mere exhibit in the Bernalian zoo, claims an equally dynamic role, in a manner radically different from, yet equivalent to, Kondratev's heroic discourse: "All right. . . . So I'll become a teacher. I'll plumb the depths of children's souls for the sake of everyone." (36) Children are as valid a way to the future as individual heroics in space.

The second section, "Homecoming," gives the narrative of human advancement a space-time twist, bringing Slavin and Kondratev, as relics of the past, back to an Earth that greatly evolved, technologically and socially, in their absence. The nine stories in this section are mostly understated narratives of daily efforts made by the "two from the Taimyr" to adapt to this new, utopian Earth, still young in biological time but old in terms of scientific and social advancement. Long thought dead, they are resurrected in a time that does not reject them, but in Bernal's sense studies them as curiosities, miraculously living forms of an old-revered humanity. Though treated with respect, they are nevertheless forbidden to leave Earth.

The key story here is "Homecoming," where dimorph and double meet and engage in dialogue. The idle and depressed Kondratev is visited by Gorbovsky, a new breed of space explorer, whose adventures will be told in later sections of *Noon*. Gorbovsky treats his double's "heroic" landing on the murderous planet Blue Sands much as one would an event in a *chanson de geste*—something magnificent yet quaintly archaic. Gorbovsky is a space scientist, not a pioneer. But he would also be a pioneer in turn, positioning himself in analogous manner on the far circumference of his own new frontier. For where other spacemen of this time pursue the hard sciences of planetology and astrophysics, or do D-principle (near-light-speed drive) research (the field Kondratev would choose if he could), Gorbovsky pursues the arcane "fourth problem," looking for traces of alien visits on distant planets.

Clearly for this space mystic, things far and near have the same mirror attraction they did for the earlier generation of spacers. When on Earth, Gorbovsky takes meals lying down in the manner of his "classic" ancestors. He sprawls in Earth's green grass, at water's edge, and catches an old-fashioned cold. In between trips to the far frontier on a D-ship, he flies settlers on a tame shuttle to nearby Venus (what was a death planet for Kondratev is now a suburb of Earth). He sees himself in fact, like Kondratev, all-too-rapidly superannuated by progress: "Now we're all ferrying volunteers. Even proud researchers of the D-principle. Now we're like the streetcar coachmen of your time." (119) Kondratev on the other hand, if he cannot return to space, is offered (in counterbalancing manner) work exploring ocean depths. As in Clarke, this is the "new" frontier that was always there, once one understands that inner space is the double of outer space.

Here as in other stories of this section, the interplay of dimorphs and doubles weaves a thread of continuity between meetings that might otherwise be catastrophic. Kondratev realizes that his encounter with Gorbovsky and the oceanographer was not fortuitous: "They're intelligent people . . . they came to help me. I need only one thing." (120) What he needs is a future, and these stories explore the undulations between desire and fate that will get us to that future, but at the rhythm of one step backward for two steps forward. In "The Moving Roads," Slavin discovers that, though these "great-grandchildren" still live very much as he did, there has been change and movement, however imperceptible. The symbol of this is the "moving roads" themselves. Unlike Heinlein's *rolling* roads, these are slow-moving conveyers of people and goods. But if they are not a "breakthrough" technology—"rolling" implies a precise technology, these roads simply "move"—they offer a significant if not spectacular advance over the old roads. A similarly slow if inexorable flow toward the future occurs in "The Conspirators," the section's pivotal story. Here, in what appears another story of teacher and pupils, a new generation of space explorers is emerging: Komov, Siderov, Sasha Kostylin, Pol Gnedykh, all names we hear in stories in the next two sections. Here they act out in childish games the roles they will take on as adults. They are future aspiring dimorphs; but their doubles, as they proclaim here, are the "heroes" of the first cycles, those they call Panin's "children."

The stories featuring our "conspirators" are of two mutually mirroring sorts. In one category, we witness "breakthrough" projects—attempts to engineer new forms of humanity—that collapse in grotesque failure. "The Mystery of the Hind Leg" takes Slavin, now a journalist, to Australia where he encounters a fantastic horde of cybernetic creatures. But these, he ultimately discovers, do not represent some future evolutionary step; instead, they are products of a Sorcerer's Apprentice prank. At the center of this story is a formidable artificial intelligence—the great CODD, Collector of Dispersed Data, a giant underground computer that gathers "traces" of past events and transforms them into images, resurrecting the past in the form of a "database." At the same time, in its role as sentient machine, it is able to expand its faculties, create and combine new elements. It appears to be advancing toward some transhuman future, ahead of its creators, a forerunner of today's "singularity" moment. At the same time, the fact that CODD remains subject to human masters is made comically evident. When given a statistical problem to solve—in this case, which trough among a series of troughs a given merino sheep will choose and why—the computer generates models—simulacra. As they input data however, programmers amuse themselves by giving the sheep seven legs. This causes this maker of forms to go berserk producing these monstrosities: "It piles absurdity upon absurdity." (207)

The mood is more somber in "Candles Before the Control Board." Here the next step in human advancement is personal immortality in the form of the "Great Encoding," the downloading of a great Academician's entire mental being into computer memory. (Computers were big objects at the time the story was written.) The recipient of this data is a massive structure: "There were . . . twenty-six squat buildings, each with a frontage, each extending six levels underground." (228) The Strugatskys are perfectly capable of extrapolating a micro-computer but chose not to in order to make a point. For not only is more space than available needed, there is not enough time to do the job. Only 98 percent of the individual biomass is downloaded before natural death sets in. In this context of human advancement, the "candles" stand for something old-fashioned, even regressive. They are necessary substitutes for the electricity that ultimately proves insufficient for the experiment and are the conventional sign of a wake. In the final image, sputtering candles, marking the futility of the labor that went into the experiment, are reflected by the control board that was to make this "next" human step happen. In this mutual play of reflections, the dimorphic impulse remains bound to its human double, the presence that sets limits to all such transhuman aspirations.

"Pilgrims and Wayfarers" offers a similar ironic mirroring. This time our future explorations themselves remain reflected in forms of our past. "Astro-archeologist" Gorbovsky meets Ivanov, an oceanographer who has discovered an Earth life form that is primitive and previously unknown. But this life form is apparently undergoing a formal evolution in the present as well. These "septipods" manifest potent changes in heart and muscle structure; for some inexplicable reason (they are all males, so reproduction is not the cause) they are now leaving their former habitat and moving onto land. The spacer Gorbovsky draws the analogy between these creatures and the new humanity he believes he represents: "They stayed in the depths for ages, and now they've risen up and entered an alien, hostile world. And what drives them? An ancient, dark instinct? . . . Or an information-processing capacity which had risen up to the level of unquenchable curiosity? After all, it would be better for it to stay home . . . but something draws it." (251) The dialogue between Gorbovsky and Ivanov is itself framed by a mirroring of the realms of sky and water. Gorbovsky reveals he too has been "tagged" by some alien force, made to emit strange radio signals, and wonders whether he and the septipod, at very different stages of evolution, are not living analogous fates. The force that marked him ("the signal goes on day and night, whether I'm happy or sad") is as indifferent to his desires as Ivanov is to the creatures he tags. The story ends with a statement by Ivanov's "forward-looking" daughter that, ironically, summons its own mirroring question: "There's a difference between an interstellar ship and wet slime in a gill bag." (253) But, given this exchange between spaceman and oceanographer, *is* there really a difference?

In other stories in this section an evolving humanity seeks out the alien, hoping the encounter will lead it to take a further step. In "The Planet with All the Conveniences," scientists arrive on distant planet Leonida in the wake of Gorbovsky's Pathfinders. Unlike other alien worlds encountered, this one seems not to need "virophages" or other terraforming devices. It is so clement in fact that the visitors, ignoring the strangeness of its structures, make themselves "at home." Head of Mission Komov suspects this may be (an echo of Bradbury's "Mars Is Heaven" [1948]) a trap. The trap however turns out to be that this world *is* so close to being another Earth—another utopian world "with all the conveniences"—that what differences there are go unheeded. The humans swim, run barefoot, trample the fauna. They even take the liberty of shooting the strange "animals" that appear to be stealing their belongings. But these, they soon realize, are intelligent beings. The Earth visitors first assumed that aliens, by definition, must be radically different from us, over-looking the fact that what appears most familiar can at the same time be the most alien.

But there is irony here. For only by associating these beings with humans can the Earth explorers pronounce them "aliens," serious objects of study. In Efremovian fashion, humans can only take humans seriously: "They're people! Animals can steal, but only people can bring back what they've sto-len." (274) Only when the observers see these creatures as "people" can they glimpse the possibility of an evolutionary "next step." They reason thus: the place has no machines or cities, only organic entities; but because its inhabit-ants, like people, seem to have morals, their alternate path must have led to a similar outcome—civilization. Assuming that "civilization" is everywhere the same, they conclude: if this is not a technological civilization, it must be a *biological* civilization, for civilization it must be, as it fits our model for such. As with all such doublings in the Strugatskys, there is neither clear advance nor retreat. A small step toward transhumanity however does occur, as the explorers come to realize their mirror dilemma: "We look for brothers in reason for 300 years, then run away as soon as we find them." (275) In this case, one of the party at least, Komov, wishes he could stay, to ask questions that might shed light on what might be a next step in human evolution. Yet, in light of what has gone before, such pretense will doubtless lead to more blindness, to further affirmation of the human form. Even so, Komov learns here by experience that, if the alien without can become familiar, what we believe to be familiar within can in an instant turn alien.

The final story in *Noon: 22nd Century*, "What We Will Be," expresses impatience with the slow rhythm of human advancement. The tilt of the story's title is forward, suggesting the desire for a dimorphic leap beyond humanity to posthuman experience. In their well-kept zoo of twenty-second century Earth, Kondratev, Slavin, and Gorbovsky gather at the seaside for a tranquil barbecue before the latter is to leave for planet Tagora. On this threshold of possible new discovery, Gorbovsky is drawn to tell a story of an old, past event. His story, however, is one of transhuman possibility. During a near-fatal accident in space, a man who calls himself Petr Petrovich, claiming to be their "remote descendent," miraculously appears inside their disabled ship. Petr is described as of "average height, thin pleasant face" and "dressed like a spacer," except for the fact that his jacket is buttoned from right to left, "like a woman's, or, according to rumor, like the Devil's." (316) This could also simply be the human form seen in a mirror. Moreover, the mysterious mirror image seems to double again. For what are these doomed spacemen facing, the Devil or Saint Peter? Are they damned or saved? Or is it possible that what they encounter is a true transhuman being, a real glimpse of things to come for humanity?

Petrovich however proves to be a Janus-faced presence as enigmatic as Bernal's dimorph or Clarke's Monolith, embodying the lure of a human future in which twin impulses toward domesticity and transcendence join in riddling tautology. Petrovich's "prediction" of human advancement is just such a riddle: "Just remember: if you are what you plan on being, then we'll become what we are. And what you, accordingly, will be." (318) But it appears that Petrovich saves the ship and crew, thus giving the crew a future. But what will that future be? Later, as these spacers engage in a half-joking exchange of views, they see the circularity of Petrovich's promise skewed toward a possible transhuman experience in an unpredictable future. Each, on this occasion, is on the verge of embarking on a new future. Their views range from the quasi-mystical to the facetious; yet buried in each lies the promise of a dimorphic moment. On one hand, there is Slavin's seriously uttered, post-Marxian prediction of a new, "completely fantastic" turn of history's wheel that has now become a spiral. On the other hand, there is Kondratev's whimsical invitation for his comrades to dive into the ocean's depths to see "the Golden Grotto," a man-made amusement park, but one with a strangely mystical name. Thus, whether the future yields something commonplace at the heart of the inconceivably new (as we see in the banality of Slavin's exclamation of visionary awe, "you haven't seen anything like it"), or something startlingly new in an undiscovered corner of what was thought to be familiar, such as the "Grotto," the possibility of future transhuman experience haunts this story. Indeed, the event that inspires these friends' predictions is a real, if modest, step forward—for Goborvsky's coming travels place him on the threshold of what is said to be possibly humanity's first genuine alien encounter.

What might such an encounter mean for the future of the human form and the rational soul it harbors? The alternating rhythm of this, and other stories in this cycle, suggests that this event, like all before it, will be banal, yet at the same time miraculously other than what we might foresee. In a later novel, the Strugatskys find a telling image for their alternating sense of things—that of the "snail on the slope."[13] In this image, Bernal's story of human advancement is rewritten in terms of continuity rather than catastrophe. The modest path of the snail advances between dimorphic extremes of immortality and monstrosity. In the form and function of its shell, world and flesh—terraforming and cyborgization—have fused, as have movement and stasis. The impasse of the "devil" seems resolved as well. With the snail, going out and staying home are no longer opposite impulses, for it carries its home wherever it goes. Even so, dimorphism is not excluded from the snail's journey. For in the story "What We Will Be," just as the snail's shell of Gorbovsky's spaceship is host to the apparition of Petrovich, so the banal "golden grotto" at the bottom of the sea may also offer a place of transhuman experience. Heinlein abandons the slow-time of future history for the deification of Lazarus Long. The Strugatskys explore this slow time here, and in subsequent novels. The alternations of fate and desire in their work remain cautious, tentative, yet profoundly dimorphic.

## THE REAL NEXT STEP: J.-H. ROSNY'S LAST MAN

I tentatively suggest that Bernal's masterplot "works" for writers in as diverse cultures as Clarke, Haraway, and the Strugatskys, because his double perpetuates the Cartesian ghost in the process of human evolution. This further indicates that, in all these cultures, reason remains the supreme, and unique, human quality. In the above examples, the transhuman moment encounters the barrier of anthropocentrism. The Strugatsky story "The Meeting" (the penultimate story of *Noon: 22nd Century*) sums this dilemma up neatly. Hunter Pol Gnedykh returns to Earth from his search for alien life to visit an "exobiological" museum tended by old friend Alexandr Kostylin. He stands before a "specimen" he hastily killed on distant Crookes' planet. He traces the word "sapiens" on the dusty plaque, then erases it. Both men however know this designation is true. Pol's guilt comes partly from having killed a *rational* alien. Such an alien might have allowed humans to bridge the gap between us and it. But at the same time the secret of this possible transhuman link must be kept. For what happens to mankind's sense of uniqueness in the universe if other genuinely sentient life forms are found?

To test Bernal's dimorph-double pattern, we turn to a writer who, following the strict logic of evolution, takes the transhuman experience as far as any science fiction writer appears ever to have done: the Belgian J.-H. Rosny aîné (Joseph-Henri Boëx). His works of speculative fiction span a period from 1887, when he published the prehistoric novel *Les Xipéhuz*, to a novel of life on Mars, *Les Navigateurs de l'infini* (1926). His most remarkable work, however, remains his Last Man story *La Mort de la Terre* (1910). Here he not only depicts a future humanity perishing in a manner plausible in evolutionary terms but locates its demise in a carefully extrapolated ecological framework.[14] Humanity is partly responsible for its own destruction, but is also caught up in a play of physical forces beyond its control. Humans survive until they can no longer do so. Their end however presents the possibility of a real next step, as the last human offers a dying gift to the form of life that will continue evolving on what was mankind's Earth. In the works above, mankind's "next step" remains a Bernalian construct: some form of hybridized "enhancement," or like Clarke's Overmind, a being of mental energy. But in neither do we see beyond the mind-matter duality which continues to insure mankind a central (if nebulous) role in future evolution. In contrast, Rosny's pluralistic sense of continuity-in-transformation of multiple life forms opens a field of speculation where process is more important than product, where *trans*-human rather than *post*-human is now the clear focus.

Rosny's novel recounts not only the death of *mankind's* Earth, but the environment in which carbon-based life in general must live.[15] Protagonist Targ is the summation and last example of all carbon-based life forms. For Targ in this role, only two possibilities remain: life as we know it perishes entirely, leaving no trace, or some aspect of that life is transmitted, passed on to the new life form, the iron-based "ferromagnetics," and possibly through them to some other, future, life form. The former seems inevitable, the latter a vague anthropocentric dream. As we follow Targ's heroic but futile efforts to find water, hoping against hope to restore the environmental conditions that support carbon life, total annihilation of the carbon kingdom seems the only outcome. Human science can posit, and perhaps verify, the feasibility of an iron-based form of life that would continue evolving on a waterless Earth. But for Targ and readers, this is scant consolation, because *our* life form will die. Targ's final moment suggests however that, within the parameters of a thoroughly scientific view of things, a transhuman event may be possible. In fact, if we consider the grammatical and situational logic of Rosny's narrative, such an event may *already* have occurred at the time of telling.

On one level, Targ is the conventional hero, the special man who struggles valiantly against impossible odds and loses. On the level of human myth, he is the chivalric knight who through his deeds claims the hand of Êre, the blonde Guinevere to his Lancelot. Rosny's Last Man is the finest example of human tenacity, ingenuity, and virtue. But no hero in previous fiction ever faced such an extreme collective tragedy. Targ's sole "enemy" is a neutral and irreversible transformation of the conditions necessary for his form of life. As hero, he is beyond good and evil. Since all forms of carbon life must perish with him, Targ knows, despite moments of hope and wishful thinking, that there is no possibility, mythical or physical, of an eternal return.

Targ clearly understands his condition and its finality. Yet his final act is a free one: he gives himself consciously and of his free will to the ferromagnetics. One could see this as an "existential" act before the fact. For Targ, in consciously accepting the *manner* of his death, frees himself to exercise a final act of will. Like his sister Arva and other Last Humans, Targ could have taken the euthanasia drug and drifted into oblivion. Instead, he chose to affirm his terminal humanity, by a willed act, in the face of the ferromagnetic successor: "Il eut un dernier sanglot; la mort entra dans son coeur et, refusant l'euthanasie, il sortit des ruines, il alla s'étendre dans l'oasis, parmi les ferromagnétaux." [He sobbed for the last time; death entered his soul and, refusing euthanasia, he left the ruins, and lay down in the oasis among the ferromagnetics.] (lxvi)[16]

All these interpretations of Targ's final heroic death, however, are subsumed in Rosny's broader sense of a transhuman act. Immediately preceding his act of giving himself to the ferromagnetics, Targ offers a short meditation on his personal relationship with Earth's environment. Mankind's Earth is now *his personal Earth*. Targ's final sense of his "condition" is an ecological one, in the basic sense of the word as *home*. His final musings do not concern his personal fate, but the fact that his fate is now that of an entire kingdom of life, which evolved to its apex in *homo sapiens*.

Let us trace the steps whereby Targ comes to accept this sweeping ecological vision, personalize it, and finally assume it. Targ makes the entire history of carbon life his own *personal story* in a vast retrospective dream, where he describes the total evolutionary sweep from primal sea to mankind mastering the atom: "'Le vainqueur capta jusqu'à la force mystérieuse qui a assemblé les atomes. Cette frénésie même annonçait la mort de la terre . . . 'la mort de la terre pour *notre* Règne,' murmura doucement Targ." ["The conqeror harnessed everything right down to the mysterious force that bound together the atoms. This frenzy itself announced the death of the Earth . . . 'the death of the Earth for our Kingdom,' Targ murmured softly.] (lxvi) Targ's final moment of despair is despair on an evolutionary scale: "Un frisson secoua sa douleur. Il songea que ce qui subsistait encore de sa chair s'était transmis, *sans arrêt*, depuis les origines. Quelque chose qui avait vécu dans la mer primitive, sur les limons naissants, dans les marécages, dans les forêts, au sein des savanes, et parmi les cités innombrables de l'homme, ne s'était jamais interrompu jusqu'à lui . . . Et voilà! Il était le seul homme qui palpait sur la face, redevenue immense, de la terre! . . ." [A shiver shook him in his pain. He reflected on the fact that what now remained in his flesh had been transmitted, without *interruption*, since the beginning. A thread of life that had lived in the primal seas, in the alluvial silt, in the swamps, the forests, in the middle of the savannas, and among the innumerable cities of mankind, had never been broken till now, with him . . . And this was it! He was the only man whose heart still beat on an earth that had now become vast and empty again.] (lxvi-lxvii) At this moment, however, Targ feels the opposite of Pascalian alienation. For one last time, he finds himself at home among familiar stars, the same stars that comforted the gaze of the trillions of humans that preceded him: "La nuit venait. Le firmament montra ces feux charmants qu'avaient connus les yeux de trillions d'hommes. Il ne restait que deux yeux pour les contempler!" [Night fell. The firmament displayed its pleasant lights that trillions of men had known. Now only two eyes were left to contemplate them!] (lxvii) Moreover, Targ does not simply contemplate. He now counts off the stars he most knows, *his stars* ("Targ dénombra ceux qu'il avait préférés aux autres" [Targ counted those he liked better than others.]). Finally, at the end of human time, he watches the rising of the most familiar of mankind's heavenly bodies, "l'astre ruineux . . . l'astre troué, argentin et légendaire" [the star of disasters . . . the star riddled with holes, silvery, the stuff of legends] (lxvii), the Moon that watched over mankind's rise and fall. Only now does Targ—fully in harmony with his mythical and physical ecology—choose to join the ferromagnetics. His act makes him a willing part of the larger evolutionary process as it unfolds.

But the novella does not end here. The account of Targ lying down among the ferromagnetics is followed by a simple, one-sentence paragraph. This paragraph clearly suggests that something more has occurred than a terminal, statistically meaningless, offering of the last carbon molecules that exist on Earth: "Ensuite, humblement, quelques parcelles de la dernière vie humaine entrèrent dans la Vie Nouvelle." [Then, humbly, several parcels of the last human life entered into the New Form of Life.] (lxvii) The preterite tense of this last paragraph tells us that, *as a consequence of* Targ's act, specifically *human* material has been transferred to the new form of life. By personifying this "Vie Nouvelle," Rosny's narrator indicates that the overarching concern in this transfer is Life in its totality, Life as the larger product of evolution, Life opposed to the realm of the inorganic. Under this general umbrella of Life, there is the possibility that Targ's transfer may result in meaningful communication between human and some future form of "intelligence." For if Targ, with his vast dream and yearning for the Moon and stars, can be said literally to *incarnate* the entire history—cultural and genetic—of carbon life, might not what he physically passes on to future life forms contain the encoding of an entire species? Might not this in turn lead, in some vastly distant future, to the development of a form of consciousness capable of decoding, and empathizing with, the story his genetic material conveys?

The final paragraph of Rosny's novella offers a sudden shift of perspective. Up to this moment we have witnessed interspecies conflict or rivalry. What now occurs is an act of what Rosny calls "sympathy." This, in the Darwinian sense, may encourage the passage of some factor—a meme, a gene, some yet unknown vector—from species to species, creating a chain of communication that will permit life forms to continue evolving. Several times during the narrative, Targ expressed sympathy with the ferromagnetics, despite his bitterness against his situation: "A Parfois, Targ l'exécrait; parfois, une sympathie craintive s'éveillait dans son âme. N'y avait-il pas une analogie mystérieuse, et même une obscure fraternité, entre ces êtres et les hommes? Certes, les deux règnes étaient moins loin l'un de l'autre que chacun ne l'était du minéral inerte. Qui sait si leur consciences, à la longue, ne se seraient pas comprises!" [At times, Targ cursed them; at other times, a timid sympathy stirred in his soul. Was there not some mysterious connection, even an obscure fraternity, between these beings and men?] (lxx) Both kingdoms share a common life. But in this final moment, humanity is the sender of the message, not the receiver. And if any such communication is to exist, there must be sympathy from the other side of the evolutionary divide as well. But how can this be? For here the kingdom that holds the future exists at best in a pre-cognitive state; it may never develop anything vaguely resembling an "intelligence" capable of understanding ours.

Despite this, there are details, in this final paragraph, specifically suggesting that Targ's act of transhuman communication *did* come to pass. Look at a few significant words in this final sentence. We first notice the narrator's choice of the strange word *parcelle*. In the earlier cited passage where Targ is presented in the situation of Pascal's reed, the word used is *particule,* which means "small part," "*petite partie.*" *Particule* implies no concern about *what* the particle is a part of. It is a word, as in "*la physique des particules,*" "particle physics," that belongs to what Pascal calls the *esprit de géometrie,* to the world as defined by the mind-matter duality. The *Dictionnaire de l'Académie française,* on the other hand, defines *parcelle* as a "petite partie *de quelque chose*" [a small part of something]. Its use indicates a broader vision. There is the idea of an assemblage of diverse parts and the suggestion that these parts remain a constituent portion of some larger, future whole.[17] The sentence affirms the finality of Targ's death as *particule.* At the same time, it suggests that, as *parcelle,* part of this larger whole, something of him may have survived. Within the *parcelles* Targ gives, the elements of a dynamic life system may persist, a system that might serve to connect past and future, and someday permit continuous transformation.

Moreover, this continuity of life forms is clearly stated. The final sentence states that some part of Targ *became* part of a larger ecology of life in evolution. Rosny insists we take the word *parcelle* at its literal meaning. He does the same, it appears, with temporal markers, in this case the past tense of the verbs in this paragraph. The adverb "*ensuite,*" "then," is followed by the verb in the preterite, "*entrèrent,*" "entered into." This verb form describes an action completed in the past. Had the narrator chosen the imperfect verb "*entraient,*" "were entering into," the reader could still place the narration on Targ's side of the void. We would have Targ lying down among the ferromagnetics, in the *act* of dying. Were the *imparfait* used, we would be able to see the final words of the narrative as Targ's thoughts presented in *style indirect libre.* The preterite verb however clearly states that the action of "entering into" occurs *after* Targ's death. If this action then is posthuman, the reader is invited to ask: who *is* speaking about Targ the Last Man? After his death, there are no humans (or carbon life forms) left to do so. More important, if the voice speaking *is* posthuman, *to whom* is it speaking? The very logic of this narrative situation asks readers to become part of the speculative process. Is it possible that a posthuman narrator and narrative audience have evolved from the ferromagnetics? If so, they would only be interested in the story of Targ's death and the carbon life he vectors, *if that life had something to do with their subsequent evolution.*

If we admit these possibilities, we must then ask by what means such impossibly distant worlds might be linked. Did Targ's final *parcelles* the contain a code, gene or other means of transferring information, that affected ferromagnetic evolution, indeed provided a determining factor leading to the creation of a form of consciousness that permits understanding across the gulf of evolutionary time? Such a transfer may appear a physical and statistical impossibility, and readers are free to reject it. In light of Rosny's final sentence, readers can also see Targ's final act as a Pascalian wager, one that, against all odds, succeeds. But if this is the case, theology trumps science. Finally, readers are free, as Rosny's narrative invites them, to entertain a strictly scientific solution, the consequence of an act that, however impossible seeming, remains within the purview of evolutionary possibility. With this single sentence, Rosny is asking his reader—perhaps for the first time in the genre's history—to *think in a science-fictional manner*, to move beyond conventions and limits to extrapolate new possibilities, new worlds.

But, even if we admit this, has Rosny's evolutionary vision succeeded in banishing anthropocentrism, of freeing Bernal's dimorph from its double? At one point in the text, Targ and Arva, contemplating the ferromagnetics, see themselves in the mirror of the future: "C'étaient les vainqueurs. Le temps était devant eux et pour eux, les chose coïncidaient avec leur volonté obscure; un jour , leurs descendants produiraient des pensées admirables et manieraient des énergies merveilleuses . . ." [They were the conquerors. Time lay before them, the way of things coincided with their obscure will; one day, their descendants would produce admirable thoughts, and wield marvelous sources of energy.] (lxxii) In light of Targ's ultimate sense of physical finality, any vision of the ferromagnetics evolving (as with Efremov) into human simulacra remains hopeless, wishful thinking. But his words can also be read as an act of trans-species sympathy that might provoke, across the void that separates carbon from ferromagnetic (or from some yet unknown) life, a corresponding expression of backward-looking sympathy. Perhaps such sympathy has always been present in the narration. Rosny's narrator may reveal its posthuman location in the final paragraph. Throughout the telling, however, this narrator increasingly seems to bond with Targ, to "focalize" on his destiny as he assumes the burden of dying humanity. In this final paragraph, this narrator openly expresses empathy for Targ by describing him as "humbly" giving over his *parcelles*. The narrator's choice of words offers a concrete clue, in evolutionary terms, to the mechanism by which some actual transfer of information between life forms may have occurred.[18]

Rosny may want us to see here, on the grander scale of posthuman destiny, an act of evolutionary altruism. Targ is not the selfish hero, nor one who sees in his terminal actions a way to "make himself" (Sartre's *se faire*). His final act of "humility" is one of selfless generosity, looking beyond self and species to the advent of new forms of life. Targ's motivation, beyond survival of the fittest, seems to be action for the good of others still to come. Today, Darwinians still ponder the possibility that such acts of selflessness may do more is to advance the evolutionary process than adversarial struggle or heroic defiance.[19] It may seem absurd to extrapolate such wide-ranging consequences from Targ's altruistic act. Yet this act sets him apart from all other last humans. This, in turn, may make his genetic, or memetic, material unique. Targ's gift may succeed in passing the evolutionary gulf, whereas similar genetic material, given reluctantly or in a selfishly defiant manner, might fail to do so.

Rosny, as rigorous evolutionist, does not minimize the immensity of the transhuman gulf. Altruism remains the improbable bottle in the evolutionary sea, and Rosny understands this. Might we not argue then that, in terms of Bernal's dimorph-double pattern, Rosny's posthuman narrator is not addressing a posthuman audience, but instead speaking to us the readers, its human double? Rosny seems to depict Targ moving beyond anthropocentrism. But is not the idea that some far distant narrator in evolutionary time would pay such attention to Targ and his *parcelles*—minuscule footnotes in vast evolutionary history   a profoundly anthropocentric vision after all? The question remains: if Rosny seems to offer one of the most rigorously evolutionary narrative accounts of the transhuman process, does he really, in the end, escape this anthropocentric impasse of Clarke and other writers issued from the evolutionary paradigm? In his final work of science fiction, *Les Navigateurs de l'infini* (1926), Rosny will openly embrace the dimorph-double dynamic that lay beneath the surface of his earlier, "evolutionary" novels.[20]

This late novel is again a tale of evolutionary fatality, where the scenario of *La Mort de la Terre* now seems to play out on Mars. Again, depletion of water—"Martian" water—results in the near-dying out of a sentient species, the *tripèdes*. This species is carbon-based and said to be "homologous" to human beings—it stands upright and has a different but comparable symmetry: three limbs, six eyes. Its evolutionary adversary is a species the Earth astronauts call the "zoomorphes." These have strange forms—strap-like shapes, chaotic amalgams of lines, amorphous "sponges" where a head should be. Like the ferromagnetics, they appear to have a different chemical composition, as their presence renders the soil of Mars infertile for *tripède* crops. Even so, Rosny's Martian scenario is quite different. Targ's Earth was locked in its evolutionary path, with no visits by voyagers across space, and no external forces intervening in a process moving uninterrupted across eons of time. But now, as a young, adventurous spacefaring species, humanity is free to intersect the evolutionary path of other "homologous" species. On Mars, it is the *tripèdes* who have reached the end of their evolutionary line and become the fatalists. Human intervention however will change this.

First describing themselves as observers, the humans only witness the decline of the *tripèdes*, and claim they are not on Mars to change the course of events. Yet the conditions they encounter on Mars force them to do just that. To survive on the planet, they must find ways to change the chemical composition of Martian food and water so their metabolism can assimilate them. They must convert Martian sources of energy, if they are to return to Earth, which they ultimately do. They are in fact "terraformers," transforming Martian elements to sustain Earth forms of life. In doing so, they make Mars an extension of their younger world. This gives them license to use their energy and knowledge to help the *tripèdes* set up defenses against the *zoomorphes*. Later, when the *tripèdes*, under attack, prove unable to adapt to contingencies and are routed, the humans step in and change the direction of the process. They do so in a way that reminds one of John W. Campbell, Jr.'s story "Twilight" (1934) written eight years after Rosny's novel. Rosny's Earth visitors re-instill in an expiring species a renewed sense of curiosity, giving them the will and means to adapt to new situations. Rosny is more subtle than Campbell, for he does not openly proclaim curiosity to be a uniquely human trait, but rather presents it as something that waxes and wanes on a given evolutionary curve, be it human or *tripède*. The curve has now waned for the *tripèdes*. The younger human species however is in full flower and can re-infuse life into an otherwise dying race. In an evolutionary context, then, Rosny's astronauts give the *tripèdes* back the will to struggle, the desire to be resourceful, intervening to reverse their demise. The Martians recognize this: "De proche en proche, votre science mettra notre espèce à l'abri des invasions. . . . Les envoyés de la Terre auront sauvé leurs humbles frères de Mars!" [Little by little, your science will shelter our species from future invasions. . . . The envoys from Earth will have saved their humble brothers on Mars.] (90)

One may wonder why this novel is entitled "Navigators of the Infinite" when its three astronauts only go as far as Mars. A guess is that Rosny's space travelers are embarking on the same new, expansive quest to transcend humanity that Bernal will set forth as science fiction's masterplot three years later. Their first encounter, in the early pages that describe their experience of space, is with Pascal's infinite void, which they rapidly leave behind as they reach Mars and the first step of Bernal's transhuman adventure—terraforming. His three astronauts, because they leave Earth for other environments, are given the possibility of reversing evolutionary conditions, if only in this localized area. The Martian *tripèdes*, because they cannot leave their planet, are now the evolutionary fatalists. Here, through the voyage of our intervening astronauts, "absolute" evolutionary time yields to a relativist sense of evolution, where mankind is now free to "navigate" the field of evolutionary possibility. The astronauts not only change the physical makeup of Mars, giving Martians the means of defeating the *zoomorphes* by reversing the depletion of their soil (which humans altered to feed themselves), but they are also on the verge of changing their own bodily makeup as well by bringing about a physical union between an Earthman and *tripède* female, which will result in offspring, a new step toward potential transhumanity.

The three astronauts, who speak of "affinités éléctives" between themselves, express a similar natural affinity for the *tripèdes*. They are not afraid to use the word "anthropocentrisme" to describe this affinity: "'Anthropocentriste!' s'écria Antoine. 'Les Ethéraux, voire les Zoomorphes, devraient nous paraître bien plus passionnants! Ceux-ci ne sont qu'une manière d'équivalent des Terriens . . .' 'C'est vrai . . . mais vous, au fond, qu'est-ce qui vous intéresse le plus?'" *Navigateurs* (65). ["Anthropocentrist!" Antoine exclaimed. "The Ethereals, even the Zoomorphes, should be of much more passionate interest to us! These [the Tripèdes] are only partially equivalent to Earthmen . . ." "That's true . . . but you, deep down, what interests you the most?"] (65) On one hand, the astronauts claim to find Martian life more fascinating than life on Earth. They see it as a possible "next step" insofar as it resembles us, yet appears to offer more evolutionary possibility: "Je le juge plus étonnant [your planet]. . . . Nous n'avons qu'une sorte de vie . . . vous en avez trois!" [I would say your planet is more astonishing. . . . We have only one form of life . . . you have three!] (84) Their Martian interlocutor answers that the contrary is true. To them, Earth is more interesting, for the reason that mankind has, at a young evolutionary age, gone into space, whereas they, over their long span of life, never did so. The reason they give in a sense foreshadows Efremov: Earth is simply a more favored place for the evolution of life: "Combien la vie de notre planète sera plus courte que celle de la vôtre! Déjà l'âge rayonnant est passé . . . et il ne fut jamais permis à nos ancêtres de franchir les abimes de l'Etendue . . . Trop petit et trop éloigné du Soleil, notre astre ne pouvait avoir une évolution comparable à celle du vôtre!" [How much shorter the life of our planet will be—compared to yours! Already the age of glory is over . . . and our ancestors will never be allowed to navigate the void of Space. . . . Our planet, too small and too distant from the Sun, can never have an evolution comparable to your planet] (84) On one hand, Mars and the Martians provide scientific mankind with a matrix for evolutionary growth toward a transhuman future. On the other hand, their "colonization" of Mars provides them with something analogous to Bernal's well-tended zoo. Human astronauts have given their planet renewed life in the image of humans, whose denizens adopt the human norm.

*Navigateurs* ends with a *union of life forms*, a cross-species "marriage," that promises a transhuman offspring. This is no longer an act where mankind gives a small, seemingly insignificant, *parcelle* of itself to a new, chemically incompatible species. It is now an act of *active* empathy on the part of narrator Jacques, who is presented as a dreamer, one who acts with his heart rather than his head. Jacques feels a "strange sympathy" toward a *tripède* female named Grâce. Her name is significant in comparison with the name of Targ's woman of promise, Êré. Êré is Eve to an Adam for whom there can be no regeneration, because the "era" of their race has been destroyed by irreversible physical change. On the other hand, "Grâce" suggests pre-destiny, a clear human overlay on the otherwise neutral process of physical evolution. She and Jacques, in terms of human reproduction, are chemically compatible. If Grâce seems grotesque by all norms of human beauty, she is supremely *attractive* to Jacques, in a vitally physical manner: "Elle me frôlait; je sentis passer je ne sais quel fluide, plus ineffable qu'un parfum, plus évocateur qu'une mélodie. Je naissais à une vie singulière et charmante qui prolongeait l'image de Grâce dans le passé et dans l'avenir." [She brushed up against me; I felt some sort of fluid pass through me, more ineffable than a perfume, more suggestive than a melody. I was reborn to a form of life both unique and charming which diffused the image of Grâce throughout my past and future existence.] (83) The fruit of this trans-species form of love—"Ces beaux frissons, ces ondes prodigieuses, comment les définir? . . . L'idée que ce pût être de l'amour, au sens humain, me semblait absurde et même répugnante. . . . Pourtant, c'est bien du désir que je ressentais auprès d'elle" [Those delightful shiverings, those mighty waves of feeling, how can I describe them? Any idea that this could be called "love" in the human sense seemed to me absurd, even repugnant. . . . And yet, it was indeed desire that I felt in her presence.] (83)—will be transhuman. But if on one hand this is mankind moving into its own dimorphic future, on the other it can be seen as anthropocentric humanity absorbing the alien into its evolutionary sphere, "diffusing the image of Grâce throughout my past and future existence." The double has again captured the dimorph.

## MAMBO CHICKENS, BEARS, AND OLDUVAI GORGE

Neither current science nor science fiction appears to have found a way beyond the Bernalian masterplot. As noted, the most recent speculations on transhumanity apply information science and artificial intelligence research to the problem. But the "cosmic superbrains" they posit still maintain contact with the human mind that gave birth to them. Kurzweil's post-singularity entities will continue to treat humans with "respect." But it is Ed Regis, in his 1990 study of "science slightly over the edge," *Great Mambo Chicken and the Transhuman Condition*, who sums up the scientific approaches to transhumanity across the same twentieth century that sees the flowering of science fiction. Regis discusses scientific speculations on terraforming, universe building, nanoengineering, and cryonics—all means of defeating

Bernal's enemies of the rational soul as mankind advances from the human to its transhuman condition.[21]

But Regis's phrase "the transhuman condition" makes explicit connection with Pascal. Human—and one assumes by extension transhuman—aspirations remain, for Pascal, mired in a state of contrariness, where mankind is an incomprehensible monster to itself. Indeed, the Great Mambo Chicken of the title, for all the advanced science that goes into its making, is nothing more than a combination of "contraries," of uplifted dimorph and monstrous double. Regis describes an experiment in which normal chickens were placed in a 3-G centrifuge for six months: "These chronically accelerated fowl were paragons of brute strength and endurance. . . . So they stomped around on the treadmills and . . . proved to one and all that, yes, here was a fabulous new brand of chicken. But the question was: *what was it good for?*" (55) Again, the conventional form of chicken, as with humans adapted to one-G, remains the norm against which we measure all such advanced forms. As with super-chimps and salamanders, the dream of surpassing the self seems always to precipitate the original form of that self. In the mirror of this original form, the new being, with all its strengths and excesses, comes to see itself as another incomprehensible monster.

We can look at several stories and novels from Regis's last decade of the Bernalian century to see how science fiction's masterplot has played out, and whether the catastrophe-continuity model still holds, and in what manner. By this decade, all the science that gives rise to the recent universe-as-mind visions was there, at least in theory. As will be seen, these stories still enact Bernal's scenario of dimorph and double. At this late date in the genre's history, however, the persistence of dimorphism points to what has become, with strong advances in "super-sciences" that describe increasingly ahuman phenomena, a major problem with the "fiction" part of science fiction—narratability. In other words, the scientific "plot" can no longer find adequate analogues to tell the story at the level of conventional narrative devices. To use Bernal's terms, the theoretical dimorphs of science no longer find their fictional double. The supermind speculations of the 2000s read like scientific descriptions. Science fiction writers who place these at the center of their narratives have not quite learned Clarke's lesson—that the Overmind has no story to tell us. But we are not quite at this point in the 1990s, which makes a look at the fate of Bernal's dimorph-double model in this decade interesting.

Rosny, in creating an "evolutionary narrator," experimented with narration at the limits of the transhuman experience. Rosny suggests that, to tell the story of the Last Man in the narrative past tense, the narrator must be telling it *from a location* that lies beyond humanity. Logically, because of its situation, the dimorph can only be addressing an audience in *its* world, for ours no longer exists. Even so, we readers exist. The transhuman story can be told to us, but only if the transcended entity addresses its untranscended double. This can be a presence in the text. An example is the Overlord listeners to Jan's account of the transcendent moment. Their presence allows readers to go to the brink of the transhuman moment by rejecting what is otherwise the logic of the situation—mankind as we know it is gone, and there should be no Jan's story because no one is left to hear and understand it. Or the double can be a visitor to our present from the other side of the transformational divide. This is, on a less vast scale, the situation of Pohl's "Day Million" (1966). The story's narrator is obviously, by the way "he" talks and thinks, from some future world; he is clearly a highly altered if not specifically transhuman being. The narration is that of a radically changed being trying to tell its story in the specific language of the time of Pohl's story, making clumsy attempts to mediate between its world and that of contemporary readers, whom it designates as its narrative audience.[22] Assuming that, in many of these science fiction works, narrators seem aware, as in Rosny, of the logical, and if we take the narrative literally, physical barriers to telling the transhuman story, the two options above seem to be those most used. Either the double approaches the dimorph, or the dimorph "returns" to resurrect its double.

These two narrative locations—this side, or that side, of the split—tend to intersect the story lines of the two models of evolutionary dimorphism: catastrophe and continuity. In one possibility, telling is from the point of view of the double. This teller is someone that had a brush with transcendence, then retreats to a human point of view to tell a story that offers a gradual approach to what proves finally untellable, at the threshold of transhuman promise. In the other possibility, the story is told from the point of view of the dimorph. Recourse to conventional suspension of disbelief allows this story to be told. Science fiction however takes the narrator's location literally. Doing so, it encounters barriers that challenge science fiction writers. Since they must adhere to the genre's material imperative, writers are snarled in questions difficult to answer. Would a posthuman entity, logically, feel the need or desire to communicate its transhuman experience back to an audience located this side of passage? Can it physically do so?

Science fiction narratives generally follow the pattern traced by Bernal's masterplot, from continuity to catastrophe. Bernal tells his story of advancement from the point of view of the rational soul, leading readers to dimorphic split; at this point he has nothing to say about the new form and falls back to the perspective of its human double. Others however take the challenge of the other direction, from catastrophe back to continuity. Haraway, for example, tries to locate her story beyond the posthuman barrier; yet her narrative, again and again, somewhat illogically addresses the cyborg's human double as necessary audience. The "copy's" story can only be told by a covert process of reattaching it to its lost "original," the only audience that actually needs to hear it.

A well-known story employing the first narrative situation is Terry Bisson's "Bears Discover Fire" (1990).[23] The narrator is located in the story's mundane present, and is even slightly behind his times, a bachelor in rural Kentucky who sells crop insurance, changes his own flat tires in the age of radials, takes care of his nephew in the summer, and has an old feeble-minded mother in a rest home. Through his point of view, readers experience what could be seen (beneath its seemingly facetious surface) as a moment of evolutionary change: the revelation that bears have discovered fire. These bears could be following in our footsteps, uplifting themselves to human status. But if we look again, a new evolutionary possibility might be occurring here, one that could lead humanity to transcend its present condition. Fire allows the bears to break free from the rhythm of hibernation, giving them the possibility of continuous memory. Newspaper accounts speculate that global warming caused the bears to discover fire. But there is the very different possibility that bears *remembered* fire, a memory perhaps awakened by the great Yellowstone fire (a detail that places the narrator close to the date of the story). Were this the case, bears could be said to have forgotten as much or more than humans ever learned. Are they then the originals of which we are copies? As such, might they not be reasserting old forgotten powers (powers we subsequently learned) while seeking to advance humanity toward some new form?

Details reported without surprise by the narrator suggest that, as a result of the bears, a new direction for humanity may be in the making. The bears occupy the medians of interstate highways going south, as if these were empty niches in the human evolutionary schema: "I had never been there, and neither had anyone else that I knew of. It was like a created country." (184) They sit around their fires eating a berry that humans identify as "the first new species in recent history" and call the "newberry." Finally, there is the "defection" of the old mother. As she loses her human memory, she finds herself summoned by the bears she sees on TV, whom she joins in the median. Oddly, the narrator and his nephew know where to find her: "I looked out the back door, and saw the firelight twinkling through the trees across the northbound lane of I-65, and realized I might just know where to find her." (186) They join her seated around the fire with the bears. As she dies in our human world, she appears to pass to a new level of consciousness, where she seems able to communicate telepathically with her son: "I leaned over to whisper something to Mother and she shook her head. *It would be rude to whisper around these creatures that don't possess the power of speech*, she let me know without speaking." (187)

The narrator himself enters this new world without the least resistance: "Inside the fire itself, things weren't so dull, either. Little dramas were being played out as fiery chambers were created and then destroyed in a crashing of sparks. My imagination ran wild. I looked around the circle at the bears and wondered what *they* saw." (187) As state troopers come the next morning to remove the body of the old woman, said to "pass away" during this night of communion, the narrator himself seems to advance to a transhuman form of seeing: "The troopers stayed behind and scattered the bears' fire ashes. . . . It seemed a petty thing to do. They were like bears themselves, each one solitary in his own uniform." (188) Humans now act as we have always thought bears do. The bears become what we always think we are—civilized, "advanced" beings. Readers looking through this narrator's eyes find themselves momentarily, as humans in Bernal's zoo, looking out upon a superior form of evolved life that has allowed humans into their fireside circle, giving them, as with the mother, a means of surpassing their present condition. The narrator however remains this side of advancement. Mother's "translation" is viewed thus: "She pointed up toward the canopy of trees, where a light was spreading, and then pointed to herself. Did she think it was angels approaching from on high? It was only the high beams of some southbound truck, but she seemed mighty pleased. Holding her hand, I felt it grow colder and colder in mine." (188) The dimorphic possibility collapses back on the human center. The narrator returns to the bears' circle two nights later, but the familiar world has righted itself: "I had taken a handful of newberries from the hubcap. . . . I tried again, but it's no use, you can't eat them. Unless you're a bear." (199)

A work attempting to narrate the story of human advancement from the opposite point of view—of the posthuman dimorph—is Mike Resnick's "Seven Views of Olduvai Gorge" (1994).[24] The narrator is a part of a classic "more-than-human" group entity that exists in a posthuman time (mankind is said to be extinct) and is ostensibly composed of different nonhuman races. Each component of this group claims to be an individual entity. Yet each does little more than augment, in specialized fashion, a faculty that once belonged to general mankind. The narrator, as part of this cluster, claims to be a transhuman extension of the human faculty of memory: "Imagine having to learn everything one knows in a single lifetime, to be totally ignorant at the moment of birth! Far better to split off from your parent with his knowledge intact in your brain, just as *my* parent's knowledge came to him, and ultimately to me." (306) Resnick suggests that many component "races" of his group entity may not have evolved from mankind at all. But if mankind is but one component among many, why is this "multi-species" entity so drawn to locate the origins of our race? Again, the subtext is that humanity is "special" and thus merits recovery, possibly due to some quality lacking in the posthuman future. Why did mankind rise to dominate the universe, then expire totally? We see in fact that humanity has not entirely expired, since "curiosity"—for writers like Campbell and Heinlein humanity's unique characteristic—drives this posthuman entity's mission to Earth.

The stated purpose of the expedition is to understand the origins of an extinct race of humans, a purely "objective" scientific mission. Resnick takes great pains to locate his narrator post-humanity. Located here, it has the task of *re-narrating* the readers' past to a narrative audience in *its world*—an audience which needs to hear this retelling of our story to help it understand a significant event in its time—an event that will occur at the end of the narrative we human readers are reading. At the same time, its narrator seeks, in the name of scientific "factuality," to get away with explaining things about itself and its function that its posthuman audience would already know, but readers do not. Here is an example: "I have no name, for my people do not use names, but for the convenience of the party I have taken the name of He Who Views for the duration of the expedition. This is a double misnomer: I am not a *he*, for my race is not divided by gender, and I am not a Viewer, but a Fourth Level Feeler." (307) Were this addressed to a transhuman audience, the speaker would have no need of categories such as "gender." It would not have to explain what it is or is not. These details are meant obliquely, by richochet, for human ears.

The "seven views" are seven vignettes in the ascent of humanity, from primitive ape to ruler of the universe, all conjured by the Feeler from artifacts found at the origin point of Olduvai Gorge. The Feeler's activity recaptures the human concept of psychometry (see Arthur Conan Doyle's story "The Leather Funnel" [1922]) that posits that objects, like time capsules, retain the emotional charge of some dramatic moment of use in the past. Physically fusing with a bone, amulet, or other archeological find, the Feeler conjures the scene in which the object played a key role, and the narrator tells its story. The gorge, then, offers a vast spatiotemporal museum, where the dimorph is physically drawn back to "original" forms, through which it advances along a path where each ensuing story is a "missing link," leading what must be a human addressee (and its double the reader) toward the transhuman moment. But as these aliens replay the human story—possibly *because they do so*—we witness the human double's *physical* resurrection from its lost past. Born of violence, leaving behind a trail of violence, humanity is born again in an equally violent eternal return.

The narrator proclaims mankind "at least as we citizens of the galaxy have come to understand him" to be extinct. The path inscribed by mankind's rise and fall, as the Feeler describes it, is a cosmic ellipse, that advanced to far limits, then returned to its place of departure: "So that was how it had ended for Man on earth, probably less than a mile from where it had begun. . . . Nothing was beyond their ability to achieve. . . . And yet they came out to the stars not just with their lusts and their hatred and their fears, but with their technology and their medicine, their heroes as well as their villains. Most of the races of the galaxy had been painted by the Creator in pastels; Men were primaries." (340) The narrator takes pride in discovering the true status of Man as the "primary" form from which all other races may have evolved, and to whose perfect functionality all yearn to return. The quest of this transhuman race to recover human origins produces in fact a step-by-step *re-constitution*—as aliens physically fuse with the artifacts that "tell" the story of a "race that refuses to die"—of this "primary" at its most violent.

The archaeological account of this re-constitution leads to a culminating event in the future of great interest to readers in our present who have just learned they are "primaries": the Exobiologist, one specialized member of this exploratory group, is killed by "lumbering, ungainly creatures of the night." Merging with the bone that seems the murder weapon, the Feeler joins with the creatures who wielded it: "As I became one with the tibia, as I felt it crashing down again and again upon our companion's head and shoulders, I felt a sense of power . . . I had never experienced before. I suddenly seemed to see the world through the eyes of the bone's possessor. . . . I saw visions of conquest against other tribes living near the gorge." (342) In a scenario that repeats over and over in science fiction, the advanced form learns it can do no better than to re-inhabit its double, to re-discover and ultimately reinvest the original form: "And finally, at the moment of triumph, he and I looked up at the sky, and *we* knew that someday all that *we* could see would be *ours*." (342) The transcended narrator, working on the dimorphic principle that original mankind is extinct, returns to the museum at the source, only to rediscover not only that Man is not gone, but that, with this new turn of the screw, Man will return to recapture its transhuman future, as part of a dynamic process whereby mankind re-energizes itself in hopes of casting a wider circumference. The spiral path of Man's advancement is "not over," and this narrative, which claims to be from the other side of the divide, proves it is not so. As the double recaptures the dimorph, Resnick's narrator demonstrates that any claim to transhumanity, at least in a story told *to humans*, is futile pretense.

## BIOLOGY AT THE END OF ITS TETHER

These stories offer fictional strategies for narrating the transhuman experience, displaying great subtlety in negotiating the divide that separates what we are and what we might become. Generally, however, they accept the limits of the double. They do not (perhaps cannot) give us a detailed description of the world transhuman entities might construct, once mind and biology as we know it have mutated into something else. Rosny, for example, gives highly detailed descriptions of the "ferromagnetics" *this side* of the barrier. Of the other side—how a transhuman entity might adapt and survive in a ferromagnetic world—he has nothing to say. The writers discussed, to one degree or another, all accept the transhuman moment as a cognitive as well as a narrative barrier, beyond which mind or imagination cannot credibly reach. Either, as with Lem, they reject as "fantasy" any attempt to see beyond the mirror of the human double, or they offer timid extrapolations, as in Pohl's and Resnick's stories, where we invariably detect, beneath the exotic surface, the hold of known forms of human mind or biology.

Recently however there have been notable attempts to model a genuinely transhuman world, especially in terms of biology. The information sciences and chemistry have been less promising. Despite new speculative concepts of the nature of mind and intelligence, the human model seems to hold. For no matter the form, there must always *be* something we recognize as "thought"; the equation remains "mind" or "non-mind." Rosny's "ferromagnetics" pushed the chemical limits for the definition of life. The arsenic component in extremophile life forms recently found at Mono Lake seems to bolster his speculations at this level. But beyond the chemistry, the question of what sort of "intelligence" an iron- or arsenic-based life form might develop goes unanswered. Indeed, the assumption that something resembling what we call "intelligence" might evolve in a chemically different life form remains a tautology. Imagining viable transformations at the level of biology however appears more promising. Recent hard science fiction has ventured into this transhuman territory, where Clarke's devils feared to tread. One of the most extraordinary of these incursions is Greg Egan's *Diaspora* (1997). In conclusion, we examine how far Egan goes, in this imaginative attempt to construct a transhuman *world*, toward freeing the dimorph from its biological double.

In the world of *Diaspora,* humanity is in the throes of detaching itself from its bodies, hence from biology and the workings of evolution as we know it. The world we enter is one of "orphanogenesis," literally birth without parents *or ancestors.* All of that long chain of carbon life Targ evoked is gone. Human political systems however are not. Beings "born" this way are called "citizens" (they are "free" in more ways than one). As expected, they live in "polises." These latter, however, are vastly "mutated" city-states which exist as the hardware of supercomputers, into whose circuits humans are "uploaded" through an elaborately described process whereby their biological bodies are disassembled and reassembled by nanomachines. The physical brain is reduced to "information states," chemical and electrical units that can be transferred to "worlds" inside the computer. "It" still has a physical locus; "we" do not. In Cartesian terms, a mind world is created inside the machine that is totally severed from any connection to bodily passions. For when biological evolution stops, we have a world not only without gender, but without human personality. Consciousness develops in durational time, yet here time produces nothing but "clones"—iterations of a same moment, the moment at which a given consciousness was "uploaded."

The world of the "polises" is one of simulated realities. Egan meticulously describes how citizens manipulate the experience of time. They can "imitate" the rate of human time, speed it up or slow it down, to the extreme of allowing one to experience the slow time of geological processes such as formation or erosion. They can choose to perceive and describe things either as linear chronology or "gestalts," all-in-one apprehension, immediately knowing things in their totality. The polises have "charters," which orient activities toward various pursuits, such as Cartesian introspection or experimental study of the "physical" world. Within these general parameters, citizens create and "live in" as many virtual worlds—ironically called "scapes"—as they like. Bodiless entities, they can choose to appear to others as "icons," visual masks they assume at will.

Humans appear to have completely left behind their "meat" existence, to have formed a well-organized "overmind." But it is clear from the terms used that Bernal's double is still present. Moreover, a *res extensa* still exists, where "orphans," somewhere, had to have biological ancestors. Their computer world still has a "hard drive," a physical location somewhere, a plug that can be pulled. Far from being totally abandoned, this physical world—for Egan's novel *does* have a plot—continues to provide evolutionary pressures that will cause the polises to leave their mind world and engage a material world that, beyond their introverted and solipsistic theories of physics, poses a catastrophic threat in real time to come.

Egan offers a detailed description of the transhuman dimorph. Side by side however we perceive its double, as he peoples his landscape with the various evolutionary "steps" that will lead to what is a classic dimorphic split. Egan rings ingenious variations on previously imagined categories of human transformation. His larger world contains "fleshers," biological humans living in places like "Atlanta," who are undergoing changes in the manner of Bernal's "flesh" or Haraway's cyborgs. There are, in contrast to fleshers, "statics," naturally evolving humans (us) living in their zoo. There are "exuberants," humans who make outlandish use of "enhancement" techniques and autoplastic transformations and shape equally strange physical environments to accommodate their auto-mutations. These beings are caught in a wildly absurd mind-matter dilemma, trying in vain to mutate themselves out of their gruesome Cartesian circle, and Egan has fun with them. For example, one group calls itself "dream apes." These use advanced techniques of selective breeding in hopes of recovering the condition of Rousseau's *bon sauvage*. Their mutations become so chaotic that, in reaction, a third species of biological humans has developed—"bridgers"—whose function is to modify their minds and bodies to bridge the increasing gap between statics and auto-mutating exuberants.

Despite these variations, this action still plays out along the axis of Bernal's world, flesh and devil. For among these variants, the normative fleshers, gradually, abandon a biological existence for the mind world of the polis. To facilitate this process, Egan has an intermediate form that in a sense functions like Clarke's Overlords—so-called "gleisners," who are software programs housed in robot bodies. In this world dimorphically divided between fleshly zoo and virtual mind cities, the robot gleisners (in an ironic twist on Bernal) assume the role of "uneven gropers" after new worlds. They live neither on Earth, nor in virtual reality, but in space habitats, from which they explore the stars. Gleisners, like the Overlords, apparently operate outside the schema of human and posthuman entities, existing to show us that, beyond arcane mind structures like "six-dimensional geometry," Pascal's infinite universe remains "out there." With their existence, Egan reveals that entropy remains a factor in the workings of the polises, where citizens in virtual realities must endlessly seek more diversity of experience at less expense of physical energy. What is more, cosmic catastrophe—not predicted by arcane "Kosuch physics"—looms. Egan's plot involves a neutron star collapse, where a gamma ray burst destroys the fleshers unable to upload in time. This event leads to the "diaspora" of the title. In one polis, the citizen protagonists shift allegiance from theory to gleisner pragmatism and mount an experiment that disperses clones of themselves across vast universes. Even so, they search for a broader *theory* that can encompass future physical events. Even in this most elaborate of transhuman futures, we do not escape the mind-matter duality.

In fact, the most Egan seems able to do, like Rosny and Clarke before him, is explore the transhuman space between dimorph and double. His post-human entities are *clones*—mental beings who appear to have split from physical humanity. Their problem is how to reach back across the gulf to embrace a spacetime in which physical events like neutron-star collapses occur, the spacetime from which their computer-worlds must draw power and energy. The posthuman clones receive help in their quest from the very human and transhuman ancestors they thought they had left behind. Egan presents this as a transhuman infusion of new life into posthuman stagnation. For example, Karpal the gleisner—a being with a human "ancestor" (a certain Gleisner created these beings)—leaves its robot body and uploads into the

Carter-Zimmerman polis, bringing with "him" a new impetus toward experiment and exploration. And the uploaded "bridger" from old Atlanta, Orlando Veneti, uses his earlier training in mediating between human "variant" species to contact aliens encountered on the diaspora. Their actions prove that, in terms of process, there is no straight line from human to posthuman. Instead, we have a series of spiral movements where each new adventure rebounds from the original human source to mount new, ever different assaults on transhuman possibility.

Egan however adds something new to the problem. Rosny, with scientific rigor, gives his reader a *possible* view of a *potential* human future, but does not take us there. Clarke abandons the Overmind to be able to take humanity, in his *2001* novels, into a future of transhuman mutations. In all these transformations, however, the double serves as nostalgic device, to remind readers constantly of what we once were and perhaps always will be. Egan on the other hand appears to offer a *dynamic* for human advancement. Mankind cannot become pure mind. But mind can extend its transhuman reach by periodically returning to its human source in flesh and physical materiality. Thought in Egan seems to reach far, but like Antaeus, the transhuman entity needs to touch Earth, to return to its energy source if it is to reach farther. Egan places us right in the middle of an extended transhuman *moment*. The art of his science fiction consists of pushing this moment as far as it can go. Within this space of promise, science *fiction* faces the problem of *telling* the transhuman moment—a task unique to science fiction storytelling that marks the genre not only as a supremely *experimental* form of narrative, but as a genre distinguished by its fascination with threshold situations, stories that, at their best, offer glimpses of ineffable otherness at the farthest limits of the human imagination.

## NOTES

1. John Desmond Bernal, *The World, the Flesh, and the Devil: An Inquiry into the Three Enemies of the Rational Soul* (London: Jonathan Cape, 1968). References are to this edition.

2. Arthur C. Clarke, *Greetings, Carbon-Based Bipeds!* (New York: St. Martins Griffin, 2000), 70. See also Olaf Stapledon, *Last and First Men and Star Maker: Two Science Fiction Novels* (New York: Dover, 1968), 198: "Certain ideas about artificial planets were suggested by Mr. J. D. Bernal's fascinating little book *The World, the Flesh, and the Devil.* I hope he will not strongly disapprove of my treatment of them." I am indebted to Eric S. Rabkin for the citation.

3. See Brenda Swann, *J. D. Bernal, A Life in Science and Politics* (London: Verso, 1999); Andrew Brown, *J. D. Bernal: The Sage of Science* (Oxford: Oxford University Press, 2005).

4. Clarke, *Childhood's End* (New York: Ballantine Books, 1953).

5. Clarke, *2001: A Space Odyssey* (New York: Signet/NAL, 1968). Clarke, *3001: The Final Odyssey* (New York: Ballantine/Del Rey, 1997). References are to these editions.

6. Clarke, *2061: Odyssey Three* (New York: Ballantine/Del Rey, 1987). References are to this edition.

7. Donna Haraway, "A Cyborg Manifesto: Science, Technology, and Socialist Feminism in the Late Twentieth Century," *Simians, Cyborgs, and Women: The Reinvention of Nature* (London: Free Association Press, 1991). References are to this edition.

8. Honoré de Balzac, "Le Chef d'oeuvre inconnu," *La Comédie humaine* (Paris: Bibliothèque de la Pléiade, 1950), IX, 389–414. References are to this edition.

9. See Istvan Csicsery-Ronay, Jr., "The SF of Theory: Baudrillard and Haraway," *Science-Fiction* Studies, 18:3 (November 1991), 387–404.

10. Arkady and Boris Strugatsky, *Noon: 22nd Century* (New York: Macmillan, 1978). Translated from the Russian by Patrick L. McGuire; references are to this translation.

11. Ivan Efremov, *The Heart of the Serpent* [*Sedtse Zmei*, 1956] (Moscow: Foreign Language Publishing House, 1960). Translated from the Russian by R. Prokofieva; references are to this edition.

12. Another source for the Strugatskys could be a work like Heinlein's juvenile *Time for the Stars* (1956). Given the Strugatskys' fascination in this story cycle with returning spacemen and temporal dislocations caused by the "twins paradox," Heinlein's novel may offer a precise locus. There is no firm evidence that they had access to the novel, but as a "juvenile" adventure, it may have passed Soviet censorship as something ideologically harmless, as simple space opera, a genre welcomed by Soviets at this early stage in their own space endeavors. In Heinlein's novel, one twin, Pat Bartlett, sweeps around the galaxy at near-light speeds, gathering many lifetimes of experience and scientific data, yet barely ageing in relation to brother Tom, who remains on Earth. Experiences at the circumference however, offering contact and possible "advancement," do not escape the center. Pat, returning to his original spacetime location, finds he has lost family and friends, yet remains *young* in relation to his old world, thus able to find new work and embark on new journeys of discovery. Upon the next return, however, the cycle will be the same, as Pat barely ages in relation to the world that serves as his recurrent center. The Strugatskys, it seems, are Heinlein's Soviet counterparts in terms of the science fiction juvenile; as such, they use this shared trope of the returning spaceman and its ever-doubling rhythm to perfection.

13. Strugatskys, *The Snail on the Slope* (New York: Bantam Books, 1980). Translated from the Russian by Alan Meyers.

14. This is certainly not the case with Jean-Baptiste Cousin de Grainville's *Le dernier homme* (1806) and Mary Shelley's *The Last Man* (1826). Grainville's novel projects the death of mankind far in the future, and the story is narrated by Time itself, a convenient way to avoid problems with narrators and narrative audiences. The last man in question has expired, and cannot tell his story, but "Time," using the past tense, apparently can. Shelley's novel ends things in 2100. Her last humans are not

evolved beings, but fictional equivalents of Percy Shelley, Byron, and others of her circle. In neither novel is there any speculation on the possibility of transhumanity.

15. J.-H. Rosny aîné, *Récits de Science-Fiction*, edited by Jean-Baptiste Baronian (Verviers, Belgium: Bibliothèque Marabout, 1975). Also see *Three Novellas of J. H. Rosny aîné: From Prehistory to the End of Mankind*, translated and annotated by George Slusser and Danièle Chatelain (Middletown, Connecticut: Wesleyan University Press, 2012); references are to this edition.

16. One could argue that the existentialist act, in Pascal's sense, is an anthropocentric act, the only and final act human beings have in the face of the material infinite. In Pascal's gambit, mankind in the act of being crushed affirms its uniqueness in perpetual opposition to this *néant*: we know, it does not know. Thus, Sartre can proclaim that *"l'existentialisme est un humanisme."* The existential act, which Sartre also sees as an act of self-creation (*"se faire"*), can therefore be seen as something quite different from Targ's ecological altruism. Again, there is the gambit that somehow snatches the uniquely human from the inevitable process of evolution: as Sartre again says, we are *condemned* to be free, and in realizing this, once again we affirm the uniqueness of rational consciousness of our situation, in opposition to certain annihilation.

17. For a similar use of this term, see Wendy Wall, *The Imprint of Gender: Authorship and Publication in the English Renaissance* (Ithaca, New York: Cornell University Press, 1993).

18. Some readers may feel that Rosny's narrator is simply the conventional "omniscient" narrator, hence all this discussion of past tense narration and narrative audience after the death of the Last Man is specious. One can make a case however for Rosny's narrator being an "evolutionary narrator," a narrator who by definition can never be omniscient, because evolution is an ever-ongoing, open-ended process. We see this in the carefully controlled focus of Rosny's narrator. It begins with a sharp focus on the last humans and their environment. In chapter two, it takes a "historical" perspective ("Depuis cinq siècles, les hommes n'occupaient plus, sur la planète, que des îlots dérisoires . . ." [For five centuries, men have only occupied those pathetic small islands]) that gradually widens to encompass the fall of mankind and its environment from its industrial apogee. Then, in the same chapter, the focus suddenly narrows, with the historical narrator, in an act of radical empathy, modulating from the pronoun "nous" to a "je" ("je pense qu'elle reflétera surtout cet étrange phénomène . . ." [I think it will mostly show that strange phenomena.]) The narrator now identifies itself as part of the last men. From this moment to Targ's final act, it maintains a steady focus on Rosny's protagonist, recounting Targ's innermost thoughts in a sort of *style indirect libre*, a penetration that culminates in Targ's great visionary dream that now spans all of carbon life. This highly mobile and evolving narrator, in the final paragraph, reveals itself a voice beyond Targ's death, thus beyond the death of that life form that culminated in Targ. This same narrator's retroactive empathy for Targ is itself proof that some aspect of the Last Man not only survived but acted as a transformatory force on the subsequent evolution of the narrating species.

19. Darwin did not use the term "altruism" but discussed the evolutionary paradox of what he called "benevolence" especially in *The Descent of Man* (1871). Eric

Strong, in an article in *The New York Times* (December 1997), sees scientists still actively debating "the causes and effects of altruistic behavior" 100 years after Darwin.

20. Rosny, *Les Navigateurs de l'infini, Récits de Science-Fiction,* 40–91. References are to this edition; translations are mine.

21. Ed Regis, *Great Mambo Chicken and the Transhuman Condition: Science Slightly Over the Edge* (New York: Addison Wesley Publishing Company, 1990). References are to this edition.

22. Frederik Pohl, "Day Million," *Day Million* (New York: Ballantine Books, 1970), 5–12.

23. Terry Bisson, "Bears Discover Fire," *The Year's Best Science Fiction,* Eighth Annual Collection, edited by Gardner Dozois (New York: St Martin's Press, 1991), 179–189. References are to this edition.

24. Mike Resnick, "Seven Views of Olduvai Gorge," *The Year's Best Science Fiction,* Twelfth Annual Collection, edited by Gardner Dozois (New York: St Martin's Press, 1995), 305–342. References are to this edition.

## Chapter Seven

# Each Man Is an Island

## *The Legacy of Emerson's Golden Age*

To finally understand the emergence of modern science fiction, we must turn to another significant paradigm, that established by the already mentioned Ralph Waldo Emerson. In Emerson's eyes, each man is literally an island— the self-reliant individual. That "island" however, according to the energy it generates and form it aspires to, proves a powerful creator of worlds. For figures like Heinlein's immortal character Lazarus Long, the circumference they seek to project is the multiverse itself. If their projections fail, they fall back on their individual dynamic centers, and project again. On one hand, Emerson's vision dynamizes the mind-matter duality of the rationalists. On the other, it short-circuits the process of evolution, for at any moment in human history a man can arise who sets humanity on a new track. Emerson's American paradigm, then, continuously challenges material, cultural, and (as we see with Heinlein) mythic limits, even if it does not overcome them. As such, it generates the Golden Age model that serves as the dynamic center of science fiction in the twentieth century.

Emerson's vision has deep roots in American romanticism. I will demonstrate how the Emersonian dynamic reinforces, through its strong presence in Golden Age science fiction, the continuity of American literature, and examine the ways in which Emerson's vision and his dynamic monad shape the science fiction of Golden Age writers like Heinlein, Asimov, and others. I also will carry the investigation into more speculative areas, notably to examine the relation between Emerson's *undulatory* process of power and form, and the propensity of science fiction's themes and technological landscapes to generate mediatized structures. Why, in films and other visual manifestations, are science fiction scenarios invariably associated with new technological feats of image dissemination? The case in point is *Star Wars*. Through a broadcasting dynamic, which seems to operate by means of an undulation of power and form analogous to the basic "plots" of Golden Age stories, science fiction has received world-wide "distribution." This may be Bruce Sterling's meaning when he remarks that, in the last decades of the twentieth century, there is no longer need to read or write science fiction because the world *has become* science fiction.

Sterling's remark is more than a *boutade*. He suggests that what was once the domain of science fiction is now being acted out in real time in locations around an increasingly globalized world. For the world to become science fiction, this latter's structures must displace and replace older, less mobile ones. These structures, Sterling tells us, are those of Alvin Toffler's "third wave," the age of global broadcasting media and the internet, instantaneous dissemination of information. These are, in a real sense, Emersonian structures. At the time *The Third Wave* was published (1980), print science fiction was just emerging from the Golden Age, but still closely tied to it. We will examine possible ways in which the dynamic of Golden Age science fiction may have encouraged the formation of Sterling's hypothetical bridge between science fiction and the advent of globalized media.

## THE EMERSON CONNECTION

Isaac Asimov and others give sole credit for American science fiction's "Golden Age" to writer-editor John W. Campbell, Jr., who began editing *Astounding Science-Fiction* in 1937 and for over two decades promoted and published writers like Heinlein and Asimov later to dominate the field. The cusp between this Golden Age and the so-called New Wave occurs in the 1960s and can be traced by looking at the famous Ace Doubles, where one finds side by side (or rather back to back) space operas by Lin Carter and early works of writers like Harlan Ellison, Samuel R. Delany, and Ursula K. Le Guin. Emerging from this pulp cauldron are Terry Carr's Ace Specials, publishing novels like Le Guin's *The Left Hand of Darkness* (1969). Campbell was certainly strong-willed, opinionated, and (in contrast to his editorial demand for "hard" science) fascinated with paranormal phenomena. Perhaps his own contradictory mindset brought Campbell to support writers as complex and diverse as Heinlein, Asimov, Sturgeon, and van Vogt. Moreover, the SF/mainstream division has led readers to accept the "ghetto" status of science fiction, when in fact Campbell's Golden Age was an essentially *American* literary movement. The science fiction being requested from, and written by, these diverse writers clearly drew heavily on nineteenth-century American themes (the frontier) and heroes (the self-reliant explorer), all seeking their personal "passage to more than India." Through Heinlein and his close relationship with Campbell, perhaps, these Golden Age writers became reconnected with Emerson's uniquely American vision.

This is the view of William H. Patterson, Heinlein's official biographer, in *Robert A. Heinlein: In Dialogue with His Century: Volume One, Learning Curve* (2010). Heinlein made few public comments about his work and its inspirations, yet Patterson states that "Emerson, Whitman and Thoreau so pervade Heinlein at a fundamental level that he rarely mentions them by name." As an example of the deep reach of Emerson into Golden Age science fiction, Patterson cites Alexei Panshin, who asserts that when Campbell famously inspired Asimov to write "Nightfall" by quoting Emerson, Heinlein was right behind Campbell giving him the quote.[1] Aside from testimony, the Emerson connection is both logical and clearly visible in Heinlein's works, where the Emerson dynamic appears to shape the "career" of a Lazarus Long and differentiate Lazarus's progress from George Bernard Shaw's evolutionary vitalism. True, Heinlein had no formal training in philosophy or literature. Even so, Emerson remained widely read and accessible both in Lazarus's and Heinlein's Missouri childhood. The form Emerson chose, in harmony with his idea of "Man writing," is the informal essay, offering thoughts and aphorisms, easy to read and cite while effortlessly presenting a powerful yet accessible vision of mankind's relation to nature. Emerson's essays could be found, side by side with the Bible, on bookshelves as disparate as those of the Heinlein family in Butler, Missouri, and Asimov's Russian immigrant family in New York City.

Exploring the origins of science fiction, I stressed the persistence of the Cartesian paradigm. In terms of Descartes's method, the doubting mind brings about a *tabula rasa*, whereby it disconnects from all material attachments, and by means of this negative action defines its existence as a thinking entity. Once this occurs, mind can pretend to rational control of the universe. Pascal however stresses the terrible isolation of the Cartesian mind, totally alone in the world of matter. In England, John Donne, standing on the firm soil of British nation and culture, responds in giving voice to the human norm: "No man is an island, entire of himself." Emerson, two centuries later, has a different response that challenges Descartes on his own terrain of mind and matter. Emerson would agree with Descartes that all men are islands, but would assert that, precisely because *they are islands,* they possess a unique power to expand their domain far beyond that of man in society, even man in nature. To Emerson, "an institution is the lengthened shadow of *one* man," the monad. If this monad is a great, or even a "representative" man, that shadow can be a great institution: "A man Caesar is born, and for ages we have a Roman Empire."[2] Descartes's method is democratic only in a restricted sense, for not every man is capable of "clear and distinct ideas."

Emerson, on the contrary, builds his vision in terms of energy, the power to secure the center. From its *single* dynamic center any monad, in principle, can make the entire world its satellite. Thus, Emerson in *The American Scholar:* "If a *single man* plant himself indomitably on his instincts, the huge world will come round to him."[3]

Emerson's monadic man, however, does not seek to found an empire in the classic, landed way. Instead, his power lies in extreme mobility, the ability to make himself insubstantial in terms of cultural and natural ties, rootless in a physical sense: "Standing on the bare ground . . . I become a transparent eyeball; I am nothing, I see all; the currents of the Universal Being circulate through me."[4] For Emerson, to become nothing in terms of society and nature (thus the "bare ground") does not lead to Cartesian separation of mind from matter, but is instead the means whereby the whole being—body and mind—can become pure expansive power: "I see all." Detaching itself from these obstacles, the individual realizes a new form of mobility that allows it to move from its center to the broadest possible circumference. Emerson replaces dualism with dynamism: "Power ceases in the moment of repose, it resides . . . in shooting the gulf, in the darting to an aim."[5] To Donne, the web holding human islands together is culture; Emerson—perhaps foreseeing today's internet, media "networks," and information "highways"—posits a situation in which things are reversed, where individual islands determine their position from inside the configuration of the net, projecting themselves as the product of energy, not substance.[6]

Emerson allows us to trace a bridge which spans what seems two disparate periods of science fiction: Campbell's Golden Age, where an impressive body of individual writers, all exercising Emersonian "power and form," created a vast web of texts, and "cyberpunk," a movement often attributed to a single author, William Gibson.[7] When Gibson describes his "matrix" in his novel *Neuromancer* (1984), he appears to extrapolate from the vast "web" of novels and stories that his Golden Age forebearers, writers of what he calls the "Gernsback continuum," bequeathed him: "Cyberspace. A consensual hallucination experienced daily by billions of legitimate operators . . . A graphic presentation of data abstracted from banks of every computer in the human system. Unthinkable complexity."[8]

Gibson's expansive vision was nurtured in a highly specific American culture. Its center lies in Emerson, and ultimately in Heinlein. Its circumference however, "incubated" by startling advances in information technologies, has expanded to areas that bear little or no external resemblance to science fiction—Hong Kong martial arts films, Jamaican reggae, Japanese manga, and cosplay—yet become fixtures of the cyberpunk landscape. Emerson's self-reliant individuals are reborn to the power of future technologies in monadic figures like Asimov's Hari Seldon and Heinlein's Lazarus, whose "circum- ference" is the spacetime universe itself.[9] Through rapid expansion of media of dissemination—film, television, personal computers, iPhones, "clouds," and wireless networks—the mythic figures of print science fiction mutate into video game superheroes and real-time film and music "legends" of the global infosphere. The capacity to create form from the power center of the individual monad has, through the extension of media, become the means of generating "cultures" with no base in land or nation, no nationality, no pass- port. Mediated legends like Bruce Lee and Bob Marley, and the global cul- tures they generate, carry on and expand a science fiction revolution, which had its origins in nineteenth-century America. This revolution was in fact an act of "dissemination." Touting the self-reliant monad, it aimed at dissolving the fabric of the European nation state, culture, and ultimately literature—the national models still dominating conventional fiction. In all domains of the mediacosm today, Emerson's monad is free, at every instant, to create new worlds for old.

## EMERSON AND THE AMERICAN GOLDEN AGE

It is perhaps a misnomer to call American science fiction, in the Campbel- lian period of the 1940s and 1950s, a "golden age," since the term denotes a traditional place of static perfection, which is not at all the fictional landscape of this period. This period is more accurately seen as the reign of Emerson's monads, dynamic, a fiction of mobile and highly expansive protagonists, whose "lengthened shadows" often aim at cosmic vastness. Heinlein's entire opus is built around the monad, but so is Asimov's classic Foundation tril- ogy—where a vast future history centers upon a monad. The trilogy is com- posed of three novels—*Foundation* (1951), *Foundation and Empire* (1952), and *Second Foundation* (1953)—that chronicle, supposedly in the manner of Edward Gibbon's *The History of the Decline and Fall of the Roman Empire* (1776), the fall of a Galactic Empire, and creation of two "foundations" designed, according to the calculations of "psychohistorian" Hari Seldon, to shorten the period of barbarism following this fall and bring about the return of civilization. In Asimov's work, however, neither the compositional nor historical process is as linear or predictable as the Gibbon analogy suggests. Each volume, in fact, is "generated" from a series of stories, previously and separately published during the 1940s in Campbell's *Astounding Science Fic- tion*. Moreover, the title of each original story claims an identity of its own. For example, the third chapter of *Foundation,* "The Mayors," appeared in the June, 1942 issue of *Astounding* as "Bridle and Saddle." Although Seldon's "plan" claims to control the trajectory and outcome of the historical process, it seems clear from Asimov's manner of constructing his trilogy that each chapter retains its status as individual monad. Each story forms an episode within the larger frame, whose general dynamic is outward expansion. Each offers a specific center within the larger net of stories that configure the space of the Foundation novels.

The same dynamic comes into play in other compilations of stories and novels. An example is the "rise" of Dr. Susan Calvin in the seminal collection *I, Robot* (1950). The first significant stories published in this compilation, "Runaround" (1941) and "Reason" (1941), feature the team of Powell and Donovan. There was a brief mention of Calvin in "Runaround," but she has no role in the story. She dominates the scene in the next story, "Liar!" (1941), which she narrates. She is a scientifically trained "robopsychologist," unlike pragmatists Powell and Donovan. They return to solve robot-generated puzzles in "Catch that Rabbit" (1944) and "Escape!" (1945) but yield the field to Calvin in the last stories. One could say here: a Susan Calvin was born, and for ages we have robots and empire. For the issues in the two Stephen Byerley stories—"Evidence" (1946) and "The Evitable Conflict" (1950)—have become so complex—a human who might be a robot, and what criteria should be employed to judge a robot who might be human and vice versa—that a person of Calvin's stature must take the helm. Throughout these stories, she emerges as the dynamic center most capable of generating the widest circumference. Asimov later adds mention of her in revising his first robot story, "Robbie," and prefaces the 1950 *I, Robot* with an "interview" wherein Calvin tells the interviewer that she herself is the narrator of all the stories.

Asimov takes this dynamic to a vaster scale in his Foundation series with its multiple centers of power, each based in a discrete monadic entity, and many circumferences. The final product reads like a number of intersecting circles, each with its own center, timeline and *raison d'être*. Hari Seldon is the primary monad in this fresco. His "psychohistory" is a discipline that deals with "mass actions," with large masses of data furnished by myriad worlds in a galactic empire. Its predictions, therefore, should be accurate for large samplings, and supposedly for the "big picture" of this expanded human history. But though psychohistory claims to "factor" in many variables, it proves unable to predict the actions of individuals, or gauge the sort of dynamic that ensues from "a man Caesar" being born. Seldon's plan is to shorten the long period of dark ages assumed to follow the fall of the Galactic Empire by establishing two foundations, one on the planet Terminus at the far end of the galaxy, the second at an undisclosed location. The First Foundation combines medieval monastery and guild, seeking to preserve human knowledge in an Encyclopedia Galactica; the other operates a trading enterprise masquerading as the religion of "scientism." Seldon's plan is less a theory than a work of social engineering projected into the future. But in for it to be "implemented," it must take into account a set of variables—the actions of strong individuals, such as "Mayor" Salvor Hardin and "Trader" Hober Mallow in the first novel, who build the First Foundation, or in adversarial fashion the General Bel Riose and telepathic Mule in *Foundation and Empire*. This is also true of Ebling Mis and Arcadia Darell, in *Second Foundation,* whose individual actions ultimately bring together the two Foundations. All that is left in the end, it seems, is for the First Speaker, the voice of the Second Foundation, to proclaim the implementation of the "plan": "It was here at Trantor that Ebling Mis discovered us; and here that we saw to it that he did not survive the discovery. To do so, it was necessary to arrange to have a normal Foundation girl defeat the tremendous mutant powers of the Mule."[10] Yet readers who followed along the way the many "undulations" from intersecting individual centers of power have difficulty accepting this overly serene statement of purpose, for Seldon's plan itself is not providence. To encompass the many variables of an essentially dynamic system, it must function as an overarching process of power and form capable of ultimately assimilating the many intersecting ripples in this Emersonian panorama of history, subject to what Emerson calls his random "lords of life."[11]

At first glance, the distribution of Foundations, one devoted to physical sciences, the other to "mental" sciences, appears to trace a Cartesian axis. Instead, what emerges from this panorama is an elastic interplay of power and form, center and circumference. The first Foundation, on far Terminus, marks the physical limits of the galaxy. Yet despite this vastness, it is revealed, the power that generated this form resided on Trantor, former center of the Empire and Seldon's home planet. Trantor, the reader discovers, has *always* provided the *elastic* center of the dynamic that shaped the events of the novels.[12] In fact, it is explicitly stated that what kept these undulating poles apart for so long is a materialist, Cartesian interpretation of Seldon's words: "In a sense, it is the irony of it all that is most amazing. For four hundred years, so many men have been blinded by Seldon's words 'the other end of the Galaxy.' They have brought their own peculiar, physical-science thought to the problem, ending up eventually either at a point in the periphery one hundred eighty degrees around the rim of the Galaxy, or back at the original point." (190) This is the Cartesian circle that has continues to trap minds. Now however a "mental science" interpretation—always clearly present in Seldon's statement yet consistently misread throughout—unlocks the energy at the center which rejoins the two poles of the Emersonian dynamic. The structure now inscribed is not the closed circle, but an open-ended spiral: "The Galaxy, you know, is not simply a flat ovoid of any sort; nor is its periphery a closed curve. Actually, it is a *double spiral*, with at least eighty percent of the inhabited planets on the Main Arm. Terminus is the extreme outer end of the spiral arm, and we are at the other—since, what is the opposite end of a spiral? Why, the center." (190)

In a nicely Emersonian turn of events, people had simply forgotten Seldon was a *social scientist* and the center was not a material point, but a *human:* "The solution could have been reached immediately, if the questioners had but remembered that Hari Seldon was a *social scientist*, not a physical scientist, and adjusted their thought processes accordingly. What could *opposite ends* mean to a social scientist? Opposite ends on the map? Of course not . . . And where is the *social opposite end of the Galaxy?* . . . Here! At the center! At Trantor, capital of the Empire of Seldon's time." (190) This statement makes it clear that the Empire, as social entity, is literally the shadow of a single man, Seldon. For Emerson, it is not the magnitude of the process, but the energy, the dynamic action, that counts. In the end of this trilogy, a "normal Foundation girl" defeats the tyrant's mind circle, realizing Seldon's plan, now seen to trace Emerson's "galvanic circuit." The perfect gloss for Asimov's trilogy is this excerpt from Emerson's essay "Experience": "A subject and object—it takes so much to make the galvanic circuit complete. But magnitude adds nothing. What imports it whether it is Kepler and the sphere, Columbus and America, a reader and his book, or puss with her tail? . . . Do you see that kitten chasing her own tail? If you could look with her eyes, you might see her surrounded with hundreds of figures performing complex dramas, with tragic and comic issues . . . many ups and downs of fate—and meantime it is only puss and her tail."[13]

Let us briefly move from Asimov to Heinlein. In works analyzed in previous chapters, his fiction is structured around the power, and perils, of the expanding monad. Interestingly, early stories by Heinlein set clear limits to individual expansiveness, while later novels allow figures like Lazarus to extend his personal circumference to what strives to be cosmic totality. Time travel would seem to offer the individual center limitless possibilities to generate circumferences. Yet in stories like "By His Bootstraps" (1942) and "'All You Zombies—'" (1958), the opposite is true. In the latter, the protagonist seeks to control the flow of personal, biological time by simply taking himself out of that flow. The idea is to tighten rather than expand the galvanic circuit, broadening its circumference just enough to encompass his own biological source, then using temporal manipulations to re-engineer his existence, making himself his own father and mother. Physically creating a world unto himself, he appears to turn Cartesian solipsism into a perpetual motion machine. Even so, one could see Heinlein's purpose in writing this despairing story as a rejection of Descartes for Emerson. For even in this extreme situation, it remains impossible for the dynamic center to close the circle. For singular events remain (a sex change that leaves a scar) that point outside the loop, displacing and moving forward the undulatory process, even if this opening has tragic consequences. Heinlein recasts this same scenario on a Gargantuan scale in his 1970 novel *I Will Fear No Evil*. In this rambling narrative, dying protagonist Johann Sebastian Bach Smith (again the name Heinlein gives provides the poles of a circuit: genius circumference, dynamic common center) has his brain transplanted in a female body, into which his seed is artificially inseminated. Not only will the product of this "union" escape a dying Earth for a new life on the Moon, but the grotesque solipsistic circle proves to be an open spiral, for the "mother," the body Smith inhabits and manipulates, remains a genetically different entity, hence a random element he cannot entirely control.

We have a variation on Heinlein's each-man-a-dynamic-world vision in Philip K. Dick's *Ubik* (1969). French critics see this novel as a series of contending mind worlds, out-of-body mental projections by characters that lie in some state of suspended animation.[14] In Dick's novel, however, one must take the term "half-life" literally. Actors in the novel are not *wholly* dead, but lie in state in a "moratorium," a condition physically suspended between life and death. In this condition, their monadic centers remain active. As in full life, the amount of (residual) physical energy they possess allows them to project "lengthened shadows" of their lives—not mental, but material, constructs. What matters is the relative strength and reach of these contending monadic worlds, as we witness the stronger projections (the "world") of young Jory interacting with, and overwhelming, the projections of Joe Chip, Runciter, and others. If, as in Heinlein, Jory's galvanic circuit were to consume that of all other characters in the narrative, we would have an "all you zombies" world, or Lazarus's great sensorium. But counterforces exist, "intercessors" such as the spray can product "Ubik," that opens circles into dynamic spirals, keeping the action open-ended. What is "ubikuitous" here is the ebb and flow of physical energy, available to all potential centers, and subject only to the process of entropy. Jory's "world" must inevitably run down.

## MEDIACOSMS

Increasingly in the popular mind, as the twentieth century progresses into the twenty-first, science fiction and technology have become entangled, as seen in a website like sciencefictionless.com, which sees itself as "spreading the word about scientific and technological advances that blur the line between SF and science fact." The "web" and "spreading the word" are important elements in the history of this interconnection between science fiction and technologies that come to dominate this post-Golden Age period. If science fiction and science are intertwined, it is less because science fiction "predicts" future developments than because it favors future selection of these develop-ments and orients their use. This was already the case with Golden Age writ-ers, fascinated with Emerson's monad and the means of empowering it. We have an example in Heinlein, where the demands of story situation generate new science and technology. If in *Methuselah's Children* (1941) space-traveling Lazarus is cut off from his base on Earth, in *Time for the Stars* (1956), Heinlein uses telepathy as a faster-than-light communications device to link Tom Bartlett with Earth-bound twin Pat. Not satisfied with vague notions like telepathy, science fiction writers of the period create imagi-nary technologies to effect FTL communication: Asimov's "hyperwaves" in *Foundation,* James Blish's "Dirac communicator," Ursula K. Le Guin's "ansible." In real technological terms, these devices are not (yet) possible, but analogous communications devices—radio satellites, the internet, wire-less networks—have become so. In the same vein, Heinlein's "Gulf" (1949) invents "speedtalk." This idea, which hearkens back to Rosny's "un autre monde" (1896), is not yet part of human technology, but zip files and other means of accelerated communication are.

Increasingly, such science fiction-driven technology does not simply pro-duce the means of broadcasting information but becomes the means of broad-casting a "self" that aspires to be a world. At the center of Toffler's "third wave" mediacosms—not just city and island-states, but banks, corporate entities, terrorist "cells," cults—individuals use broadcast technology to real-ize Emerson's dictum: "Why not realize your world? But far be from me the despair which prejudges the law by a paltry empiricism,—since there never was a right endeavor but it succeeded."[15] We think of Osama Bin Laden, holed up in front of a television set, endlessly recording and viewing his own speeches, promoting his own "right endeavor."

Corollary to this idea of expandable monad is the sense of insubstantiality of locus. The "transparent eyeball" stands on bare ground—a place purposely void of history, culture, or nation. But, projecting itself toward the totality of its own circumference, it becomes "nothing," the self becomes the mes-sage, the medium becomes both. When Sterling, in *Islands in the Net* (1988), speaks of his "islands" as both parts of an "official" network—the United Na-tions, satellites following fixed orbits, international corporations—and rogue entities—floating drug labs, pirate ships—he reiterates Emerson. The "net" Emerson envisions, composed of both the "largest and solemnest things" and "the history of every man's bread," is in fact a structure of no fixity and end-less plasticity: "Like a bird that alights nowhere, but hops perpetually from bough to bough, it is the Power which abides in no man and in no woman, but for a moment speaks from this one, and for another moment from that one."[16] No longer is it just fictional protagonists—like Lazarus—whose stories are amplified. Instead, we have, empowered by the broadcasting media that have become the subject of science fiction, the stories of any person capable of generating a space—myspace—within the circumference of the broadcast media. The more powerful and prevalent of these figures can assume, as they become centers of the mediacosm that grows up around them, the stature of "legends." As such, they strive to seize the Power that abides in no man or woman to generate a "culture" that, in its speed and compression, claims to vie with conventional genres and great nation-states of the past.

But can these mediacosms, issued from Emerson's prophetic dynamic, pretend to be a "culture" in the conventional sense of the word? An answer is suggested in the shift in meaning of the word "satellite." The old meaning is rooted in the Latin *satelles*: a thing attendant upon, and vassal to, a central power. The satellite today works in an opposite, and centrifugal, manner. From its mobile, evanescent center, it broadcasts a circumference of forms, be they images or, in the science-fictional sense, "worlds." Types of satellites in the latter sense have emerged as part of Toffler's "third wave." Two in particular have been prominent. There is the oxymoronic "island nation," small ex-colonies that declare independence from a "motherland," island or city states like Singapore or Dubai, who have no material resources (again "bare ground") but compensate for this by using the new window of mobility offered by broadcast technologies. And there is the science fiction technocosm, either a "runaway" colony of Earth or other larger bodies—moons, asteroids and such—or a space or way station, or even an exploration-bound "generation starship," a flying Noah's Ark destined to settle some distant, unknown world.

Those who attack the old, nation-based "second wave" culture tend to associate such islands in the sky or elsewhere with serious utopian experiments.[17] But science fiction, in many cases, stresses in Emersonian manner the mediacosmic activity of these locations. An example is Le Guin's "ambiguous utopia" *The Dispossessed* (1974). Here we have twin worlds in the Ceti system, Urras and Annares, whose relation remains (in classic science-fictional manner) that of Earth to its Moon. Urras has the material resources and has evolved a capitalist system; Annares, more or less barren, has developed a classless society, which in turn is devolving toward its own form of totalitarianism. But because Annarians are "dispossessed," they are more inherently mobile. Protagonist Shevek is a physicist from Annares, working on theories of time and communication. He is the expanding monad, who travels to Urras and there develops the theory of the "ansible," an FTL

communications device that ultimately connects these two contending systems of government to the larger net of the Hainish people and their intergalactic history. Utopia is not the subject of Le Guin's novel; it is Shevek, the
bird that alights nowhere, and the breakthrough of a single dynamic center
to a larger circumference. With the discovery of the ansible, all personal and
political struggles are instantaneously elided. In this communications net,
utopias are again "no-places." At best, they are way stations, insubstantial
places briefly inhabited, then abandoned by the Emersonian power—ephemeral products of technological energy as it "shoots the gulf."

## THE WORLD AS SCIENCE FICTION

If works like Sterling's *Islands in the Net* can present the world as science
fiction, it is because the world described is one that issues from the same
dynamic as Emersonian science fiction. The relation between the real and fictional has become undulatory. The dynamic center of many "island-worlds"
is a single legendary figure. In turn the circumference each such figure
projects claims to being a "culture," a world unto itself. These are "worlds"
within island worlds. In Hong Kong, for example, the nexus of finance and
film has generated—in the mediatized image of a Bruce Lee—a widely received "third world" political vision. Or take Jamaica, where tourism and
electronically enhanced music produce, via Bob Marley, a product claiming
to be a post-diaspora religion. Ultimately Lee and Marley, like the worlds
they project, lose their physical locus and come to exist entirely through the
powerful but ephemeral media of broadcasted sound and light.

Clearly, there is a shared dynamic behind the function of modern city-
states like Hong Kong, and that of science fiction's "islands" that stretch from
Heinlein's Luna City to Samuel R. Delany's Triton to the Tessier-Ashpool
satellite Villa Straylight in Gibson's *Neuromancer*. It no longer seems to
matter if one "world" is real and the others come from fiction. For in both we
find a similar interrelation between generative and disseminative elements,
between the plastic powers of the single individual and the extrapolative circumference. Be it the soaring skyscrapers of the real city, or vast structures of
the imagination, both seem made of sound and light, projections of some central force. The technology of dissemination, deployed by a figure like Delos
D. Harriman ("Delos" is the central island in the Greek Cyclades) way back
in Heinlein's "The Man Who Sold the Moon" (1950), is fed back into science
fiction, via non-science fiction theoreticians like Toffler and Ilya Prigogine,
where it informs the early works of Sterling or a novel like John Shirley's *City
Come A-Walkin'* (1976), where the entire city of San Francisco is incarnate

as a single power center—the character "City" who takes on the literal task of "cleaning up the streets." A persistent theme in Heinlein's novels is the creation and operation of a Moon city-state (which due to physical conditions is a highly restricted territorial space). Beyond this, there are his other points of cultural "dissemination" on future geo- and cosmo-political maps, such as Farnham's infamous "freehold." In all these cases, against unwieldy nations or government bureaucracies, freedom and power equate with mobility of information—the rapid movement of what Delos calls "intangibles." Sterling extrapolates these power points to offshore banks, crime networks, terrorist groups moving nuclear weapons like peas in a shell game. We still find this fascination with islands as locus of undulating power and form in a more recent work like Howard V. Hendrix's *Empty Cities of the Full Moon* (2002). Hendrix's title itself is an echo of previous media events, looking back to the title of Lewis Shiner's *Deserted Cities of the Heart* (1988), itself the title of a song by the rock group Cream. In Hendrix's novel, a man-caused epidemic has all but decimated humanity, and a group of scientists whose research was in some unknown way responsible for the disaster find safe haven on a Caribbean island. From this center, protagonist Simon Lingham embarks on a journey to restore the lost narrative of this disaster, moving from encounter to encounter up the American East Coast, until the tale is finally told as he, now himself a figure of legend, reaches the far point on the former circumference, the empty world city of New York.

Just as the power that emanates from Hong Kong resides in the mediated figure of Bruce Lee, so in science fiction works such as Gibson's *Neuromancer* and its sequel *Count Zero* (1986) the dynamic center detaches itself from all specific physical and cultural moorings, indeed from concrete "characters," to abide in evanescent figures of legend. So, it is with the "console cowboy" Pauley McCoy in the former novel. This McCoy proudly claims that he is not "the real McCoy." Having been "iced" during a hacking expedition in the matrix, McCoy is resurrected as Dixie Flatline, the computer program Case and Molly need to crack the Tessier-Ashpool "core" and bring about the merger of AIs Wintermute with Neuromancer, completing the galvanic circuit of the matrix and unifying "the whole show." As the circuit forms, Dixie Flatline will also "shoot the gulf" and his legend fade as he becomes an integral part of the matrix, with no further dependence on a "meat" hand to slot his program. The same process occurs as amateur hacker Bobby Newmark becomes Count Zero. The name itself is a fascinating shape-changer à la Heinlein. The nullity in question can be the zero center—"count zero interrupt." Or it can be *Count* Zero, the everyman become legendary figure who makes contact with Angie Mitchell in the matrix—the girl with the Zeiss-Icon eyes—and in doing so closes the galvanic circuit of the narrative. This same sort of legend-making, with evanescent "heroes" shooting the gulf of their own fictional beginnings, is a trademark of the later "steampunk" movement. For example, in Alan Moore's graphic series *The League of Extraordinary Gentlemen* (1999- ), figures from various nineteenth-century fictions are resurrected, most notably Verne's Captain Nemo. But the island here is no longer Cyrus Smith's Mysterious Island, which was conquered as U.S. territory. Now Nemo himself becomes the island. As such he has become the archetypal example of Emerson's dynamic, disseminative center. For he is now—by name—the "I am nothing" who becomes everything in the many hypertextual adventures he generates.

## SCIENCE FICTION'S REPRESENTATIVE MEN

Emerson's Transcendentalism is often seen as a Western adaptation of Hinduism and concepts such as Brahma and karma, where the individual captures world energy, projects, then loses it, as it passes to another subject. In this Eastern tradition, the individual is simply the vessel that contains and projects this energy. The Golden Age science fiction version of this dynamic however draws on Emerson's thoroughly Western version of the individual *doer*, termed his "representative man." Its origin however is Western technological man, the creator of devices that use natural forces to his own end. In a sense, the first incarnation of this figure to act in a fictional context that pits individual mobility against fixed cultural forces is Prospero in Shakespeare's *The Tempest* (1611). This play breaks with the conventional world order presented in earlier plays. In history plays, Shakespeare worked hard to build a solid and coherent tradition of kingship, as institution rooted in the English nation and in divine, and thus natural, authority. But in *The Tempest*, Shakespeare challenges this rooted authority by creating in Prospero's "white magic" an art or technology of mobility that vies with a natural order of things that was violated by his ouster from "rightful" rulership in Milan. Landing on an island by fortune, he not only takes possession, but in doing so declares himself rival with, indeed superior to, the old landed order of things: "Know for certain that I am Prospero, thrust forth from Milan, who most strangely on this shore . . . was landed, to be lord on't."[18] On this bare ground, void of tradition and "civilization," Prospero's magic, by means of his intermediary and agent Ariel, is in fact a technology of broadcasting, a "realized" form of the power that is conventionally diminished as "fantasy," but here is restored to its primal meaning as *phantasein*, the causing to appear of images that rival, and perhaps outdo, solid forms of nature.[19]

Prospero is a prime example of Emerson's "representative man" who anchors the dynamic of the transparent eyeball, the abstract process of power and form, in a precise historical context; "he" is Napoleon, Goethe, other figures of history or story who "represent" categories of self-reliant men. The representative man provides, for Golden Age writers, a meeting point between individual action and world creation. Such "men" provide the *fictional* anchor for this process. As fictional characters, they inhabit the middle ground between nothing and all. In doing so, they provide the specific path whereby power unites with form. The dynamic center of Golden Age science fiction is held by such representative men. In Heinlein, they are identified by names that, like Lazarus Long, combine a physical process ("length" of spacetime expansion) with a historical figure whose substantive nature cannot be "mediatized" away as a mere legend. It is the difference between Prospero the actor and the insubstantial "cloud capp'd towers" he projects.

But a question arises, given the evolution of this Emersonian dynamic in science fiction, as to the fate of the print medium itself. Has print, in more recent science fiction, become a superseded technology? Science fiction films since *Star Wars* (1977) are judged by the technological sophistication of their "special effects," not on "print" qualities such as character or plot. If Heinlein's protagonists remain fictional "characters" in a conventional sense, science fiction films seem to generate "legends." For example, Harrison Ford, who assumed roles in films from *Star Wars* to *Blade Runner* (1982), remains better known today as himself, rather than any named protagonist in these stories. A step further is the "animated" figure, completely assembled like a Cartesian machine in an animation laboratory. Animation today, in a film like *A Scanner Darkly* (2006, based on Philip K. Dick's 1977 novel), generates jerky replicas of the human form, dispensing with the need for human actors at all. We appear to witness the demise of the "character" as solid center of the process of narrative. And can we speak of "story," or even narrative, when their conventional anchor—the character—is gone, and the spatial coordinates of "plot" is disseminated in ephemeral displays of light and sound? To answer this, we must examine how print science fiction has evolved in this age of mediatized world fiction. Arguably, science fiction's use of the representative man allows its printed form to evolve as dynamic force that refuses to yield to the forces of "dissemination," retaining the basic Emersonian elements of subject and object that continue to sustain the conventional fictional medium—the printed text—in which science fiction evolved.

There are two main ways print science fiction has dealt with the dynamics of mediatisation and concomitant dissolution of the fictional subject. One is to follow the philosophical and academic trend of deconstruction, to abolish both the Cartesian and monadic subject alike. The material imperative of science fiction—the supremely *referential* world of Emerson's power and form—gives way to "non-referential" worlds. The Derridian idea of "dissemination"—that it is not the subject who controls language, but the language system that creates the subject—leads to fictions where the *res extensa* of science is seen as an *effet de réel* and human actions are subsumed in an empire of signs or codes. This is the path followed by Delany's fiction. *Nova* (1968) is presented as a "meta-fictional" space opera. His later novel, *Triton: An Ambiguous Heterotopia* (renamed *Trouble on Triton*) (1976), puts Michel Foucault in the title, and is overtly patterned to read like a "deconstruction" of both Le Guin's "ambiguous utopia" and Seldon's "psychohistory." With the "modular calculus" of nominal protagonist Bron Helstrom, mathematics is no longer the means of predicting undulating centers and circumferences, but of reducing human personalities to "constructs" with no location in the physical world. Foucault's "heterotopia" defines "places of difference," such as museums and train stations, where we escape from the forms and strictures of the dominant culture, and become, in relation to those structures, non-entities. Emerson's "transparent eyeball," on the other hand, is a dynamic construct. For in the *act* of becoming nothing we affirm our place in the physical world and embrace that world as an "all." Such action requires an actor, a subject in time and space. In contrast, Bron's quest to sample all the heterotopic aspects of Neptune's moon Triton—a place where all is possible: political variance, sexual deviance, bodily transformations—results in progressive dispersion of self, the loss of a defined center or "subject" in a limitless web of possible meta-transformations.

## EFFING THE INEFFABLE

Few science fiction writers have followed Delany. The other, science-fictional way is to follow material science and its forays into physical concepts that are equally disseminative of the subject: quantum theory, "string theory," the many-worlds hypothesis. In these works of science fiction, dissemination of subject and story comes not from a segue into textual or metafictional realms. Here the physical world itself the characters inhabit denies the human condition any possibility of continuity. They must somehow "live" in a quantum world, and the author must find an impossibly consistent narrator to tell their story. The visual media to some extent can present a hopelessly fragmented human experience. The print medium, on the other hand, must rely on some degree of continuity of personality and story. In Emersonian terms, at each quantum moment, the center generates a circumference. The wholly self-reliant man would be torn apart by this dynamic. But Emerson's "representative" figures—in the roles of character and/or narrator—offer a way for stories to be told, and narrative constructed, in physical worlds that are otherwise totally alien to common human experience. Gregory Benford sees such fiction writing as confronting the challenge of "effing the ineffable."[20] To test this, we examine the function of the representative man in two later works whose "worlds" are modeled on quantum premises—Greg Egan's *Quarantine: A Novel of Quantum Catastrophe* (1992) and Benford's "Matter's End" (1991). In these works, use of the representative man allows print science fiction to modulate between conventional and "disseminative" fictional structures.

Greg Egan is an Australian writer, who publishes exclusively under the science fiction label at its "hardest" edge. As an Australian, he is not, like Heinlein, the product of a specifically Emersonian cultural matrix. But his work, on the new world stage of science fiction, attaches itself, via cyberpunk writers like Gibson, to the "Gernsback continuum," the Emersonian current that flowered in Golden Age works which clearly remain his models. This may explain why his fiction, which gives itself the seemingly impossible task of depicting entities like quantum "worlds" in conventional narrative forms, continues to exploit the dynamics of center and circumference as possible means of doing so. Egan's science is at the far edge of narratability. The possibility, at this juncture, of telling the quantum story must rely on Emerson's "representative man."

Quantum theory is a *description* of a world, one with little relevance to the story of the human condition. As such, it does not meet the minimal requirements for a narrative as outlined by Gerald Prince in *Dictionary of Narratology*.[21] For Prince a statement like "the cat sat on its mat" is not a narrative, but "the cat sat on the dog's mat" is. In quantum theory, as with Emerson's transparent eyeball, each cat is on its own mat. Emerson however, in essays like "Experience" and *Representative Men,* sought to relocate his self-reliant individual within the sphere of history and society, in other words, to give him a narrative presence, to adapt his theoretical model of center and circumference to a realm of activity governed by comparatives rather than superlatives: a world where great men can become *greater* men. Such men represent categories. Egan chooses such a man—a private eye—to narrate his story, and in doing so to mediate between quantum and consensus (i.e., our) realities, to put cats back on dog's mats. Science fiction is often faulted for using "clichéd" generic characters of this sort. But it is precisely this sort of "representative" figure that allows Egan to restore a narrative presence to his world of quantum catastrophe.

Egan's novel is narrated by Nick Stavrianos, Master Detective for the quantum age, who is investigating the disappearance of a certain Laura, who escaped from a mental institution by apparently walking through walls. Nick works in the category of figures, like C. Auguste Dupin in Poe's "Murders in the Rue Morgue" (1841), whose function is to find rational explanations for phenomena that seem to have none. In this case, the explanation leads Nick to a vision of chaos, of uncontrollable dissemination of monadic entities. Laura, in the language of quantum theory, is said to be "smeared." In the reader's world, "reality" (the context or circumference of observation) is a question of consensus. In relation to the quantum world, Laura is an indeterminate entity because she remains "uncollapsed," choosing not to choose between the wave or particle. In such a quantum world, Descartes's method appears to work in reverse. Individual subjects do not fix their centers so much as dislocate them. Here, if Laura's action reveals the idea of "subject" to be consensual illusion, it also frees her from any story context. The result, it seems, is a Brownian motion of free monads: "one isolated consciousness per eigenstate, like the many worlds model brought to life."[22] A passage from Emerson suggests he himself was but a step away from what could be called a "many worlds model," whereby the dynamic subject not only generates a circumference, but in undulating back and forth from its center can create an entire world unto itself, at which point the single "consciousness per eigenstate" offers each unit access to its own "closet of God": "In ascending to this primary and aboriginal sentiment, we have come from our remote station on the circumference instantaneously to the center of the world, where, as in the closet of God, we see causes, and anticipate the universe."[23] As in Emerson, each monad in Egan can and does, at every instant, generate a world. The act of doing so, however, detaches the monad from all possibility of a stable or consensus reality, because center and circumference have themselves become probabilities. Each act, at every minute, puts God in Schröedinger's closet. In Egan's novel the monads have seemingly become "smeared," stochastic presences. Their dissemination presents a situation that, in terms of the readers' logic, cannot be narrated.

But narrative there must be. And to allow for narrative, the conventional stories previously discussed—the detective scenario, the God scenario—sneak back into this quantum world. With these scenarios, the Emersonian dynamic, at the level of "representative man," is reinstated, even though the very idea of something "representative" is meaningless in the quantum order of things. Nick is "hired" to find Laura for a simple reason: she *represents* the explorer who pushed beyond the borders of human consensual reality: "she was left unobserved long enough to smear to a degree of complexity which enabled her to mount expeditions." (233) Logically, in the world of eigenstates, each quantum instant is its island, nothing represents anything, no "expeditions" can be mounted. But in Nick's narrative, connections are made, the contours of a story begin reappearing. It is feared that other "explorers"—monads who follow Laura—will group together to form a new consensus world. Such order, however improbable, is needed to restore a narratable space within this quantum reality: "With ten thousand, or a hundred thousand people smeared, how long before the smeared selves learn to suppress the collapse of the rest of the city? And with twelve million people smeared . . ." (251) Theoretically there should be, at this smeared center, unlimited quantum dispersion preventing any knowledge of a "self." Even so the narrator continues to speak as a subject, an entity who somehow knows it exists: "But if I'm smeared, all patterns occur—so I'm decreasing the intrinsic probability of the eigenstate that constitutes success, and creating ever more versions of myself who *know* that they won't be chosen." (221) The narrative of causality creeps back here. For who or what is doing the "choosing"? Logically, these quanta cannot claim a "self," for a self is a continuous entity, and the eigenstate cannot "know" anything beyond its current version, if the word "know" applies at all. Yet the speaking subject refers to itself as "I." With this "I" as center, guaranteeing the continuity of a circumference, narrative returns in this vacuum. The narrative in this case appears that of Emersonian undulation. In Nick's eyes, "smearing" restates "I am nothing." Yet with the proliferation of such entities now seen as "versions of myself," an expansion occurs that "causes" some sort of God response, whereby their "explorations" cause some higher force of equilibrium to impose order—the "quarantine" of the title—in the form of a circumference—the "Bubble"—a dark sphere surrounding Earth and blocking out the stars. In Nick's words, we witness an otherwise impossible return of the galvanic circuit. Narrative again becomes possible.

What is more, this Bubble proves less a fixed limit than an invitation to dynamic undulation, as Nick, the representative man, pursues his "investigation." For Emerson, representative men are "great men" because they are *useful* in terms of the process of human expansion: "We may say great men exist that there may be greater men."[24] Here, amidst the possibility of quantum catastrophe, we witness the resurgence of other "representative" scenarios—those of human initiative, and human hubris. Whatever forces create the Bubble now appear fixed, "cast" as hostile god-figures—the Bubble Makers. Laura is described as their "avatar." This may mean that Laura, by remaining hidden, indeterminate, is forcing a story on the quantum world, causing it to take "sides," with the "unsmeared"—our consensus "reality"—on one side, and the "smeared"—those who choose not to collapse the wave—on the other. She becomes then, *de facto,* a dynamic presence at the center of this process. Nick's description reinforces this sense of a quantum "drama": "Smearing is an exponential process. Within a day or two, remaining unobserved would have required her to suppress the collapse of everyone on Earth. And after a day or two of *that* . . . the depleted region would be filled. Humanity would tunnel through the Bubble and make contact with the rest of superspace. What would happen *then* is hard to predict, but one possibility is that the wave function in this region would never be collapsed again." (233) Like all offspring of gods come to Earth, she may be the one to set clear limits to this process. Nick at least offers this hypothesis: "So . . . Laura didn't stay smeared, to avoid dragging us into this catastrophe?" (233) Nick is offering conventional, "unsmeared" scenarios to unconventional actions. As he does, a story in the conventional sense builds up around Laura's initial act. For it is implied that, though Laura walked through the limited walls of her asylum, other beings—here the shadowy organizations and mad scientists of some standard cyberpunk plot—might vie with her example by *organizing* a walk through the walls of the Bubble. We now have volition and conflict in a world that should have none, and randomness impossibly *directed* toward some larger and—for the sake of the detective story—as yet undiscovered destiny.

The great manipulator is a certain Lui Kiu Chung, who claims to be a quantum version of Fu Manchu. When Nick confronts him—"you're talking about blasting twelve billion people into some kind of metaphysical nightmare"—Lui begins talking about a new "heaven on earth" beyond the quantum dispersion: "I'm talking about the end of twelve billion people dying every microsecond. I'm talking about the end of the death of possibilities." (261). The discourse turns to mad visions of implicate design beyond the collective smear—a quantum "I am the resurrection and the life": "Once the planet is smeared, everyone will be linked. The smeared human race can decide for itself whether or not to recollapse." (262) This is not Clarke's vision of the once-and-for-all transcendence of the Overmind. Instead, with talk of "collapsing" and "recollapsing," we have an insane version of Emerson's undulating, ever-expanding dynamic: "The collapse has a finite horizon; there are always eigenstates beyond it. Do you think none of them contain human beings? The Bubble Makers are the residues of ourselves—they're made up of versions of us so improbable that they've escaped the collapse. All I want to do is to give us the chance to rejoin them." (263)

Nick's narrative, ultimately, replays Emerson's dynamic of center and circumference. In this quantum version, the world contains nothing but monads—eigenstates—but no matter how many there are, each retains its representative role as potential center of some larger activity. Emerson sees each monad as having a trade: "Every man, inasmuch as he has any science, is a definer and map-maker of the latitudes and longitudes of our condition."[25] If Emerson, in "Experience", sees each man as "a center for nature, running out threads of relation through everything, fluid and solid, material and elemental," he also foresees their quantum fate, where each monad loses its *place*, its location in a commonly accepted scheme of things: "Ghostlike we glide through nature, and should not know our place again."[26] But even in this condition, the monad does not lose its power to form a center, to become a map-maker rather than one defined by someone else's map, in this case the theoretical map of quantum theory. In Emerson's scheme of things, we must look to the representative man to re-establish an *operative place* in a world of increasingly dislocated subjects: "Is a man in his place, he is constructive, fertile, magnetic. . . ."[27] Nick may first seem to evoke nothing more substantial than a radio voice, a disembodied "private eye" in the realm of the Shadow who clouds men's minds so they cannot see him. Yet this insubstantial being takes on the improbable role of narrator. Egan gives him—as consistent voice—an operative location in the quantum scheme of things. Thus does Egan, through his quantum investigator, reconnect with the tradition of print science fiction, linking him to figures like Heinlein's science fiction detective, Ted Randall, in "The Unpleasant Profession of Jonathan Hoag" (1942).[28]

Egan's Nick comes close to compromising his representative role by over-theorizing the instability, the non-locality of his existence: "So I wait like a human: sick with pointless, unproductive fears. Trying to imagine the unimaginable. If the whole planet smeared, permanently . . . what exactly would people experience? *Nothing*—because there is no collapse to make anything real? Or *everything*—because there is no collapse to make anything less than real? . . . Or *everything simultaneously*—a cacophony of superimposed possibilities? . . . Once there's nothing to make the past unique, the whole experience could be radically different." (253) But this is precisely what the Representative Man does—establish the point that makes the past unique. Without such a past, there can be no future. Without such "circuits," the narrator is little more than a Newtonian ghost in a quantum world.

Yet Nick's presence, as detective, causes this world of theoretical probability to collapse into a series of conventional situations—"plots." He posits shadowy "groups" seeking to create a supermind à la Gibson's Sprawl novels. These forces will either create a "post-smear" dystopian world or lead mankind beyond the Bubble Maker to contact with some unimaginable deity—"states beyond the Bubble full of the most incredible things!" But beyond all this, Nick's search has a personal motivation. In "The Unpleasant Profession of Jonathan Hoag," the "soul" of Ted's wife Cynthia is taken from her body and placed in a vial. His quest is to recapture and restore this soul, which essentially raises her from the dead. Nick's wife is also dead; this time however he possesses the "soul" but does not have the body, for by means of an implant she dwells in his consciousness as his cyberpartner. In another example of a revived science fiction plot, Nick sees the universal smear offering him the means of retrieving her physical body through time travel: "Once the world stops collapsing, anything is possible. The collapse is the source of time asymmetry; you might be able to tunnel back to a time before her death . . ." Nick the stochastic man would restore the galvanic circuit by directing probability to a specific, personal end, this time using the breakdown of the old "consensual" world of time to restore his personal corner of that world: "No, *versions of me* might—while others wouldn't. . . . I couldn't live that way: creating billions of copies of myself, just so that some tiny fraction of them could get what I wanted. *Couldn't I? I've done just that tonight."* (266)[29]

In the end, Nick comes through his quantum adventure only to reaffirm that he remains a dualist. But the terms he uses are more Emersonian than Cartesian. He does not describe his condition as: I think therefore I am, but rather: I am because I am thinking. Nick, in fact, restores Emerson's circuit in solidly existential terms: "But if smeared humanity couldn't face what lay beyond the Bubble . . . then it had no choice but suicide. Smearing is exponential growth, increase without bounds. A single, unique reality was the only stable alternative. There could be no middle ground." (279) In saying this, Nick places himself, as representative man, at the center of quantum chaos: "Every dream, every vision, has been brought to life. Heaven and Hell on Earth. . . . Every dream, every vision. This one included, mundane as it seems, halfway between infinite happiness and infinite suffering." This is not a restatement of Pascal's human condition, but an Emersonian re-placing of self. Nor is this re-located self doomed to remain alone, in its Cartesian stove: "So here I am, gazing up into the darkness, unable to decide if I'm staring at infinity, or the backs of my own eyelids. . . . But I don't need to know the answer. I just recite to myself, over and over, until I can choose sleep: *It all adds up to normality."* (280) Normality is the sphere of representative men, a realm in which dissemination is controlled by restoration of the dynamic center of man acting.

In Benford's "Matters End" the dispersion of the human center is the result of a culminating experiment in particle physics.[30] But here again, what reins in the ensuing possibility of chaos is the restoration of Emerson's galvanic circuit. Benford chooses an Indian venue for his scientific discovery that matter—the seemingly unbreachable barrier set by Western science to human endeavor—does indeed "die." Benford's story in a sense repatriates Emerson. For if Emerson's dynamic vision has roots in Indian philosophy, whose cycles of reincarnation and eternal return he fashioned into a thermodynamically regulated process whose energy source remains the self-reliant man, Benford reverses this trajectory. For now, in a "new" East that adopted Western scientific methods, his Western scientist witnesses the "end" of matter. Matter is the source of Emerson's energy, the bedrock of his dynamic of power and form. With the end of matter, the hegemonic mind-matter opposition of Western science simply dissolves. Another situation is created where there is no longer either subject or object, thus no possibility of creating the galvanic circuit.

Benford also reverses the direction taken by another Western writer connected to Indian culture and religion—Arthur C. Clarke in "The Nine Billion Names of God" (1953). Here, Western computer scientists succeed in naming the nine billion names. When they do so, a barrier is breached. They look up and "overhead, without any fuss, the stars were going out."[31] Western scientists here solve an Eastern problem. The seemingly infinite names constitute the veil of illusion. Once it is lifted, behind it lies a catastrophe that is (as in *Childhood's End* [1953]) a genuine death of matter. In Benford the illusion, for Western science, is the permanence of matter, what it believes to be reality's substantial bedrock. Once this is gone, there remain only "interpretations" of reality. We have a quantum situation where, this time as in Egan, the stars go out because there is no longer a consensual body present to perceive them.

Clarke's story stops short of narrating what comes after the naming of names. It is enough to know that skeptical Western scientists unwittingly brought it about. Benford takes on the same task as Egan—to tell a story beyond the firm anchor of the mind-matter duality. If the physical world is in flux, Benford like Egan locates its telling in a representative figure, given the task of providing a narrative center to a radically delocalized, post-matter world. If reality is now a matter of interpretation, Benford chooses the point of view of a Western scientist. As matter and mind become one, time as we know it, as a function of matter, ends. Even so, the narrator's story, telling the end of matter as a sequence of events, re-locates this process of fusion back in the Western world of time.

Egan's first-person narration is the perfect medium to anchor Nick as voice in the midst of quantum white noise. Benford chooses a third-person narrator, but one tightly focalized on his representative man of Western science, Professor Robert Clay. The narration, from the beginning, enfolds both a center and circumference, a circuit that will be asked to hold even as the Western concept of order—the mind-matter duality—breaks down. Clay is thoroughly a part of the Western scientific establishment—"established" in the sense of safely circumscribed by the holy grail of Western science—the permanence of matter. Even so, Clay (despite his material name) proves a mobile center. He is first of all a black man, by his origins a man not quite at home in the world of European science. Moreover, he proves a strange representative of Western reason, for his initial contact with an India ravaged by Western technology is both intuitive and highly sensual. His "mobility" will allow him to secure a new galvanic center when the old order vanishes, when matter becomes energy.

Clay goes to India to report on a proton experiment conducted by Indian scientists who claim they have measured the lifetime of matter. He confirms their data in the Western manner—they have hard numbers: "And at the end, all cases reviewed, he said quietly: 'You have found it. The proton lifetime is nearly 10 to the 34th years.'" (239) Clay sees this as Nobel Prize work. The Indian scientist Singh sees much vaster consequences: "*This world*—this universe!—has labored long under the illusion of its own permanence. . . . We might die, yes, the sun might even perish—but the universe went on. Now we prove otherwise. There cannot help but be profound reactions." (238)

It is fascinating how Emerson's text glosses this story. Clay in this story becomes Man displaced. As such, he fits Emerson's definition of a "great man": "I count him a great man who *inhabits* a higher sphere of thought, into which other men rise with labor and difficulty; he has to keep his eyes open to see things in a true light and *in large relations*, while they [other humans, in this case those who adhere to Western science] must make painful corrections and keep a vigilant eye on many sources of error." Clay moves from great to greater as he comes to incarnate the end of the Cartesian subject as seen by Emerson: "I find him [representative man] greater when he can abolish himself, and all heroes, by letting in this element of reason, irrespective of persons; this subtiliser, and irresistible upward force, into our thought, destroying individualism."[32] Clay's name seems to predestine him to unite Western science and Eastern religion, for he will recapture physically his nominal origins and with this recapture learn to speak and reason anew. Here is Emerson: "Man, made of the dust of the world, does not forget his origin; and all that is yet inanimate will one day speak and reason. . . . Shall we say that quartz mountains will pulverize into innumerable Werners, Von Bachs and Beaumonts . . ."[33]

One could simply say here, as with Clarke's *Childhood's End*, that once the barrier of matter is abolished, a new order of Brahma ascending transcends the old. Benford's Clay however presents the apotheosis in terms of the formation of a new galvanic circuit, where we experience undulation between technology and mysticism, between visions East and West: "The anxious clouds caught blue and burnt-yellow pulses and seemed to relay them, like the countless transformers and capacitors and voltage drops that made a worldwide communications net, carrying staccato messages laced with crackling punctuations." (246) The protagonists—Westerner Clay and Indian scientist Mrs. Buli—see their opposite views of reality become an undulating process, rather than the ascension of one over the other: "We have always argued, some of us, that the central dictate of quantum mechanics is the interconnected nature of the observer and the observed." [Clay] "We always filter the world . . . and yet are linked to it. How much of what we see is in fact taught us, by our bodies, or by the consensus reality that society trains us to see . . ." [Mrs Buli] The product of this "interconnection" here is the "we" shared by opposite views of nature now seen fusing into one.

In this dynamic anchoring of things in a new subject, the finality of a timeless moment, ending the opposition of matter and consciousness, is but another illusion: "Time that was no time did not pass, and he and she and the impacted forces between were pinned to the forever moment that cascaded through them . . ." (250) The "forever moment" proves unstable, as forces "cascade" through their combined existence to form the center of a new, as yet defined, galvanic circuit. If opposite views of physics and nature appear to fuse in the realization that it is not the world, but our perception of the world, that changes, there remains the very real sense that the perceiver is also an actor, with the power (in Emerson's sense) to further "collapse" the reality wave. As with Nick and the Bubble, Clay comes to see that, if matter is a barrier we have created, he still, as dynamic center, retains the power to generate new circumferences. Furthermore, because he is not just Man acting, but a *representative* man, he remains connected to other such men and their visions—in this case to Plato: "the underlying Platonic beauties . . . the underlying forms. Perhaps that one Western idea was correct after all." (249) From Clay's new dynamic perspective, acceding to timeless perfection is but one circumference among many. Clay's activity points to a different possibility, one where, once we come to see matter as energy, we further liberate the Emerson monad. If the old consensus world is abolished, might not Man create a new one, born of greater power, with greater reach?

The illusion here is belief in absolutes. "Apprehension" remains a comparative process, one that produces greater visions, rather than absolutes. Clay considers the results of spreading the news of the proton experiment: "So what? Just some theoretical point about subnuclear physics. How's that going to . . ." Dr. Singh replies, "The point is that we were believed. Certain knowledge, universally correlated, surely has some impact—" (248). The train of thinking is clear here: if the observer does affect the observed, and if every observer *believes* that matter is dead—that is to say, creates a new consensus reality—then matter effectively "dies." This is another totalitarian "collapsing of the wave," a "quantum" tyranny in the manner of Egan's Bubble Makers. Instead, with Clay's remark "So what?" the dynamic center of this and all "worlds" possible in the wake of matter's death remains the single individual—Benford's representative man who, as Emerson before him, negotiates boundaries between East and West, matter and energy, reality and illusion. In this story, the old circumference goes, but a new center is identified, which in turn will generate its own circumference. If the Emersonian pattern holds, then the end is neither Platonic nor Brahman eternity. There is no end, only the endless process of undulation. In the "hard" science fiction of Egan and Benford, the striving monad continues to occupy "places" in the quantum landscape, to invest "representative" forms, using them to move on and up, subject to Emerson's law of "rotation."[34] The proclamation "Within the limits of human education and *agency*, we may say great men exist that there may be greater men" defines not only Heinlein, but the work of Australian Egan and American Benford, separated by continents, but united by both science and the tradition of print science fiction that nourishes their craft. Emerson appears to offer the bridge between theories and technologies of "dissemination," and the print medium and its traditional fictional structures.

## EMERSONIAN EXPERIMENTS

From the outset, I argued that science fiction is a literature of experiments, shaped in the cauldron of ongoing dialogue between ever-changing, science-driven "world views" and conventional, human based themes and structures of fiction. In terms of twentieth-century fiction however, and especially post-World War II fiction, this view is not commonly accepted. Science fiction is widely faulted for formulaic plots and conventional characters. To the contrary, I have shown that incorporating advanced scientific concepts of spacetime into fiction requires a plasticity and mobility of "character" and "plot" unheard of in Northrop Frye's "novel proper." The Emersonian dynamic gives human agents a place in a quantum universe where, logically, they have none. In such contexts, writers make use of "representative men"—stock characters—to operate in, and to narrate, situations far beyond the reach of psychology and the "deep" characters of Virginia Woolf, Faulkner, and other writers.

To conclude, let us look at a couple of examples of science fiction experiments where the legacy of Emerson's vision is clearly visible. Both works are post-cyberpunk, but strongly reveal an "Emerson continuum." First, Ted Chiang's "Story of Your Life" (1999) is a dialogue between two forms of dissemination, both products of writing, thus of the print medium itself. On one hand, there are the deconstructionist philosophies that seek to remove the dynamic speaking subject from the linguistic web it no longer controls. On the other hand, there is the Emersonian subject and its disseminative structure of power and form. The story places both visions in a new light by examining grapho- and phono-centric visions with an alien language, in the understanding of which linguistics and physics, human subjects and textual systems, must learn to interact. Second, Robert Silverberg's "Enter a Soldier. Later: Enter Another" (1989) takes up the question of dissemination in terms of media technology and culture, the dispersal and subsequent restoration of the subject as vital agency. It offers a response in the print medium to the Frankensteinian creations of industrial light and magic.

"Story of Your Life" is a fascinating example of how a basic science fiction trope—the alien encounter—provides a framework, not only for dialogue between "hard" and "soft" science—physics and linguistics—but for restoring the dynamic circuit between two realms seemingly driven apart by the technology of dissemination: writing and the spoken word.[35] The story is told by linguist Louise Banks. She recounts how she, with the help of physicist Gary Donnelly (with whom she will have a child), deciphers an alien language, whose written form, Heptapod B, is "semasiographic," conveying meaning without reference to speech: "It was strange trying to learn a language that had no spoken form. Instead of practicing my pronunciation, I had taken to squeezing my eyes shut and trying to paint semagrams on the insides of my eyelids." (145) Chiang's story takes up—from a point of view of expanding rather than "deconstructing" the role of language in human expression—the central question posed by the master philosopher of dissemination Jacques Derrida: which was there in the beginning—the spoken word or written "text"? Derrida would dissolve the duality of writing and speaking which he feels, in Western culture, has favored the latter. Plato, in his *Phaedrus*, described the *logos* as "living" as opposed to the "dead" discourse of written text. Derrida inverts this priority: the "text"—dead discourse—is primary element. But Chiang, on the broader speculative playing field of alien encounter, is not trapped in this question of origins. His question is a comparative one: how does *their* sense of language reflect the way *they* conceive the world; how does our sense of language do likewise? How do they, and how do we, describe the role of subject to object, of speaker to writer? The relation now is between of centers and circumferences, in linguistic worlds that, through contact, have become relative to one another. But can a galvanic circuit be established between two divergent linguistic universes? In other words, can Louise Banks tell the story of her life, the written story we are reading, in Heptapod B?

The title of Chiang's story literally inscribes the duality—graphocentric/logocentric—that Derrida seeks to "deconstruct." Is this the story of *your* life, Louise's personal story as speaking subject (she is the "first person" narrator)? Is it the story of your *life*, the *big story*, the once-in-a-lifetime story that creates the broad circumference—the story of the alien encounter, which Louise, as university professor, is doomed to tell over and over to generations of students in the post-encounter world (the aliens go away as mysteriously as they came)? Or can it be both? Chiang's title seems to directly challenge Derrida's famous *différence/différance* pair, where the difference between the two terms, in speech, is inaudible, where we need the written text to distinguish between them. In Chiang's title, the same *written* sentence, when inflected according to the *speaker*'s meaning, both re-invokes the old duality between speaking and writing, and places these opposite visions in a dynamic, interactive relation to each other.

What emerges in Chiang's story is a clear difference between the Emersonian dynamic that marks science fiction writing and Derrida's project of "deconstruction." Derrida conceives of "arche-writing"—the text as field of human activity—as the means of "deconstructing" the hegemony of the speaking subject in Western thought and literature. This written text cannot be fixed or controlled by the volition of a subject; there is no pure "now" moment such as phenomenology claims, for this is always compromised by "traces" of previous experience. In fact, there is similarity between Derrida's arche-text and Egan's scientific metaphor of "smearing" and collapsing. In Derrida's graphocentric world, due to absence of an effective subject able to collapse the wave and tell its story, there reigns an "undecidability" principle, a realm of endless hesitation, where there is no way to choose between subject and object, or (as in the famous example of Plato's *pharmakon*—medicine and poison) between life and death. As in Egan's smeared world, the question is the same: how can one tell a story at all in Derrida's disseminated text—in his Heptapod-B?

The problem is laid out differently in Chiang's story. The two forms of story in the title designate two different positions from which a story can be told, two different ways the human story may be narratable. The story of *your* life is a story in what we believe to be the organic unfolding of events, in a world of free will and chance, where what lies ahead as the story is being told is essentially unpredictable. The *story* of your life, however, suggests the story has already been told, and all its events—"beginning" and "end"—coalesce around this center, creating a point from which the so-called "stages" of life radiate outward. The alien encounter in Chiang's story brings to the forefront the Whorfian hypothesis that the linguistic patterns of a given culture reveal how it perceives and thus conceives the world. Humans and heptapods share a same physical world, with like chemical elements and basic life functions. These facts are conveyed to Louise and Earth's scientists and linguists through the aliens' spoken language—Heptapod A. But physicist Connelly is first to see the radical difference in the way we perceive our physical world and they theirs: "We tried to demonstrate basic physical attributes like mass and acceleration so we could elicit their terms for them, but the heptapods simply responded with requests for clarification." (142) The search for equivalencies leads to total divergence: "If their version of the calculus of variations is simpler to them than their equivalent of algebra, that might explain why we've had so much difficulty talking about physics; their entire system of mathematics may be topsy-turvy compared to ours." (148)

The "breakthrough" comes with the evocation of Fermat's Principle of Least Time. In terms of our physics, Fermat's principle, which states that the path a light ray takes is always the shortest possible one, seems coun-terfactual. Yet, no matter how we challenge the actual path light takes with hypotheses based on physical variables—shorter vectors, refraction—that path proves to be always the shortest: "Any hypothetical path would require more time to traverse than the one actually taken." (147) The implications of Fermat's principle have proven profoundly upsetting to our mechanistic way of conceiving the natural world: "The thing is, while the common formulation of physical laws is causal, a variational principle like Fermat's is purposive, almost teleological." (155) The conclusion Louise draws from this, as she works on deciphering the nature of Heptapod B, is more troubling yet: "I thought to myself, *the ray of light has to know where it will ultimately end up before it can choose the direction to begin moving in.*" (154) As every element of Derrida's graphocentric world is always connected by traces, in-finitely rewritten by "supplements," so here every beginning knows its end, every story has already been written before it begins.

Louise begins to learn this written Heptapod B language, which bears no relation to the spoken language, as if for the aliens speaking and writing were totally separate operations. A speech act can only occur in a world of before and after, of statement and reception, message and meaning. But Heptapod B, the written language, is formed of "semagrams" that "sprout like frost on a window pane." (327) The Heptapod sentence is a single continuous line, where, as speaker becomes writer, it must know all events on the line, *at the exact same moment* it makes the first stroke, just as light, in Fermat's Principle, must know where it is going before it begins its trajectory: "That's right; the notion of a 'fastest path' is meaningless unless there's a destination specified. And computing how long a given path takes also requires informa-tion about what lies along that path, like where the water's surface is." (157)

To assume "foreknowledge" is to deny the possibility of free will. If Gary can tell Louise that "the fundamental laws of physics were time-symmetric, that there was no difference between past and future," she responds that this may be *theoretically* true, but for humans in an existential situation, it is not true, because of free will. She invokes the ancestor of Derrida's arche-text: *The Book of Ages*, "the chronicle that records every event, past and future." This problem enters science fiction with time travel, notably Wells's vision of the future death of humanity in *The Time Machine* (1895). Did the Traveller, playing the text of evolution, know his destination before he started? Heinlein's scientist Hugo Pinero, in "Life-Line" (1939), offers an Emersonian solution. Pinero invents a machine that measures the length of each individual lifeline. Like a Heptapod B sentence, each lifeline is a "pink worm" on the "vine" of existence. Pinero's heroism is to know his own end and to *enact it.* He leaves behind the dilemma posed by Heptapod B. The other scientists hold in their hands a box, in which Pinero has placed papers on which their lifelines are measured. Instead of opening it, they destroy it, preferring uncertainty to foreknowledge. Pinero's "free will" is to know, yet to do.

Heinlein, like Emerson, knows the monad is subject to the iron laws of matter—energy and entropy—and their logic is linear. Louise realizes that, as she becomes proficient in Heptapod B, she is entering an entirely opposite universe: "With Heptapod B, I was experiencing something just as foreign: my thoughts were becoming graphically coded. . . . As I grew more fluent, semagraphic designs would appear fully formed, articulating even complex ideas all at once. . . . There was no direction inherent in the way propositions were connected, no 'train of thought' moving along a particular route; all the components in an act of reasoning were equally powerful, all having identical precedence." (158) Learning a language is one thing; but using that language to tell a story in *our* medium of narration is something else. Are we bound by our physical existence to live, and tell stories about our life, in sequential order? Or is the physical universe, in fact, a "language with a perfectly ambiguous grammar," where "every physical event was an utterance that could be parsed in two entirely different ways, one causal, and the other teleological, both valid, neither one disqualifiable no matter how much context was available?" (165) Indeed, as Gary says of physics: "In all branches of physics, almost every physical law can be restated as a variational principle. The only difference between these principles is in which attribute is minimized or maximized." (149)

We appear to restate the wave-particle problem in the realm of linguistics: two languages, two worlds; choose one or the other, and collapse the wave either way. We saw how difficult it was for Egan's narrator to tell his story in such a world, how he relied on a constant relocation of narrative voice to sustain a dynamic undulation between subject and object, a relationship the "smeared" universe denies. In Chiang's story, if each set of laws is written in its own language, how can the monad break out of one system and establish the galvanic circuit with another? "There is no 'correct' interpretation; both are equally valid. But you can't see both at the same time." (169) Yet Louise's narration seems to alternate between these two "universes"—causal and teleological. One narrative strand is completely linear, that of the *arrival and departure* of the alien Heptapods. It unfolds in the classic manner of the detective story, with an account of the gradual discovery of the mystery of their language and their departure. It comprises one of the "stories" of her life. The other story is the birth and death of her daughter, presented to the reader in the "radial" manner of the semagram. Here Louise addresses her dead daughter as someone alive, perusing her entire lifeline in the future tense: "I'd love to tell you the story of this evening, the night you were conceived, but the right time to do that would be when you're ready to have children of your own, and we'll never get that chance." (117) But if we look closely, we see these two strands are intertwined in the narrative from the first utterance: "I know how this story ends. I think about it a lot. I also think a lot about how it began, just a few years ago, when ships appeared in orbit and artifacts appeared in meadows. . . . And then I got a phone call, a request for a meeting." (118)

The narrator, in the act of telling, experiences a gradual re-positioning of herself as subject in the alien linguistic system: "The existence of free will meant that we couldn't know the future. And we knew free will existed because we had direct experience of it. Volition was an intrinsic part of consciousness. Or was it? What if the experience of knowing the future changed a person?" (163) Physical death draws a circumference around her story as it struggles to free itself from causality. What Louise does, in her search to write in Heptapod B, is shift places, take up a new position from which she can interact dynamically with a new circumference. At the end of her physical narration, in the linear time of the reader's world, she summons a beginning, the instant of the child's birth, only to suspend time as narrative knows it, to escape the hold of the future in the very process of narrating in the future tense: "Once you begin nursing, everything will reverse. . . . NOW is the only moment you'll perceive; you'll live in the present tense." (169)

At this moment, Louise realizes the profound implications of the Heptapod way of narrating. Human narratives appear trapped in the opposition of fate or free will. Either they accept the tyranny of linear human time or they "free" themselves from this tyranny by "deconstructing" the active subject as disseminated "text." But the Heptapod narrative, as Louise describes it, seems to escape this duality by following Emerson's model of undulation: "The heptapods are neither free nor bound as we understand those concepts; they don't act according to their will, nor are they helpless automatons. What distinguishes the heptapods' mode of awareness is not that their actions coincide with history's events; it is also that their motives coincide with history's purposes. They act to *create* the future, to *enact* chronology." (169, my italics) The extremes of Fermat's principle have become "actions" and "purposes." As such they seem to create a new galvanic circuit, where the duality of speech and writing is transformed in what Louise calls an act of "performative" linguistics. Louise reminds readers that "a morphological relative of 'performative' was 'performance,' which could describe the sensation of conversing when you knew what would be said: it was like performing a play." (171) This is not, as in the disseminated mediacosm, performance from a previously written script we ritually recite each time we experience a media presence in image and sound. Instead, it is a *re-activation*, the restoration of a vital circuit between extremes in a world that appears static, self-contained: "For the heptapods, all language was performative. Instead of using language to inform, they used language to actualize. Sure, heptapods already knew what would be said in any conversation; but in order for their knowledge to be true, the conversation would have to take place." (170)

This raises the question of solipsism. Striving in linear time to encompass his own first and final cause, Heinlein's Lazarus aspires to a heptapod situation. Louise's narrative seems to end at the moment it began, with her addressing a daughter who is both dead and waiting to be born. The first line is: "Your father is about to ask me the question." The final paragraph appears to close this circle: "These questions are in my mind when your father asks me: 'Do you want to make a baby?' And I smile and answer: 'Yes,' and I unwrap his arms from around me, and we hold hands as we walk inside to make love, to make you." (178) In this ouroboric speech, Louise's world, like the Heptapod semagram, seems to close on itself. The conversation presented takes place only to realize something that has already been written, the "you" it addresses "already" dead. In this context of the solipsistic circle, it seems of no matter whether each man *is* his world, or dynamically *enacts* his world; the result would still be solipsism. Here is Louise summing up her life: "Working with the heptapods changed my life. I met your father and learned Heptapod B, both of which make it possible for me to know you, here on the patio in the moonlight. Eventually, many years from now, I'll be without your father, and without you. All I will have left from this moment is the heptapod language." (178)

But "having left" the Heptapod language may be the means of breaking the solipsistic circle, of restoring Emerson's galvanic circuit. Heinlein himself clearly realized the danger of performative self-enactment in his story "'All You Zombies—.'" Here too, though the solipsistic circle seems to close, the possibility of a further galvanic circuit remains. For within the circle there are events—the "Mistake of 1972"—showing that events cannot be entirely bent to personal laws of time. Here is Louise reflecting on the child she simultaneously, in her Heptapod narrative, has already created and is about to create: "You won't be a clone of me; you can be wonderful, a daily delight, but you *won't be someone I could have created by myself.*" There are moments when she acts causally in the world of simultaneity, as when she buys in the "present" of her narrative the same salad bowl she knows will "later" fall and injure her daughter. She may be performing her script; but in this case it is clear that she *chooses* to re-enact the scenario, even though she *knows* it is painful. As she admits of her daughter: "Living with you will be like aiming for a moving target; you'll always be further along than I expect." (144) Her final statement restates Fermat's principle, but the declaration of closure has become interrogative query. The human dynamic is restored within the Heptapod circumference: "From the beginning I knew my destination, and I chose my route accordingly. But am I working toward an extreme of joy, or of pain? Will I achieve a minimum, or a maximum?"(178) The road is already traced. But the magnitude of the experience remains open-ended.

In Silverberg's delightfully profound "Enter a Soldier. Later: Enter Another,"[36] two computer engineers replay the Frankenstein script by creating holographic figures of two very disparate-seeming "soldiers"—Francisco Pizarro and Socrates—who through "virtual" interaction with each other free themselves from the manipulation of their creators and become independent entities. The supervisor Tanner describes Richardson's experiment in clear Frankensteinian terms:

> You breathed life in. Life of a sort, anyway. But you breathed free will in too. That's what this experiment is all about, isn't it? All your talk about volition and autonomy? You're trying to re-create a human mind—which means to create it all over again—a mind that can think in its own special way, and come up with its own unique responses to situations, which will not necessarily be the responses that its programmers might anticipate . . . and you simply have to allow for that risk, just as God, once He gave free will to mankind, knew that He was likely to see all manner of evil deeds being performed by His creations as they exercised that free will . . . (522)

Previously discussed stories dealt with identifying a circumference, its breaching, and subsequent re-establishing of a new galvanic circuit between a displaced subject and its repositioned object. In Egan, smeared humanity breaches the Bubble; in Benford, the death of matter removes the barrier that preserves Western science; in Chiang, the barrier Louise breaches in telling the story of her life is that of the sequency-simultaneity paradox. The barrier in Silverberg's story is the Frankenstein barrier, the barrier that, since publication of Mary Shelley's book, has continued to constrain science fiction. It exists in clear violation of Emerson's statement that "great men exist so that there may be greater men," for Frankenstein refuses to yield his place to the creature he created, though it may be physically and cognitively superior to him. The bride is refused and with it the creation of a new race; the creature can only turn on its creator. Each remains an isolated monad, a subject without any vital object except the adversary that has become its double. Mankind is separated from its other, its future.

Richardson's Frankenstein experiment takes place in a near future dominated by media "events." The program he uses to create his holograms was first used by French scientists to generate "son et lumière" events: "Imagine Louis XIV demonstrating the fountains of Versailles . . . or Picasso leading a tour of Paris museums. . . . Napoleon! Joan of Arc! Alexandre Dumas!" (516) But these are mere simulacra. The French programmers have a more ambitious project in mind: to re-create Don Quixote for a state visit by the Spanish king. They fail for a specific reason: "The knight of La Mancha was a mere fragment; but had Cervantes not provided far more detail about Don Quixote's mind and soul than was known of Richelieu, or Molière, or Louis XIV?" (517) The implication is that, when re-constituting the genes and memes that comprise such figures, the literary story—fiction—is a far richer "text" than historical accounts: "The Don—like Oedipus, like Odysseus, like Othello, like David Copperfield—had come to have a reality far more profound and tangible than most people who had indeed actually lived." Re-creating Don Quixote is what Louise would call a performative act, re-activation of an already written script. But this re-activation is now seen as failing in terms that are clearly Emersonian: "He [the Don] had no *capacity* for independent life and thought—no way to perceive the world that brought him into being, or to comment on it, or to interact with it. . . . Any actor could dress up in armor and put on a scraggly beard and recite snatches of Cervantes." (518). Silverberg's new Frankenstein would substitute for the process of media dissemination a character "resurrected" from a richer, more life-containing print narrative. The media "legend" (the *son et lumière* Joan of Arc) comes up short when compared with the creature of print (Don Quixote). Even so this creature, though "born" of a text, is asked to step out of it to assume a new existence. By means of an act of hologramic "life" creation, the new Frankenstein would summon, from its text, the independent striving monad Emerson called his representative man.

Emerson, when enumerating his representative men, made no distinction between the inanimate and animate, dead and living, "imaginary" and "real": "Man, made of the dust of the world, does not forget his origin; and all that is yet inanimate will one day speak and reason. . . ."[37] Only the galvanic circuit, with its power to generate a dynamic relation between subject and object, can span a gulf such as this. Taking lessons from past mistakes in hologram creation—"we aren't necromancers, we're programmers, and we have to figure out how to give the program what it needs"—the American Richardson proposes that his first "subject" to enter holographic limbo be ruthless conquistador Francisco Pizarro, who is simultaneously a figure whose *motives* are unfathomable and whose *energy* and self-reliance are undeniable: "His drive. His courage. His absolute confidence. The other side of ruthlessness . . .

is a total concentration on your task, an utter unwillingness to be stopped by any obstacle." (519) In another story of the same period, "A Sleep and a Forgetting" (1988), Silverberg "rotates" Genghis Kahn from his original historical location as Mongol scourge, having him abducted as a child and taken to Constantinople to be raised a Byzantine Christian. This information is picked up by a scientist in our time, who devised a means of "listening" to other places on our historical timeline. But what he taps into here is an *alternate* timeline, where Genghis Kahn grows up in Byzantium. As with Pizarro, this story is about centers and circumferences. Genghis Kahn is simply re-positioned as power center: "Listen to the way he speaks. He's scary. Even if you can't understand a word of what he's saying, can't you feel the power in him? The coiled-up anger? That's the voice of somebody capable of conquering whole continents." (500) In his new world, he may lead another sweeping crusade, but this time in the name of the Christian God. We simply displace the center of power, and in doing so generate a new "form," a possible new world.

The "rebirth" of Pizarro as hologram is just such a relocation of power. As the figure of the conquistador stands, a small speck, in the limbo of holospace, Tanner, the supervising scientist, shows him a vision of America in 2130. Pizarro is amazed, yet at the same time, "watching all of this, he felt the fine old hunger taking possession of him again: he wanted to grasp this strange vast place, and seize it, and clutch it close, and ransack it for all it was worth." (524) Pizarro does not understand the science but relocates himself quickly: the speaker from the void, he says, must be a sorcerer; and if he is so, then he has raised me from the dead; in that case, let him tell me how I died. The illiterate Pizarro, adapting with alacrity, now shows he is capable of Heptapod B thinking: he wants to know how he died in one world so he can understand his position in this new world, where he seems simultaneously dead and yet alive: "He's got it all figured out pretty much as it's going to happen. As it *did* happen, I should say." (528) Fearfully, Tanner sees his new Pizarro on the brink of the Frankenstein barrier: "He can't manufacture that kind of knowledge by magic, but he can assemble what looks to us like irrelevant bits and come up with new information. . . . That's what we mean by artificial intelligence." (529) Tanner reiterates Frankenstein's fear: "I don't want any of your goddamned *simulations walking* out of the tank and conquering *us*." (520) Tanner however does not want to destroy "Pizarro"; rather, he wants "to try to learn what that kind of drive and determination is really like." In effect, he proposes to breach the Frankenstein barrier by allowing his new creation to express self-reliance, thus giving it the power to enact the Emersonian dynamic, "something that we don't understand in this country anymore." (530)

Tanner does not give his Pizarro a new object—a near-future America—to conquer. Instead, he proposes to give him a dialogue partner, another simulacrum of a soldier—this time "Socrates." The "soldier" nexus is important, for it is, in the beginning, the sole common ground upon which these highly disparate representative men can initially stand—the "bare ground" upon which a never-before-seen galvanic circuit will be formed. But this time the circuit will involve an undulation between two beings who, through dialogue, begin to change in their present, moving beyond the limits of legend, even of text, returning their holographic death to a life in mutual understanding.

Emerson says it is "within the limits of human education and agency" to create greater from great men. In the holotank, we push beyond human limits. The Socrates we know is Plato's creation, the great dialectician of "I don't know." Here he is removed from this context, given a new start in a yet-unwritten realm, as a soldier talking to a soldier. Bloody conqueror Pizarro, in responding to unknown phenomena, has shifted positions, has become a mighty reasoner. The ensuing dialogue is a marvelous exchange between two self-discovering, self-affirming *presences.* In terms of what we know about them from their written pasts, "their basic assumptions are too far apart." (539) We first see Socrates's famous dialectical method, his argument from doubt and false humility, at once confounded by Pizarro's bluntness, his sense that, though he killed the Aztec king and sacked the land, he merely did what he had to do. But a regenerated Socrates, in turn, draws forth from Pizarro a vision of life that, though it remains deeply dynamic, redirects its energy toward a new sense of life self-questioning and contemplative, yet affirmative: "They tell us to strive, to conquer, to gain—and for what? For a few years of strutting around. Then it's taken away, as if it had never been. . . . Did I say all that just now? Did I mean it? Well, I suppose I did. Still life's all there is, so you want as much of it as you can. Which means getting gold, and power, and fame." (544)

The human "handlers" who observe their holograms taking on new existence prove incapable of understanding the implications of what is occurring. They remain products of their media age, hoping to use their holograms to create some new kind of sporting spectacle or "game show": "A new way of settling political disputes . . . like a medieval tournament . . . with each side using champions that we simulate for them—the greatest minds of all the past, brought back and placed in competition . . ." (544) Yet as they ponder this, the dialogue pursues its own organic path, turning on the question of why Pizarro killed King Atahuallpa. For Pizarro it was necessity: "There weren't even two hundred of us, and twenty-four million of them. . . . So *of course* we had to get rid of him if we wanted to conquer them." (545) To Pizarro this was a simple act: "This way I made his death useful: to God, to the Church, to Spain. . . . Can you understand that?" (545) But "soldier" Socrates brilliantly turns the argument: "I think so," said Socrates. "But do you think King Atahuallpa did?" "Any king would understand such things." "Then he should have killed you the moment you set foot in his land." (545) Pizarro's rebuttal should be a draw—"Unless God meant us to conquer him, and allowed him to understand that." (545). But Socrates segues, and effectively, physically, breaks out of the dialectical circle their handlers have placed them in: "'Perhaps he is in this place, too, and we could ask him' . . . Pizarro's eyes brightened. 'Mother of God, yes! A good idea! And if he didn't understand why, I'll try to explain it to him. Maybe you'll help me.'" (545)

In Silverberg's story, we trace the trajectory of modern science fiction and media culture from *Frankenstein* to the hologram. Silverberg transposes two such "creations" into the mediacosm, where they are asked to become virtual structures striving to create their own infosphere. But Silverberg, in *writing* a story about the relation of disseminated images to text—and particularly about Socrates (Derrida's nemesis as incarnation of *logos*) as a *literary* creation now resurrected from its text, given *new life* as it breaks free of the prison house of the disseminated image—is an example of print science fiction offering an Emersonian response to the insubstantial pageant of media culture. Brilliantly Silverberg, by making this connection between Frankenstein and the "disseminations" of our media culture, restores the power of the word—both spoken and written—to the equation. "Pizarro" and "Socrates" would be helpless holograms—figures of *son et lumière*—were it not for the words they speak that represent resurrected script or "text," words that create their particular form of galvanic circuit within the medium of prose narrative. Their creators realize they cannot put the right Spanish pronunciation in Pizarro's mouth (or Greek in Socrates's mouth) as no one living had ever heard seventeenth-century words spoken. Yet here, in a shift of perspective worthy of Cervantes's dogs in his *Coloquio de los perros* (1613), both Pizarro and Socrates, supposedly summoned from the void back to a new void, free themselves as dynamic subjects because they somehow *know* they are not speaking correctly. Going further, in the final scene they tacitly realize that they should not be speaking to each other. Yet the reader, before his eyes, sees them *interacting*. In doing so, they effectively break the circle imposed by the modern media Frankensteins—not only coming alive but *coming together*. In doing so, they form the center of a new galvanic circuit. Silverberg here breaks the Frankenstein barrier by creating two figures that walk together out of the world of "texts" and images alike, operating now a refurbished world of print *science fiction*. At the same time, in restoring this Emersonian dynamic, Silverberg reminds us of Spider's admonition to Lo Lobey in Delany's *The Einstein Intersection* (1967), made likewise in a world where disembodied images seek new substance: why settle for two when you can have three? Physicist A. S. Eddington says much the same thing about doing science: when you think you have circumscribed nature, made it into a fixed deck of cards with which you play games—or manipulate images—nature always adds a new card to your deck.[38] Emerson's dynamic may contribute to the mediatization of forms, but this dynamic is not limited to the dissemination of images alone. The monads central to Emerson's dynamic are *both* mobile *and* vital—representative *men* whose mobility allows them to use the new cards dealt by nature to generate new centers of power and form. Silverberg's Socratic dialogue for the information age demonstrates how this dynamic works in the deepest sense of the *science fiction* tradition. Doing so, it shows us what it might really be like to *live* in Sterling's science-fictional world.

## NOTES

1. William H. Patterson, private email correspondence with the author, May 10, 2011.

2. Ralph Waldo Emerson, *Self-Reliance, The American Tradition in Literature*, edited by Sculley Bradley, Richmond Croom Beatty, and E. Hudson Long (New York: W. W. Norton, 1967), I, 1136–1137.

3. Emerson, *The American Scholar, The American Tradition*, I, 1113.

4. Emerson, *Nature, The American Tradition*, I, 1067.

5. Emerson, *Self-Reliance*, I, 1140.

6. Emerson constantly speaks in dynamic terms. An example is when he attributes an anecdote to Confucianist philosopher Meng-tse concerning the term "fast-flowing vigor": "'The explanation,' replied Mencius, 'is difficult. This vigor is supremely great, and in the highest degree unbending. Nourish it correctly and do it no injury, and it will fill up the vacancy between heaven and earth.'" See Emerson, *Experience, The American Tradition*, I, 1177.

7. See *Fiction 2000: Cyberpunk and the Future of Narrative*, edited by George Slusser and Tom Shippey (Athens: University of Georgia Press, 1992). In this forum on cyberpunk, almost every essay focuses on William Gibson and *Neuromancer*. There is a real sense here that this entire "movement" is the lengthened shadow of a man.

8. William Gibson, *Neuromancer* (New York: Ace Books, 1984), 5.

9. Numerous statements in Emerson gloss Lazarus's career. For example, this one from *The American Scholar:* "The world, this shadow of the soul, or *other me*, lies wide around." (I, 1104). There is also a caveat in "Experience", which Heinlein did not heed: "Life itself is a mixture of power and form, and will not bear the least excess of either." (I, 1171)

10. Isaac Asimov, *Second Foundation* (New York: Avon Books, 1964), 191. References are to this edition.

11. Emerson, "Experience".

12. The word "elasticity" is a key word in Emerson. See "Experience," I, 1169.

13. Emerson, "Experience".

14. Michel Jeury's novel *Le temps incertain* (1973) takes Dick's idea that each person creates (or is) his or her own world and develops a story about completely disembodied beings who exist in the "subjective eternity" of "chronolysis." The protagonist's problem is to relocate the exact physical moment of his death, so as to rejoin his material existence and escape this prison of endlessly recurring mental forms.

15. Emerson, "Experience," I, 1182.

16. Emerson, "Experience," I, 1170.

17. For a thorough treatment of the space station theme in science fiction, see Gary Westfahl, *Islands in the Sky: The Space Station Theme in Science Fiction Literature,* Second Edition (Holicong, Pennsylvania: Borgo Press/Wildside Press, 2009).

18. Shakespeare, *The Tempest, The Riverside Shakespeare*, edited by G. Blakemore Evans (Boston: Houghton Mifflin Company, 1974), 1611–1636.

19. An interesting recent variation on Ariel's powers is the story by Serge Brussulo, "Aussi lourd que le vent" (1981), where an artist's vocal cords are transformed in such a way that, when the artist utters the vilest language, beautiful "cloud-capp'd" structures are generated. We learn that this "art" is in fact subsidized by building contractors, who thus erect vast apartment complexes, which (as expected) eventually collapse.

20. Gregory Benford, "Effing the Ineffable," *Aliens: The Anthropology of Science Fiction*, edited by Slusser and Eric S. Rabkin (Carbondale: Southern Illinois University Press, 1987), 13–25.

21. Gerald Prince, *Dictionary of Narratology* (Lincoln: University of Nebraska Press, 1967); see article on "Narrative," 58–59. See also Danièle Chatelain, *Perceiving and Telling: A Study of Iterative Discourse* (San Diego: San Diego State University Press, 1998).

22. Greg Egan, *Quarantine: A Novel of Quantum Catastrophe* (New York: Harper Prism, 1995), 253. References are to this edition.

23. Emerson, *The Over-Soul, The American Tradition*, 1154.

24. Emerson, *Representative Men: Seven Lectures* (London: George Routledge & Co., 1850), Lecture I, "The Uses of Great Men," 21.

25. Emerson, *Representative Men,* 7.

26. Emerson, *Experience.*

27. Emerson, *Representative Men,* 13.

28. Let us revisit Hoag again. Heinlein's story, in its pre-quantum world, prefigures much of Egan's narrative world. For instance, the Sons of the Bird are presented as a corporate entity whose job is to exploit this botched world by making sure it remains what Egan would call our consensus reality. The Sons come and go through mirrors, suggesting it is human vanity that holds the consensus together. Heinlein prefigures Egan here in having Hoag "smear" the Sons' world—our world—as "bad art." In the final scene Hoag, as he savors the "good" things of this world for one last time, tells Ted and Cynthia to drive south. As they pass through Chicago with windows rolled up, they see the familiar landscape. When they roll down the window, however,

they see a gray void. Given the quantum choice, they first "collapse" the situation by rolling the window up. But as with Emerson's map-maker, they go further—they learn to control the experiment by leaving the window half up, half down. Hoag the "art critic" is an early version of the Bubble Makers, for he polices the circumference of a world where each human, trapped in his mirror condition, remains an eigenstate, and the Sons of the Bird exploit this condition to dominate humanity. The Randalls are the mobile center, representative "men" who learn to control the dynamic of the "switch" that keeps the wave-particle function open. Heinlein's characters only seem to live in a simpler narrative world than that of Egan's Nick. In Heinlein, however, "many worlds" come to life as magic or thaumaturgy, and an "art critic" is given power to alter the consensus world. Emerson's galvanic circuit here is subject to random dissemination based on "connoisseurship" rather than quantum theory. In both Heinlein's and Egan's narrative worlds, the counterforce remains a version of Emerson's representative man. Both protagonists are beings whose activity, and example, confirm Emerson's dictum that "we must not deny . . . the substantial existence of other people." ("The Uses of Great Men," 11) The model "man" in Heinlein, who works to hold the consensual center, is two people, detectives Ted and Cynthia, who represent as dynamic entities all those who work in this archetypal profession, whose "use" is to resolve mysteries on the concrete, human level.

29. This is eerily reminiscent of the 1992 film *Grand Tour: Disaster in Time* (David Twohy), based on Henry Kuttner and C. L. Moore's "Vintage Season" (1946). The story is about time travelers whose "tourism" consists of visiting disaster sites in the past. They are connoisseurs of horror, "eigenstates" detached from spacetime causality. In the film the protagonist has survived a meteor strike in which his daughter is killed. Accepting to detach himself from his timeline, he takes the time-travel device of one "tourist" and jumps back before the disaster to save his daughter. He does not use the device to go back and warn the townspeople to flee. Their timeline remains fixed in disaster. However, for selfish ends, he "smears" his temporal being and brings his daughter back from the dead. In this film, the protagonist cannot escape the iron law of causality. His "smeared" self simply vanishes, leaving his daughter behind.

30. Gregory Benford, "Matter's End," *Matter's End* (New York: Bantam Books, 1995), 236–288. References are to this edition.

31. Arthur C. Clarke, "The Nine Billion Names of God," *The Nine Billion Names of God* (New York: Harcourt Brace Jovanovich, 1967), 11.

32. Emerson, *Representative Men,* 12, 28.

33. Emerson, *Representative Men*, 17.

34. See Emerson, *Representative Men*, 24: "Rotation is the law of nature. When nature removes a great man, people explore the horizon for a successor; but none comes, and none will. His class is extinguished with him. In some other and quite different field, the next man will appear." This dance of forms is a dance of monads. The great man remains the representative of his category, not surpassed by another, but *superseded* by a new "field" of activity, whose great man in turn will "rotate" to some other category.

35. Ted Chiang, "Story of Your Life," *Stories of Your Life and Others* (New York: Orb Books, 2003). References are to this edition.

36. Robert Silverberg, "Enter a Soldier. Later: Enter Another," *The Collected Stories of Robert Silverberg, Volume 1, Secret Sharers* (New York: Bantam Books, 1992), 511–546. References are to this edition.

37. Emerson, *Representative Men*, 17.

38. A. S. Eddington, *New Pathways of Science* (New York: Macmillan, 1935), 68.

# Conclusion

## *The Fortunes of Science Fiction*

In the twenty-first century, science fiction seems firmly established as a world literature, with new national forms regularly becoming prominent. But can we still say, in terms of Goethe's dialectic of local cultures and general science, that these fictions simply come "on line" as a given national culture comes to grip with a Western science indisputably the worldwide norm? A subtle shift in this dynamic seems to have occurred. For today, the local component of Goethe's dialogue appears to be *sciences* in the plural, alternate models of apprehending material nature that writers openly call "science." These represent a cognitive method that no longer aspires to objectivity, but rather to a cultural specificity that is the opposite of what science claims to be today. Heinlein could calmly, in referencing scientific method, assume it was *the* scientific method and understood as such by his audience. Today the literary form he is seen to incarnate must consider many methods, many sciences, in the science fiction equation. All the paradigm shifts previously discussed are products of the development of the idea of science as observation of nature and verifiable experiment. Somewhat ironically, the coming of age of science fiction as a world literature has caused it to question, for the first time, the nature and purpose of what science might be.

In Emerson's Golden Age, science and technology were seen as the motors for expanded exploration of nature, pushing the envelope of human experience ever farther in search of its nebulous grail of "sense of wonder." Its popular media incarnations in turn purveyed space adventure, with special effects using sophisticated technology to render this same wonder. In the 1970s and 1980s, however, we see a clear pullback from the Golden Age model. The reasons are many and complex. The space program fades. Attention turns to pressing environmental and social issues. Readers tire of engineering feats such as Larry Niven's *Ringworld* (1970) and turn instead to mythic and cultural extrapolations like Frank Herbert's *Dune* (1965). Political and cultural "wars" erupt around the dystopian landscapes of cyberpunk and meta-escapism of "steampunk." The computer replaces the spaceship as central icon, which leads to the creation of "cyberspace," itself perhaps a Cartesian import via the French *bandes dessinées* conveyed by magazines like *Heavy Metal*. We have a form of literature that falls to Earth. As it does, Western science, its former enabler, is either rejected or displaced by what are called "alternate" systems of knowledge, but in reality, seem little more than magic or paranormal science. Novels like Dan Simmons's *The Hollow Man* (1992) place side by side highly sophisticated quantum theory and phenomena such as telepathy. If, as Arthur C. Clarke says, any sufficiently advanced science may seem to be magic, then cannot magic in its own right be seen as a "science"? Such a science remains (for now) one of effects, a descriptive model without causal explanations.

In recent science fiction, these alternate systems challenge Western scientific and rationalist orthodoxy. In this, however, there is a second twist on Goethe's dialectic between local and general tendencies. In the development of what proponents call "global" science fiction, local belief systems displace Western science. Yet the general element in the equation now appears linguistic—the appearance of a series of science fictions, in variational English, from Anglophone countries. Writers working in other national languages often complain of a "hegemony" of English-language, mostly American, science fiction. Here is an interesting variation on this, where the science of American science fiction is contested by an Anglophone literature using the "SF" designation. We have essentially a "commonwealth" literature, a generic diaspora whose newfound homeland is the English language of the former colonizer. It espouses local scientific systems, yet in opposing "American" science it claims to represent the "global" aspirations of the all, against the domination of the One.

## THE ROAD TO GLOBAL SF

Before the late 1970s, science fiction, especially the great mass of literature produced in the United States before and during its "Golden Age," was a literature ignored by literary pundits and university scholars. This slowly changed as academics began to study the form, fascinated especially by its presence as cultural phenomenon. To approach it in this context, however, there was a need to remove the word "science" from its designation. This word connected it to that other culture, that of the engineer and builder, the Emersonian self-reliant monad. Thus was promulgated the abbreviation

"SF." Up till now, I avoided using this term, as its slippery nature leads away from facing the central dynamic of the form—the impact of science. Its use, originally, may have been to counter the term "sci-fi," which retains popular currency. But "SF" became a way of shifting valence to court respectability in academic circles. *Science Fiction Studies*, as editorial policy, insisted on "SF" or "sf." Excluding "space opera" and other forms of "fantasy," the term could reference a more serious "*speculative* fiction." Robert Scholes moved farther afield with "structural fabulation." "SF" allows recent writers identified with the "global SF" movement to reposition very different elements in what was once science's commanding position in science fiction's dynamic. For example, writer Nalo Hopkinson tells us in her website (nalohopkinson. com) that "sf" means "subversive fiction." Asked in interviews and on blogs by naïve readers why and if she writes science fiction, she offers oblique answers—because she read fantasy as a child, because she is interested in social change, or just because she wanted to do "something different."

The letters and social sciences, in American and British academia, experienced an influx of French theory in the 1980s and 1990s, and one offshoot was the use of metaphysical issues to launch politically motivated attacks on science and the scientific method—the so-called "science wars" that came to a head with Alan Sokal's and Jean Bricmont's book *Fashionable Nonsense* (1998).[1] The Anglophones have retaken this territory with the current fashion of "postcolonial studies," implementing a similar agenda by giving "voice" to writers and intellectuals from former British colonies. Fiction labeled "science fiction" by Anglophone writers is published today by mainstream publishing houses and in magazines like *The New Yorker* that never previously touched a work of science fiction. To do so, they convert the "alternate history" of science fiction into a vehicle for revisionism. One thing most frequently "rewritten" is the impact of Western technology and science.

"Deconstructionist" tactics are still at work in many postcolonial rewrites of science fiction. An example is British writer China Miéville, who came on the scene in the first decade of the twenty-first century with his Bas-Lag novels: *Perdido Street Station* (2000), *The Scar* (2002), and *Iron Council* (2004). Miéville is a Marxist intellectual who wrote a scholarly treatise on law in the globalized world, *Between Equal Rights* (2007). His fiction was instantly picked up by academics who hailed him as a writer "re-inventing" an otherwise worn-out genre. In a sense, however, both the genre and the science that enabled it have been simply removed from the equation. Carl Freedman calls this "weird fiction" and gives a telling description: "[It is] a version of speculative fiction that blends science fiction, Surrealism, fantasy, magic realism, and Lovecraftian horror, and . . . the whole tradition of the Western from Zane Grey to Cormac McCarthy."[2] Science in any form is nearly absent from this generic stew. Yet articles on Bas-Lag are increasingly frequent in journals like *Science Fiction Studies*. The entire Summer, 2009 issue of *Extrapolation* focuses on Miéville's work, described as "beyond steampunk," itself a form of literary pastiche, which resurrects "extraordinary" figures from nineteenth-century popular fiction of all genres, allowing them to play in the fields of the industrial and technological century that supposedly set the (wrong) direction for modern science fiction. Miéville's work, in fact, is a personal form of urban fantasy whose purpose, it seems, is to confound genre readers while delighting critics, spurring them to invent ever more surprising and unstable descriptive compounds, such as "post-cyberpunk Tolkien." For Miéville, Western science at best is the negative and destructive force that gave rise to bourgeois humanism in its postmodern globalized form.

Miéville's work is heralded as part of a "global SF" movement. But he epitomizes the critic as writer. Let us look instead at two works by writers, working in the "diasporic" English of their native cultures, who openly call their works "science fiction." First is *The Calcutta Chromosome* (1995), written in English by Indian-Bengali Amitav Ghosh. A long-time professor of Comparative Literature at NYU and Harvard, he is hailed by critics as bringing to the genre a rich field of intercultural comparison, lauded for providing new ways of assessing, from an Indian and colonial point of view, both the tropes of Western science fiction and scientific ideas (here medicine and temporality) that shape it. For this, the novel received the 1997 Arthur C. Clarke Award.

Ghosh's novel takes up two common themes of science fiction—alternate timelines and the scientific quest for life extension—that converge in a rewrite of the story of British doctor Sir Ronald Ross, who won the Nobel Prize in 1902 for discovering that malaria was transmitted by a certain kind of mosquito. In terms of the "established" history of science, Ross seems an extraordinary figure, the kind of scientist praised by Claude Bernard, whose discoveries led to not only an understanding of the mechanisms of a disease but the means of eradicating (if not curing) it. Ross's methods have been seen as controversial. It is claimed that he "experimented" on Indian patients, though others counter that the patient he used, Hussain Khan, was already infected with malaria. There was rancor at the fact that Ross got the Nobel Prize, while his Indian assistant got only a gold medal. These are the elements upon which Ghosh's alternate history turns: we learn that responsible for Ross's discovery is the activity of a group of Indian scientists, conducting higher research on a form of "chromosome transfer," which allows individual human traits to pass to new bodies, allowing single individuals to prolong their existence indefinitely. The "real" science here—with cosmic rather than simply practical goals—is conducted in Indian ways by Indian scientists.

This, on the surface, seems a perfectly orthodox thought experiment: What if a secret society of Indian scientists did find the cause of malaria? What if they used this discovery to greater, quasi-spiritual ends? What if life extension is nothing more than transmigration of souls? Even so, the extrapolative reach of this novel seems weak when compared with a work like Benford's "Matter's End" (1991), published years before Ghosh's novel. For Benford, there is a new physics born of the Indian scientists' discovery that matter is finite. But it represents a fusion of two systems of physical analysis, where neither can function without the other. In Ghosh's novel, there is the sense that one system is *corrected* by the other, that we are unveiling the "secret history" of Western science. Despite all the practical consequences of Ross's discovery, all the many lives saved (and the fact that Ross himself could be a formidable science fiction hero in his own right), the novel closes the window on his kind of "colonialist" science, as former inequalities are redressed.

Commentators see Ghosh's novel developing "indo-nostalgic" visions. And it is true that, as alternate history, it takes place, not in some future or alternate timeline, but the cultural memory of the author. Another writer who mines this deep racial realm of "alternate histories" is Canadian-Jamaican Nalo Hopkinson. Her relation to science fiction is curiously instructive. Her first novel, *Brown Girl in the Ring* (1998), is set in a vaguely near-future Toronto. Her "inner city" resembles Samuel R. Delany's Bellona in *Dhalgren* (1975), an anarchic terrain inhabited by the left-behinds of modern society. There are issues of poor people being "organ-farmed" and other dystopian clichés. But the real core of the novel is what reviewer David Soyka calls Hopkinson's "voice grounded in the rhythms, myths and vernacular of Caribbean culture." Another reviewer, Neil Walsh, describes the novel as "a supernatural horror tale." Reviewer Donna McMahon states emphatically that this is NOT a science fiction novel.[3] The novel however was nominated for a Philip K. Dick award and won the Locus Award for Best New Writer.

Her subsequent *Midnight Robber* (2000), nominated for a Hugo Award that year, has more obvious science fiction elements: it takes place on another planet (called Toussaint); there is a group-mind utopia, talk of nanotechnology, and multi-dimensional travel. Hopkinson, in an interview in *SF Site*, explains her extrapolative purpose. Assuming there was a Caribbean diaspora to another planet, how would these people conceive and name the new technologies they are obliged to develop? But there is more naming than conceiving here. Hugo Gernsback in *Ralph 124C 41+* (1911–1912, 1925) creates neologisms. But in his case, the new name given seeks to describe the form and *function* of the new technology. Here Hopkinson names the AI that controls the world of Toussaint "Granny Nanny"—a name from Caribbean folk myth given to what is a *known* technology. One can retort that this is common practice, and that even Heinlein does the same. For example, when he calls his central computer "Mycroft" in *The Moon Is a Harsh Mistress* (1966), he calques a cultural face on the machine, rather than offering a description of its technical specifications and function. And if this novel is primarily, as Hopkinson says, a "coming of age" story, isn't this the case with Heinlein's *Citizen of the Galaxy* (1957) as well? New and challenging science does not have to be the focus of a novel for it to be called "science fiction." Even so, it is hard to follow James Schellenberg when he calls this a "hard science fiction novel."[4] A scientific theory or scientific method, in the classical sense, is clearly not writing the fiction here. Instead, fiction is *renaming* known science and technology in a new cultural context, one supposed to *re-humanize* it. In doing so, she is, in the eyes of reviewer Geoffrey Dow (*Edifice Rex Online*, 2009), offering an alternative to a science he simply dismisses as "male, mainstream, western, and white," with a further comment that "most SF reads like it was written by some White Guy in a small apartment somewhere in Middle America." Given such observations, it is difficult to dismiss the ideological message of such fiction.[5]

Hopkinson's subsequent novels have only a marginal connection with science fiction. Walsh rightly calls *Brown Girl in the Ring* "a supernatural horror tale," focused on obeah sorcerers and the resurgence of folk magic in a postmodern world. Her *The Salt Roads* (2003) is presented to the reader as an "alternate-history novel." The novel, again, has little in common with the classic science fiction "uchronia," novels that examine the "what if" of Napoleon winning at Waterloo. There are many examples of such in science fiction, from Ward Moore's *Bring the Jubilee* (1953), where the South wins the Civil War, to Gregory Benford's *Timescape* (1980), where the non-assassination of John F. Kennedy marks a splitting of timelines in a sophisticated network of many-world possibilities. The motor for such spatiotemporal displacements is generally an "invention," a time machine, or a theory of tachyons. Hopkinson's novel is a simple historical novel, with stories told from perspectives that are different from those of "official" history. There are three sections: the first takes place in times of colonial slavery; the second in nineteenth-century Paris, where the story of Charles Baudelaire is told from the point of view of his Creole mistress Jeanne Duval; the third offers a fictional portrait of Thais, the Nubian prostitute, in times of Roman occupation of Palestine. The whole story turns around the eternal presence of magic fertility goddesses. The emphasis has totally shifted away from interaction or dialogue between new world views imposed by science and conventional human categories. Now there is simply the wrongness of human institutions, and the rightness of basic forces of life. The novel turns its back completely on science, never even suggesting the link between technology and the institution of slavery.

The title of *The New Moon's Arms* (2007), attributed to Leonardo da Vinci, suggests that Western science may have a redeemable side, but only if poetry and magic replace its cold equations.

## SCIENCE FICTION AS LINGUISTIC CROSSROADS

Writers like Ghosh and Hopkinson benefit from the world-wide use of English as "universal" language, which gives them an immediate readership and a critical and academic establishment ready to engage their work. They also benefit from writing under the "SF" or "science-fiction" banners, in the sense that this allows them to claim the status of "science"—another universally accepted term—for elements of their particular cultural world views that would otherwise be rejected by Western science as religion, myth, supernaturalism, or at best paranormal phenomena. Yet this same dialogue between local and universal science(s)—contending visions of what science is and how it functions—is at the core of the many national, non-English-language science fictions developing today. Because most of this literature is not translated into English, it remains *terra incognita* for most science fiction scholars. Consider two significant examples: China and Israel. Both are "diasporic" cultures. Yet at the same time both provide vibrant crossroads for disparate scientific visions, cultures, and literary traditions. English-language science fiction is not excluded, but rather assimilated into the production of science fiction in other languages that challenge its (stated or unstated) hegemony.

Today, Chinese-language science fiction is growing by leaps and bounds. Because of the vast and varied geographical reach of the language, the landscape of Chinese science fiction has rapidly become complex. On one hand, a sophisticated, "postmodern" form of science fiction is being written in Chinese enclaves outside the mainland, a form clearly engaged in dialogue with its Anglophone counterpart. But rather than being subservient to it, because of the rapidity of its growth, it seems poised to move beyond it in terms of its "modernity." The diasporic Chinese science fiction of Hong Kong, Singapore, and Taiwan seems to have leapt over space travel and the Golden Age to embrace cyberpunk as yardstick for measuring the futuristic urbanization underway in these places. The role of science fiction in this Chinese diaspora was the topic of two recent East-West colloquia, held at the Chinese University of Hong Kong in 2001 and 2003. The first conference produced a significant collection of essays by scholars from all five continents—*World Weavers: Globalization, Science Fiction and the Cybernetic Revolution* (Hong Kong University Press, 2002), edited by the East-West team of Wong Kin-Yuen, Gary Westfahl, and Amy Kit-sze Chan. The essays from the 2003 conference, edited by the same team, appeared a decade later, in 2011, under a now "world" umbrella, as *Science Fiction and the Prediction of the Future*. The "future" discussed here is the future Asia of Gibson and Greg Egan, played off against Chinese-language writers' views of a future, multicultural, "Asianized" America. Even so, emerging from the post-modern landscape of these colloquia, is the undercurrent, noticed by scholars East and West, of Chinese myth and legend. There is fascination with (and participation in) Chinese martial arts, discussion of the role of Shaolin "science" in technically sophisticated Hong-Kong film. Lisa Raphals, a scholar of ancient Chinese and Greek, considers the role of Chinese legend and "science" in the work of Cordwainer Smith. Connections between ancient systems and "postmodern" futures, East and West, are being made here only because many of the participants are "fluent" in both cultures and languages.

In the science fiction of the "new" cosmopolitan Asia, ancient belief systems invade the postmodern digitalized megatropolis; super-futures dialogue with ancient pasts. In contrast to this, science fiction from the Chinese mainland appears to remain (for the moment at least) technocratic and utilitarian. As described by Jie Lu, the spirit of this fiction, produced in increasing volume, is that of Jules Verne—a literature of scientific adventure in the Western sense, designed to lure talented young people into scientific and technological careers.[6] In this sense, China is aping the West, creating its own "industrial revolution." But whether this is an accurate assessment, and how and in what ways the path of nation-state Chinese science fiction will vary from its European and American counterparts, are questions the future will answer. For now (with conspicuous exceptions like the novels of Cixin Liu), the prodigious amount of mainland Chinese science fiction currently being produced remains basically unread in the West.

On a smaller scale, Israeli science fiction is another diasporic literature. The small size however may be made up for by a much broader cultural and linguistic input. Israel, through immigration, is a microcosmic world culture, with immigrants from Europe, the United States, Africa, and Russia, each bringing with them strong national cultures. American science fiction was naturally introduced into Israel by means of its large English-speaking population. In his MA thesis (Tel Aviv University, 1999), Inbal Sagiv isolates two spikes in translation of American science fiction into Hebrew: 1976–1978, and 1996–1999. The first wave of translation was "classic" Golden Age, the second wave more recent cyberpunk and "globalized" science fiction. Israel has an active fan network and recent writers like Ladvie Tidhar and Nir Yaniv are well versed in the Anglo-American tradition and write in both Hebrew and English. One collection is Yaniv's *One Hell of a Writer*, published by Odyssey Press in English (2006). A second good example of the cultural and linguistic polyvalence of recent Israeli science fiction writers is Guy Hasson, whose name is French, writes plays in Hebrew, and science fiction in English.

At the same time however, through a recent influx of immigrants from Russia, the alternate tradition of *nauchnaya fantastika* has made strong inroads. In terms of science, this tradition mixes the rigors of experimental method and high technology of space adventure with folk magic and "over-the-edge" science—especially teleportation, theories of overlapping "dimensions" and "homeostatic" universes. We see this mix in the Strugatskys's story "Natural Science in the Spirit World" (1962), which involves an "Institute of Discrete Science" running experiments on extrasensory perception and the "theory of interpenetrating spaces." In Israel, this vision of science—which because of the "cold war" remained throughout the Soviet period the sole purview of Russian-language science fiction—encounters the strong current of American-inspired science fiction, in English and Hebrew. Because of this a vital dialogue between cultures—impossible before—is created. We find it working in writers like Daniel Kluger, who writes in Russian. His science fiction brings to the mix science fantasy in the manner of Bulgakov, or the Strugatskys's *Monday Begins on Saturday* [*Ponedel'nik nachinaetsia v subbotu*] (1965), which immerses readers in the doings of a Soviet Institute of Witchcraft and Magic, where Baba Yaga jostles with Einstein. The surge of recent Israeli science fiction written in Russian is the subject of a book, *The Future of the Past: On Russian and Non-Russian SF* (2006) by Elana Gomel, a Russian-speaking professor of English and American Studies at Tel Aviv University. Described here is the possibility of belated, but meaningful, fictional dialogue between the different scientific visions of the two major space age powers.

Even so, despite this capacity for intercultural dialogue, we see in Israeli science fiction today a similar phenomenon to that of mainland Chinese science fiction. For the country today is producing a large number of science fiction novels whose purpose is utilitarian and often propagandistic. This science fiction (written in Hebrew, English, and Russian) tends to extrapolate from current political reality to imagine nuclear armageddon, or future wars with Iran and other menaces to Israeli statehood in the here-and-now.

## PARADIGM REDISCOVERED: DDR SCIENCE FICTION

Chinese-language science fiction is the product of a new-century technological revolution, Israeli science fiction of a crossroads of strong cultures with a will to create a future. I turn now to two European science fictions—East German and Romanian—that developed in relative isolation. Cut off from any meaningful exchange with postwar American science fiction, East German writers were obliged to look back to their national past, for both a sense of the nature of science and fictional models that engaged the questions it posed. The problem they rediscovered appears to be Kant's Copernican revolution, the literary model Hoffmann's scientific fantastic. Romanian science fiction is a rediscovery of another sort. Unlike Germany, Romania in the nineteenth and early twentieth centuries had a tradition of popular science fiction second only to France in continental Europe. Geopolitical reasons kept Romanian science fiction isolated, and Romanian remained a secondary language. Communism further isolated Romania. Yet through these years Romanian science fiction continued developing its own unique form. Unlike East Germany, which had to rediscover and re-establish somewhat tenuous links between Hoffmann and science fiction, Romania not only kept its form alive, but through the dark years of communism kept reaching out to the West, engaging in a creative dialogue that flowered in the post-communist years.

Stacked against "classical" literature, any science fiction in prewar Germany was seen as "entertainment." Postwar West Germany did not produce original science fiction, and unlike France, did not dialogue with American science fiction. Instead, it simply published it, again as entertainment. In an ironic turn of events, the creation of the DDR (Deutsche Demokratische Republik), physically walled off from the West, caused writers interested in science fiction to search their own national past for models on which to create a literature of scientific speculation. They needed to look beyond bourgeois realism, which dominated German-language fiction from Goethe up to Thomas Mann, but instead of Kant's attempts at rational certainty, they found the science-driven uncertainly of Hoffmann's world and apparently made the link from this to the meaningless mathematics of Kafka's stories and parables. On the other hand, prewar Nazi German fascination with technology—making war machines and rockets—did not disappear in the DDR. On the eve of World War II, Nazi scientists smuggled magazines like *Astounding Science-Fiction* into Germany. In the postwar era of electronic media, the Wall could not stop dissemination of the icons of American space science—the machines and decors of its science fiction. In the cultural island of East Germany, the coming together of local and international elements—in the hothouse of a highly censored society—produced a unique form of science fiction.

The writers' guilds of the DDR mandated that this "scientific" fiction, which did not have a fixed name until post-Wall Western houses began publishing it, be written in "literary" German. In the early 1990s, with the fall of the Wall, DDR writer Olaf Spittel published two anthologies of science fiction stories from East Germany—one with the former DDR house Verlag Das Neue Berlin, *Die Zeitinsel: SF-Erzählungen aus einem Land das es mal gab* (1991) [An Island in Time: SF Stories from a Land that Once Was], the other, *Zeit-Spiele: Ex-oriente Science Fiction* [Time Games: Ex-Eastern Science Fiction] (1992), from West German publisher of science fiction (mostly American and labeled "Unterhaltungsliteratur" [entertainment literature]), the Wilhelm Heyne Verlag in München. These revealed to the German-speaking world a full-blown tradition of *German* science fiction. Since 1950, it was Neue Berlin that published much of what became a flourishing DDR literature. In addition to DDR writers, its editors published selected international works, by Wells, Alexei Tolstoy, West German writer Wolfgang Jeschke, and the Strugatskys. There were "safe" American writers: Bradbury, Asimov, Pohl, Sheckley, Le Guin, as well as a number of Polish writers (significantly Lem is not among them). Following the lead of the Soviet Union, space became a dominant theme. Even so, a glance at the covers and illustrations of Neue Berlin books reveals a strong cultural resistance to the space-age icons both of Western and Soviet science fiction. An example is the 1987 collection of Erik Simon, *Mondphantome, Erdbesucher* [Moon Phantoms, Earth Visitors]. The drawings of house artist Michael de Maizière (whom Spittel reprinted in his two post-DDR anthologies) bear scant resemblance to other known models—the nuts-and-bolts "realism" of American space art, the retro-futurist Soviet visions, the surreal figures of French covers. They suggest instead the sketches and drawings, in his own hand, that accompany Hoffmann's stories. Satirical and grotesque, they focus on human faces and forms, struggling to keep their shape as they deal with inhuman forces: close-ups of sweating astronauts, spacemen with swinish, terrified faces. De Mazière represents the order beyond humanity as series of numbers, as triangles; a giant eye directly alludes to the "spirit of music" in Hoffmann's "Ritter Gluck" (1809). These represent superhuman entities, alien and indifferent to human activity.

The thread that connects Simon's sketches and stories is space and alien encounter. Again, this theme is treated much differently from either American science fiction or other Soviet bloc science fictions. In Lem's *Solaris* (1961), alien encounter is an encounter with human cognitive limits. In Tarkovsky's film version (1971), the encounter instead is with the protagonist's affective and cultural past. Lem's spaceship is haunted by mind phantoms; Tarkovsky's ship is a material junkyard, which forces Kelvin's psychic activity back to an inverted Earth dreamscape which, by film's end, becomes one with planet Solaris. Simon on the other hand is fascinated with parables, the conundrum, open-ended mathematical postulates on the order of Gödel's theorem.

A title like "Der Untergang der Erde, von Mond aus betrachtet" [The Sinking/Downfall of the Earth, as Seen from the Moon] (1987), for instance, suggests a puzzle in the manner of Kafka's "Silence of the Sirens" (1931). Here the unanswerable question is: did the sirens sing? For if Odysseus stopped his ears, how could he know whether they sang or not? Simon's title is a similar relativistic puzzle. The word "Untergang" can mean "downfall" [die Untergang des Abendlandes], or simply the "setting" of the Earth. But humans have never seen Earth "set." It is stated that the Earth sets (or is perhaps being destroyed), and someone is watching. But we cannot verify this, hence cannot know what is happening to us. These cognitive paradoxes are of the same order as Kant's "synthetic apriori," the unstable product of the attempt to bridge the unbridgeable gap between mind and "thing in itself." This quandary is brought about on one hand by the irresolvable encounter of Baconian skepticism and rationalist certainty, and on the other by human science's need to make "judgments," timid steps forward in a material universe whose "real" workings we cannot understand. This disjunct, in Hoffmann's fiction, drives protagonists to transgression and madness.

Here, one sees the paradigm shift of Hoffmann's Copernican revolution, once thought lost in the context of German fiction, rediscovered in what appears a uniquely *German* form of science fiction. What is more, this discovery allows us to trace a line not traced by German scholars, from Kant's response to the impact of science, to Hoffmann, to the unique fictions of Kafka, to the large body of DDR science fiction represented by Simon. Hoffmann's terrain was that of paranormal forces such as music, which in stories like "Don Juan" (1813) pushes its protagonist beyond known limits of physical law, but leaves the workings of material reality as inscrutable as the "ding an sich." Kafka's terrain is myth. It is some form of "weariness"—inexplicable by known cosmic laws—that wears down the forces holding Prometheus to his rock of punishment. They simply tire of holding him, and he walks away to an inscrutable future. Simon's terrain (and that of his fellow writers) seems this same paradigm shift that informs the work of both. Its subject is a radical disjunction between science's object—advancing knowledge of the physical world—and science's subject—the fatal limits of its perceptual apparatus. The characters of Simon's stories, like those of Hoffmann, invariably find themselves in the situation of the builders of Kafka's Great Wall of China: this Wall, like human science, is built piecemeal, with sections starting here and there, building outward on each side, but never joining another, never finding the nature of the plan, or whether there was any plan at all.

One notices that, if Spittel calls his anthologized stories (which range from the early 1960s to the later 1980s) "science fiction," many stories originally had other designations. Simon's collection, for example, bears the subtitle "phantastische Geschichten," fantastic stories. Karl-Heinz Tuschel calls his story "Angriff aus 100 Jahren Distanz" [Attack from a Hundred Years Away]

(1984), a "wissenschaftlich-phantastischer Bericht" [a scientific-fantastic report]. One might explain the use of such generic terminology as an attempt to elevate science fiction in the DDR, to distinguish it from the space opera tradition of Karl May and ultimately from the decadent science fiction of the United States. Yet the terms "science-fiction" and "SF" were widely used, in the 1970s and 1980s, by Verlag Das Neue Berlin. Simon himself used the term in his 1982 essay and lexicon of writers, "Science-fiction. Personalia zu einem Genre in der DDR" [News about the People in the Science Fiction Genre in the DDR]. The more tempting explanation is that writers themselves were both aware of, and desirous to make readers aware of, their connections with Hoffmann's scientific "fantastic" and the German tradition of the "ghost story" [Gespenstergeschichte] that traces its roots back to early nineteenth century pseudo-scientific treatises such as Gotthilf Heinrich Schubert's *Ansichten von der Nachtseite der Naturwissenschaft* (1806). Titles such as "Para Noah" (Rainer Klis, 1983), "Widofried geht einkaufen, oder der Zauberspruch des Jahrhunderts" [Widofried Goes Shopping, or the Magic Spell of the Century] (Berit Neumann), or "Der tintenschwarze Spiegel" [The Ink-Black Mirror] (Angela Steinmüller) deal playfully with this tradition. Others, like Hartmut Mechtel's "Verhör" [Trial] (1985), point in the direction of Kafka. The first four pages of Johanna and Günter Braun's "Cantorville, 1990" (written sometime in the 1970s or 1980s but only copyrighted by Spittel in 1992), a story that bears the subtitle "Gespenstergeschichte," present the description of a room-world reminiscent of Kafka's *Das Schloss* (1926), or the famous drawers within drawers in *Amerika* (1927). Just as Hoffmann used the non-canonical form of the *Märchen* or fairy tale to test the impact of sophisticated science-driven ideas on human beings, and Kafka used the parable, so these writers use the outwardly seeming conventional science fiction story, with its future and/or space age décor, as means of confronting human beings with forces and systems of order that have no relevance to, or cognizance of, its situation. In the unlikely place of East German science fiction, of a land that once was and is no more, we seem to recover Hoffmann's paradigm. There is much more investigating to do here. Of course, one must read German to do it.

## DRACULA SPEAKS ROMANIAN

Most readers of science fiction know Romania as the land of Bram Stoker's *Dracula* (1897). They know Transylvania, Borgo Pass, the Children of the Night. Count Dracula however is not just an incarnation of Vlad the Impaler. The word "drac" in Romanian means "dragon," or "devil"; the suffix "ulea" means "son of." We have a name that points to a powerful folk culture, one with a full-fledged cosmology, full of violence and supernatural occurrences. Romanian folk tales are not, like the German *Märchen*, a literary device. They plunge their roots in a powerful and persistent world view.

What is more, unlike Germany, Romania has a long tradition of science fiction works. At the end of the nineteenth century and beginning of the twentieth century, Romania, among all European countries, could be said to rival France and England. A Romanian writer, Victor Anestin, wrote *Un Român in Luna* [*A Romanian on the Moon*] in 1914, in the wake of Verne and Wells. Interestingly, during the Communist dictatorship of Nicolae Ceausescu, not only did a uniquely Romanian science fiction literature remain vigorous, but despite severe ideological constraints, a flourishing science fiction criticism as well. As for the science fiction, the native folk tradition seemed able to negotiate, and to some extent reshape, the Socialist state's emphasis on practical technology. At the same time Romanian critics, with close linguistic ties to France, and clear fascination with the growing Anglophone academic criticism, kept abreast of the changing nature of both science fiction and its critics in those countries.

In 1989, constraints were lifted, and numerous English- and French-language works were immediately translated into Romanian. Romanian writers and critics at once placed themselves between the two major currents in science fiction, in the position of linguistic mediators between traditions that to this day tend to ignore each other. Several things are particularly interesting about this Romanian science fiction "renaissance." One is a concerted effort to breach the translation gap. Wishing to write in Romanian, but at the same time realizing that Romanian is not a widely read language, Romanian science fiction writers, in a series of anthologies published by Nemira, have offered their own English translations. Their model may be the Soviet Foreign Language Publishing House, but this is a private enterprise, with authors translating their own or others' works. The result is not-always-orthodox English, yet represents a brave grass-roots enterprise, given that almost no English-language publisher today will pay to translate science fiction from "foreign" languages.

The other notable aspect of Romanian science fiction is the interplay between writer and critic. Even under Communism, Romanian critics such as Ion Hobana and Cornel Robu were reaching out to the Western critical establishment, offering articles and reviews to the journals *Foundation* (U.K.) and *Science-Fiction Studies* (U.S.). Post-1989, Romanian critics appear to have voraciously acquired knowledge of Anglophone primary texts and critical studies. The result is works such as Bodgan Aldea's *Worlds in the Making: Science Fiction between Fabulation and Mannerism* (2006). Aldea sees science fiction, and its international history, as an ongoing dialectic between literary and speculative goals ("fabulation"), and the commercial and formulaic aspect of the genre (what he calls "mannerism," which he defines as science fiction's "appetite for consecrated formulas").[7] The sweep of his knowledge—of Anglo-American science fiction criticism, literature, and fan activity—is vast (from Panshin to Delany, from Aldiss to Jameson, from Suvin to *Star Wars*). He is also highly conversant with postwar French theoreticians. All this however is neatly balanced against a Romanian vision of the genre (there are numerous citings of Hobana and Robu, as well as discussions of critical works virtually unknown to Anglophone readers, such as Sorin Antohi's study of utopia and science fiction, *Civitas imaginalis: Istorie si utopie in cultura româna* [1994]). The Romanian vision, as it emerges here, is pragmatic, eclectic, and visionary, as befits a strong culture repressed by over-theoretical cultural tsars. This is the subject of Robu's *Teoria Pierde Omenia* [Theory Kills Sympathy] (2009). Robu's book is bilingual. It reproduces, in almost antiphonal manner, significant critical statements from Anglophone critics and comments and analyses by Romanian scholars, including Robu's own seminal essay, "A Key to Science Fiction: The Sublime" (1988), originally written in English. The book assumes readers who can read both Romanian and English. As this is hardly the case for Anglophone scholars, the format calls for a new linguistic culture—Romanian and polyglot at the same time—to recapture both science fiction and the study of science fiction. Robu's title openly rejects theory—the current mainstay of French and Anglophone cultures—in favor of old-fashioned literary history and analysis of concrete texts, the kind of critical approach he and Aldea (and many other Romanian writer-critics) use. At the same time, Robu calls for new, multilingual readers of science fiction, capable of penetrating to the core of a literary tradition through the door of language, and his idea of the "sublime" refocuses the study of science fiction on the American Golden Age and its "sense of wonder," a vision still alive in the American popular mind today, if not in science fiction.

Again, little space remains. But let us take a rapid look at some stories published in these Nemira volumes, which are dated by year ("*Nemira '94*") with each story published in Romanian and English recto verso, in the manner of Ace Doubles. The second volume, *Nemira '95*, features stories by writers like Iulia Anania, Ovidiu Bufnila, Sebastian Corn, Florin Pitea, and others. A couple of writers were born before World War II, like Camil Baciu, and moved abroad to avoid Communism. Most however were born around 1960, under the Communists, and describe themselves as the "new wave" of Romanian writers, all trained in science or technology "because all of our authors have a BSc in some technical stuff." Editor Romulus Barbulescu offers this introduction: "For the English-speaking reader, this second Nemira Anthology of Romanian SF may sound exotic. It comes from a far-off geographical and spiritual realm, where the fabulous—under all its hypostases—has always been . . . a palpable presence. It is but natural that Romanian culture easily adopted SF, and it is with pride that it may look back to a history of over one hundred years."[8]

Norman Spinrad prefaced *Nemira '95* with the following comment: "You can read a paragraph of just about any story in this book, and know that you are reading Romanian science fiction and not something else." (1) These stories—from both postwar and post-communism writers—offer a unique crossroads of science fictions, and scientific systems as well, conventional and folk science alike. Several stories remind one of French science fiction, with its carceral futures, shadowy entities controlling populations through organ and mind "transplants." In Iulia Anania's "Civilized Illusions," however, there is both a haunting vagueness about the world presented, and (with its central symbol of the phoenix) a feeling that traditional nature remains strong, that love is still possible, even if we do not know between who or what. Corn's "Substitute" throws the reader in the middle of a future world (a Zamyatin-like city, populations driven underground due to some environmental degradation) where diverse power factions are waging seemingly pointless wars of propaganda. "Substitutes" are trained to kill important news persons, literally become them by shaping themselves physically into their bodies, and thus "infiltrate" and disseminate false information. This world however is not that of Kafka, nor Philip K. Dick, nor the Soviet bureaucracies of the Strugatskys. As with the closed cosmology of Iulia Anania's story, where body parts and organs are recycled endlessly, here substitutes are taken over by countersubstitutes, so ultimately no one knows who is who. There are multiple versions of a same killing, shifts in wording from one tract to another. The narrator's death is re-narrated over and over, his first-person narrator becomes another, female narrator. The word "I" becomes meaningless, as does the entire "plot." This is neither dystopia, nor satire, nor political commentary, but rather a fantasia on a sense of things as perpetual motion, where no matter how microcosmic or closed the playing field, there is always energy to play.

This same dynamic is recast in terms of thermodynamics and universal force fields in Barbulescu and George Anania's "Your Fares, Please." Two rogue scientists invent Sisyf, a creator of closed force fields, like Sisyphus and his rock, where actions summon equal and opposite actions, so that no action is ever finished, no friend ever lost, no death final. But this does not have to be a material hell enforced by the iron laws of science: "It is either the eternal wheel of ingratitude and hatred, or the salvation of love." This leads to the possibility of a larger "scientific" world view where human desires matter: "If this is true, then the fundamental field in mathematics and physics can be much more than an aggregate of forces crushed into each other and bearing such a simple name." (43) Camus's existential Sisyphus pales in comparison, for here returning to the same place may allow the roller of the rock to push it in a different direction: "A world with Sisyf? . . . Without sinful women abandoning their infants on the doorstep of the church? Without old parents forgotten by their sons and daughters . . ." (44) We find much the same vision in Bogdan Ficeac's "The Last Gateway to Hope," a monologue by a lone astronaut who travels to some unidentified frontier planet. Here he finds other lone astronauts from a multitude of planets, seekers like himself of "THE GREAT PASSAGE to the OTHER UNIVERSE": "Another loner, just like me and many others, who chose of his own accord to lead a murderously monotonous life on this frozen land of illusions, waiting for the unique and unpredictable day." (118) His account begins with a vision of Ada among the green hills of Earth. It ends with his finding this unique day and being chosen to pass into the other world. We are reminded of Arthur's cry—HAPPINESS FOR ALL—as he rushed toward the Golden Ball in the Strugatskys's *Roadside Picnic* (1972). But Arthur is deluded, whereas here there is transcendence. With its "Obelisk [seeming] to expand infinitely, tilting slightly toward the unfathomable canopy," the experience resembles that of Bowman in *2001: A Space Odyssey* (1968). At the same time, it echoes the musical apotheosis in Hoffmann's story "Ritter Gluck" (1809): "Waves of soft blue light shimmer . . . in front of me . . . and from the immeasurable Universe an eerie music flows over us in solemn tones of organ, crushing us all." (136) Both Bowman and "Gluck" fail to escape their Earthly existence, their fall is tragic. But here, as with Sisyf, the end is always a new beginning, the green forest of the beginning awaits at the end, the loop is once more sustained by love: "Wait for me, Ada, I shall return."

However, Romania is also the land of Dracula the dragon, Vlad the Impaler, "immeasurable" violence and terror. The dragon in world culture seems to represent the dynamic, ever-mutating forces of nature. Attempts to "slay" it fail. Yet science, if it cannot master it, can in a sense form a pact with its dragons. Le Guin's Earthsea dragons are cast as patterning agents, vital yet controlled forces in opposition to the sterile cobwebs of rational thought. The dragons of Cordwainer Smith, in "The Game of Rat and Dragon" (1955), become scientific mankind's means of interfacing with terrors of the void. But here apparently, in Romanian cosmology, the dragon seems the eternal enemy of the feedback systems of internal harmony promised by the science of the above two stories. The cover art of *Nemira '95* depicts this struggle. On the English verso side, we have an arena, suspended over a yawning chasm suggesting a serpent's maw, where mechanical arms hold up two contending fighters. One is a metal-clad "spaceman," the other a fierce red dragon figure, smaller than the armored human, but flailing a tail that is in the process of sawing through the metal arm that holds up its adversary. The dragon's "face" is sheer unrelenting cruelty. On the recto Romanian side, a spaceman modeled on Gray Lensman enters an area where giant cylinders contain figures in suspended animation. He is followed by a magician figure. Half his dress is a space uniform, the other half a sorcerer's robe. The front tank holds a monstrous figure with claws and distorted cranium. The rear tank holds a Nosferatu-like figure, with red eyes and long teeth and claws. These drawings are emblematic of the dynamic that informs the stories presented within. In each, to one degree or another, two "sciences" confront each other. One is modern science, as either theory (unified field theory, information theory) or its resultant technology. The other is mythic or magic "science," the idea of a never-ending struggle between chaos and suffering, and redemptive love.

Two stories develop this dragon cosmogony. In Pitea's "ANCALAGON," an old blind man takes his young protegé through a cyberpunk and "snow crash" landscape to engage in a final battle between the blind warrior, sword in hand, and Ancalagon, a rogue computer program that metamorphoses into a terrifying dragon: "The twitching tail hit him, knocked the sword out of his hand. . . . Ancalagon's hideous face split into a grin, a strange reptilian grimace." (188). Here the human defeats the dragon. But the hero is old and blind, running out of energy: "One more victory like this one and we'll be done for." (189) The other story, Bufnila's "Legion of the Devil," literally raises the dragon-Dracula from the dead, sending him on a mission to destroy the legions of another devil, the cruel General Ib Hassan, a pop incarnation of Vlad. The landscape here is bric-a-brac: the new Dracula speaks hip slang; on his way he meets a mermaid, the Blind Fish (a cross between Poseidon and a funky water demon), the sax-player Belbo—all gatekeepers to the realm of Beauburg. Here the forces of Ib Hassan are busy impaling and disemboweling women, children, and old people: "The General was splitting his sides with laughter. He waved a silver ax above his head." (55) The cycle this time is one of blood and extreme violence. Ib Hassan's forces earlier killed the narrator; now he returns from the dead to avenge: "I turned everything into a slaughterhouse! I quartered the bone breakers. I washed the walls with their blood." (55) The conflict rises to cosmic proportions: "Ib Hassan raised his legion and waylaid me on the shore. . . . The power of the water grew inside my body. Huge waves poured out of me and drowned the soldiers." (56) What remains of science fiction here is a dance of primeval elements—earth, fire, water—and the Dracula principle, the monster who cannot be killed— "They make up stories about me."

This is but a sampling of what today is a flourishing literature of science fiction in Romania. These stories are available in relatively accurate translations, yet the great body of works remains untranslated. The stories examined merit comparison with the Anglophone works of Ghosh and Hopkinson, for here, in terms of a many-sciences paradigm shift, we do not simply replace modern science with "primitive" knowledge systems such as voodoo or animism. Instead, equal weight is given to modern science (most writers have scientific backgrounds) and belief systems of folk "science" still strong today in their culture. These two currents seamlessly mix in the stories. Neither colonialism nor communism has "suppressed" the local cosmogony. It remains a vital partner in a powerful dialectic between systems of thought. Once again, the key to this fascinating realm of world science fiction is language— the ability to read Romanian.

## THE MANY SCIENCES OF SCIENCE FICTION

These foreign-language science fictions may shed light on where science fiction is going today. In these national traditions, clearly one pole of their fictional dialogue is with science in "classic" American science fiction and the now universally recognized science that shapes it. They do not reject this science, but instead seek to expand its reach. At the same time, experimental science is beginning to explore areas previously relegated to the realm of the paranormal or magical, such as FTL communication, telepathy, and telekinesis, as neuroscientists experiment with mind-computer communication to remotely move objects programmed to human brain waves. In this range, a combination of the paranormal and classical mechanics can be narrated. But these areas of investigation may prove either more exciting than science fiction or essentially un-narratable because they have nothing to do with the "human condition." Arthur C. Clarke could imagine a God Particle, but scientists at CERN *actually found it*. There is the possibility the lights *really* could go out. On the other hand, the NASA discovery of "extremophile" life forms at Mono Lake and perhaps in Martian soil reawakens a real possibility of Rosny's "ferromagnetics." But just as the latter would be so alien as to be inscrutable, so extremophile life forms (though more within the range of our chemistry) have little to do with us, hence little possibility as subjects of fiction. The *double entendre* of Gregory Benford's title *The Martian Race* (2002) reveals the problem of making science fiction out of extremophiles. On one hand, there are technical descriptions of the "Marsmats," bona fide Martian life, yet the sole role this entity can play in the fictional structure is that of "prize" for the other Martian "race," governments vying for control of Mars, a classic mystery plot.

If science is outpacing fiction, science fiction seems to have turned back from attempting to fictionalize these extreme visions. Readers felt that Robert L. Forward's *Dragon's Egg* (1980), however ingenious, went too far in this direction. Forward meticulously designs a life form—the Cheela—capable of existing on a neutron star. Their integration into a physical environment conceivable but fundamentally "other" to the human form of life is impeccable. Cheelas have about the mass of humans, but gravity flattens them to the size of a speck. Their life span is some forty minutes; since vast numbers of Cheela lives occur within the span of one human life, these accelerated lives (relative to ours) allow their science to advance at a dizzying pace. The need to create an interface with a human spaceship leads them to develop a means of "manipulating gravity." Our two life forms improbably meet. However, we never learn how any meaningful exchange between *sentient* entities might occur. It seems impossible for Forward to conceive how conditions of life on a neutron star might shape how *they understand* the physical world. He falls back on classic science-fictional situations: the Cheela live the life of Sturgeon's "Microcosmic God" (1941); our encounter with them is a repeat of Murray Leinster's "First Contact" (1945); the Cheela are unwilling to give us their superior science; in the end we trick them into revealing just enough so we can take it "back home" and use it for further human advancement. Forward was upfront in calling *Dragon's Egg* "a textbook on neutron star theory disguised as a novel."[9] He likened his creative process to writing a scientific paper; when finished, the novel is written. In terms of narrative, he places us at a final barrier—that of description and fiction. Science describes. Fiction experiments with such descriptions in the crucible of human experience. In light of the extreme visions of science, what strategies must science fiction invent to do this?

When we look at much recent American science fiction, we see it turning away from this question. The focus in many cases is on how known technology (rather than speculative science) *feels* from the inside, giving us life within the belly of the beast which is today's world-wide social "network." An example is Cory Doctorow's *Makers* (2009). The libertarian spirit of Heinlein is alive in this novel, a paean to the backyard engineers, inventors, and manipulators of the web. Their "science" however is limited to exploring the *uses* of today's technology, telling the story of those who work in the interstices of mega-corporate structures, in the contemporary world of global warming, dwindling resources, and vanishing possibilities for creative enterprise.

Yet some American writers today have both extensive knowledge of new developments and speculations in the experimental sciences, as well as the propensity to explore alternate systems of knowledge, "occult" sciences, numerology, superstition—and link these together via what has become the world-wide "information" network. Their worlds are scientific extrapolations, but their uses of science are different from those of the classic "hard" science fiction writer. Let us conclude with two writers with extensive knowledge of Western scientific tradition and the new sciences—Neal Stephenson and Howard V. Hendrix. Both seem to approach the original dynamic of science fiction—the impact of new world views on human beings—from a "meta-scientific" angle, working within the many-sciences paradigm. But the question—on which the fortunes of a future science fiction rest—is whether this paradigm will, as in the past, allow scientific discovery to further *shift* paradigms to open new fictional avenues, or simply reduce science fiction to a shuffling of systems. For Golden Age science fiction, the essential product of the dialogue between science and fiction is "sense of wonder," the result of open-ended human encounters with the unknown. The dynamic is alive in Robu's statement that science fiction's encounters are with the "sublime." But is this still true for the "new" American science fiction of the twenty-first century?

Stephenson's first major novels—*Snow Crash* (1992) and *The Diamond Age* (1995)—were heralded respectively as "post-cyberpunk" and "steampunk" classics. But unlike most such novels, Stephenson builds his worlds around scientific extrapolation, however quirky the science. *Snow Crash* takes place in the post-nation-state Los Angeles, now a "burbclave." Protagonist Hiro combines Gibson's Case and Bruce Lee—master hacker and martial artist. The novel tells of two worlds—one virtual, the other real—comprising the "metaverse" (a bow to Heinlein's "multiverse"). The link between these worlds is a mysterious narcotic, "snow crash," both a computer "virus" and mind-altering virus. The link is an ingenious extrapolation—worthy of a world science fiction vision—relating two "languages"—ancient Sumerian and binary. Sumerian is literally a "basic" language, seen as programmed into the human brain stem and transmitted to subsequent humans in the form of an "information virus" through the vector of Babylonian prostitutes. Awareness of language permeates *Snow Crash.* As with Gibson's novels, it is a linguistic tour de force. But here language and scientific knowledge merge, as verbal texture and tone reflect the deep and detailed knowledge of computer science and linguistics that underlies its construction.

Stephenson calls himself a "maximalist," evoking the large, all-inclusive panoramas of writers like Thomas Pynchon. This causes him, in subsequent novels, to expand his generic field to science-mystery. The link is the science of cryptology, a domain where mathematics and mystery interact. Cryptology today is a popular place of genre crossover: witness films like Michael Apted's *Enigma* (2001) about the Bletchley Park codebreakers, or Ron Howard's

*A Beautiful Mind* (2001) about mathematician John Nash and codebreaking, and of course Dan Brown's *The Da Vinci Code* (2003). Stephenson's *Cryptonomicon* (1999) is infinitely more knowledgable, and works more cleverly with this crossover science, using it to blend metaphysical mystery (as in Gene Wolfe's *Book of the New Sun* [1980–1983] or Umberto Eco's labyrinthine *Foucault's Pendulum* [1988]) with the technothriller and alternate history novel. There is interpenetration of historical and fictional timelines, one a "historical" account of Turing and World War II codebreakers, the other a contemporary thriller about data security and cyber-terrorism. It is a fascinating book, but as fiction, with its many undigested didactic passages, it only exacerbates Forward's dilemma between science as description and fiction as action. Stephenson's subsequent Baroque Cycle is essentially a massive rewriting of the history of Western science, focused on the age of Newton. It is full of didactic passages; many are textbook-like descriptions of issues and problems in the development of experimental science. As such, they differ from Forward's scientific paper, which works out the details of a physical problem to engineer a coherent world and life form, with which human protagonists can hopefully interface. They constitute instead a history text.

The history, of course, on the level of fiction, claims to be an "alternate" history. Stephenson insists on calling his work science fiction. But it is not the conventional alternate history as uchronia or time-travel conundrum. Nor is it a work (like Silverberg's "Enter a Soldier" [1989]) that physically resurrects, as a result of media technology, historical figures, allowing them, as artificial constructs, to resume their lives. Its fictional nature is more that of a mega-steampunk-adventure.[10] Amidst a cast of fictional characters are numerous historical figures, upon which semi-fictional personal histories are constructed. The central figure is Newton himself, who comes alive as protagonist in a narrative about "doing science." The science done however is not the theoretical problems that make Newton a key figure in the development of Western science. We do not have, as in a story like Benford's "Exposures" (1981), a narrative that weaves together personal issues and scientific discovery. The theory is generally relegated to didactic passages. Newton's life, on the other hand, provides the meeting point between two major thematic strands: his dispute over calculus with Leibniz, and the question of monetary systems (Newton's life as Warden of the Royal Mint and instigator of the gold standard). All this leads to fascinating speculation on forgotten, even potential aspects of history. But there is a distance between this triptych and William Gibson and Bruce Sterling's steampunk classic, *The Difference Engine* (1990). For their novel still follows the classic alternate history scenario: Babbage *does succeed* in creating his "difference engine" in Victorian England, and the entire Western world is transformed. There is no such bifurcation of alternate timelines in Stephenson's vast work. There remains the retelling of historical byways, interlarded with informative, often brilliant, speculations.

A later Stephenson novel, the 900+-page *Anathem* (2008), returns to a classic science fiction venue—a distant planet in a web of overlapping, contradictory worlds and universes, one of which (in the spirit of "renaming" the known) is called "Laterre." This planet, predictably, provides a major character named Jules Verne Durand. The center of action is a planet called Arbre, quite Earth-like, where for 7000 years there has been a dizzying series of rises and falls of empires, all observed by a group of monastic intellectuals called *saunts* [saints + savants] safe inside their "concents." The comparison critics often make with Walter M. Miller, Jr.'s classic *A Canticle for Leibowitz* (1960), is inaccurate. For Miller, there is the real possibility that, in the cycles of scientific advancement and return to barbarism he chronicles, humanity might actually destroy itself once and for all. In *Anathem* however, over a preposterous 7000-year history, Earthly things are endlessly recycled. We have the "fraa" and "suurs" [*frères* and *soeurs*] of French medieval monasticism. These "avouts" still adhere to the rationalist vision of Saunt Cartas—Descartes—founder of the "mathic" world. The linguistic mutation that produces "anathem" from our words "anthem" and "anathema" is another example of his use of *faux amis.* The components of this new word, however, are so obvious that they immediately take us back to our origins: Earth, France, Descartes. For an American science fiction writer, this could be seen as a "world move," constructing a future world entirely on the foundations of French thought and science fiction, placing rationalist thought, rather than empirical science, at its conceptual center.

Anthony Burgess's *A Clockwork Orange* (1962) and Russell Hoban's *Riddley Walker* (1980) are often cited as models for Stephenson's language-building, which permeates the novel. In the case of Burgess, however, language is in the process of evolving. Here, in contrast to the narrative profusion of alternate "worlds," the movement remains centripetal. Not only has French remained, but it affirms itself as the central element in wordplay. This unabashedly signals that the wash of multi-dimensionality is a vast game, that speculation on "other worlds" is useless, because for human readers everything must come back to Earth models (Plato, a host of significant figures in the history of Western rational thought) given vaguely disguised names. When Asimov located the world of *Foundation* 30,000 years in our future, he posed the problem of Seldon's theory with such literary skill that readers suspended disbelief, ignoring the fact that none of our institutions (or shape of our bodies or nature of our minds) could possibly endure over such a sweep of evolutionary space time. In Stephenson, we have passed through

Delany's "poststructuralist" future in *Nova* (1968), where such egregious anachronisms—jet set tourists in the year 3000—are offered as narrative conventions rather than physical probabilities. In Stephenson's novel, this play with cultural counters reaches colossal proportions. Yet there remains a fine line between the ludic and didactic. For all his far-future thinkers are easily identifiable (there is a glossary to help readers) and thus become "talking heads." The far future world becomes little more than the terrain for a giant lesson in the science and philosophy of "laterre."

For half the novel, the situation remains static. The situation is one of theory inside the monastery, praxis outside. Then, in medias res, an alien starship is sighted. This well-balanced zoo must confront a third ("dimorphic") term, and the narrative segues into an elaborate space opera wherein characters quest for answers through a dizzying series of "worlds," working with an "on-the-edge" physics structured in terms of alternate time "rates." Reviewer Gary K. Wolfe sees this book taking off in its second half, giving us a "full bore SF tale." For Wolfe, Stephenson shows "a sparkling talent for sequences of flat-out adventure." This is the half of his novel inspired by the world of "Jules Verne Durand," scientific adventure and good old "sense of wonder," with "polycosms" harkening back to Heinlein's "multiverses."[11]

Wolfe is correct however in saying that this massive novel has two very different faces. Whereas Verne gave readers a palatable mix of adventure and didacticism, Stephenson amplifies the proportion of each until the novel seems to break in two. On one hand, the weaving of alternate realities is a virtuoso performance. The didactic passages, on the other, seem tailored to the Wikipedia generation and new auto-didacticism of internet users. We learn about neo-rationalist philosophy, the new physics of Roger Penrose—indeed, there are many learned "teaching moments" on diverse, often highly specialized and topical issues of interest to today's readers. These ideas and systems no longer "impact" or transform the ground rules of their fictional world, as in previous science fiction. Instead, fictional characters and settings have become stage props for conveying information that educated people *should know*. If Verne's didacticism was aimed at attracting talented students to scientific careers, Stephenson's new didacticism strikes one as an alternate means of educating readers who, in today's educational climate, never encounter physics or rationalist philosophy. This is probably why a novel like *Anathem*, so hard to read for someone seeking a story, has been so popular. The autodidacts of the internet age seem willing to wade through its 900 pages to "download" the wealth of information therein contained. With its CD of music and other accompanying materials, the novel reminds one of the new "multimedia" methods for learning a foreign language, where users must wade through a maze of technical and theoretical details before they finally get to the core—the words by which we tell stories.

Howard V. Hendrix burst onto the science fiction scene with an extraordinary trilogy of novels: *Lightpaths* (first version 1990, new version published in 1997), *Standing Wave* (1998), and *Better Angels* (1999). In a 1999 interview, Hendrix describes his abiding fascination with writers like Clarke and Alfred Bester, the former for his combination of science and cosmic "mysticism," the latter for his exuberant imagination in works like *The Stars My Destination* (1956). Hendrix presents his work as that of a "secular mystic": "In these novels, humanity is ever seeking a broader and open-ended future, which means re-writing forms such as utopia and apocalypse (as in Clarke) in terms of continual change and future transformation. . . . Utopias are often seen as a static non-changing future, while apocalypses are the abrupt end. In *my* utopia [*Lightpaths*], it is not something that ends—it changes, shifts, a constant goal that's never really achieved." Despite the "mystical" tone, what he describes here are paradigm shifts, "revelations" of new ways of conceiving the world that, from Descartes to Darwin and Emerson, forever change our sense of our place in the universe: "When epiphanies happen in these novels, when something breaks through from the other side, usually, it's a way of showing that all our little concerns are not the whole picture, that there is something much larger. It's hard for us to get at it, to reach it, to touch it, but it's there."[12] This is the profession of faith of a classic science fiction writer, and Hendrix in these novels proves that his vision is as "hard" and new-science-driven as any discussed.

Hendrix's novels however operate in the same information-loaded world as Stephenson. In form, they are long, complex meta-narratives, with the same interest in decryption of scientific "mysteries" and fascination with intersecting parallel universes. There are many moments when the story line bogs down in interesting, but digressive, scientific flights of imagination. McMahon levels the same charges against *Lightpaths* (and, later, *Empty Cities of the Full Moon* [2001]) that many reviewers level against Stephenson's Baroque Cycle and *Anathem*: that these novels are one big digression, full of lectures on science, social organization, and a myriad of learned topics.[13] Many are sheer intellectual delights but detract from conventional aspects of narrative such as character-building and clarity of plot. Often, in Hendrix, the story does not get underway until mid-novel, and Hendrix does not have the flair for action and adventure we see in Stephenson. He does rival Stephenson when it comes to verbal razzle-dazzle and outdoes him in the creation of names—in *Standing Wave* we find the character Phelonious Manque and a humanoid computer named Hugh Manatee.

Both, in fact, seem to be science fiction writers for the age of Dan Brown. What sets them apart is their encyclopedic knowledge of current issues in science and technology and ability to spin out extrapolative ideas from this store of knowledge, resisting the shallow knowledge and best-seller facileness of a work like *The Da Vinci Code*. Both work on a far higher intellectual level. By his own admission however, Hendrix aspires to be a hard science fiction writer in the classic sense. His novel *Better Angels* (1999), for instance, relocates the cyberpunk theme of the designer drug—the "snow crash"—back in the world of Dick's Can-D, and farther back yet in the world of Heinlein's *The Door into Summer* (1957), where expansion of consciousness and time travel conflate. Hendrix also takes from Heinlein the idea of multi-novel characters, who serve as links between worlds in Hendrix's ever-expanding multiverse. For example, a character from the parallel world of *Better Angels* is, in the first pages, simply "dumped" into the world of Hendrix's subsequent novel, *Empty Cities of the Full Moon*. This latter novel, though structured around numerous characters and multiple plot-universes, nonetheless retains a sharp focus on a single extrapolative idea—the *prion,* or prionides, proteins whose altered shape become contagious to other proteins. This is not a fanciful idea like Stephenson's sexually transmitted Sumerian meme; it is the biochemistry of "mad cow disease," a current physical phenomenon being studied in a scientific field Hendrix knows inside and out. He brilliantly extrapolates from this shape-changing protein to a devastating epidemic of "shape-shifting" forms of humanity, which results in the near-extinction of humanity. Hendrix's treatment of this theme draws inspiration from a classic novel like Clarke's *Childhood's End* (1953). His utopian New Atlantis has survived general extinction. Instead of a Last Man, Hendrix presents a "post-extinction" utopian colony, where he gathers together characters from parallel worlds, then disperses them, under the leadership of a Jan-like figure, in a quest to understand, and ultimately, like Jan, to be able to tell the story of this devastation. In the latter half of this novel, Hendrix gives us an "on the road" situation, the endpoint of which is nothing less than science fiction's holy grail: transhumanity.

Hendrix's next novel, *The Labyrinth Key* (2004), seems another Borgesian metaphysical mystery in the manner of *Cryptonomicon*. The plot is hypercomplex, and range of disciplines—historical and pseudo-scientific—overwhelming: cabalism, alchemy, Knights Templar, codes, the Grail quest. Yet this novel is no *Foucault's Pendulum* (which Geoffrey Sauer calls a "long, erudite dry joke"[14]). Hendrix does not turn in endless circles of the paranormal, nor does he "bring to life" historical figures to engage in a hologramic lecture series. The search in this novel is for something called a "quantum computer," and Hendrix makes this hypothetical device and complex speculative science behind it the sharp focus of his mystery. Despite the sheer weight of ideas in this novel, it remains an example of extrapolation in the classic science fiction manner.

Readers and reviewers of Hendrix's novels, pro or con, invariably note the divorce between the science and fiction, between speculative *discourse* and the action-adventure-mystery. This split seems to mark "post-cyberpunk" science fiction, with its technobabble and fascination with cabals, secret societies, codes, cyber-attacks, and defenses. Despite this, Hendrix's novels appear to evolve along classic lines of the apocalypse-transhumanity axis he defined in his interview. His deep inspiration is Bernal and Clarke. In another novel, *Spears of God* (2006), he uses recent discoveries (and speculations) in evolutionary biology to explore new avenues of this "masterplot." The outer form of the novel is again a complex "thriller." Its core is purest extrapolation: the possibility that meteorites contain a "fungus" (an extraterrestrial multicellular life form) capable of triggering a transformation of humans into a collective entity that gains paranormal powers and is ultimately able to transcend its human condition. The scientist-protagonists discover, in an isolated micro-ecosystem in South America, three children, survivors of a massacre, who through use of this meteorite fungus have fused into a symbiotic entity capable of telepathy. From this kernel, Hendrix's plot evolves in labyrinthine manner, as scientists seek to protect the secret of these children from corporate and military-industrial cabals, and from religious fanatics hell-bent on bringing about apocalypse on their own terms.

Reviewer Bill Mason sees Hendrix displaying a "command of diverse and intertwined scientific and spiritual disciplines" not seen "since the Hyperion series by Dan Simmons."[15] More striking is Hendrix's skillful intertwining of multiple science-fictional strands: a blend of "Chariots of the Gods" fiction with René Barjavel's *La nuit des temps* [(1968) translated as *The Ice People*], of magic realism and the Latin American landscapes of Pat Murphy and Lucius Shepard, of scientific thrillers such as Benford's *Eater* (2000) and (more germane) the bacteria-driven evolution of Greg Bear's *Darwin's Radio* (1999). Hendrix is working in the speculative mainstream of science fiction. Most significantly, his novel constitutes another new-millennium rewrite of Clarke's *Childhood's End.* Hendrix's novel is a worthy addition to the literature of imagination at the transhuman threshold.

The work of Stephenson and Hendrix is very different from earlier "hard" science fiction in sweep and magnitude. Its eclecticism and verbosity stand out against the streamlined elegance of a classic like Poul Anderson's *Tau Zero* (1970) or the sparse "scientific" prose of Hendrix's model Clarke. Yet the massive presence of science in both works, as well as Hendrix's skill in extrapolating fictional situations from extreme science, shows that the process that has produced a science fiction since Descartes is still very much alive. One does not, as Roger Luckhurst does in his "The Many Deaths of Science Fiction: A Polemic" (1994), need a resurrection argument to explain science fiction's enduring nature.[16] As long as science has, and continues, to impact fictional worlds, there will be science fiction in some form. Hendrix and Stephenson write for the well-educated, the scientifically knowledgeable. Their work at times seems to reinforce the divide between scientific description and human adventure, to the point that the science, fascinating in itself, appears to have no relevance to human situations. Hendrix however still strives to extrapolate new worlds for old, to confront the unknown with the same "sense of wonder" that Claude Bernard, echoing the excitement of Galileo and Descartes, saw as the product of open-ended scientific investigation of nature and our role in it.

In this study, we have sought to trace the *process* of science fiction from points of origin that functioned long before the genre we call "science fiction" had a name. Not only did a world view both empowering and terrifying displace conventional religious and moral paradigms, but a new standard for fiction came about. Science demands of its hypotheses and world views that they be taken literally, as physical facts. Just as science, in Benford's term, requires we "play with the net up," so must fiction. In science fiction, there is no escape from science's material imperative. Transcendence can only occur at the end of a long physical process. Increasingly, on that road, the cold equations of the physical world may come to have no relevance to us. But it is this search for relevance, the ability to adapt to change, to overcome physical and mental barriers limiting human advancement, that mark the deep current of science fiction. In fact, to say that science fiction no longer need exist because the world itself is science fiction is to deny the very nature of science fiction. For it is never co-extensive with any given world. Instead, it invites us to extrapolate worlds and modes of being from new discoveries, to seek to live and grow under new sets of "laws." In Descartes, a new human faculty—unaided reason—and new method of analysis were first tested in the crucible of fiction. The possibility of a science fiction was born. If the net of science seems increasingly high, science fiction invites us to hit the ball over it. It is by playing the "game" of science that this form of fiction found its generic identity and flourished. This "game" of science is best defined by Claude Bernard as the *unending* pursuit by the rational mind of the physical unknown. It is such an open-ended pursuit that I have traced, from Descartes and Pascal, to Verne, Wells, Clarke, Heinlein, Benford, and finally Hendrix. It will certainly continue, in one form or another, as long as science itself continues.

## NOTES

1. Editor's note: Slusser indicated that he planned to write a note discussing "Derridisme a l'americaine," perhaps along the lines of a comment from an interview with Gregory Benford about why he decided to focus on science fiction instead of his original field of study: "To make matters worse, American academia was invaded by French theoreticians, which opened the door to 'le derridisme a l'americaine,' a lot of neo-scholasticism and amateur politics. I wanted to get my hands on something concrete, a large body of texts and a vast cultural vision." ("An Interview with Professor George Slusser—by Cristian Tomas," posted on Gregory Benford's blog, August 9, 2014, at http://www.gregorybenford.com/blog/page/3/).

2. Carl Freedman, *Art and Ideas in the Novels of China Miéville* (Canterbury: Glyphi, 2015), 70.

3. David Soyka, review of *Midnight Robber*, SF Site, posted 2000, at https://www.sfsite.com/05b/mr81.htm; Neil Walsh, review of *Brown Girl in the Ring*, SF Site, posted 1998, at https://www.sfsite.com/07b/brow37.htm; Donna McMahon, review of *Brown Girl in the Ring*, SF Site, posted 2002, at https://www.sfsite.com/01b/bg120.htm.

4. James Schellenberg, review of *Midnight Robber*, Challenging Destiny: Science Fiction and Fantasy Reviews, posted March 22, 2001, at https://www.challengingdestiny.com/reviews/midnightrobber.htm.

5. Geoffrey Dow, review of *Midnight Robber*, Edifice Rex Online, posted 2009, no longer available online.

6. See Jie Lu, "Science Fiction in China: A Report on the World's Largest SF Magazine." *Extrapolation*, 43:2 (Summer, 2002), 219–225.

7. Bodgan Aldea, *Worlds in the Making: Science Fiction between Fabulation and Mannerism* (Napoca-Star: Cluj-Napoca, 2006), 178.

8. Romulus Barbulescu, introduction, *Nemira '95: Romanian SF Anthology*, edited by Barbulescu and George Anania (Bucharest: Nemira Publishing Group, 1995), 2. The two introductions differ in that the English-language introduction reaches out to English readers, while the Romanian-language introduction, aimed at Romanian readers, gives facts leading to the anthology and describes the participation of authors and critics in various academic gatherings in United Kingdom and elsewhere. References are to this edition.

9. Leonard David, "Robert Forward, Space Futurist, Dies at Seventy," Space.com, posted September 23, 2002, at https://web.archive.org/web/20060218003005/http://space.com/news/ robert_forward_020923.html.

10. It was published in 3 "volumes" in 2004–2005, with *Quicksilver* (Volume One) winning the Arthur C. Clarke Award (2004) and *The Confusion* (Volume Two) and *The System of the World* (Volume Three), each winning the Locus Award for 2005. The "volumes" are divided into eight "books."

11. Gary K. Wolfe, review of *Anathem*, Locus Online, posted September 27, 2008, at http://www.locusmag.com/Features/2008/09/locus-magazines-gary-k-wolfe-reviews.html.

12. "Howard V. Hendrix: Secular Mystic," *Locus*, 42:6 (June 1999), 6, 77–78.

13. McMahon, review of *Lightpaths*, SF Site, posted 2001, at https://www.sfsite .com/11b/lp116.htm; review of *Empty Cities of the Moon*, SF Site, posted 2002, at https://www.sfsite.com/02b/ec122.htm.

14. Geoffrey Sauer, "*Foucault's Pendulum* and Postmodern Focus," *Humanitas*, 12:3 (February 12, 1990).

15. Bill Mason, Amazon.com review, posted March 26, 2007, at https://www .amazon.com/Spears-God-Howard-V-Hendrix/product-reviews/0345455983.

16. "It is my polemical proposal that these regularly issued panic narratives, these apocalyptic warnings and calls to arms in fact conceal the opposite concern: that SF wants to die, that it is ecstatic at the prospect of its own death and desires nothing else." Roger Luckhurst, "The Many Deaths of Science Fiction," *Science-Fiction Studies*, 21:1 (March 1994), 36.

# Afterword

## *Knowing George*

### Gregory Benford

When George Slusser phoned me around 1980 with the idea of a conference built around the J. Lloyd Eaton collection, I thought back to the Lloyd I had known. He was a physician and solid SF fan. I spoke at meetings in his home of the Little Men, the Bay Area SF fan group. George was interested in what Lloyd thought so that, as a Harvard-trained literary scholar, he could build a conference "that guy, our donor, would like to attend."

He felt that SF was the product a number of cultures as they react in specific ways to onrushing paradigm shifts brought about by the development of science and tech. He specified the Cartesian paradigm, the Evolutionary Paradigm, and for Americans the Emersonian Paradigm. Science fiction flourished in America because this Emersonian vision is both dynamic and open-ended, thus better able to negotiate scientific discoveries that impact the people. Emerson's vision of center-circumference and power and form, a dynamic focused on the individual monad, seems marvelously adaptable to the advent of visual and electronic media, the principal venue of SF today. I recall him saying, "That's not an American 'invention,' but as Emerson says, we have built a better mousetrap."

He felt that perhaps that was why cyberpunk made such an impact. It offered a quite new vision. This was in several ways depressing, and also has proved often to be wrong: we aren't worried about zaibatsus anymore, the notion of fading governmental power is laughable, hackers aren't masters of the universe (except as virus builders). Events like the dotcom collapse have shown that street smarts don't necessarily outweigh the power and resources of the suits. Still, it was plausible because it offered accelerating growth of information-flow, something which was and is actually happening. Cyberpunk is still going strong, as a flavor, not a following.

After the Eaton Conference on this we thought that "biopunk" was the coming vision. We were going to get SF capitalizing on a big breakthrough of our lifetime, DNA discovery. But biopunk hasn't taken off the way cyberpunk did: it hasn't gone "collective" in the same way. Such social dynamics George pondered but could not explain; such is the vigorous swamp of the field.

Brian W. Aldiss once told me that his idea of heaven was a big console up in the sky, where you could just sit, whisky in hand, and watch to see what happened next: always more unexpected and more interesting than anything you could think up for yourself. What should SF be predicting? There's global warming, of course. George saw that we've got an energy crisis coming, along with food/population/resources crises. None of these is insoluble, of course, but our big deficiency is in political will. Are our political structures capable of adapting? George cited to me the 1970s paradigm: moving to the Niven and Pournelle scenario of genuine habitats and serious industry in space. He quoted the end of the Niven story, "At the Bottom of a Hole," which goes like this:

> *Young Guy:* "There's everything in space. Monopoles. Metal. Vacuum. . . . Free fall. . . . Room to test things. . . . A place to learn physics . . ."
>
> *Old Guy:* "Was it all that obvious before we got here?"
>
> *Young Guy:* "Of course it was. [Then he realizes how old the old guy is. Ancient!] Wasn't it?"

No, it wasn't. Only to SF readers. George deplored that since Harry Truman, and then somewhat in Reagan, politicians haven't been SF readers—which he thought a great pity.

When George negotiated the buying of a big SF collection in Switzerland, he wondered at the different light cast on European SF, now shored up in Riverside. American culture had always flourished, and created art, in the matrix of consumerism. The great jazz of the 1950s moved silently among jazz clubs during the dull Eisenhower 1950s. The same is true for Hollywood cinema. The great directors became greater because they had to struggle against studio bosses. The artistic phoenix springs from consumerist soil. Science fiction was no exception. It moved in its own circles, where writers in order to live have to sell books. Editors and publishing houses are an integral part of the creative picture. where creative editors like Terry Carr and David Hartwell moved the genre in significant directions. That's why he insisted that writers, editors, and even lowly fans be in the Eaton conference.

He studied European intellectuals, especially their tending to think of artistic creation from the top down, and to often see theory preceding practice. George intently studied French-language SF as a genuinely alternate tradition, known here only to a handful of readers. Marginalized by its own culture, it has few adherents in France itself, though the way it operates is central to the Cartesian vision that shapes it. I personally have had the same experience with Russian SF and the Strugatskys, since I knew Russian. (I read German SF too, but found it fairly poor, with exceptions.)

He realized a gulf in understanding: European cultures create "schools" of literature, or cultural tsars orient and subsidize writer's guilds. In the past, American culture has grown very nicely from the soil of consumerism. SF invented fandom and fanzines, as a byproduct of being a literature primarily of ideas. It's still the only literature that features many collaborations, mirroring science, where multi-author papers are the majority. Hence, Eaton hosted mostly hard sf writers' papers and it began massing fanzines even before the huge program of fanzines and even fan photos, courtesy of the J. Kay Klein endowment.

In his last years he deplored that from academic "respectability" and the growing groupthink of political correctness, the writers of the American Golden Age are rarely mentioned. Nor even are Verne and Wells. Nor Stapledon and Rosny. Nor the vastly popular figures that came later. These writers do not merely play mind-games with the universe, but are, as I say, "playing with the net up," a lift from Robert Frost. For George and myself, the criterion, rather than literary "excellence," is adherence to the forms and conventions of the genre, building on the past. Science and its history are definitely Whig, for real progress is possible and often done—and so is sf.

He abounded in insights:

"To Bradbury, science is the forbidden fruit, destroyer of Eden."

"Heinlein's later work is self-indulgent but his early works draw students because it's like *Huckleberry Finn* redone. He represents a certain strain in our culture, a kind of secular Calvinist vision of the world of the elect and the damned."

"The New Wave was small, so as we learn in surfing, it crashed quickly."

"Nobody who reads science fiction comes out with this crap about the end of history."

A classic remark George made to me: "Soon there will be no courses on Shakespeare, but many seminars on theoretical issues such as 'fill-in-the-blank studies.' This plays right into the hands of the technocrats looking for an excuse to get rid of things that don't prepare students for the 'workaday world.' The whole idea of a broad humanist education goes out the window."

As well: "Gérard Klein recently declared to me via an interview that he is very concerned about the phenomenal rise in sales of the so-called 'BitLit'

(Bite Literature) featuring vampires, zombies and werewolves, this meaning to him that the traditional superstitions and the irrational had conquered the young generations' mind."

These catch a flavor of thought that we have lost, alas.

# A Brief Bibliography
# of the Works of George Slusser

This bibliography lists all of the books authored, edited, or co-edited by George Slusser, followed by a summary of his numerous other publications and scholarly achievements. A complete bibliography will be posted at the Lexington Books website.

## BOOKS AUTHORED, EDITED, OR CO-EDITED

*Aliens: The Anthropology of Science Fiction.* Edited by George Slusser and Eric S. Rabkin. Carbondale: Southern Illinois University Press, 1987. 243 pp.

*The Bradbury Chronicles.* By George Slusser. San Bernardino, California: Borgo Press, 1977.
Japanese translation as *The World of Ray Bradbury.* Tokyo: Toppan Publishing, 1981.
Republished. [Rockville, Maryland]: Borgo Press/Wildside Press, 2006.

*Bridges to Fantasy.* Edited by George Slusser, Eric S. Rabkin, and Robert Scholes. Carbondale: Southern Illinois University Press, 1982.

*Bridges to Science Fiction.* Edited by George Slusser, George R. Guffey, and Mark Rose. Carbondale: Southern Illinois University Press, 1980.

*The Centenarian, or, The Two Beringhelds.* By Honoré de Balzac as Horace de Saint-Aubin. Translated by George Slusser. New York: Arno Press, 1976.

*The Centenarian, or, The Two Beringhelds.* By Honoré de Balzac as Horace de Saint-Aubin. Translated and annotated by George Slusser and Danièle Chatelain. Middletown, Connecticut: Wesleyan University Press, 2005.

*The Classic Years of Robert A. Heinlein.* By George Slusser. San Bernardino, California: Borgo Press, 1977.
Excerpts republished in *Contemporary Literary Criticism.* Volume 14. Detroit, Michigan: Gale Research Company, 1980, 246–251.
Republished. [Rockville, Maryland]: Borgo Press/Wildside Press, 2006.

*Coordinates: Placing Science Fiction and Fantasy*. Edited by George Slusser, Eric S. Rabkin, and Robert Scholes. Carbondale: Southern Illinois University Press, 1983.

*The Delany Intersection: Samuel R. Delany Considered as a Writer of Semi-Precious Words*. By George Slusser. San Bernardino, California: Borgo Press, 1977.
Excerpts republished in *Contemporary Literary Criticism*. Volume 14. Detroit, Michigan: Gale Research Company, 1980, 143–147.
Republished as *The Delany Intersection: Samuel R. Delany*. [Rockville, Maryland]: Borgo Press/Wildside Press, 2006.

*The Fantastic Other: An Interface of Perspectives*. Edited by Brett Cooke, George Slusser, and Jaume Marti-Olivella. Amsterdam and Atlanta, Georgia: Editions Rodopi, 1998.

*The Farthest Shores of Ursula K. Le Guin*. By George Slusser. San Bernardino, California: Borgo Press, 1976.
Excerpts republished in *Contemporary Literary Criticism*. Volume 13. Detroit, Michigan: Gale Research Company, 1980, 345–348.
Excerpt republished as "The Earthsea Trilogy." *Ursula K. Le Guin*. Edited by Harold Bloom. New York: Chelsea House, 1986, 71–84.
Republished. [Rockville, Maryland]: Borgo Press/Wildside Press, 2006.

*Fiction Two Thousand: Cyberpunk and the Future of Narrative*. Edited by George Slusser and Tom Shippey. Athens: University of Georgia Press, 1992.

*Fights of Fancy: Armed Conflict in Science Fiction and Fantasy*. Edited by George Slusser and Eric S. Rabkin. Athens: University of Georgia Press, 1993.

*Foods of the Gods: Eating and the Eaton in Fantasy and Science Fiction*. Edited by Gary Westfahl, George Slusser, and Eric S. Rabkin. Athens: University of Georgia Press, 1996.

*Genre at the Crossroads: The Challenge of Fantasy*. Edited by George Slusser and Jean-Pierre Barricelli. Riverside, California: Xenos Press, 2003.

*Gregory Benford*. By George Slusser. Modern Masters of Science Fiction. Urbana: University of Illinois Press, 2014.

*Hard Science Fiction*. Edited by George Slusser and Eric S. Rabkin. Carbondale and Edwardsville: Southern Illinois University Press, 1986.

*Harlan Ellison: Unrepentant Harlequin*. By George Slusser. San Bernardino, California: Borgo Press, 1977.
Excerpts republished in *Contemporary Literary Criticism*. Volume 13. Detroit, Michigan: Gale Research Company, 1980, 204–208.
Republished. [Rockville, Maryland]: Borgo Press/Wildside Press, 2006.
Excerpt republished as "Myth." *Critical Insights: Harlan Ellison*. Edited by Joseph Francavilla. Pasadena, California: Salem Press, 2012, 181–193.

*H. G. Wells's Perennial Time Machine: Selected Essays from the Centenary Conference "The Time Machine: Past, Present, and Future," Imperial College, London, July 26–29, 1995*. Edited by George Slusser, Patrick Parrinder, and Danièle Chatelain. Athens: University of Georgia Press, 2001.

*Immortal Engines: Life Extension and Immortality in Science Fiction and Fantasy*. Edited by George Slusser, Gary Westfahl and Eric S. Rabkin. Athens: University of Georgia Press, 1996.

*Intersections: Fantasy and Science Fiction.* Edited by George Slusser and Eric S. Rabkin. Carbondale: Southern Illinois University Press, 1987.

*Mindscapes: The Geographies of Imagined Worlds.* Edited by George Slusser and Eric S. Rabkin. Carbondale: Southern Illinois University Press, 1988.

*No Cure for the Future: Disease and Medicine in Science Fiction and Fantasy.* Edited by Gary Westfahl and George Slusser. Westport, Connecticut: Greenwood Press, 2002.

*Nursery Realms: Children in the Worlds of Science Fiction, Fantasy, and Horror.* Edited by Gary Westfahl and George Slusser. Athens: University of Georgia Press, 1999.

*A Priest in 1935.* By Jules Verne. Translated and annotated by George Slusser and Danièle Chatelain. Edited by Brian Taves. Albany, Georgia: BearManor Fiction, 2016.

*Robert A. Heinlein: Stranger in His Own Land.* By George Slusser. San Bernardino, California: Borgo Press, 1976. Second Edition. San Bernardino, California: Borgo Press, 1977.
Second Edition Republished. [Rockville, Maryland]: Borgo Press/Wildside Press, 2006.

*Science Fiction and Market Realities.* Edited by Gary Westfahl, George Slusser, and Eric S. Rabkin. Athens: University of Georgia Press, 1996.

*Science Fiction and the Two Cultures: Essays on Bridging the Gap Between the Sciences and the Humanities.* Edited by Gary Westfahl and George Slusser. Jefferson, North Carolina: McFarland Publishers, 2009.

*Science Fiction, Canonization, Marginalization, and the Academy.* Edited by Gary Westfahl and George Slusser. Westport, Connecticut: Greenwood Press, 2002.
Unauthorized translation into Slovenian as *Znanstvena Fantastika, Kanonizacija, Marginalizacija in Akademsko.* Ljubljana: Zalozniski atelje Blodnjak, 2004 or 2005.

*Shadows of the Magic Lamp: Fantasy and Science Fiction in Film.* Edited by George Slusser and Eric S. Rabkin. Carbondale: Southern Illinois University Press, 1985.

*The Space Odysseys of Arthur C. Clarke.* By George Slusser. San Bernardino, California: Borgo Press, 1978.
Excerpts republished in *Contemporary Literary Criticism.* Volume 13. Detroit, Michigan: Gale Research Company, 1980, 151–155.
Republished. [Rockville, Maryland]: Borgo Press/Wildside Press, 2006.

*Storm Warnings: Science Fiction Confronts the Future.* Edited by George Slusser, Colin Greenland, and Eric S. Rabkin. Carbondale and Edwardsville: Southern Illinois University Press, 1987.

*Styles of Creation: Aesthetic Technique and the Creation of Fictional Worlds.* Edited by George Slusser and Eric S. Rabkin. Athens: University of Georgia Press, 1992.

*Three Science Fiction Novellas: From Prehistory to the End of Mankind.* By J.-H. Rosny Aîné. Translated and annotated by George Slusser and Danièle Chatelain. Middletown, Connecticut: Wesleyan University Press, 2012.

*Transformations of Utopia: Changing Views of the Perfect Society.* Edited by George Slusser, Paul Alkon, Roger Gaillard, and Danièle Chatelain. New York: AMS Press, 1999.

*Unearthly Visions: Approaches to Science Fiction and Fantasy Art.* Edited by Gary Westfahl, George Slusser, and Kathleen Church Plummer. Westport, Connecticut: Greenwood Press, 2002.

*Visions of Mars: Essays on the Red Planet in Fiction and Science.* Edited by Howard V. Hendrix, George Slusser, and Eric S. Rabkin. Jefferson, North Carolina and London: McFarland Publishers, 2011.

*Worlds Enough and Time: Explorations of Time in Science Fiction and Fantasy.* Edited by Gary Westfahl, George Slusser, and David Leiby. Westport, Connecticut: Greenwood Press, 2002.

*The Xipehuz and the Death of the Earth.* By J.-H. Rosny Aîné. Translated by George Slusser. New York: Arno Press, 1978.

Slusser also edited or co-edited special issues of the journals *Science Fiction Studies* and *Verniana.*

## FILM AND TELEVISION APPEARANCES

Appeared as interviewed expert in documentaries "Beyond the War of the Worlds" (2005), episode of *UFO Files*; "H. G. Wells" (1995), episode of *Biography*; "Isaac Asimov" (2012), episode of *Prophets of Science Fiction*; *Jules Verne & Walt Disney: Explorers of the Imagination* (2003); *Leonard Nimoy: Science Fiction: The Gold Collection* (2005); and *New Visions of the Future: Prophecies III* (1996).

## OTHER PUBLICATIONS

28 essays (some with Danièle Chatelain) in *Annals of Scholarship, Arts and Architecture, Canadian-American Slavic Studies, Comparative Literature, Extrapolation, Foundation: The International Review of Science Fiction, Historical Reflections, Mississippi Review, Nature, Science Fiction Studies, Special Collections, Verniana*, and *Yearbook of English Studies.*

36 essays (one with George R. Guffey; others with Danièle Chatelain) in critical anthologies published by AMS, Blackwell, Continuum, University of Georgia Press, Greenwood Press, Hong Kong University Press, Liverpool University Press, McFarland Publishers, Modern Language Association, Pennsylvania State University Press, Prentice-Hall, St. Martin's Press, Salem Press, Southern Illinois University Press, and Xenos Press.

7 book reviews published in *Canadian Review of Comparative Literature, Extrapolation, Nineteenth-Century Fiction, Science Fiction and Fantasy Book Review*, and *Utopian Studies.*

16 entries in reference books published by Greenwood Press, St. James Press, Salem Press, Charles Scribner's Sons, and Thomson Gale.

31 introductions or afterwords (some with Danièle Chatelain, Colin Greenland, George R. Guffey, Howard V. Hendrix, Eric S. Rabkin, Robert Scholes, or Gary Westfahl) to books published by Arno Press, BearManor Fiction, Borgo Press, Easton Press, University of Georgia Press, Greenwood Press, G. K. Hall, Mc-Farland Publishers, Newcastle Publishing Company, Southern Illinois University Press, Wesleyan University Press, and Xenos Press.

## OTHER SCHOLARLY ACTIVITIES

Coordinated or co-coordinated 29 scholarly conferences on science fiction in College Station, Texas; Leeds, England; London, England; Long Beach, California; Paris, France; Riverside, California; Seattle, Washington; and Yverdon-les-Bains, Switzerland.

Wrote and edited website "Balzac's Paris: A Guided Tour" at http://www.balzacsparis.ucr.edu/index.html with Daniéle Chatelain.

Prepared book display and catalog for the Antiquarian Book Fair, Los Angeles, California, 1998.

## SELECTED AWARDS AND HONORS

1986: Winner, Pilgrim Award, Science Fiction Research Association, for lifetime contributions to science fiction and fantasy scholarship.

1987: Nominee, Locus Award, best nonfiction work, for *Hard Science Fiction* (with Eric S. Rabkin).

1993: Nominee, Locus Award, best nonfiction work, for *Fiction 2000: Cyberpunk and the Future of Narrative* (with Tom Shippey).

1999: Honorable Mention (Second Place), Pioneer Award, best article on science fiction, for "The Perils of an Experiment: Jules Verne and the American Lone Genius" (*Extrapolation*).

2013: Nominee, SF&F Translation Award, best long form, for Three Science Fiction Novellas: From Prehistory to the End of Mankind by J.-H. Rosny Aîné (with Daniéle Chatelain).

# Works Cited

## PRIMARY TEXTS

Aldiss, Brian W. *Cryptozoic!* New York: Avon Books, 1969.

Aristotle. *Physics*. Translated by R. P. Hardie and R. K. Kaye. New York: Dover Publications, 2017.

Arnold, Matthew. *The Portable Matthew Arnold*. Edited by Lionel Trilling. New York: Viking Press, 1949.

Asimov, Isaac. *Second Foundation*. New York: Avon Books, 1964.

Bacon, Francis. *Selected Writings of Francis Bacon*. Introduction and notes by Hugh G. Dick. New York: The Modern Library, 1955.

Balzac, Honoré de. *The Centenarian, Or, The Two Beringhelds*. Translated and edited by Danièle Chatelain and George Slusser. Middletown, Connecticut: Wesleyan University Press, 2005.

———. *La Comédie humaine*. Paris: Bibliothèque de la Pléiade, 1950.

———. *Sur Catherine de Médicis*. Paris: Calmann Lévy, 1892.

Barbulescu, Romulus, and George Anania, editors. *Nemira '95: Romanian SF Anthology*. Bucharest: Nemira Publishing Group, 1995.

Benford, Gregory. "Matter's End." *Matter's End*. New York: Bantam Books, 1995.

———. *Timescape*. New York: Simon and Schuster, 1980.

Bernal, John Desmond. *The World, the Flesh, and the Devil: An Inquiry into the Three Enemies of the Rational Soul*. London: Jonathan Cape, 1968.

Bernard, Claude. *Introduction à l'étude de la médecine expérimentale*. Paris: Garnier-Flammarion, 1966.

Bisson, Terry. "Bears Discover Fire," *The Year's Best Science Fiction*, Eighth Annual Collection. Edited by Gardner Dozois. New York: St Martin's Press, 1991, 179–189.

Bradbury, Ray. "No Particular Night or Morning." *The Illustrated Man*. New York: Bantam Books, 1952, 106–114.

Bradley, Sculley, Richmond Croom Beatty, and E. Hudson Long, editors. *The American Tradition in Literature*. New York: W. W. Norton, 1967.

Chaucer, Geoffrey. *The Tales of Canterbury, Complete*. Edited by Robert A. Pratt. Boston: Houghton-Mifflin Company, 1974.

Chiang, Ted. "Story of Your Life." *Stories of Your Life and Others*. New York: Orb Books, 2002, 117–178.

Clarke, Arthur C. *Childhood's End*. New York: Ballantine Books, 1953.

———. "The Nine Billion Names of God." *The Nine Billion Names of God*. New York: Harcourt Brace Jovanovich, 1967.

———. *3001: The Final Odyssey*. New York: Ballantine/Del Rey, 1997.

———. *2001: A Space Odyssey*. New York: Signet/NAL, 1968.

———. *2061: Odyssey Three*. New York: Ballantine/Del Rey, 1987.

Compton, D. G. *The Steel Crocodile*. New York: Ace Books, 1970.

———. *Synthajoy*. New York: Ace Books, 1968.

Constant, Benjamin. *Political Writings*. Translated and edited by Biancamaria Fontana. Cambridge: Cambridge University Press, 1988.

Defoe, Daniel. *Robinson Crusoe*. New York: Signet New American Library, 1961.

Descartes, René. *Descartes: Oeuvres et lettres*. Edited by André Bridoux. Paris: Éditions de la Pléiade, 1987.

Dorémieux, Alain. *Promenades au bord du gouffre*. Paris: Éditions Denoël, 1978.

Efremov, Ivan. *The Heart of the Serpent* [*Sedtse Zmei*, 1956]. Moscow: Foreign Language Publishing House, 1960.

Egan, Greg. *Quarantine: A Novel of Quantum Catastrophe*. New York: Harper Prism, 1995.

Emerson, Ralph Waldo. *Representative Men: Seven Lectures*. London: George Routledge & Co., 1850.

Gibson, William. *Neuromancer*. New York: Ace Books, 1984.

*Grand Tour: Disaster in Time*. Channel Communications, 1991.

Hawthorne, Nathaniel. *The Complete Novels and Selected Tales of Nathaniel Hawthorne*. Edited by Norman Holmes Pearson. New York: Random House, 1937.

Heinlein, Robert A. "By His Bootstraps." *The Menace from Earth*. New York: Signet Books, 1959), 39–88.

———. *Have Space Suit, Will Travel*. New York: Ace Books, [1969].

———. *The Moon Is a Harsh Mistress*. New York: Berkley Medallion Books, 1968.

———. *Starman Jones*. New York: Ballantine Books, 1975.

———. *Time for the Stars*. New York: Scribner's, 1956.

———. "Waldo." *Waldo and Magic, Inc.* New York: Pyramid Books, 1963.

Hoffmann, E. T. A. "Der Sandmann." Full text available at Project Gutenberg, https://www.projekt-gutenberg.org/etahoff/sandmann/sandman1.html and following pages.

Hume, David. *Enquiries Concerning the Human Understanding and Concerning Principles of Morals*. Oxford: Clarendon Press, 1902.

Jeury, Michel. *Le temps incertain*. Collection Ailleurs et demain. Paris: Robert Laffont, 1973.

Lem, Stanislaw. *The Invincible*. Translated from the German by Wendayne Acker-man. New York: Ace Books, 1968.

Marlowe, Christopher. *The Complete Plays of Christopher Marlowe*. Edited by Irving Ribner. New York: Odyssey Press, 1963.

Maupassant, Guy de. *Contes et nouvelles II*. Edited by Louis Forestier. Paris: Édition de la Pléiade, 1988.

Mill, John Stuart. *August Comte and Positivism.* London: N. Trübner & Co., 1865.

Mills, Robert P., editor, *The Worlds of Science Fiction*. New York: Paperback Library, 1965.

Molina-Galiván, Yolanda, and Andrea Bell, editors. *Cosmos Latinos: An Anthology of Science Fiction from Latin America and Spain*. Middletown, Connecticut: Wesleyan University Press, 2003.

Montellier, Chantal. *Shelter*. Paris: Les Humanoïdes associés, 1979.

Moore. C. L. "Shambleau." *The Wesleyan Anthology of Science Fiction*. Edited by Arthur B. Evans, Istvan Csicsery-Ronay, Jr, Joan Gordon, Veronica Hollinger, Rob Latham, and Carol McGuirk. Middletown, Connecticut: Wesleyan University Press, 2010, 110–135.

Pascal, Blaise. *Pensées*. Edited by Louis Lafuma. Paris: Éditions du Seuil, 1962.

Perkins, David, editor. *English Romantic Writers.* New York: Harcourt, Brace & World, 1967.

Pohl, Frederik. "Day Million," *Day Million.* New York: Ballantine Books, 1970, 5–12.

Resnick, Mike. "Seven Views of Olduvai Gorge." *The Year's Best Science Fiction, Twelfth Annual Collection*. Edited by Gardner Dozois. New York: St Martin's Press, 1995, 305–342.

Rosny aîné, J. H. *Récits de Science-Fiction*. Edited by Jean-Baptiste Baronian. Verviers, Belgium: Bibliothèque Marabout, 1975.

———. *Three Novellas of J. H. Rosny aîné: From Prehistory to the End of Mankind.* Translated and annotated by George Slusser and Danièle Chatelain. Middletown, Connecticut: Wesleyan University Press, 2012.

Ruellan, André. *Mémo.* Paris: Denoël Présence du futur, 1984.

Shakespeare, William. *The Riverside Shakespeare*. Edited by G. Blakemore Evans. Boston: Houghton Mifflin Company, 1974.

Shelley, Mary. *Frankenstein; or, The Modern Prometheus*. Boston: Sever, Francis, & Co., 1869.

Silverberg, Robert. "Enter a Soldier. Later: Enter Another." *The Collected Stories of Robert Silverberg, Volume 1, Secret Sharers.* New York: Bantam Books, 1992, 509–546.

Stapledon, Olaf. *Last and First Men and Star Maker: Two Science Fiction Novels.* New York: Dover, 1968.

Stephens, James, Edwin L. Beck, and Royal H. Snow, editors. *Victorian and Later English Poets*. New York: American Book Company, 1934.

Strugatsky, Arkady and Boris. *Noon: 22nd Century.* Translated from the Russian by Patrick L. McGuire. New York: Macmillan, 1978.

———. *The Snail on the Slope*. Translated from the Russian by Alan Meyers. New York: Bantam Books, 1980.

Tennyson, Alfred Lord. *Tennyson's Poetry* . Edited by Robert W. Hill, Jr. New York: W. W. Norton, 1971.

Valéry, Paul. "Le cimetière marin." *Oeuvres I*. Edited by Jean Hytier. Paris: Éditions de la Pléiade, 1957, 74–78.

Verne, Jules. *Journey to the Centre of the Earth*. Translated and annotated by William Butcher. Oxford: Oxford World Classics, 1992.

———. *Hector Servadac: Voyages et aventures a travers le monde solaire*. Paris: Hetzel, 1877.

Voltaire. *Lettres philosophiques*. Edited by Raymond Naves. Paris: Garnier, 1962.

———. *Micromégas. Zadig et Micromégas*. London: George Routledge and Sons, 1886.

Wells, H. G. *The Time Machine: An Invention*. New York: Bantam Books, 1968.

Woodring, Carl R., editor. *Prose of the Romantic Period.* Cambridge: Houghton Mifflin Company, 1961.

## SECONDARY SOURCES

Aldea, Bodgan. *Worlds in the Making: Science Fiction between Fabulation and Mannerism*. Napoca-Star: Cluj-Napoca, 2006.

Alkon, Paul K. *Origins of Futuristic Fiction*. Athens: University of Georgia Press, 1987.

Asimov, Isaac. "Social Science Fiction." *Modern Science Fiction: Its Meaning and Its Future*. Edited by Reginald Bretnor. New York: Coward-McCann, 1953, 157–198.

Auerbach, Erich. *Mimesis: Dargestellte Wirklichkeit in der abendländischen Literatur*. Bern: A. Francke AG, 1946.

Barthes, Roland. *Mythologies.* Paris: Éditions du Seuil, 1957.

Benford, Gregory. "Effing the Ineffable." *Aliens: The Anthropology of Science Fiction*. Edited by George Slusser and Eric S. Rabkin. Carbondale: Southern Illinois University Press, 1987, 13–25.

———. "Pascal's Terror." *Mindscapes: The Geographies of Imagined Worlds.* Edited by Slusser and Rabkin. Carbondale: Southern Illinois University Press, 1989, 271–277.

Blanc, Bernard. *Pourquoi j'ai tué Jules Verne*. Paris: Éditions Stock, 1978.

Bohm, David, and Basil J. Hiley. "On the Intuitive Understanding of Non-Locality as Implied by Quantum Theory." *Birkbeck College Writings on Science*. London: University of London, 1974.

Bozzetto, Roger. "Le Horlà: histoire d'alien ou récit de l'altérité?: Une double approche de l'altérité." Montpellier: *Cahiers de l'Irea*, 1996. Available online at https://www.noosfere.org/icarus/articles/Article.asp?numarticle=369.

Brown, Andrew. *J. D. Bernal: The Sage of Science.* Oxford: Oxford University Press, 2005.

Changeux, Jean-Pierre. *L'homme neuronal*. Paris: Fayard, 1983.

Chatelain, Danièle. *Perceiving and Telling: A Study of Iterative Discourse.* San Diego: San Diego State University Press, 1998.

Clarke, Arthur C. *Greetings, Carbon-Based Bipeds!* New York: St. Martin's Griffin, 2000.

Conry, Yvette. *L'Introduction du Darwinisme en France au XIXe siècle.* Paris: Corti, 1974.

Csicsery-Ronay, Istvan, Jr. "The SF of Theory: Baudrillard and Haraway." *Science-Fiction Studies*, 18:3 (November 1991), 387–404.

David, Leonard. "Robert Forward, Space Futurist, Dies at Seventy." Space.com, posted September 23, 2002, at https://web.archive.org/web/20060218003005/http://space.com/news/ robert_forward_020923.html.

Dow, Geoffrey. Review of *Midnight Robber*. Edifice Rex Online, posted 2009, no longer available online.

Eddington, A. S. *New Pathways of Science.* New York: Macmillan, 1935.

Evans, Arthur B. "The Vehicular Utopias of Jules Verne." *Transformations of Utopia*. Edited by Slusser, Roger Gaillard, Alkon, and Chatelain. New York: AMS Press, 1999, 99–108.

Forward, Robert L. "When Science Writes the Fiction." *Hard Science Fiction*. Edited by Slusser and Rabkin. Carbondale: Southern Illinois University Press, 1986, 1–7.

Foucault, Michel. *Histoire de la folie à l'âge classique.* Paris: TEL Gallimard, 1972.

Franklin, H. Bruce. *Robert A. Heinlein: America as Science Fiction.* Oxford: Oxford University Press, 1980.

Freedman, Carl. *Art and Ideas in the Novels of China Miéville.* Canterbury: Glyphi, 2015.

Haraway, Donna. *Simians, Cyborgs, and Women: The Reinvention of Nature.* London: Free Association Press, 1991.

Heinlein, Robert A. "Science Fiction: Its Nature, Faults and Virtues." *The Science Fiction Novel: Imagination and Social Criticism*. Edited by Basil Davenport. Chicago: Advent: Publishers, 1959, 14–48.

Hendrix, Howard V. "Howard V. Hendrix: Secular Mystic" *Locus*, 42:6 (June, 1999), 6, 77–78. Interview; interviewer unidentified.

Knight, Damon. *In Search of Wonder: Essays on Modern Science Fiction.* Revised and Enlarged. Chicago: Advent: Publishers, 1967.

Leach, Clifford. "Marlowe's Humor." *Essays on Shakespeare and Elizabethan Drama in Honor of Hardin Craig*. Edited by Richard Hosley Columbia: University of Missouri Press, 1962. Reprinted in *Marlowe: A Collection of Critical Essays*. Edited by Leach. Englewood Cliffs, New Jersey: Prentice-Hall, 1964.

Lu, Jie. "Science Fiction in China: A Report on the World's Largest SF Magazine." *Extrapolation*, 43:2 (Summer 2002), 219–225.

Luckhurst, Roger. "The Many Deaths of Science Fiction." *Science-Fiction Studies*, 21:1 (March 1994), 35–50.

Mason, Bill. Review of *Spears of God*. Amazon.com, posted March 26, 2007, at https://www.amazon.com/Spears-God-Howard-V-Hendrix/product-reviews/0345455983.

McMahon, Donna. Review of *Brown Girl in the Ring*. SF Site, posted 2002, at https://www.sfsite.com/01b/bg120.htm.

————. Review of *Empty Cities of the Moon.* SF Site, posted 2002, at https://www .sfsite.com/02b/ec122.htm.

————. Review of *Lightpaths.* SF Site, posted 2001, at https://www.sfsite.com/11b/ lp116.htm.

Miller, Norbert. *Die empfindsame Erzähler.* Munich: Hanser Verlag, 1968.

Molina-Galiván, Yolanda, Andrea Bell, Miguel Ángel Fernández-Delgado, M. Elizabeth Ginway, Luis Pestarini, and Juan Carlos Toledano Redondo. "A Chronology of Latin-American Science Fiction, 1775–2005." *Science Fiction Studies*, 34:3 (November 2007), 369–431.

Murphy, Patricia. *Time Is of the Essence.* Albany: State University of New York Press, 2001.

Muscatine, Charles. *Chaucer and the French Tradition: A Study in Style and Meaning.* Berkeley: University of California Press, 1957.

Paul, Harry W. *From Knowledge to Power: The Rise of the Science Empire in France, 1860–1939.* Cambridge: Cambridge University Press, 1985.

Prince, Gerald. *Dictionary of Narratology.* Lincoln: University of Nebraska Press, 1967.

Regis, Ed. *Great Mambo Chicken and the Transhuman Condition: Science Slightly Over the Edge.* New York: Addison Wesley Publishing Company, 1990.

Ricardou, Jean. *Le nouveau roman.* Paris: Éditions de Seuil, 1990.

Roberts, Adam. *The History of Science Fiction.* London: Palgrave Macmillan, 2006.

Rousseau, G. S. "The Hunting of the Leviathan and Awakening of Proteus." *Genre at the Crossroads: The Challenge of Fantasy.* Edited by George Slusser and Jean-Pierre Barricelli. Riverside, California: Xenos Books, 2003, 56–59.

Sauer, Geoffrey. "*Foucault's Pendulum* and Postmodern Focus." *Humanitas*, 2:3 (February 12, 1990).

Schellenberg, James. Review of *Midnight Robber.* Challenging Destiny: Science Fiction and Fantasy Reviews, posted March 22, 2001, at https://www.challenging-destiny.com/reviews/midnightrobber.htm.

Serres, Michel. *Jouvenances de Jules Verne.* Paris: Editions du Minuit, 1974.

Slusser. "The Beginnings of *Fiction*." *Science-Fiction Studies*, 16:3 (November 1989), 307–337.

————. "Why They Kill Jules Verne." *Science Fiction Studies*, 32:1 (March 2005), 61–80.

————, and Tom Shippey, editors. *Fiction 2000: Cyberpunk and the Future of Narrative.* Athens: University of Georgia Press, 1992.

————. Patrick Parrinder, and Chatelain, editors. *H. G. Wells's Perennial Time Machine.* Athens: University of Georgia Press, 2001.

Soyka, David. Review of *Midnight Robber.* SF Site, posted 2000, at https://www .sfsite.com/05b/mr81.htm.

Svendsen, Kester. *Milton and Science.* Cambridge: Harvard University Press, 1956.

Swann, Brenda. *J. D. Bernal, A Life in Science and Politics.* London: Verso, 1999.

Thomas, Pascal. "French SF and the Legacy of Philip K. Dick." *Foundation: The Review of Science Fiction,* No. 34 (Autumn, 1985), 22–35.

Todorov, Tzvetan. *Introduction à la littérature fantastique.* Paris: Éditions de la Pléiade Points, 1970.

Tomas, Cristian. "An Interview with Professor George Slusser—by Cristian Tomas." Gregory Benford's blog, posted on August 9, 2014, at http://www.gregorybenford .com/blog/page/3/.

Wall, Wendy. *The Imprint of Gender: Authorship and Publication in the English Renaissance.* Ithaca, New York: Cornell University Press, 1993.

Walsh, Neil. Review of *Brown Girl in the Ring.* SF Site, posted 1998, at https://www .sfsite.com/07b/brow37.htm.

Westfahl, Gary. *Islands in the Sky: The Space Station Theme in Science Fiction Literature.* Second Edition. Holicong, Pennsylvania: Borgo Press/Wildside Press, 2009.

Wolfe, Gary K. Review of *Anathem.* Locus Online, posted September 27, 2008, at http://www.locusmag.com/Features/2008/09/locus-magazines-gary-k-wolfe -reviews.html.

Zukav, Gary. *The Dancing Wu Li Masters: An Overview of the New Physics.* New York: Bantam Books, 1979.

# Index

# About the Authors

**George Slusser** (1939–2014) long served as a professor of comparative literature, and Curator of the J. Lloyd Eaton Collection of Science Fiction and Fantasy Literature, at the University of California, Riverside. In addition to numerous scholarly articles, reviews, and television appearances, he authored, edited, or co-edited 39 books about science fiction and fantasy, including the author study *Gregory Benford* (2014) for the University of Illinois Press, and he coordinated or co-coordinated 29 academic conferences focused on that subject. He earned the Science Fiction Research Association's 1986 Pilgrim Award for his lifetime contributions to science fiction and fantasy scholarship.

**Gary Westfahl**, now professor emeritus at the University of La Verne, has written, edited, or co-edited 31 books about science fiction and fantasy, most recently the two-volume *Science Fiction Literature through History: An Encyclopedia* (2021), while also publishing over 100 scholarly articles and reviews. He worked with George Slusser for two decades, co-coordinating the annual J. Lloyd Eaton Conferences on Science Fiction and Fantasy Literature and co-editing the resulting Eaton volumes, and he also earned the Pilgrim Award in 2003.

Lightning Source UK Ltd.
Milton Keynes UK
UKHW010404200422
401751UK00002B/10

9 781666 905359